The Pearson Textbook Reader

Reading in Applied and Academic Fields

compiled and edited by
Dawn Lee

Longman

Boston   Columbus   Indianapolis   New York   San Francisco   Upper Saddle River
Amsterdam   Cape Town   Dubai   London   Madrid   Milan   Munich   Paris   Montreal   Toronto
Delhi   Mexico City   Sao Paulo   Sydney   Hong Kong   Seoul   Singapore   Taipei   Tokyo

Editor-in-Chief of Developmental English: Eric Stano
Editorial Assistant: Lindsey Allen
Senior Supplements Editor: Donna Campion
Electronic Page Makeup: Grapevine Publishing Services, Inc.
Marketing Manager: Thomas DeMarco
Cover Photo: www.iStockphoto.com

The Pearson Textbook Reader: Reading in Applied and Academic Fields, compiled and edited by Dawn Lee.

1 2 3 4 5 6 7 8 9 10–QDB–13 12 11 10

Longman
is an imprint of

www.pearsonhighered.com

ISBN 13: 978-0-205-78051-8
ISBN 10:   0-205-78051-2

Contents

Introduction for Instructors and Students

This book is intended to serve as a companion text to your course's primary text. It is not a reading text per se. The purpose of *Reading Strategies for Academic and Applied Disciplines* is to provide instructors with an opportunity to demonstrate to their students the strategies needed to read textbooks in the historically difficult disciplines and to give students an opportunity to learn and practice using those strategies before they are enrolled in the courses. While the primary course text explains reading skills in general, this text will apply discipline-specific strategies so that students will be able to see that, for example, a science text must be approached differently than a history text or a business text. Being armed with these discipline-specific strategies before enrolling in the course should then help the student become a more efficient and effective reader more rapidly than one having to learn through trial and error.

This text contains complete chapters from textbooks in several of the historically difficult disciplines and some of the popular applied disciplines, as well as a few works to illustrate literature and the visual arts. "Historically difficult" disciplines are typically regarded as those courses that have the highest failure rates, such as psychology, mathematics, and history. Many reading texts contain excerpts from various textbooks from across the disciplines, but in order for the student to receive the greatest benefit, it is most helpful to view an entire chapter, from the learning objectives on the first page through to the review materials on the last page. This text also allows all of the students to have the same chapter in front of them, so it does not matter if students are currently enrolled in the discipline under consideration or not.

The chapters herein represent the most commonly required and/or selected courses taken by incoming college freshmen. Each chapter is reproduced in its entirety; the complete original text, all photographs and graphic art, and pedagogical features are included. The end-of-chapter questions to assess the student's comprehension of the chapter materials have been included for just that purpose. In addition, a series of exercises and activities have been included following each chapter with which to review the discipline-specific strategies and critical thinking about the information and its presentation. If these questions seem repetitious, it is because they are, for two reasons. First, the questioning pattern is designed to help the students recognize the patterns used in textbook organization. There is a methodical approach to reading textbooks, and recognizing patterns helps. In addition, regardless of what order the professor uses to select chapters, the strategies will be the same, so it enables skipping around instead of having to cover chapters in chronological order.

A final consideration in the selection process was to give consideration to the level of interest for the topic, practicality (how beneficial the material itself may be for the students regardless of whether or not they actually go on to study the subject), and the degree to which the strategies are best represented. The intent is to make the chapters useful on several levels and not just be an object lesson.

Therefore, in order to present the students with the experience they will be able to apply to the actual assignments they will have in their college courses, the chapters in *Reading Strategies for Academic and Applied Disciplines* have been drawn from tested textbooks, with permission from Pearson Education's authors. These chapters are:

- Allied Health & Nursing: Chapter 6, "Health Care Delivery Systems." From Berman, Audrey, et al. *Kozier & Erb's Fundamentals of Nursing: Concepts, Process, and Practice*, 8/e. C. 2008, by Pearson/Prentice-Hall.
- Business & Foodservice: Chapter 14, "Marketing Foodservice." From Gregoire, Mary B., and Marian C. Spears. *Foodservice Organizations: A Managerial and Systems Approach*, 6/e. C. 2007, by Pearson/Prentice Hall.

- Humanities (History, Literature, & Visual Arts): History/Visual Arts—Chapter 14, "European Cultural and Religious Transformations." From Brummett, Palmira, et al. *Civilization: Past & Present (Volume I: To 1650)*, 11/e. C. 2007, Pearson/Longman. Literature—"Salvation" by Langston Hughes and "The Masque of the Red Death" by Edgar Allan Poe. From Sisko, Yvonne Collioud. *American 24-Karat Gold: 24 Classic American Short Stories*, 2/e. C. 2006, Longman. "Richard Cory" by Edwin Arlington Robinson and "Sympathy" by Paul Laurence Dunbar. From Barnet, Burto, and Cain, *An Introduction to Literature*, 14/e. C. 2006, Longman.
- Mathematics & Automotives: Chapter 14, "Math, Charts and Calculations." From Halderman, James D. *Automotive Technology*, 3/e. C. 2009, Pearson/Prentice Hall.
- Natural Sciences: Chapter 21, "Nutrition, Digestion, and Excretion." From Audesirk, Teresa, Gerald Audesirk, and Bruce E. Byers. *Life on Earth*, 5/e. C. 2009, by Pearson/Benjamin Cummings.
- Social Sciences & Criminal Justice: Chapter 17, "Terrorism and Multinational Criminal Justice." From Schmalleger, Frank. *Criminal Justice Today: An Introductory Text for the 21st Century*, 10/e. C. 2009, Pearson/Prentice Hall.
- Technical Fields & Computer Science: Chapter 15, "Getting Started with Microsoft PowerPoint 2007." From Gaskin, Shelley, et al. *GO! With Microsoft Office 2007 Introductory*, 2/e. C. 2008. Pearson/Prentice Hall.

The Instructor Answer Key is available for download via Pearson's Instructor Resource Center (www.pearsonhigered.com/irc). Simply log in using your login and password, and search by ISBN 020512089X. If you do not know your login and password, please contact your Pearson Representative (www.pearsonhighered.com/replocator).

May *Reading Strategies for Academic and Applied Disciplines* be beneficial to you all.

—Dawn Lee

Reading Strategies for the Disciplines

Reading a textbook is different than reading for pleasure. Regardless of what you are reading for your own interest or enjoyment, the fact that you are reading what you want to read makes even challenging material more interesting or enjoyable. Your professors know that by virtue of the fact that they have assigned reading, even an enjoyable novel for your literature class, they have basically drained any enjoyment out of the reading and made it a chore. *Having* to read is less enjoyable than *wanting* to read. And, if you are not someone who reads for pleasure, this has made the reading even drier. But you know what? You and your classmates are all in the same boat, and you chose to pursue a college degree, so regardless of whether or not you want to do assignments, you are required to do them. Now that the cold truth of the matter is out of the way, how do you make the best job out of it? Well, knowing what to look for helps.

TEXTBOOK DESIGN

The first thing to keep in mind about textbooks is that they are "information-dense." This means that they contain a great deal of information between their two covers. In fact, your introductory course level textbooks are like having a library in your hand on any given subject because you are given so much background knowledge within one book; therefore, take your time. Expect to have to read slowly and carefully, even that novel for literature. Why? Because you will be tested on the material, and you will have to apply the material. Since you have to remember and use the material, you will recall it better if you take some time up front to *preview your assignment before actually reading it* to see what the assignment contains, how it is organized and how the material is presented, and if there are any study aids within the chapter. When you preview, you go through the assignment page by page, reading only certain items word-for-word at this stage: the learning objectives or goals, the introduction, headings and subheadings, captions for all the graphics, margin notes, and the summary and/or review questions if they are provided. After you have previewed the chapter, *then go back to the beginning and read the entire chapter,* section by section. This means to start with the first heading, read to the next heading, then stop, review what you have read, make notes of or highlight the important material, then read from the second heading to the third, repeating the process until you complete the chapter. When you have finished reading the entire chapter, *review what you have read.* Make notes. Ideally, you should take notes on your reading so you can work yourself out of the book and study from your text notes. Once you weed out what you don't need for the test, why re-read it every time you are back in the text? Text notes take care of this problem. (If you later consolidate your text and lecture notes, you will have a very efficient study guide to review from.) Answer the review questions. Recite your notes to yourself. Follow the suggestions in your accompanying text about reading strategies.

The next thing to keep in mind is that most textbooks are set up in an *outline format.* In fact, you could write an outline of the chapter yourself during your preview of it just by reading the headings, subheadings, supporting points, and so on. The key here is to pay attention to the font and size of the lettering used for the headings. The largest font used in the chapter will be your main topics, which are usually designated with Roman numerals when outlining. The next size down will be your subheadings, which are usually designated with capital letters in outlines. If the headings continue in smaller and smaller print, just keep following the outline pattern of Arabic numerals, then lower-case letters, and so on. Spotting the outline pattern will help you recognize shifts in topics in the chapter. The headings also give you good stopping points if you need to break up the reading assignment into manageable chunks, which would be a good idea. Trying to read forty pages of any textbook in one sitting seems overwhelming. It is also a great deal of information to process at once, so breaking the chapter into smaller portions, maybe five to ten pages, will make the task more productive for you. Another idea is to break the assignment down based on time. Read for thirty minutes, then take a short break (without the television or the computer!), and then come back and read for another thirty minutes, and so on. One other strategy would be, if your textbook includes exercises within the chapter itself, to read to a set of exercises, complete the exercises/answer the questions while the information is fresh in your mind, then take a short break before continuing on in the chapter.

Another element to look for is the use of *graphics*. During your preview, pay attention to the illustrations used in the chapter. Look at the pictures, photos, tables, charts, and so on. Read the captions. Note what you are being shown. By looking at the graphics during the preview, you reduce their ability to distract you when you read. If you see them for the first time when you read, then you will lose your train of thought and what the author was telling you. In addition, we remember best when things are familiar to us. Our brains do not really recognize how long we have known something, just that we know it. Therefore, when you turn the page while reading, your eyes will see the illustration, your brain will recognize it as familiar, and then the text you are reading that relates to the illustration will be connected to it in your mind. This will help you retain information.

As mentioned previously, also note during your preview the *study aids* in the chapter. Use them! Begin by reading over the list of learning objectives at the beginning of the chapter. They list the major concepts to be covered. If they are included, read the chapter summary and the questions at the end of the chapter *before* you read the chapter itself. They also give you an overview of what is important before you start reading. The questions will also help you spot the information when you read because, as with the graphics, your mind will recognize that this is something you have seen before, so it will catch your attention. Then you can note the material to help you find it again when you answer the questions.

One other tip: do not skip reading the *boxed* information. Your professors know that unless they tell you to specifically read something, you won't. They often turn to these boxed sections, and chapter footnotes, to develop quiz or test questions in order to make the point that *you are responsible for the entire reading assignment before coming to class*. Therefore, be proactive. Read the entire chapter. Remember, forewarned is forearmed.

Finally, when taking on a new discipline, understanding the field into which one is heading often helps to make the transition from what is familiar into that which is new. Therefore, understanding how scholars in different disciplines approach their subject and the *thought processes* they use most often can help you adapt to their methods more quickly.

COMMON THOUGHT PROCESSES

The most common thought processes are a good place to begin. While most of these are used in most disciplines, some disciplines rely on some processes more than others. The thought processes you will come across most often are *definition*, *enumeration* or *listing*, *order* or *sequence*, *classification*, *comparison and contrast*, and *cause and effect*. By being able to recognize a pattern, you can then arrange your own thought process to prepare yourself for what is to come.

Definition is used to explain what something is or what a term means. Oftentimes the same words will be used in several disciplines, but in each discipline they may have a different meaning. Therefore, in order for you to understand the jargon of a discipline, you need to understand how the speakers define their terms. Your professor is going to expect you to learn and be able to use the terminology of the field you are studying, and the text is an excellent place to learn the language, so to speak. While the books often have a glossary at the end of the text to define terms, the terms will also be used in the context of the chapters. Granted, your context clues will help you determine meaning, but texts often highlight definitions in a variety of ways to be sure you know a term is important and learn it, as you will see in the chapters included here.

Enumeration, or *listing*, is used to provide informational items by naming one following another. This process is often closely associated with the *order*, or *sequence*, thought process. Information could be listed in *order of importance*, which means information is listed in ranked order from first to last or most to least important, or vice versa, and is usually enumerated by including words such as *first, second, next*, and *finally*. Dates or events are often listed in *chronological order*, so you can know the sequence of events based on time. Listing is also used for a *process*, such as the order to follow to perform the steps in your science lab experiments. Process is also important for *problem solving*, so you will know in which order to perform the mathematical operations to solve a math problem. Finally, listing may be used when discussing *spatial order*, which is when authors describe how a space is filled, such as from left to right, north to south, foreground to background, and so on.

All of these lead to *classification*. Human beings need things named and categorized. Our minds do have some limits, and in order to communicate, we need a common denominator: language. By naming things we can make specific references. By classifying things into categories, we can organize information. For example, in biology, all living creatures are classified, which is helpful when trying to separate mammals from fish. Then there are sub-classifications, such as canines. They are mammals, but a specific type of mammal, and then canines can become more specified by breaking the category down further into species, separating wolves from dogs, and then further into breeds, such as by separating dogs into Golden Retrievers and Labrador Retrievers. Since every discipline has its component parts, they all use classification.

One thought process that helps in classification is *comparison and contrast*. Comparison looks primarily for similarities, and contrast looks for differences. To go back to the above example of canines, we can compare in what ways wolves and dogs are similar to see why they are classified as canines and not felines, but there are differences between the two species. By contrasting them, we can then separate these canines from each other into different species. Comparison and contrast are also used to help introduce us to new information. Comparison is used to explain in what ways the new information is similar to something you already know. Since we learn more quickly when we recognize things, this connecting of ideas or information is important. Contrast is then used to show you how the new material is different from the old, and therefore something new. However, by attaching this new information to the old information, we are more likely to retain it for use later.

The remaining thought process, *cause and effect*, is a bit more of a challenge. When considering cause and effect, you need to be sure that one event did actually lead to, or cause, the outcome, or effect. Just because two events may occur simultaneously does not mean one necessarily caused the other. Be prepared to consider carefully the evidence you have been presented. Cause and effect is used to demonstrate a relationship between two or more events that seem to be connected. This is not the same as chronological order in which events simply occur one after the other, as one day leads into the next. Cause and effect means that one thing actually led to another outcome. Cause and effect is used in the disciplines because this is essentially what is being studied: how did one action or event bring about another development?

There are some other methods used to think about information that may be more specific to particular disciplines. For example, the social sciences and business often use the *case study*, which will explain to you all the information relating to one specific case, situation, business, individual, and so on. *Models* are used in business to show you, for example, how a plan would work when put into action, how a device works, how an organizational plan is set up. Models are often accompanied by diagrams or flow charts to help demonstrate the plan in action. *Theories* are included in all of the sciences and business. The *scientific method* is used in all of the sciences, natural and social. There are other processes as well, so be sure to read your textbook's explanations carefully. Remember that these books are written by experts in their fields of study, so when they offer you advice concerning how to learn and apply the material, take it.

One other thing to keep in mind is that you will usually have combined thought processes at work. For instance, often definitions include lists and comparison or contrast. The thought patterns do not usually occur in isolation. When trying to determine which process dominates, consider the entire explanation you are reading, not just the list within the definition. Below is a table indicating which thought processes are used most commonly by each discipline:

	Natural Sciences	Social Sciences	Business	Math	History	Humanities & Arts
Definition	X	X	X	X	X	X
Enum./listing	X	X	X		X	
Order/Seq.	X			X	X	X
Classification	X	X	X			
Comp/Cont	X	X	X	X	X	X
Cause/Effect	X	X			X	X
Process	X	X	X	X		X
Problem Solving	X		X	X		

Another thing to keep in mind is to buy a new textbook or a used one that is relatively unmarked. It is important to have an unmarked text so that you do your own work and without distractions. You need a book you can mark up yourself. Since many campus bookstores are self-service stores, if you must buy a used text, look through the ones that are in good shape on the outside. Often they are pretty clean on the inside, too. If your used text has markings, remove them if you can. If not, assume the previous owner was the weak student and not the strong one so you are not tempted to cheat and rely on the previous owner's work. The previous owner will not be taking your test for you, so you need to do the work yourself. This advice applies to the purchase of any course text.

ACADEMIC VS. APPLIED DISCIPLINES

If you are not already aware of it, there is a difference between academic disciplines and applied disciplines. Academic disciplines provide the material you need to know about your field of study. This is the core knowledge that anyone working within the discipline should have. Applied disciplines basically do what the name suggests: they teach you how to apply the core knowledge to a job. For example, when one studies history, the student learns history, not how to do history. On the other hand, in fields such as education, nursing, cosmetology, and automotives, the student not only learns about the subject, but how to actually do the job as well. Education majors will have practicums and student teaching to get experience in the classroom before graduating and being given their own students. Nursing majors will have clinical practices and hands-on training in hospitals. Students majoring in cosmetology, automotives, dental hygiene, foodservice, et cetera, will also have practicums, internships, clinical, or other situational job-related experiences to provide hands-on training. These disciplines not only provide background knowledge but also job training so one is prepared to do the job upon graduating.

This text includes chapters from textbooks from both academic and applied fields, and some of the applied ones actually do double-duty. For example, the mathematics/automotive chapter provides strategies for both, and the chapter itself covers information beneficial for anyone, regardless of which direction one is heading in with their course of study. In this way, the text can offer assistance to any student regardless of their academic program of study.

Unit I
Reading Strategies for Allied Health and Nursing

from

Kozier & Erb's Fundamentals of Nursing: Concepts, Process, and Practice

Eighth Edition

by

Audrey Berman, Shirlee J. Snyder, Barbara Kozier, and Glenora Erb

Allied health fields, such as nursing and other health care professions, will combine academic classes in the sciences and mathematics with applied courses to supply students with the skills they will need to perform the jobs in their chosen fields. For the science and mathematics courses, use the strategies found in those units in this text.

The chapter provided here explains the "Health Care Delivery Systems," which means this chapter would be a good overview of the health care fields. In many respects, this chapter is very similar to the chapters you will find in the business unit. A similar organization pattern is used for the chapter material, and similar graphics are used as well. Like the chapter in the social sciences unit, this chapter draws from multiple fields, including fields such as economics and sociology. As you will find, there is a great deal of cross-over in your disciplines. Knowledge should not be compartmentalized, and you need to learn to be a flexible thinker. This means, for example, to consider how science ties in with literature. How does mathematics tie in with criminal justice? And so on. The more connections you can find between the disciplines, the more efficient and productive you will be. To be good at your chosen career, you will need to learn to "think on your feet," which means being flexible and becoming adept at flipping through the huge hard drive of information in your brain to find the information you need quickly. You also need to be able to see how to use different areas of knowledge in perhaps unexpected places. This flexibility will help you serve your patients—or clients, customers, et cetera—better than if you compartmentalize knowledge.

CHAPTER 6

Health Care Delivery Systems

LEARNING OUTCOMES

After completing this chapter, you will be able to:

1. Differentiate health care services based on primary, secondary, and tertiary disease prevention categories.

2. Describe the functions and purposes of the health care agencies outlined in this chapter.

3. Identify the roles of various health care professionals.

4. Describe the factors that affect health care delivery.

5. Compare various systems of payment for health care services.

KEY TERMS

case management, *18*

coinsurance, *20*

critical pathways, *18*

diagnosis-related groups (DRGs), *21*

differentiated practice, *19*

health care system, *9*

health maintenance organization (HMO), *21*

independent practice associations (IPAs), *22*

integrated delivery system (IDS), *22*

licensed vocational (practical) nurse (LVN/LPN), *13*

managed care, *18*

Medicaid, *20*

Medicare, *20*

patient-focused care, *18*

preferred provider arrangements (PPAs), *22*

preferred provider organization (PPO), *21*

Supplemental Security Income (SSI), *20*

team nursing, *19*

A **health care system** is the totality of services offered by all health disciplines. It is one of the largest industries in the United States. Previously, the major purpose of a health care system was to provide care to the ill and injured. However, with increasing awareness of health promotion, illness prevention, and levels of wellness, health care systems are changing, as are the roles of nurses in these areas. The services provided by a health care system are commonly categorized according to type and level.

TYPES OF HEALTH CARE SERVICES

Health care services are often described in a way correlated with levels of disease prevention: (a) primary prevention, which consists of health promotion and illness prevention, (b) secondary prevention, which consists of diagnosis and treatment, and (c) tertiary prevention, which consists of rehabilitation, health restoration, and palliative care.

Primary Prevention: Health Promotion and Illness Prevention

Based on the notion of maintaining an optimum level of wellness, the World Health Organization (WHO) developed a project called Healthy People. The U.S. Department of Health and Human Services (2000) project that evolved from the original work is called *Healthy People 2010* and has two primary goals: (a) increase quality and years of healthy life and (b) eliminate health disparities.

Health promotion was slow to develop until the 1980s. Since that time more and more people are recognizing the advantages of staying healthy and avoiding illness. Primary prevention programs address areas such as adequate and proper nutrition, weight control and exercise, and stress reduction. Health promotion activities emphasize the important role clients play in maintaining their own health and encourage them to maintain the highest level of wellness they can achieve.

CLINICAL ALERT

As insurance companies have realized that keeping people healthy is less expensive than treating illnesses, their insurance plans have begun to pay for preventive health care activities. ∎

Illness prevention programs may be directed at the client or the community and involve such practices as providing immunizations, identifying risk factors for illnesses, and helping people take measures to prevent these illnesses from occurring. Illness prevention also includes environmental programs that can reduce the incidence of illness or disability. For example, steps to decrease air pollution include requiring inspection of automobile exhaust systems to ensure acceptable levels of fumes. Environmental protective measures are frequently legislated by governments and lobbied for by citizens groups.

Secondary Prevention: Diagnosis and Treatment

In the past, the largest segment of the health care services has been dedicated to the diagnosis and treatment of illness. Hospitals and physicians' offices have been the major agencies offering these complex secondary prevention services. Hospitals continue to focus significant resources on patients requiring emergency, intensive, and around-the-clock acute care.

Freestanding diagnostic and treatment facilities have also evolved and serve ever-growing numbers of clients. For example, magnetic resonance imaging (MRI) and related radiological diagnostic procedures are commonly performed at physician- or corporate-owned centers. Similar structures exist in outpatient surgical units (surgi-centers).

Also included as a health promotion service is early detection of disease. This is accomplished through routine screening of the population and focused screening of those at increased risk of developing certain conditions. Examples of early detection services include regular dental exams from childhood throughout life and bone density studies for women at menopause to evaluate for early osteoporosis. Community-based agencies have become instrumental in providing these services. For example, clinics in some communities provide mammograms and education regarding the early detection of cancer of the breast. Voluntary HIV testing and counseling is another example of the shift in services to community-based agencies. Some malls and shopping centers have walk-in clinics that provide diagnostic tests, such as screening for cholesterol and high blood pressure.

Tertiary Prevention: Rehabilitation, Health Restoration, and Palliative Care

The goal of tertiary prevention is to help people move to their previous level of health (i.e., to their previous capabilities) or to the highest level they are capable of given their current health status. Rehabilitative care emphasizes the importance of assisting clients to function adequately in the physical, mental, social, economic, and vocational areas of their lives. For example, someone with an injured neck or back from an automobile crash may have restrictions in the ability to perform work or daily activities. If the injury is temporary, rehabilitation can assist in return to former function. If the injury is permanent, rehabilitation assists the client in adjusting how to perform activities in order to achieve maximum abilities. Rehabilitation may begin in the hospital, but will eventually lead clients back into the community for further treatment and follow-up once health has been restored.

Sometimes, people cannot be returned to health. A growing field of nursing and tertiary prevention services is that of palliative care—providing comfort and treatment for symptoms. End-of-life care may be conducted in many settings, including the home.

TYPES OF HEALTH CARE AGENCIES AND SERVICES

Health care agencies and services in the United States and Canada are both varied and numerous. Some health care agencies or systems provide services in different settings; for example, a hospital may provide acute inpatient services, outpatient clinic or ambulatory care services, and emergency room services. Hospice services may be provided in the hospital, in the home, or in another agency within the community (see Figure 6-1 ■). Because the array of health care agencies and services is so great, nurses often need to help clients choose that which best suits their needs. Clients may be seen by any number and type of nurses and other providers, depending on their care and ability to pay for the services.

Public Health

Government (official) agencies are established at the local, state, and federal levels to provide public health services. Health agencies at the state, county, or city level vary according to the need of the area. Their funds, generally from taxes, are administered by elected or appointed officials. Local health departments have responsibility for developing programs to meet the health needs of the people, providing the necessary nursing and other staff and facilities to carry out these programs, continually evaluating the effectiveness of the programs, and monitoring changing needs. State health organizations are responsible for assisting the local health departments. In some remote areas, state departments also provide direct services to people.

The Public Health Service (PHS) of the U.S. Department of Health and Human Services is an official agency at the federal level. Its functions include conducting research and providing training in the health field, providing assistance to communities in planning and developing health facilities, and assisting states and local communities through financing and provision of

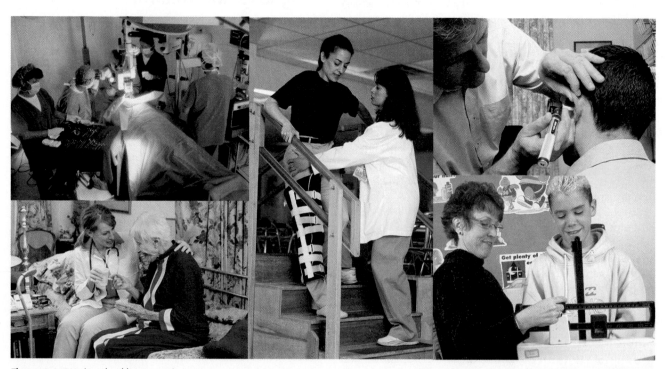

Figure 6-1 ■ Various health care settings.

trained personnel. Also at the national level in the United States are research institutions such as the National Institutes of Health (NIH). The National Institute on Drug Abuse, the National Institute on Alcohol Abuse and Alcoholism, and the National Institute of Mental Health work with federal, regional, and state agencies. The Centers for Disease Control and Prevention (CDC) in Atlanta, Georgia, administer a broad program related to surveillance of diseases and behaviors that lead to disease and disability. By means of laboratory and epidemiological investigations, data are made available to the appropriate authorities. The CDC also publishes recommendations about the prevention and control of infections and administers a national health program. The federal government also administers a number of Veterans Affairs (VA) services in the United States.

Physicians' Offices

In North America, the physician's office is a primary care setting. The majority of physicians either have their own offices or work with several other physicians in a group practice. Clients usually go to a physician's office for routine health screening, illness diagnosis, and treatment. People seek consultation from physicians when they are experiencing symptoms of illness or when a significant other considers the person to be ill.

In some medical office practices, such as those of family practice physicians or specialists such as dermatologists or surgeons, nurse practitioners practice alongside physicians. Often, physicians' offices do not require the expertise of registered nurses. Where there are RNs, they have a variety of roles and responsibilities, including client registration, preparing the client for an examination, obtaining health information, and providing information. Other functions may include obtaining specimens, assisting with procedures, and providing some treatments. In offices without RNs, these tasks may be performed by medical assistants.

Ambulatory Care Centers

Ambulatory care centers are used frequently in many communities. Most ambulatory care centers have diagnostic and treatment facilities providing medical, nursing, laboratory, and radiological services, and they may or may not be associated with an acute care hospital. Some ambulatory care centers provide services to people who require minor surgical procedures that can be performed outside the hospital. After surgery, the client returns home, often the same day. These centers offer two advantages: They permit the client to live at home while obtaining necessary health care, and they free costly hospital beds for seriously ill clients. The term *ambulatory care center* has replaced the term *clinic* in many places.

Occupational Health Clinics

The industrial (occupational) clinic is gaining importance as a setting for employee health care. Employee health has long been recognized as important to productivity. Today, more companies recognize the value of healthy employees and encourage healthy lifestyles by providing exercise facilities and coordinating health promotion activities.

Community health nurses in the occupational setting have a variety of roles. Worker safety has always been a concern of occupational nurses. Today, nursing functions in industrial health care include work safety and health education, annual employee health screening for tuberculosis, and maintaining immunization information. Other functions may include screening for such health problems as hypertension and obesity, caring for employees following injury, and counseling.

Hospitals

Hospitals vary in size from the 12-bed rural hospital to the 1,500-bed metropolitan hospital. Hospitals can be classified according to their ownership or control as governmental (public) or nongovernmental (private). In the United States, governmental hospitals are either federal, state, city, or county hospitals. The federal government provides hospital facilities for veterans and merchant mariners (VA hospitals). Military hospitals provide care to military personnel and their families. Private hospitals are often operated by churches, companies, communities, and charitable organizations. Private hospitals may be for-profit or not-for-profit. Although hospitals are chiefly viewed as institutions that provide care, they have other functions, such as providing sources for health-related research and teaching.

Hospitals are also classified by the services they provide. General hospitals admit clients requiring a variety of services, such as medical, surgical, obstetric, pediatric, and psychiatric services. Other hospitals offer only specialty services, such as psychiatric or pediatric care. An acute care hospital provides assistance to clients whose illness and need for hospitalization are relatively short term, for example, several days.

The variety of health care services hospitals provide usually depends on their size and location. The large urban hospitals usually have inpatient beds, emergency services, diagnostic facilities, ambulatory surgery centers, pharmacy services, intensive and coronary care services, and multiple outpatient services provided by clinics. Some large hospitals have other specialized services such as spinal cord injury and burn units, oncology services, and infusion and dialysis units. In addition, some hospitals have substance abuse treatment units and health promotion units. Small rural hospitals often are limited to inpatient beds, radiology and laboratory services, and basic emergency services. The number of services a rural hospital provides is usually directly related to its size and its distance from an urban center.

Hospitals in the United States have undergone organizational changes in order to contain costs or to attract clients. Some hospitals have merged with other hospitals or have been purchased by large multihospital for-profit corporations (e.g., Columbia/HCA Healthcare Corporation, Humana, and Tenet, Inc.). Other hospitals are providing innovative outpatient services, such as fitness classes, day care for elderly people, nutrition classes, and alternative birth centers.

Subacute Care Facilities

Subacute care is a variation of inpatient care designed for someone who has an acute illness, injury, or exacerbation of a disease process. Clients may be admitted after, or instead of, acute hospitalization or to administer one or more technically complex treatments. Generally, the individual's condition is such that the care does not depend heavily on high-technology monitoring or complex diagnostic procedures. Subacute care requires the coordinated services of an interdisciplinary team including physicians, nurses, and other relevant professional disciplines. Subacute care is generally more intensive than long-term care and less than acute care.

Extended Care (Long-Term Care) Facilities

Extended care facilities, formerly called nursing homes, are now often multilevel campuses that include independent living quarters for seniors, assisted living facilities, skilled nursing facilities (intermediate care), and extended care (long-term care) facilities that provide levels of personal care for those who are chronically ill or are unable to care for themselves without assistance. Traditionally, extended care facilities only provided care for elderly clients, but they now provide care to clients of all ages who require rehabilitation or custodial care. Because clients are being discharged earlier from acute care hospitals, some clients may still require supplemental care in a skilled nursing or extended care facility before they return home.

Because chronic illness occurs most often in the elderly, long-term care facilities have programs that are oriented to the needs of this age group. Facilities are intended for people who require not only personal services (bathing, hygiene, eating) but also some regular nursing care and occasional medical attention. However, the type of care provided varies considerably. Some facilities admit and retain only residents who are able to dress themselves and are ambulatory. Other extended care facilities provide bed care for clients who are more incapacitated. These facilities can, in effect, become the client's home, and consequently the people who live there are frequently referred to as residents rather than patients or clients.

Specific guidelines govern the admission procedures for clients admitted to an extended care facility. Insurance criteria, treatment needs, and nursing care requirements must all be assessed beforehand. Extended care and skilled nursing facilities are becoming increasingly popular means for managing the health care needs of clients who do not meet the criteria for remaining in the hospital. Nurses in extended care facilities assist clients with their daily activities, provide care when necessary, and coordinate rehabilitation activities.

CLINICAL ALERT

Elders may move among levels of care several times—from independent living, to a hospital, to a rehabilitation center, to long-term care, and hopefully back to independent or assisted living. The sequence varies as will the length of time in each setting. ∎

Retirement and Assisted Living Centers

Retirement or assisted living centers consist of separate houses, condominiums, or apartments for residents. Residents live rela-

tively independently; however, many of these facilities offer meals, laundry services, nursing care, transportation, and social activities. Some centers have a separate hospital to care for residents with short-term or long-term illnesses. Often these centers also work collaboratively with other community services including case managers, social services, and a hospice to meet the needs of the residents who live there. The retirement or assisted living center is intended to meet the needs of people who are unable to remain at home but do not require hospital or nursing home care. Nurses in retirement and assisted living centers provide limited care to residents, usually related to the administration of medications and minor treatments, but conduct significant health promotion activities.

Rehabilitation Centers

Rehabilitation centers usually are independent community centers or special units. However, because rehabilitation ideally starts the moment the client enters the health care system, nurses who are employed on pediatric, psychiatric, or surgical units of hospitals also help to rehabilitate clients. Rehabilitation centers play an important role in assisting clients to restore their health and recuperate. Drug and alcohol rehabilitation centers, for example, help free clients of drug and alcohol dependence and assist them to reenter the community and function to the best of their ability. Today, the concept of rehabilitation is applied to all illness and injury (physical and mental). Nurses in the rehabilitation setting coordinate client activities and ensure that clients are complying with their treatments. This type of nursing often requires specialized skills and knowledge.

Home Health Care Agencies

The implementation of prospective payment (discussed later in this chapter) and the resulting earlier discharge of clients from hospitals have made home care an essential aspect of the health care delivery system. As concerns about the cost of health care have escalated, the use of the home as a care delivery site has increased. In addition, the scope of services offered in the home has broadened. Home health care nurses and other staff offer education to clients and families and also provide comprehensive care to acute, chronic, and terminally ill clients.

Day-Care Centers

Day-care centers serve many functions and many age groups. Some day-care centers provide care for infants and children while parents work. Other centers provide care and nutrition for adults who cannot be left at home alone but do not need to be in an institution. Elder care centers often provide care involving socializing, exercise programs, and stimulation. Some centers provide counseling and physical therapy. Nurses who are employed in day-care centers may provide medications, treatments, and counseling, thereby facilitating continuity between day care and home care.

Rural Care

Rural primary care hospitals were created as a result of the 1987 Omnibus Budget Reconciliation Act to provide emergency care to clients in rural areas. In 1997, the Balanced Budget Act authorized the Medicare Rural Hospital Flexibility Program in order to continue to make available primary care access and improve emergency care for rural residents. This program established a new classification called critical access hospitals, which receive federal funding to remain open and provide the breadth of services needed for rural residents, including interfaces with regional tertiary care centers. Each state has an Office of Rural Health Programs that assesses and identifies interventions for the health care needs of the local population. Nurses in rural settings must be generalists who are able to manage a wide variety of clients and health care problems. Due to their training in providing comprehensive primary care across the life span, nurse practitioners are particularly suited to these roles.

Hospice Services

Originally, a hospice was a place for travelers to rest. Recently the term has come to mean interdisciplinary health care service for the dying, provided in the home or another health care setting. The hospice movement subsumes a variety of services given to the terminally ill, their families, and support persons. The central concept of the hospice movement, as distinct from the acute care model, is not saving life but improving or maintaining the quality of life until death. Hospice nurses serve primarily as case managers and supervise the delivery of direct care by other members of the team. Clients in hospice programs are cared for at home, in the hospital, or in skilled nursing facilities. The place of health care delivery may vary as the client's condition declines or the ability of the family to care for the client changes. The hospice nurse does ongoing assessments of needs of the client and family and helps to find the appropriate resources and additional services for them as needed.

Crisis Centers

Crisis centers provide emergency services to clients experiencing life crises. These centers may operate out of a hospital or in the community, and most provide 24-hour telephone service. Some also provide direct counseling to people at the center or in their homes. The primary purpose of the center is to help people cope with an immediate crisis and then provide guidance and support for long-term therapy.

Nurses working in crisis centers need well-developed communication and counseling skills. The nurse must immediately identify the person's problem, offer assistance to help the person cope, and perhaps later direct the person to resources for long-term support.

Mutual Support and Self-Help Groups

In North America today, there are more than 500 mutual support or self-help groups that focus on nearly every major health problem or life crisis people experience. Such groups arose largely because people felt their needs were not being met by the existing health care system. Alcoholics Anonymous, which formed in 1935, served as the model for many of these groups. The National Self-Help Clearinghouse provides information on current support groups and guidelines about how to start a self-

help group. The nurse's role in self-help groups is discussed in Chapter 27. ∞

PROVIDERS OF HEALTH CARE

The providers of health care, also referred to as the health care team or health professionals, are nurses and health personnel from different disciplines who coordinate their skills to assist clients and their support persons. Their mutual goal is to restore a client's health and promote wellness (Figure 6-2 ■). The choice of personnel for a particular client depends on the needs of the client. Health teams commonly include the nurse and several different personnel. Nurses' roles are described in Chapter 1 ∞ and throughout this textbook. The non-nurse providers that follow are in alphabetical order and are not an all-inclusive list of possible providers.

Nurse

The role of the nurse varies with the needs of the client, the nurse's credentials, and the type of employment setting. A registered nurse (RN) assesses a client's health status, identifies health problems, and develops and coordinates care. A **licensed vocational nurse (LVN),** in some states known as a **licensed practical nurse (LPN),** provides direct client care under the direction of a registered nurse, physician, or other licensed practitioner. As nursing roles have expanded, new dimensions for nursing practice have been established. Nurses can pursue a variety of practice specialties (e.g., critical care, mental health, oncology). Advanced practice nurses (APNs) provide direct client care as nurse practitioners, nurse midwives, certified registered nurse anesthetists, and clinical nurse specialists. These nurses have education and certifications that—depending on state regulations—

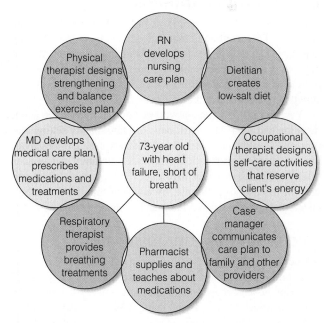

Figure 6-2 ■ Although all members of the health care team individualize care for the client based on the expertise of their own discipline, there are areas of overlap facilitated through teamwork.

may allow them to provide primary care, prescribe medications, and receive third-party (insurance) reimbursement directly for their services.

Alternative (Complementary) Care Provider

Alternative or complementary health care refers to those practices not commonly considered part of Western medicine. See Chapter 19 ∞ for detailed description of these. Chiropractors, herbalists, acupuncturists, massage therapists, reflexologists, holistic health healers, and other health care providers are playing increasing roles in the contemporary health care system. These providers may practice alongside Western health care providers, or clients may use their services in conjunction with, or in lieu of, Western therapies.

Case Manager

The case manager's role is to ensure that clients receive fiscally sound, appropriate care in the best setting. This role is often filled by the member of the health care team who is most involved in the client's care. Depending on the nature of the client's concerns, the case manager may be a nurse, a social worker, an occupational therapist, a physical therapist, or any other member of the health care team.

Dentist

Dentists diagnose and treat dental problems. Dentists are also actively involved in preventive measures to maintain healthy oral structures (e.g., teeth and gums). Many hospitals, especially long-term care facilities, have dentists on staff.

Dietitian or Nutritionist

A dietitian, often a registered dietitian, has special knowledge about the diets required to maintain health and to treat disease. Dietitians in hospitals generally are concerned with therapeutic diets, may design special diets to meet the nutritional needs of individual clients, and supervise the preparation of meals to ensure that clients receive the proper diet.

A nutritionist is a person who has special knowledge about nutrition and food. The nutritionist in a community setting recommends healthy diets and gives broad advisory services about the purchase and preparation of foods. Community nutritionists often function at the preventive level. They promote health and prevent disease, for example, by advising families about balanced diets for growing children and pregnant women.

Occupational Therapist

An occupational therapist (OT) assists clients with impaired function to gain the skills to perform activities of daily living. For example, an occupational therapist might teach a man with severe arthritis in his arms and hands how to adjust his kitchen utensils so that he can continue to cook. The occupational therapist teaches skills that are therapeutic and at the same time provide some fulfillment. For example, weaving is a recreational activity but also exercises the arthritic man's arms and hands.

Paramedical Technologist

Laboratory technologists, radiological technologists, and nuclear medicine technologists are just three kinds of paramedical technologists in the expanding field of medical technology. *Paramedical* means having some connection with medicine. Laboratory technologists examine specimens such as urine, feces, blood, and discharges from wounds to provide exact information that facilitates the medical diagnosis and the prescription of a therapeutic regimen. The radiological technologist assists with a wide variety of x-ray film procedures, from simple chest radiography to more complex fluoroscopy. The nuclear medicine technologist uses radioactive substances to provide diagnostic information and can administer therapeutic doses of radioactive materials as part of a therapeutic regimen.

Pharmacist

A pharmacist prepares and dispenses pharmaceuticals in hospital and community settings. The role of the pharmacist in monitoring and evaluating the actions and effects of medications on clients is becoming increasingly prominent. A clinical pharmacist is a specialist who guides physicians in prescribing medications. A pharmacy assistant is also recognized in some states. This person administers medications to clients or works in the pharmacy under the direction of the pharmacist.

CLINICAL ALERT

Significant overlap may occur among those providers who can perform certain health care activities. For example, an anesthesiologist (MD), a neonatal care nurse, or a respiratory therapist may be responsible for assisting a newborn baby with breathing problems. All providers perform client teaching. ■

Physical Therapist

The licensed physical therapist (PT) assists clients with musculoskeletal problems. Physical therapists treat movement dysfunctions by means of heat, water, exercise, massage, and electric current. The physical therapist's functions include assessing client mobility and strength, providing therapeutic measures (e.g., exercises and heat applications to improve mobility and strength), and teaching new skills (e.g., how to walk with an artificial leg). Some physical therapists provide their services in hospitals; however, independent practitioners establish offices in communities and serve clients either at the office or in the home. Physical therapy aides also work with PTs and clients.

Physician

The physician is responsible for medical diagnosis and for determining the therapy required by a person who has a disease or injury. The physician's role has traditionally been the treatment of disease and trauma (injury); however, many physicians are now including health promotion and disease prevention in their practice. Some physicians are general practitioners (also known as primary care or family practitioners), while others are dermatologists, neurologists, oncologists, orthopedists, pediatricians, psychiatrists, radiologists, or surgeons—to name a few.

Physician Assistant

Physician assistants (PAs) perform certain tasks under the direction of a physician. They diagnose and treat certain diseases, conditions, and injuries. In many states, nurses are not legally permitted to follow a PA's orders unless they are cosigned by a physician. In some settings, PAs and nurse practitioners have similar job descriptions.

Podiatrist

Doctors of podiatric medicine (DPM) diagnose and treat foot conditions. They are licensed to perform surgery and prescribe medications.

Respiratory Therapist

A respiratory therapist is skilled in therapeutic measures used in the care of clients with respiratory problems. These therapists are knowledgeable about oxygen therapy devices, intermittent positive pressure breathing respirators, artificial mechanical ventilators, and accessory devices used in inhalation therapy. Respiratory therapists administer many of the pulmonary function tests.

Social Worker

A social worker counsels clients and their support persons regarding problems, such as finances, marital difficulties, and adoption of children. It is not unusual for health problems to produce problems in day-to-day living and vice versa. For example, an elderly woman who lives alone and has a stroke resulting in impaired walking may find it impossible to continue to live in her third-floor apartment. Finding a more suitable living arrangement can be the responsibility of the social worker if the client has no support network in place.

Spiritual Support Personnel

Chaplains, pastors, rabbis, priests, and other religious or spiritual advisors serve as part of the health care team by attending to the spiritual needs of clients. In most facilities, local clergy volunteer their services on a regular or on-call basis. Hospitals affiliated with specific religions, as well as many large medical centers, have full-time chaplains on staff. They usually offer regularly scheduled religious services. The nurse is often instrumental in identifying the client's desire for spiritual support and notifying the appropriate person.

Unlicensed Assistive Personnel

Unlicensed assistive personnel (UAPs) are health care staff who assume delegated aspects of basic client care. These tasks include bathing, assisting with feeding, and collecting specimens. UAP titles include certified nurse assistants, hospital attendants, nurse technicians, patient care technicians, and orderlies. Some of these categories of provider may have standardized education and job duties (e.g., certified nurse assistants), while others do

not. The parameters regarding nurse delegation to UAPs are delineated by the state boards of nursing.

FACTORS AFFECTING HEALTH CARE DELIVERY

Today's health care consumers have greater knowledge about their health than in previous years, and they are increasingly influencing health care delivery. Formerly, people expected a physician to make decisions about their care; today, however, consumers expect to be involved in making any decisions. Consumers have also become aware of how lifestyle affects health. As a result, they desire more information and services related to health promotion and illness prevention. A number of other factors affect the health care delivery system.

Increasing Number of Elderly

By the year 2020 it is estimated that the number of U.S. adults over the age of 65 years will be more than 53 million (U.S. Census Bureau, 2004). Long-term illnesses are prevalent among this group, and they frequently require special housing, treatment services, financial support, and social networks. The frail elderly, considered to be people over age 85, are projected to be the fastest growing population in the United States and will number over 76.5 million by 2020 and almost 90 million by 2030 (U.S. Census Bureau). Because only 5% of older people are institutionalized with health problems, substantial home management and nursing support services are required to assist those living in their homes and communities.

Older people also need to feel they are part of a community even though they are approaching the end of their lives. The feeling of being a useful, wanted, and productive citizen is essential to every person's health. Special programs are being designed in communities so that the talents and skills of this group will be used and not lost to society.

Advances in Technology

Scientific knowledge and technology related to health care are rapidly increasing. Improved diagnostic procedures and sophisticated equipment permit early recognition of diseases that might otherwise have remained undetected. New antibiotics and medications are continually being manufactured to treat infections and multiple drug-resistant organisms. Surgical procedures involving the heart, lungs, and liver that were nonexistent 20 years ago are common today. Laser and microscopic procedures streamline the treatment of diseases that required surgery in the past.

Computers, bedside charting, and the ability to store and retrieve large volumes of information in databases are commonplace in health care organizations. In addition, as a result of the Internet and World Wide Web access from numerous public and private locations, clients now have access to medical information similar to that of health care providers (although not all websites provide accurate information). One example of a reliable source of health care information for clients is the Agency for Healthcare Research and Quality (AHRQ) website: *Guide to Health Care Quality* (2005).

MediaLink — Where Do Elders Live Application

MediaLink — Nursing Assistants Video

MediaLink — Physician Assistant Video

These discoveries have changed the profile of the client. Clients are now more likely to be treated in the community, utilizing resources, technology, and treatments outside the hospital. For example, years ago a person having cataract surgery had to remain in bed in the hospital for 10 days; today, most cataract removals are performed on an outpatient basis in outpatient surgery centers.

Technological advances and specialized treatments and procedures may come, unfortunately, with a high price tag. Some diagnostic equipment may cost millions of dollars. Due to this expenditure plus the expense of training specialized personnel to perform the tests, each procedure can cost consumers hundreds or thousands of dollars.

Economics

Paying for health care services is becoming a greater problem. The health care delivery system is very much affected by a country's total economic status. According to the Centers for Medicaid and Medicare Services (CMS, 2006), health spending in 2004 was $1.8 trillion in the United States and projected to reach $3.6 trillion by 2014, increasing an average of 7.1% per year. This is currently equal to over $5,000 per year for every man, woman, and child and will more than double to $11,000 by 2014. About 33% are inpatient hospital expenses, 21% physician office and clinic expenses, 15% prescription drug expenses, and the remainder emergency department, home care, dental, and related services. Approximately 42% of these costs are paid through private insurance, 45% through public programs, and 14% out-of-pocket (paid directly by the person) (Kashihara & Carper, 2005).

The major reasons for cost increases are as follows:

■ Existing equipment and facilities are continually becoming obsolete as research uncovers new and better methods in health care. Health care providers and patients want the newest and the best, and these cost more each year.
■ Inflation increases all costs.
■ The total population is growing, especially the segment of older adults who tend to have greater health care needs than younger persons.
■ As more people recognize that health is everyone's right, large numbers of people are seeking assistance in health matters. The average American sees a doctor three times per year, but infants less than 12 months of age and elders over 65 average almost seven visits per year (Hing, Cherry, & Woodwell, 2005).
■ The relative number of people who provide health care services has increased.
■ The numbers of uninsured persons are increasing: approximately 25% of persons under age 65 are uninsured at some time during a year and 13% are uninsured for the entire year (Rhoades, 2006a). Although these percentages have not changed dramatically in the past decade, since the population has increased, the total number of persons affected is rising.
■ The cost of prescription drugs is increasing. As of January 2006, Medicare recipients are eligible for prescription drug coverage to help cover some basic and catastrophic medication costs.

Women's Health

The women's movement has been instrumental in changing health care practices. Examples are the provision of childbirth services in more relaxed settings such as birthing centers, and the provision of overnight facilities for parents in children's hospitals. Until recently, women's health issues focused on the reproductive aspects of health, disregarding many health care concerns that are unique to women. Investigators are beginning to recognize the need for research that examines women equally to men in health issues such as osteoporosis, heart disease, and responses to various treatment modalities. Current provision of health care shows an increased emphasis on the psychosocial aspects of women's health, including the impact of career, delayed childbearing, role of caregiver to older family members, and extended life span.

Uneven Distribution of Services

Serious problems in the distribution of health services exist in the United States. Two facets of this problem are (a) uneven distribution and (b) increased specialization. In some areas, particularly remote and rural locations, there are insufficient health care professionals and services available to meet the health care needs of individuals. Rural clients may need to drive large distances to obtain the services they require. Uneven distribution is evidenced by the relatively higher number of nurses per capita in the New England states and the lowest number in California and Nevada (see Figure 6-3 ■). Physicians are also unevenly distributed: In 2003, Mississippi, Idaho, Iowa, and Oklahoma had the fewest physicians per 100,000 people, whereas the District of Columbia, Massachusetts, Maryland, and Vermont had the most (National Center for Health Statistics, 2005).

An increasing number of health care personnel provide specialized services. Specialization can lead to fragmentation of care and, often, increased cost of care. To clients, it may mean receiving care from 5 to 30 people during their hospital experience. This seemingly endless stream of personnel and paperwork required is often confusing and frightening.

Access to Health Insurance

Another problem plaguing individuals is access to health insurance. Data from 2004 show that one in seven Whites, one in five Blacks, and more than one in three Hispanics are uninsured (Rhoades, 2006b). Lack of health insurance is related to income. Persons with incomes below or near the poverty level are at least three times as likely to have no health insurance coverage as those with incomes twice the poverty level or higher (National Center for Health Statistics, 2005). Low income has been associated with relatively higher rates of infectious diseases (e.g., tuberculosis, AIDS), problems with substance abuse, rape, violence, and chronic diseases. Thus, those with the greatest need for health care are often those least able to pay for it. Even though some government assistance is available, eligibility for government insurance programs and benefits varies considerably from state to state and is continually being reevaluated. Other aspects of variations in health beliefs and practices among people of different cultures are found in Chapter 18. ∞

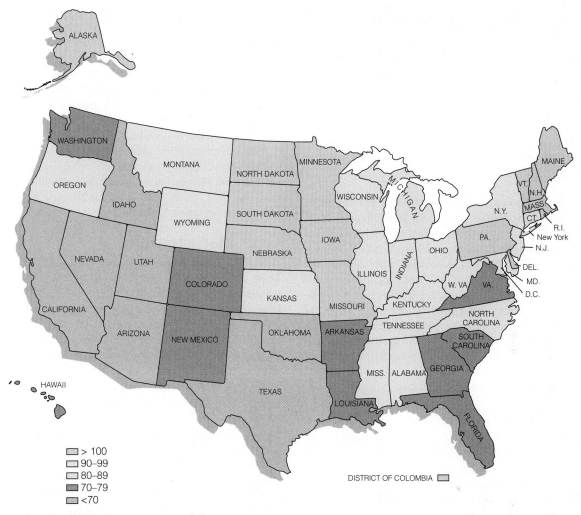

Figure 6-3 ■ Number of nurses per 100,000 population map.

Source: Data from Department of Health & Human Services, Bureau of Health Professions, Division of Nursing. (2004). *The registered nurse population: National sample survey of registered nurses March 2004. Preliminary findings.* Retrieved January 11, 2006, from http://bhpr.hrsa.gov/healthworkforce/reports/rnpopulation/preliminaryfindings.htm

The Homeless and the Poor

Because of the conditions in which homeless people live (in shelters, on the streets, in parks, in tents, under temporary covers and dwellings, in transportation terminals, or in cars), their health problems are often exacerbated and sometimes become chronic. Physical, mental, social, and emotional factors create health care challenges for the homeless and the poor (see Box 6–1). These persons may lack convenient or timely transportation to health care facilities—especially if repeated visits are necessary. Limited access to health care services significantly contributes to the general poor health of the homeless and poor in the United States.

Health Insurance Portability and Accountability Act (HIPAA)

One of the major alterations in how health care is practiced in this country may be attributed to the Health Insurance Portability and Accountability Act of 1996 (HIPAA). These new regulations were instituted to protect the privacy of individuals by safeguarding individually identifiable health care records, in-

cluding those housed in electronic media (see Box 6–2). Protection of individual medical records extends not only to clinical health care sites but also to all ancillary health care providers such as pharmacies, laboratories, and third-party payers. Each

---

BOX 6–1 Factors Contributing to Health Problems of the Homeless and the Poor

■ Poor physical environment resulting in increased susceptibility to infections
■ Inadequate rest and privacy
■ Improper nutrition
■ Poor access to facilities for personal hygiene
■ Exposure to the elements
■ Lack of social support
■ Few personal resources
■ Questionable personal safety (physical assault is a constant threat for the homeless)
■ Inconsistent health care
■ Difficulty with adherence to treatment plans

BOX 6–2	**Intent of HIPAA Regulation**

- Provides individuals with more control over their health information.
- Establishes limits for appropriate use and release of health care information.
- Requires the majority of health care providers and their agents to comply with safeguards to protect individual privacy related to health care information.
- Delineates a set of civil and criminal penalties holding HIPAA regulation transgressors accountable for actions if the client's health care privacy is violated.

health care provider dealing with client health care information must, by HIPAA regulations, provide for secure limited access to that information. This is accomplished by restricting access to only those individuals who truly need to possess the information to aid the client, by locking documents in file cabinets, and by limiting computer access to health care files. The regulated privacy has altered the way health care providers share information. Each client is provided a notice of privacy practices for each type of health care provider. These notices clearly state how and under what conditions individual health care records will be shared with other persons or agencies. Violation of HIPAA regulations by health care providers or agencies can result in heavy fines for this breach of trust.

Demographic Changes

The characteristics of the North American family have changed considerably in the last few decades. The numbers of single-parent families and alternative family structures have increased markedly. Most of the single-parent families are headed by women, many of whom work and require assistance with child care or when a child is sick at home.

Recognition of the cultural and ethnic diversity of the United States and Canada is also increasing. Health care professionals and agencies are aware of this diversity and are employing means to meet the challenges it presents. For example, more agencies are employing nurses who are bilingual and who can communicate with clients whose primary language is not English.

FRAMEWORKS FOR CARE

A number of configurations for the delivery of nursing care support continuity of care and cost-effectiveness. These include managed care, case management, patient-focused care, differentiated practice, shared governance, the case method, the functional method, team nursing, and primary nursing. These have evolved, some from each other, for reasons such as the need to decrease health care costs and to improve the utilization of limited human and physical resources. A particular agency may use more than one configuration—for example, team nursing on the medical-surgical units and primary nursing on the cardiac surgery unit.

Managed Care

Managed care describes a health care system whose goals are to provide cost-effective, quality care that focuses on decreased costs and improved outcomes for groups of clients. The care of a client is carefully planned from initial contact to the conclusion of the specific health problem. In managed care, health care providers and agencies collaborate to render the most appropriate, fiscally responsible care possible. Managed care denotes an emphasis on cost controls, customer satisfaction, health promotion, and preventive services. Health maintenance organizations and preferred provider organizations are examples of provider systems committed to managed care.

Managed care can be used with primary, team, functional, and alternative nursing care delivery systems. Although managed care has been embraced as a model for health care reform, many question the application of this business approach to a commodity as precious as health.

Case Management

Case management describes a range of models for integrating health care services for individuals or groups. Generally, case management involves multidisciplinary teams that assume collaborative responsibility for planning, assessing needs, and coordinating, implementing, and evaluating care for groups of clients from preadmission to discharge or transfer and recuperation. A case manager, however, may be a nurse, social worker, or other appropriate professional. In some areas of the United States, case managers may be referred to as discharge planners. Key responsibilities for case managers/discharge planners are shown in Box 6–3.

Case management may be used as a cost-containment strategy in managed care. Both case management and managed care systems often use **critical pathways** to track the client's progress. A critical pathway is an interdisciplinary plan or tool that specifies interdisciplinary assessments, interventions, treatments, and outcomes for health-related conditions across a time line. Critical pathways are also called critical paths, interdisciplinary plans, anticipated recovery plans, interdisciplinary action plans, and action plans.

Patient-Focused Care

Patient-focused care is a delivery model that brings all services and care providers to the clients. The supposition is that if activities normally provided by auxiliary personnel (e.g., physical therapy, respiratory therapy, ECG testing, and phlebotomy) are moved closer to the client, the number of personnel involved and the number of steps involved to get the work done are decreased. Cross-training, development of multiskilled workers who can perform tasks or functions in more than one discipline, is an essential element of patient-focused care.

BOX 6–3	**Responsibilities of Case Managers/Discharge Planners**

- Assessing clients and their homes and communities
- Coordinating and planning client care
- Collaborating with other health professionals
- Monitoring clients' progress
- Evaluating client outcomes

Differentiated Practice

Differentiated practice is a system in which the best possible use of nursing personnel is based on their educational preparation and resultant skill sets. Thus, differentiated practice models consist of specific job descriptions for nurses according to their education or training, for example, LVN, associate degree RN, BSN RN, MSN RN, or APN. The model is customized within each health care institution by the nurses employed there. The institution must first identify the nursing competencies required by the clients within the specific practice environment. This model further requires the delineation of roles between both licensed nursing personnel and UAPs. This enables nurses to progress and assume roles and responsibilities appropriate to their level of experience, capability, and education. As with managed care and case management, differentiated nursing practice seeks to provide quality care at an affordable cost.

Shared Governance

The shared governance model can be used in concert with other models of nursing delivery. It is an organizational model in which nursing staff are cooperative with administrative personnel in making, implementing, and evaluating client care policies. The focus of this model is to encourage participation of nurses in decision making at all levels of the organization. Individuals may participate either at their own request or as part of their job role criteria. More commonly, nurses participate through serving in decision-making groups, such as committees and task forces. The decisions made may also address employment conditions, cost-effectiveness, long-range planning, productivity, and wages and benefits. The underlying principle of shared governance is that employees will be more committed to the organizational goals if they have had input into planning and decision making.

Case Method

The case method, also referred to as total care, is one of the earliest nursing models developed. In this client-centered method, one nurse is assigned to and is responsible for the comprehensive care of a group of clients during an 8- or 12-hour shift. For each client, the nurse assesses needs, makes nursing plans, formulates diagnoses, implements care, and evaluates the effectiveness of care. In this method, a client has consistent contact with one nurse during a shift but may have different nurses on other shifts. The case method, considered the precursor of primary nursing, continues to be used in a variety of practice settings such as intensive care nursing.

Functional Method

The functional nursing method focuses on the jobs to be completed (e.g., bed making, temperature measurement). In this task-oriented approach, personnel with less preparation than the professional nurse perform less complex care requirements. It is based on a production and efficiency model that gives authority and responsibility to the person assigning the work, for example, the head nurse. Clearly defined job descriptions, procedures, policies, and lines of communication are required. The

functional approach to nursing is economical and efficient and permits centralized direction and control. Its disadvantages are fragmentation of care and the possibility that nonquantifiable aspects of care, such as meeting the client's emotional needs, may be overlooked.

Team Nursing

Team nursing is the delivery of individualized nursing care to clients by a team led by a professional nurse. A nursing team consists of registered nurses, licensed practical nurses, and unlicensed assistive personnel. This team is responsible for providing coordinated nursing care to a group of clients.

The registered nurse retains responsibility and authority for client care but delegates appropriate tasks to the other team members. Proponents of this model believe the team approach increases the efficiency of the registered nurse. Opponents state that inpatients' high acuity of illness leaves little to be delegated.

Primary Nursing

Primary nursing is a system in which one nurse is responsible for overseeing the total care of a number of clients 24 hours a day, 7 days a week, even if he or she does not deliver all the care personally. It is a method of providing comprehensive, individualized, and consistent care.

Primary nursing uses the nurse's technical knowledge and management skills. The primary nurse assesses and prioritizes each client's needs, identifies nursing diagnoses, develops a plan of care with the client, and evaluates the effectiveness of care. Associates provide some care, but the primary nurse coordinates it and communicates information about the client's health to other nurses and other health professionals. Primary nursing encompasses all aspects of the professional role, including teaching, advocacy, decision making, and continuity of care. The primary nurse is the first-line manager of the client's care with all its inherent accountabilities and responsibilities.

FINANCING HEALTH CARE

Although efforts have been made to control the costs of health care, these costs continue to increase. Employers, legislators, insurers, and health care providers continue to collaborate in efforts to resolve the issues surrounding how to best finance health care costs. Among these efforts, the United States has implemented some cost-containment strategies including health promotion and illness prevention activities, managed care systems, and alternative insurance delivery systems. The U.S. Center for Outcomes and Effectiveness Research (COER) conducts and supports studies on the outcomes and effectiveness of diagnostic, therapeutic, and preventive health care services and procedures, including cost.

Payment Sources in the United States

In most situations, a health care agency receives funding from several of the available payment sources. For example, an elderly client may have Medicare coverage and supplement Medicare with private insurance plus the need to pay some out-of-pocket

 MediaLink The Competent Case Manager Application

RESEARCH NOTE

Do the Types of Nurses and Delivery Models in Hospitals Influence Client Outcomes?

Researchers in this study correlated the number of professional nursing staff on a total of 77 medical, surgical, and obstetrical units in 19 hospitals with costs and quality of care. Quality of care was measured through the client outcomes: rates of medication errors, falls, and certain infections. Over 1,000 nurses were surveyed for the care delivery model used on their units. These models included total care, team nursing, and primary care nursing. They were also asked about communication and coordination within the nursing unit.

Quality, coordination, and communication were statistically superior on those units that had all registered nurse staffing as opposed to staffing that included unlicensed assistive personnel and practical nurses. Quality was lower on those units that used the total care delivery model.

IMPLICATIONS

This is one of several significant nursing research studies that have shown a relationship between the composition of the nursing staff and the quality of client care. In every case, the larger the percentage of registered nurses among the total care staff, the lower the incidence of adverse client outcomes such as falls, errors, and preventable infections. It is more difficult to correlate outcomes with care delivery models in that each unit may employ slight variations in the model and comparisons among units are difficult. However, it is important to continue to examine delivery models and their effectiveness in order to allow optimal deployment of registered nurses in a time of a shortage.

Note: From "Nurse Staffing Models, Nursing Hours, and Patient Safety Outcomes," by L. M. Hall, D. Doran, and G. H. Pink, 2004, *Journal of Nursing Administration, 34,* pp. 41–45.

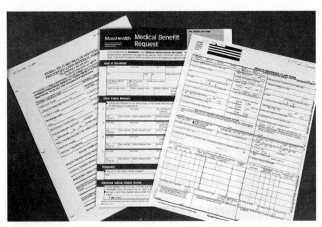

Figure 6-4 ■ Medicare helps defray the costs of health care.

expenses (see Figure 6-4 ■). Almost all insurance plans include a per-visit or per-prescription copayment.

Medicare and Medicaid

In the United States, the 1965 **Medicare** amendments (Title 18) to the Social Security Act provided a national and state health insurance program for older adults. By the mid-1970s, virtually everyone over 65 years of age was protected by hospital insurance under Part A, which also includes post-hospital extended care and home health benefits. In 1972, its coverage was broadened to include workers with permanent disabilities and their dependents who are eligible for disability insurance under Social Security. In 1988, Congress expanded Medicare to include extremely expensive hospital care, "catastrophic care," and expensive drugs.

The Medicare plan is divided into parts: Part A is available to people with disabilities and people 65 years and over. It provides insurance toward hospitalization, home care, and hospice care. Part B is voluntary and provides partial coverage of outpatient and physician services to people eligible for Part A. Part D is the voluntary prescription drug plan begun in January 2006. Most clients pay a monthly premium for Parts B and D coverage.

All Medicare clients pay a deductible and coinsurance. **Coinsurance** is the percentage share (usually 20%) of a government-approved charge that is paid by the client; the remaining percent is paid by the plan.

Medicare does not cover dental care, dentures, eyeglasses, hearing aids, or examinations to prescribe and fit hearing aids. Most preventive care, including routine physical examinations and associated diagnostic tests, is also not included. However, as part of the 1997 Balanced Budget Act, annual screening mammograms for women over age 40 are now a fully covered cost under Medicare.

Medicaid was also established in 1965 under Title 19 of the Social Security Act. Medicaid is a federal public assistance program paid out of general taxes to people who require financial assistance, such as people with low incomes. Medicaid is paid by federal and state governments. Each state program is distinct. Some states provide very limited coverage, whereas others pay for dental care, eyeglasses, and prescription drugs.

In 1972, Congress directed the Department of Health, Education, and Welfare to create professional standards review organizations to monitor the appropriateness of hospital use under the Medicare and Medicaid programs. In 1974, the National Health Planning and Resources Development Act established health systems agencies throughout the United States for comprehensive health planning. In 1978, the Rural Health Clinics Act provided for the development of health care in medically underserved rural areas. This act opened the door for nurse practitioners to provide primary care.

Supplemental Security Income

Persons with disabilities or those who are blind may be eligible for special payments called **Supplemental Security Income (SSI)** benefits. These benefits are also available to people not eligible for Social Security, and payments are not restricted to health care costs. Clients often use this money to purchase medicines or to cover costs of extended health care.

State Children's Health Insurance Program (SCHIP)

The SCHIP was established by the U.S. government in 1997 to provide insurance coverage for poor and working-class children. The program expands coverage for children under Medicaid and subsidizes low-cost state insurance alternatives. Coverage includes visits to primary health care providers, prescription medicines, and hospitalization. State eligibility requirements vary, but generally, children 18 years and under who live in families earning less than $34,100 per year (for a family of four) are eligible. Many children have been protected from loss of health insurance when a parent loses a job, but over 7 million children remain uninsured (Cawley & Simon, 2005) and outreach efforts are not as effective as they could be. Research indicates that if families are offered application materials when they are seen in the emergency department, enrollment increases significantly (Gordon, Emond, & Camargo, 2005).

Prospective Payment System

To curtail health care costs in the United States, Congress in 1983 passed legislation putting the prospective payment system into effect. This legislation limits the amount paid to hospitals that are reimbursed by Medicare. Reimbursement is made according to a classification system known as **diagnosis-related groups (DRGs).** The system has categories that establish pretreatment diagnosis billing categories.

Under this system, the hospital is paid a predetermined amount for clients with a specific diagnosis. For example, a hospital that admits a client with a diagnosis of uncomplicated asthma is reimbursed a specified amount, such as $1,300, regardless of the cost of services, the length of stay, or the acuity or complexity of the client's illness. Prospective payment or billing is formulated before the client is even admitted to the hospital; thus, the record of admission, rather than the record of treatment, now governs payment. DRG rates are set in advance of the prospective year during which they apply and are considered fixed except for major, uncontrollable occurrences.

Insurance Plans

A variety of plans have come into existence to finance health care in the United States. These include private insurance and group insurance. Each individual and group plan offers different options for consumers to consider when choosing a prepaid health care program. The Institute of Medicine issued six research reports from 2001 to 2004 identifying the scope of the problem of the underinsured in America. They recommended five principles for addressing the problem:

1. Health coverage should be for everyone.
2. Health coverage should be ongoing/uninterruptible.
3. Individuals and families need to have coverage they can afford.
4. A national approach must be cost effective and able to be maintained by the society.
5. The care provided under this coverage must ensure care that is "effective, safe, timely, patient centered, and equitable" (Jennings, 2004, p. 101).

Private Insurance

In the United States, numerous commercial health insurance carriers offer a wide range of coverage plans. There are two types of private insurance: not-for-profit (e.g., Blue Shield) and for-profit (e.g., Metropolitan Life, Travelers, and Aetna). Private health insurance pays either the entire bill or, more often, 80% of the costs of health care services. With private insurance health plans, the insurance company reimburses the health care provider a fee for each service provided (fee-for-service). The term *third-party reimbursement* refers to the insurance company that pays the client's (first party) bill to the provider (second party).

These insurance plans may be purchased either as an individual plan or as part of a group plan through a person's employer, union, student association, or similar organization. For private insurance not covered by an employer, the individual usually pays a monthly premium for health care insurance. Group plans offer lower premiums that may be paid for completely by the employer, completely by group members, or some combination of the two.

Group Plans

Health care group plans provide blanket medical service in exchange for a predetermined monthly payment. A variety of group plans have come into existence to finance health care in the United States. These include health maintenance organizations, preferred provider organizations, preferred provider arrangements, independent practice associations, and physician/hospital organizations. Each group plan offers different options for consumers to consider when choosing a prepaid health care program.

HEALTH MAINTENANCE ORGANIZATIONS. A **health maintenance organization (HMO)** is a group health care agency that provides health maintenance and treatment services to voluntary enrollees. A fee is set without regard to the amount or kind of services provided.

The HMO plan emphasizes client wellness; the better the health of the person, the fewer the HMO services that are needed and the greater the agency's profit. Members of HMOs choose a primary care provider (PCP): an internal medicine physician, general practitioner, or nurse practitioner who evaluates their health status and coordinates their care. If the primary care provider cannot treat a particular problem because of its special nature, he or she may decide to make a referral to a specialist provider. For example, a client with a skin problem sees a PCP. After evaluating the client, the PCP has two options: treat the condition or refer the client to a dermatologist. To reduce costs, HMOs will pay for specialty services only if the PCP has made a referral to the specialist. It is an expectation between the HMO and PCPs being reimbursed under their plans that PCPs will treat clients and reduce costs whenever possible.

Thus, under HMO plans, clients are limited in their ability to select health care providers and services, but available services are at reduced and predetermined cost to the client. Because health promotion and illness prevention are highly emphasized in HMOs, nurses in HMOs focus on these aspects of care. Companies that provide HMO plans such as Kaiser Permanente, United Healthcare, and Aetna have been established across the United States, although not in every community.

PREFERRED PROVIDER ORGANIZATIONS. The **preferred provider organization (PPO)** consists of a group of providers and perhaps a health care agency (often hospitals) that provide an insurance company or employer with health services at a discounted rate. One advantage of the PPO is that it provides clients with a choice of health care providers and services. Providers can belong to one or several PPOs, and the client can choose among the providers belonging to the PPO. A disadvantage of PPOs is that they tend to be slightly more expensive than HMO plans, and if individuals wish to join a PPO, they might have to pay more for the additional choices.

PREFERRED PROVIDER ARRANGEMENTS. **Preferred provider arrangements (PPAs)** are similar to PPOs. The main difference is that the PPAs can be contracted with individual health care providers, whereas PPOs involve an organization of health care providers. A PPA plan can be limited or unlimited. A limited PPA restricts the client to using only preferred providers of health care; an unlimited PPA permits the client to use any health care provider in the area who accepts the contractual agreement of the plan. Again, with PPAs, more choices in health care providers may mean more cost to the enrollee.

INDEPENDENT PRACTICE ASSOCIATIONS. **Independent practice associations (IPAs)** are somewhat like HMOs and PPOs. The IPA provides care in offices, just as the providers belonging to a PPO do. The difference is that clients pay a fixed prospective payment to the IPA, and the IPA pays the provider. In some instances, the health care provider bills the IPA for services; in others, the provider receives a fixed fee for services given. At the end of the fiscal year, any surplus money is divided among the providers; any loss is assumed by the IPA.

PHYSICIAN/HOSPITAL ORGANIZATIONS. Physician/hospital organizations (PHOs) are joint ventures between a group of private practice physicians and a hospital. PHOs combine both resources and personnel to provide managed care alternatives and medical services. PHOs work with a variety of insurers to provide services. A typical PHO will include primary care providers and specialists.

A PHO may be part of an **integrated delivery system (IDS).** Such a system incorporates acute care services, home health care, extended and skilled care facilities, and outpatient services. Most integrated delivery systems provide care throughout the life span. Insurers can contract with IDSs to provide all required services, rather than the insurer contracting with multiple agencies for the same services. Ideally, an IDS enhances continuity of care and communication between professionals and various agencies providing managed care.

LIFESPAN CONSIDERATIONS   Assessing Elders' Functional Levels

Assessing the functional levels of elders on an ongoing basis will provide guidelines for detecting needs for special care, resources, and services. It helps to determine their level of independence and changes as they occur. The two most common assessments are to evaluate the following activities of daily living and instrumental activities of daily living:

ACTIVITIES OF DAILY LIVING

- Bathing
- Dressing
- Toileting
- Transferring
- Continence
- Feeding

INSTRUMENTAL ACTIVITIES OF DAILY LIVING

- Ability to use the telephone
- Shopping
- Food preparation
- Housekeeping
- Laundry
- Mode of transportation
- Responsibility for own medication
- Ability to handle finances

The case study in this chapter in the Critical-Thinking Checkpoint is an example of how these assessments and needs might change for elders. Mobilizing appropriate resources to help maintain elders' functioning ability is important in providing nursing care.

CRITICAL THINKING CHECKPOINT

Mr. Mendel is an 83-year-old married man. He has a history of severe osteoarthritis leading to bilateral hip replacements and one knee replacement. He has mild hypertension controlled by oral medication. His last orthopedic surgery was done to replace a hip component that failed due to repeated dislocations. At that time, he developed a severe urinary tract infection resulting in weight loss, fatigue, and weakness. After stabilizing, he was sent to the skilled nursing unit of the hospital for 2 weeks until ready to go back home. Occupational therapists consulted with him and his wife during his hospitalization.

He lives in a three-story house with the bedrooms on the top floor, kitchen and living room on the middle/main floor, and family room on the bottom floor. He has not driven since the last operation, but would like to. He has smoked cigars for years and sits on the front porch to smoke. Physical therapists have come to the house three times a

week for several months. A home health nurse has also been consulted periodically to assist with nutrition and elimination difficulties.

1. In what ways has Mr. Mendel used (a) health promotion and illness prevention (primary prevention), (b) diagnosis and treatment (secondary prevention), and (c) rehabilitation and health restoration (tertiary prevention) health care services?
2. Name three types of health care agencies he has used. What are the strengths of each of these?
3. Mr. Mendel's insurance company has assigned him a case manager. What would this person's responsibilities be in his particular case?
4. What other members of the health care profession would most likely be on the case manager's team and why?

See Critical Thinking Possibilities in Appendix A.

CHAPTER 6 REVIEW

CHAPTER HIGHLIGHTS

- Health care delivery services can be categorized by the type of service: (1) primary prevention: health promotion and illness prevention, (2) secondary prevention: diagnosis and treatment, and (3) tertiary prevention: rehabilitation, health restoration, and palliative care.
- Hospitals provide a wide variety of services on an inpatient and outpatient basis. Hospitals can be categorized as for-profit or not-for-profit, public or private, acute care or long-term care. Many other settings, such as clinics, offices, and day-care centers, also provide care.
- Various providers of health care coordinate their skills to assist a client. Their mutual goal is to restore a client's health and promote wellness.
- The role of the nurse in providing care to clients will vary depending on the employment setting, the nurse's credentials, and the needs of the client.
- The many factors affecting health care delivery include the increasing number of elderly people, advances in knowledge and

technology, economics, increased emphasis on women's health, uneven distribution of health services, access to health care, health care of the homeless and poor, HIPAA, and demographic changes.
- Delivery of nursing care that supports continuity of client-focused care and is cost-effective may be implemented by any of the following methods: managed care, case management, patient-focused care, differentiated practice, shared governance, case method, functional method, team nursing, or primary care nursing.
- In the United States, health care is financed largely through government agencies and private organizations that provide health care insurance, prepaid plans, and federally funded programs. Government-financed plans include Medicare and Medicaid. Private plans include Blue Cross and Blue Shield. Prepaid group plans include HMOs, PPOs, PPAs, IPAs, and PHOs.

TEST YOUR KNOWLEDGE

1. Which of the following is an example of a primary prevention activity?
  1. Antibiotic treatment of a suspected urinary tract infection
  2. Occupational therapy to assist a client in adapting his or her home environment following a stroke
  3. Nutrition counseling for young adults with a strong family history of high cholesterol
  4. Removal of tonsils for a client with recurrent tonsillitis

2. Which of the following statements is true regarding types of health care agencies?
  1. Hospitals provide only acute, inpatient services.
  2. Public health agencies are funded by governments to investigate and provide health programs.
  3. Surgery can only be performed inside a hospital setting.
  4. Skilled nursing, extended care, and long-term care facilities provide care for the elderly whose insurance no longer covers hospital stays.

3. In most cases, clients must have a primary care provider in order to receive health insurance benefits. If a client is in need of a primary care provider, it is most appropriate for the nurse to recommend which of the following?

  1. Family practice physician
  2. Physical therapist
  3. Case manager/discharge planner
  4. Pharmacist

4. The most significant method for reducing the ongoing increase in the cost of health care in the United States includes controlling which of the following?
  1. Number of children according to the family's income
  2. Numbers of uninsured and underinsured persons
  3. Number of physicians and nurses nationwide
  4. Competition among drug and medical equipment manufacturers

5. A client is seeking to control health care costs for both preventive and illness care. Although no system guarantees exact out-of-pocket expenditures, the most prepaid and predictable client contribution would be seen with:
  1. Medicare.
  2. An individual fee-for-service insurance.
  3. A preferred provider organization (PPO).
  4. A health maintenance organization (HMO).

See Answers to Test Your Knowledge in Appendix A.

EXPLORE MEDIALINK www.prenhall.com/berman

DVD-ROM
- Audio Glossary
- NCLEX Review
- Videos
    Long-Term Care Facilities
    Using Health Care Technology Systems

COMPANION WEBSITE
- Additional NCLEX Review
- Case Study: Delivery Systems
- Application Activities:
    Where Do Elders Live?
    Issues Plaguing Women and Children
    Health Care and Indigents
    The Competent Case Manager
- Links to Resources

READINGS AND REFERENCES

SUGGESTED READINGS

DeLenardo, C. (2004). Web-based tools steer patient-focused care. *Nursing Management, 35*(12), 60–64.
This article depicts methods to utilize Web-based information to improve understanding of potential treatment venues to cancer patients.

Frist, W. H. (2005). Overcoming disparities in U.S. health care. *Health Affairs, 24*, 445–451.
The many dimensions of health disparities include race, ethnicity, socioeconomic status, and geography. This article suggests strategies for policy makers to address health security for all regardless of socioeconomic characteristics.

RELATED RESEARCH

Agency for Healthcare Research and Quality. (2004). Hospital nurse staffing and quality of care. *Research in Action, Issue 14.* AHRQ Publication No. 04-0029. Retrieved June 9, 2006, from http://www.ahrq.gov/research/nursestaffing/nursestaff.htm

Furaker, C., Hellstrom-Muhli, U., & Walldal, E. (2004). Quality of care in relation to a critical pathway from the staff's perspective. *Journal of Nursing Management, 12*, 309–316.

Short, P. F., & Graefe, D. R. (2003). Battery-powered health insurance? Stability in coverage of the uninsured. *Health Affairs, 22*, 244–255.

REFERENCES

Agency for Healthcare Research and Quality. (2005). *Guide to health care quality.* Retrieved June 24, 2006, from http://www.ahrq.gov/consumer/guidetoq

Department of Health & Human Services, Bureau of Health Professions, Division of Nursing. (2004). *Preliminary findings: 2004 national sample survey of registered nurses.* Retrieved June 25, 2006, from http://bhpr.hrsa.gov/healthworkforce/reports/rnpopulation/preliminaryfindings.htm

Cawley, J., & Simon, K. I. (2005). Health insurance coverage and the macroeconomy. *Journal of Health Economics, 24*, 299–315.

Centers for Medicaid and Medicare Services (CMS). (2006). *National health expenditure data.* Retrieved June 11, 2006, from http://www.cms.hhs.gov/NationalHealthExpendData/03_NationalHealthAccountsProjected.asp#TopOfPage

Gordon, J. A., Emond, J. A., & Camargo, C. A. (2005). The State Children's Health Insurance Program: A multicenter trial of outreach through the emergency department. *American Journal of Public Health, 95*, 250–253.

Hall, L. M., Doran, D., & Pink, G. H. (2004). Nurse staffing models, nursing hours, and patient safety outcomes. *Journal of Nursing Administration, 34*, 41–45.

Hing, E., Cherry, D. K., & Woodwell, D. A. (2005). National ambulatory medical care survey: 2003 summary. *Advance data from vital and health statistics;* No. 3645. Retrieved June 25, 2006, from http://www.cdc.gov/nchs/data/ad/ad365.pdf

Jennings, C. P. (2004). Insuring America's health: Principles and recommendations: IOM report. *Policy, Politics, and Nursing Practice, 5*, 100–101.

Kashihara, D., & Carper, K. (2005). *National health care expenses in the U.S. civilian noninstitutionalized population, 2003.* Statistical Brief No. 103. Rockville, MD: Agency for Healthcare Research and Quality. Retrieved June 25, 2006, from http://www.meps.ahrq.gov/papers/st103/stat103.pdf

National Center for Health Statistics. (2005). *Health: United States, 2005.* Hyattsville, MD: Author.

Rhoades, J. A. (2006a). *The uninsured in America, 1996–2005: Estimates for the U.S. civilian noninstitutionalized population under age 65.* Statistical Brief #130. Rockville, MD: Agency for Healthcare Research and Quality. Retrieved June 25, 2006, from http://www.meps.ahrq.gov/papers/st130/stat130.pdf

Rhoades, J. A. (2006b). *The uninsured in America, First half of 2005: Estimates for the U.S. civilian noninstitutionalized population under age 65.* Statistical Brief No. 129. Rockville, MD: Agency for Healthcare Research and Quality. Retrieved June 25, 2006, from http://www.meps.ahrq.gov/papers/st129/stat129.pdf

U.S. Census Bureau. (2004). *U.S. interim projections by age, sex, race, and Hispanic origin.* Retrieved June 24, 2006, from http://www.census.gov/ipc/www/usinterimproj/natprojtab02a.pdf

U.S. Department of Health and Human Services. (2000). *Healthy people 2010: Understanding and improving health* (2nd ed.). Washington, DC: U.S. Government Printing Office.

SELECTED BIBLIOGRAPHY

American Association of Colleges of Nursing. (1995). *A model for differentiated nursing practice.* Washington, DC: Author.

Brown, G. (2004). Nursing and its future status. *Minority Nurse Newsletter, 11*(1), 1.

Cutler, D. M. (2004). *Your money or your life: Strong medicine for America's health care system.* New York: Oxford University Press.

Erickson, J. I., & Miller, S. (2005). Caring for patients while respecting their privacy: Renewing our commitment. *Online Journal of Issues in Nursing, 10*(2), Manuscript 2. Retrieved June 11, 2006, from http://www.nursingworld.org/ojin/topic27/tpc27_1.htm

Feuer, L. (2004). The growing population of uninsured: Are you prepared for the challenge? *Case Manager, 15*, 19–21.

Hall, L., & Doran, D. (2004). Nurse staffing, care delivery model, and patient care quality. *Journal of Nursing Care Quality, 19*(1), 27–33.

Harrington, C., & Estes, C. L. (Eds.). (2004). *Health policy and nursing: Crisis and reform in the U.S. health care delivery system* (4th ed.). Boston: Jones & Bartlett.

Institute of Medicine. (2004). *Uninsured in America.* Retrieved June 6, 2006, from http://www.iom.edu/Object.File/Master/21/040/0.pdf

Kovner, A. R., & Knickman, J. R. (2005). *Jonas & Kovner's health care delivery in the United States* (8th ed.). New York: Springer.

Simpson, S. H., Majumdar, S. R., & Marrie, T. J. (2003). Physician-related barriers to the adoption of a critical pathway for community-acquired pneumonia: A qualitative analysis. *Journal of General Internal Medicine, 18* (Suppl. 1), 275–280.

Chapter 6: Health Care Delivery Systems

CHECKING YOUR READING STRATEGIES
DISCUSSION AND CRITICAL THINKING QUESTIONS

1. **Preview the chapter** as you have been instructed. *Without reading the chapter itself*, write an outline of the chapter. Leave room to fill in the details later. Use your typographical cues to help you. (Do not include the "Chapter Review" section in your outline.)

2. **Preview the chapter again**, this time focusing on all the graphic illustrations. Read all the captions and information in tables; look carefully at all photographs and drawings. Next, let your eyes scan over the columns of text. See if you can find where in the paragraphs the illustrated material is explained. What cues are given in the text to tie the illustrations to the words?

3. *Circle the best answer for each of the following questions.*

   1. According to the outline listed at the beginning of the chapter, this chapter will cover how many points?
      a. Four
      b. Ten
      c. Five
      d. Not enough information to answer the question

   2. What is the *overall purpose* of the chapter's introduction?
      a. To define a term
      b. To offer a case study
      c. To set up the focus for the chapter
      d. To demonstrate how health care works

   3. How many types of graphic illustrations are used in this chapter? Look through the entire chapter. Select all that apply.
      a. Photographs
      b. Charts
      c. Graphs
      d. Organizational charts
      e. Shaded boxes (of formulas, theories, etc.)
      f. Maps
      g. Branching/tree diagrams
      h. In-chapter assessments/quizzes
      i. Diagrams
      j. Tables
      k. Flow charts
      l. Pie charts
      m. Process diagrams
      n. Margin notes

   4. What typographical cues are used in the chapter to highlight important information for you? Select all that apply.
      a. Boldface print
      b. Font size
      c. Bulleted lists
      d. Color of print
      e. Shading
      f. Symbols (light bulb, question mark, star, etc.)
      g. Italicized print
      h. Font style
      i. Underlining
      j. Boxes
      k. Arrows to show direction/order

4. **Preview** the "Chapter Highlights" and the "Test Your Knowledge" questions. Read over the review of the concepts and the questions. These are the key points the authors feel you should draw from the chapter. How do the authors tie the concepts back to the text so you would know where to find the information? Go back and look for it. Make a checkmark in the margin so you will remember this is a key point when you read the chapter.

5. Now go back to the first page of the chapter and read the chapter. Move through the chapter section by section. Read first, then decide what information is important for you to know and what is explanatory to illustrate the point. Next, return to the outline you drafted for question 1. Fill in the outline with the information you have determined to be important for you to remember. Consider your method as well. **How** did you determine which information was important enough to record?

6. Did you read the "Clinical Alert" inserts? If not, go back and do them. Why do you think these are included in the text? Of what benefit are they to you and your reading of the chapter?

7. Did you read the "Research Note" boxes? How are these relevant to you? Why do you think the authors included them? How do they help you learn?

8. Did you read the "Critical Thinking Checkpoint"? If not, go back and do so now. Answer the questions as well. Why is this included at this point in the chapter? How does it help you learn?

9. Finally, **after reading** the chapter, answer the questions at the end under "Test Your Knowledge." How well did you do?

GROUP PROJECTS

1. Compare your outline with that of your classmates. Are they all the same? If not, how do they differ? Why do you think that may be? Next, compare how well you and your classmates did when answering the questions at the end of the text's chapter. Did those of you with the more detailed outline do better? Why or why not?

2. Within your group, discuss the benefits of previewing the illustrations in the text before reading, as opposed to waiting to explore them as they come up in the reading.

3. As a group, consider what the authors do to make this chapter interesting and appealing to you. Consider both the visual components and the information itself. How do page layout and writing style make assigned reading more enjoyable?

4. Discuss with your groups which health tips you might adopt and why.

5. Discuss with your group how helpful the chapter's information will be for you to care for your own health. Have the authors left out any systems/providers you have had to consider in your experience?

6. As a group, consider the different types of assessments supplied in the text. Why are they included? How do they aid your reading?

Unit II
Reading Strategies for Business and Foodservice

from

Foodservice Organizations: A Managerial and Systems Approach
Sixth Edition

by

Mary B. Gregoire and Marian C. Spears (deceased)

While business is a discipline that is considered a social science, it is often in a separate category. Business usually encompasses accounting, business, economics, management, and marketing courses. The focus here is on human interaction with commerce and finance. Studying business may help you with your own business plans, but it could surely help you with your own money management. Understanding how commerce and finance work will be beneficial regardless of what your major field of study is.

Business courses often focus on the *organization* of business structures and the *management* of business operation systems. *Branching diagrams* often accompany these so that you can see how steps in a process or the departments in a company connect to each other. *Flow charts* are easy to spot because they are branching diagrams that use arrows to connect the related parts so you can readily see the flow, or direction, of the process. Another branching diagram, the *organizational chart,* is often used to depict how a business is organized. In addition, business *models* are often included to provide prime examples of, for example, how business systems work or how business plans are put into action, as the name suggests. *Case studies* may also be used to provide an example of a particular situation. The model may be more of a representation, and the case studies show the model put into practice.

The chapter included here ties together business and foodservice. In "Marketing Foodservice," you get the marketing information you would learn in a business course applied to the field of foodservice. In this way, you can see marketing strategies put into practice in a particular field.

One other thing to consider about this particular text chapter is that it is printed in black and white. You might want to consider what effect, if any, color printing has on enhancing your digestion of the material in a text.

CHAPTER

14

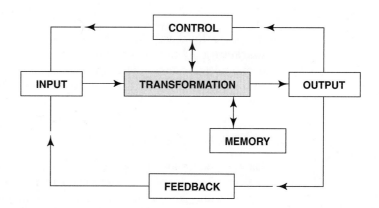

Marketing Foodservice

Enduring Understanding
- Marketing is more than advertising and promoting products or services.
- Marketing involves determining customer wants and needs and designing products/services that will be profitable and meet those wants/needs.

Learning Objectives
After reading and studying this chapter, you should be able to

1. Define core marketing terms such as marketing mix, target market, market segmentation, and promotion.
2. Develop a marketing plan for a foodservice operation.
3. Describe ways a market may be segmented, based on demographic, geographic, or psychographic characteristics.

Marketing has become a philosophy and a way of doing business in many industries, including the foodservice industry. In this chapter, you will see that marketing is much more than advertising and selling. You will be introduced to basic marketing concepts and definitions and will learn strategies and techniques that foodservice managers can use to develop a strong marketing program for their operation.

SYSTEMS APPROACH TO MARKETING MANAGEMENT

Managers in all types of foodservice operations, whether commercial or onsite, recognize marketing as a component of management. Marketing is an integral component of the management functions that transform inputs into outputs (see Figure 14.1). Marketing, long defined in terms of a product, now includes a much stronger emphasis on the consumer. Achieving customer satisfaction as an output of the foodservice system depends in part on the success of a foodservice manager's ability to apply marketing principles in his or her operation.

DEFINITION OF MARKETING

Marketing has been defined in many ways. The American Marketing Association, the professional association for those interested in the marketing discipline, defines **marketing** as "an organizational function and a set of processes for creating, communicating, and delivering value to customers and for managing customer relationships in ways that benefit the organization and its stakeholders" (see www.marketingpower.com).

Marketing Products

Many activities are needed to market products or goods. Producers, sellers, and buyers of products are all involved in marketing. Because of escalating costs in products and labor in the past decade, noncommercial foodservice managers have become cognizant of the value of using marketing principles. Competition for survival has become a priority for healthcare organizations, universities, and other institutions. Commercial foodservice managers learn early to be competitive because of the high failure rate of restaurants.

For an *exchange* to occur between two or more individuals or organizations, each must be willing to give up "something of value" for "something of value" (Pride & Ferrell, 1997). Both the buyer and seller have to communicate with each other to make their "something of value" available, as shown in Figure 14.2. In most situations, the seller has products, and the buyer has financial resources such as money or credit. In an exchange, products are traded for other products or money. The exchange must be satisfying to both the buyer and the seller. The

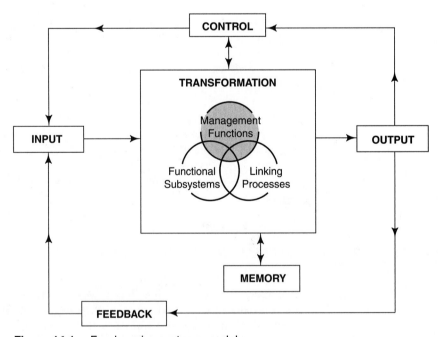

Figure 14.1. Food service systems model.

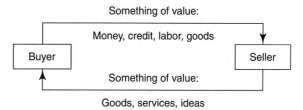

Figure 14.2. Exchange between buyer and seller.
Source: Pride, William, & Ferrell, O. C. *Marketing: Concepts and Strategies,* 10th edition. Copyright © 1997 by Houghton Mifflin Company. Used by permission.

buyer must be pleased with the product received from the seller and the seller with the reimbursement.

MARKETING CONCEPT

The **marketing concept** is a management philosophy about how an organization views customers and the sale of their product. In marketing terms, a "product" is a good, service, or idea. Kotler, Bowen, and Makens (1999) categorize marketing philosophies into five concepts:

- **Manufacturing/production concept**—based on the belief that customers favor products that are available and highly affordable; thus, companies should focus on production and distribution efficiency.
- **Product concept**—based on belief that customers prefer existing products and product forms; thus, companies should develop good versions of these products.
- **Selling concept**—based on the belief that customers will not buy enough of the organization's product unless the organization undertakes a large selling and promotion effort.
- **Marketing concept**—based on the belief that organizations should determine the needs and wants of target markets and deliver desired satisfaction more effectively and efficiently than competitors.
- **Societal marketing concept**—based on the belief that organizations should determine needs and wants of target markets and deliver desired satisfaction more effectively and efficiently than competitors in a way that maintains or improves the consumer's and society's well-being.

Evolution of Marketing

Satisfying customers has not always been the philosophy of business. This concept was preceded by the production and sales eras. During the late 1800s, the Industrial Revolution marked the beginning of the modern concept of marketing. With mass production, better transportation, and more efficient technology, products could be manufactured in greater quantities and sold at lower prices. In the initial stages of the Industrial Revolution, output was limited, and marketing was devoted to the physical distribution of products. Because demand was high and competition low, businesses did not have to conduct consumer research, modify products, or otherwise adapt to consumer needs. The production era of marketing had the goal of increasing production to keep up with demand (Evans & Berman, 1996).

Once a company was able to maximize its production capabilities, it hired a sales force to sell its inventory. The sales era began in the 1920s, as businesses sought to alter customers' desires to accept the products being produced. Business executives decided that advertising and sales were the major means of increasing profits.

By the early 1950s, business executives recognized that efficient production and promotion of products did not guarantee that customers would buy them. The marketing era began with the creation of the marketing department to conduct consumer research and advise management in how to design, price, distribute, and promote products. During the past 20 years, marketing managers have been represented on organizations' decision-making teams because of their ability to conduct consumer research.

Competition is intense, and companies must draw sophisticated customers to their products and retain them (Evans & Berman, 1996). According to Pine (1993), today's competitive edge is found in the concept of mass customization, which is the development, production, marketing, and delivery of affordable goods and services with enough variety that most people will find exactly what they want. For example, Burger King's advertising campaigns have included anti-mass-production slogans such as "Have It Your Way!" and "Sometimes You've Gotta' Break the Rules." The marketing concept, with its emphasis on satisfying the customer, thus forms the basis of the marketing era.

Marketers must have a good understanding of customer satisfaction and loyalty to be successful. Harrell (2002) defined **customer satisfaction** as a customer's positive, neutral, or negative feelings about the value received from a product. **Customer loyalty** refers to the frequency with which a customer consistently purchases a specific brand.

Implementation of Marketing

Once the management of an organization has adopted a marketing philosophy, the development and implementation of that philosophy is based on the marketing concept. According to Lewis, Chacko, and Chambers (1997), the marketing concept derives from the premise that the customer is king, has a choice, and does not have to buy the product. Thus the best way to earn a profit is to serve the customer better.

The marketing concept affects all types of business activities and should be adopted entirely by top-level management. These executives must incorporate the marketing concept into their personal philosophies of business management so completely that customers become the most important concern in the organization. Support of managers and employees at all levels of the organization is required for implementation of the marketing concept (Pride & Ferrell, 1997).

First, management must establish an information system to determine the customers' real needs and use the information to develop products that satisfy them. This is expensive and requires money and time to make the organization customer oriented. Second, the organization must be restructured to coordinate all activities.

Customer satisfaction: Positive, neutral or negative feelings about the value received from a product.

Customer loyalty: Frequency with which a customer consistently purchases a specific brand.

The head of the marketing department should be a member of the top-level management team in the organization (Pride & Ferrell, 1997).

Problems can occur with this new marketing approach. Most operations cannot make products specific to the needs of each customer in our mass-production economy. Regardless of the great amount of time and money spent for research, products still are produced that do not sell. Occasionally, satisfying one segment of the population makes another dissatisfied. Limited-menu restaurants realized early that one menu would not appeal to all members of a family. Applebee's Neighborhood Grill and Bar and Denny's have capitalized on this fact by recognizing that young families will become repeat customers if children are occupied and prices are low (Chaudhry, 1993).

MARKETING MANAGEMENT

Marketing management is a process of planning, organizing, implementing, and controlling marketing activities to facilitate and expedite exchanges effectively and efficiently (Pride & Ferrell, 1997). The managerial functions in the transformation element of the foodservice system have an important role in marketing management. **Effectiveness** refers to the degree to which an exchange helps to achieve an organization's objectives; the quality of the exchanges may range from highly desirable to highly undesirable. **Efficiency** refers to the minimization of resources that an organization must spend to achieve a specific level of desired exchanges. Pride and Ferrell (1997) summarized these definitions by stating that the overall goal of marketing management is to facilitate highly desirable exchanges and to minimize, as much as possible, the costs of doing so.

To achieve the goal of facilitating and expediting desirable exchanges, marketing management is responsible for developing and managing marketing strategies. Strategy encompasses key decisions for reaching an objective. A **marketing strategy** pertains to the selection and analysis of a group of people, identified as a target market, which the organization wants to reach; it includes the creation and maintenance of an appropriate marketing mix that will satisfy those people.

Marketing Mix

Marketing mix: Combination of product, price, place, and promotion to satisfy target market.

Target market: Customer with common characteristics for which an organization creates products/services.

To manage marketing activities, managers must deal with variables relating to the marketing mix and the marketing environment. The **marketing mix** is defined as the specific combination of marketing elements used to achieve an organization's objectives and satisfy the target market (Evans & Berman, 1996). The marketing mix decision variables are product, price, place, promotion, and other factors over which an organization has control. These variables are constructed based on buyer preferences. The **target market** is a group of persons for whom an organization creates a marketing mix that specifically meets the needs of that group (Pride & Ferrell, 1997). The marketing environment variables are political, legal, regulatory, societal, economic, competitive, and technological forces. Many decisions must be made concerning the activities required for each element included in the mix.

Product

A **product** can be a good, a service, or an idea (Hsu & Powers, 2002). Even though the manufacturing of products is not a marketing activity, research on customer needs and product designs is. Product decisions focus on which products to develop, which current products to promote, and which products to discontinue. The term **new product** means it is a genuine innovation because it has not been served commercially (such as the McGriddle® syrup-infused pancake). Products referred to as **new to the chain** such as Chicken McNuggets® are really an imitation of a successful product offered by another chain, such as KFC's chicken nuggets.

Price

Price is the amount of money charged for a product. Price competition has become very common in foodservice operations. In 1989, Taco Bell introduced value pricing. More than half of Taco Bell's menu was priced under $1.00 and company sales tripled. Once the success of value pricing became clear, McDonald's and many others followed. Marketing managers usually are involved in establishing pricing policies for various products because consumers are concerned about the value obtained in the exchange. Price is a critical competent of the marketing mix and often is used as a competitive tool. Price also helps establish a product's image. The goal is to set the price at a point that customers perceive value yet the company achieves the volume and profit it desires.

Promotion

This element is used to facilitate exchanges by informing prospective customers about an organization and its products. **Promotion** is used to increase public awareness about a new product or brand; also, it is used to renew interest in a product that is waning in popularity. Upscale restaurants spend less on advertising than mid-scale and quick-service restaurants (Powers, 1995). The foodservice industry is one of the largest advertisers in the United States. The strategic change in foodservice promotion took place in the 1980s, when advertising increased four times over the previous decade. The level of advertising in the quick-service restaurant has become quite large—McDonald's spends over $1 billion on marketing each year. In upscale foodservice operations, promotion plays a less crucial role.

Place

In marketing, **place** refers to the location, the place where food or services are offered. Increasingly, food is prepared elsewhere. Food manufacturers are preparing, packaging, and distributing menu items for restaurants and contract companies. Each is intruding on the turf of others, making foodservice competitive. Many foodservice operations are downsizing traditional distribution operations to fit into kiosks and mobile carts that are much less expensive. Baskin Robbins ice cream is being sold from kiosks in malls and airports, and Pizza Hut is delivering pizza to several thousand school lunch programs and hospitals. Customers have many options to purchase food when they are away from home.

Environmental Forces

As shown in Figure 14.3, the **marketing environment** surrounds the buyer and the marketing mix (Pride & Ferrell, 1997). Political, legal, regulatory, societal, economic, competitive, and technological forces in the environment affect the marketing manager's ability to facilitate and expedite change. The marketing environment influences customers' preferences and needs for products. These forces also directly influence how a marketing manager should perform certain marketing activities. Finally, a manager's decisions may be affected by environmental forces that influence customers' reactions to the organization's marketing mix.

Political forces influence the country's economic and political stability and decision making, which in turn affects domestic matters, negotiation of trade agreements, and determination of foreign policy. Political trends can have tremendous impact on the hospitality and healthcare industries. Organizations such as the National Restaurant Association, American Hotel and Lodging Association, American Dietetic Association, and School Food Service Association maintain lobbyists in Washington, D.C.

Legal forces are responsible for legislation and interpretation of laws. Marketing is controlled by numerous laws designed to preserve competition and protect the consumer; interpretation of laws by the marketers and courts has a great effect on marketing mix components.

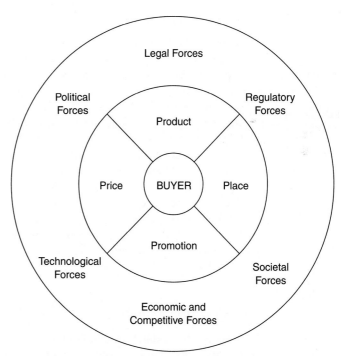

Figure 14.3. Components of the marketing mix and marketing environment.
Source: Pride, William, & Ferrell, O. C. *Marketing: Concepts and Strategies,* 10th edition. Copyright © 1997 by Houghton Mifflin Company. Used by permission.

Local, state, and federal regulatory forces develop and enforce regulations that can affect marketing decisions. Quite often, regulatory agencies, especially at the federal level, encourage industries to develop guidelines to stop questionable practices. Industry leaders usually cooperate to avoid government regulations. Individual industries and trade organizations also put regulatory pressures on themselves and their members.

Societal forces cause marketers to be responsible for decisions. Thousands of consumer groups have been formed to discuss such issues as environmental pollution and the use of pesticides on fruit and vegetable crops. Consumer groups also have been active in discussions on food labeling.

Economic forces have a major influence on competition, which is affected by the number of industries controlling the supply of a product, the ease by which a new operation can enter the industry, and the demand for the product relative to the supply. Demand is determined by buyers' abilities and willingness to purchase.

Technological forces have an impact on everyday living, influencing consumers' desires for products and the stability of the marketing mix. The technologies of communication, transportation, computers, and packaging influence the types of products being produced.

Managers must be able to adjust marketing strategies to major changes in the environment. If they want to develop effective strategies, managers must recognize the dynamic environmental forces that cause marketing problems and opportunities.

Market Segmentation

Market segmentation: Division of total market into groups of customers who have similar needs, wants, values, and buying behavior.

Swinyard and Struman (1986) stated that separating customers into "natural" market groups provides the basis for successful strategy development in marketing a restaurant. **Market segmentation** is the process of dividing a total market into groups of people with similar needs, wants, values, and buying behvaiors (Harrell, 2002). A market, in the context used here, is not a place but rather a group of people; as individuals or organizations, the group needs products and possesses the ability, willingness, and authority to purchase them. A market segment is a mixture of individuals, groups, or organizations that share one or more characteristics, which causes them to have similar product needs.

In a homogeneous market, which consists of individuals with similar product needs, a marketing mix is easier to design than one for a heterogeneous group with dissimilar needs. Choosing the correct variable for segmenting a market is important in developing a successful strategy. Variables have been grouped into four categories for the segmentation process: geographic, demographic, psychographic, and behavioristic. Examples of each are shown in Table 14.1.

Geographic Variables

Geographic variables include climate, terrain, natural resources, population density, and subcultural values that influence customers' product needs. In addition, the size of the region, city, county, or state and whether the area is urban, suburban, or rural have an effect on the market. Population in these areas, customer preferences, and spending patterns also need to be considered in marketing decisions. As an example of geographical variables, Cajun food, which is part of the

Table 14.1   Major Segmentation Variables for Consumer Markets

Variable	Typical Breakdown
Geographic	
Region	Pacific, Mountain, West North Central, West South Central, East North Central, East South Central, South Atlantic, Middle Atlantic, New England
City or metro size	Under 5000; 5000–20,000; 20,000–50,000; 50,000–100,000; 100,000–250,000; 250,000–500,000; 500,000–1,000,000; 1,000,000–4,000,000; 4,000,000 or over
Density	Urban, suburban, rural
Climate	Northern, southern
Demographic	
Age	Under 6, 6–11, 12–19, 20–34, 35–49, 50–64, 65+
Gender	Male, female
Family size	1–2, 3–4, 5+
Family life cycle	Young, single; young, married, no children; young, married, youngest child under 6; young, married, youngest child 6 or over; older, married, with children; older, married, no children under 18; older, single; other
Income	Under $10,000; $10,000–$15,000; $15,000–$20,000; $20,000–$30,000; $30,000–$50,000; $50,000–$100,000; $100,000 and over
Occupation	Professional and technical; managers, officials, and proprietors; clerical, sales; craftspeople, foremen; operatives; farmers; retired; students; housewives; unemployed
Education	Grade school or less; some high school; high school graduate; some college; college, graduate
Religion	Catholic, Protestant, Jewish, Muslim, Hindu, other
Race	White, Black, Asian
Nationality	American, British, French, German, Italian, Japanese
Psychographic	
Social class	Lower lowers, upper lowers, working class, middle class, upper middles, lower uppers, upper uppers
Lifestyle	Straights, swingers, longhairs
Personality	Compulsive, gregarious, authoritarian, ambitious
Behavioral	
Occasions	Regular occasion, special occasion
Benefits	Quality, service, economy, speed
User status	Nonuser, ex-user, potential user, first-time user, regular user
Usage rate	Light user, medium user, heavy user
Loyalty status	None, medium, strong, absolute
Readiness stage	Unaware, aware, informed, interested, desirous, intending to buy
Attitude toward product	Enthusiastic, positive, indifferent, negative, hostile

Source: Marketing for Hospitality and Tourism, 2nd edition, by Kotler, Bowen, and Makens. Reprinted by permission of Pearson Education, Inc., Upper Saddle, NJ.

culture in Louisiana, has been accepted in New York City and in California. The astute foodservice manager knows when and where to introduce such food items on the menu by doing a market analysis before making a decision.

Demographic Variables

Demographic variables consist of population characteristics that might influence product selection, such as age, gender, race, ethnicity, income, education, occupation, family size, family life cycle, religion, social class, and price sensitivity. Only those demographic variables pertinent to the population segment under consideration must be ascertained.

Psychographic Variables

Psychographic variables include many factors that can be used for segmenting the market, but the most common are motives and lifestyles. When a market is segmented according to a *motive,* it recognizes the reason a customer makes a purchase. *Lifestyle* segmentation categorizes people according to what is important to them and their mode of living.

A useful classification system for segmenting customers in terms of a broad range of lifestyle factors is the **Values and Life-Styles (VALS)** research program, which is sponsored by SRI International in Menlo Park, California (see www .sric-bi.com). The current version of the program seeks to predict customer behavior by defining segments, based on resources and primary motivation.

Resources include the psychological, physical, demographic, and materials means and capabilities that people have. Resources are viewed on a continuum from low to high. Motivation is viewed on a continuum from low to high innovation and is divided into three components in the VALS model:

- **Ideals**—Consumers make choices based on their knowledge and principles.
- **Achievement**—Consumers make choices based on what they perceive will show their success to their peers.
- **Self-expression**—Consumers make choices based on a desire for social or physical activity, variety, or risk.

Combining the dimensions of resources and primary motivation results in the categorization of consumers into one of eight groups defined by SRI (see www .sric-bi.com) as follows:

- **Innovators**—Highest level of resources and motivation. They are characterized as change leaders who are active consumers and receptive to new ideas. They tend to prefer upscale, niche products and services.
- **Thinkers**—These consumers are characterized as mature, reflective, well-informed individuals who are motivated by ideals. They value order, knowledge, and responsibility and base decisions on their principles. Although their income allows abundant choices, they tend to look for durability, functionality, and value in products they purchase.
- **Achievers**—These individuals have high levels of resources and are motivated by achievement. They are characterized as work-oriented, conservative, and value-conscious consumers who favor established, prestige products that demonstrate success to their peers.
- **Experiencers**—These consumers have high levels of resources and are motivated by self-expression. They seek variety, excitement, new and risky activities. They tend to be young, impulsive, and rebellious individuals who spend much of their income on products such as fashion, entertainment, and socializing.
- **Believers**—These consumers have low amounts of resources and are motivated by ideals. They tend to be conservative, follow established routines, and organize their lives around home, family, and social or religious organizations. They favor American products and established brands.

- **Strivers**—These consumers have limited resources and are motivated by achievement. They often emulate those who own more impressive possessions, but usually lack the financial resources to purchase what they would like.
- **Makers**—These consumers have limited resources and are motivated by self-expression. They are characterized as practical, self-sufficient, and traditional. They experience the world by working on it (i.e., by building a house, fixing a car, canning vegetables, etc.). They purchase products that have practical or functional purpose.
- **Survivors**—These consumers have the lowest resources and motivation. They are very cautious consumers whose chief concerns are for security and safety. They are loyal to favorite brands purchased at a discount.

Behavioristic Variables

Behavioristic variables are the basis of some feature of consumer behavior toward and use of a product. They include variables such as purchase volume, purchase readiness, loyalty, and shopping behavior. To satisfy a specific group of customers, a special product might need to be produced, such as caffeine-free diet cola. How the customer uses a product also may determine segmentation. Frozen menu items are being packaged in single servings to meet the needs of people living alone.

Niche Marketing and Micromarketing

Newer strategies for market segmentation are niche marketing and micromarketing. Niche is a narrowly defined portion of the market with unique interests or characteristics. **Niche marketing** focuses on identifying small but profitable segments of the market and making products specifically for this segment. **Micromarketing** is marketing to the single customer, the smallest niche.

SERVICE MARKETING

In the definition of marketing used in this chapter, a *product* refers to a good, a service, an idea, or any combination of the three. A *good* is a tangible product that a customer can physically touch; a *service* is the application of human or mechanical efforts to people or objects. The most satisfactory definition of service is that given by Kotler (1996): A service is any act or performance that one party can offer to another that is essentially intangible and does not result in the ownership of anything.

Manufacturing firms still exist, but services have replaced goods in the U.S. economy, accounting for 67% of the **Gross Domestic Product (GDP)** and 57% of consumer expenditures (www.bea.gov, 2002). Several reasons for this growth in the services sector are apparent. The United States now is an information rather than an industrial society; services are the primary material of an information society. Services are no longer byproducts in a manufacturing or production process but often are the products. A third reason is the prosperity in the United States that has led to growth in financial, travel, entertainment, and personal-care services. Lifestyle changes, such as more women in the workforce, have created increased demand for child care, domestic, and other time-saver services including meal preparation. The elderly require increased healthcare services, and at the same time the younger population demands increased fitness and health maintenance services. The technology explosion has created more complex goods that require servicing and repair; the business environment is more specialized, justifying more business and industrial services.

Lewis, Chacko, and Chambers (1997) emphatically stated that marketing and management in a service business, such as the hospitality industry, are one and the same. Many marketing experts argue that service marketing is different from goods marketing and requires different strategies and tactics; they contend that a pure good without some elements of service attached to it is impossible.

Characteristics of Services

Zeithaml, Parasuraman, and Berry (1985) stated that the problems of service marketing are not the same as those of goods marketing. A look at the four basic characteristics of service marketing—intangibility, inseparability of production and consumption, perishability, and heterogeneity—explains why. Services generally are sold before they are produced, and goods generally are produced before they are sold (Berry & Parasuraman, 1991). Moreover, services marketing has a more limited influence on customers before purchase than goods marketing.

Intangibility

Intangibility of services: Inability of services to be seen, touched, tasted, smelled, or possessed before buying.

Atmospherics: Physical elements in an operation's design that appeal to customers' emotions.

Generally, **intangibility of services** is defined in terms of what services are not; they cannot be seen, touched, tasted, smelled, or possessed (Pride & Ferrell, 1997). Services are performances and, therefore, intangible; products are tangible. Services, however, have a few tangible attributes. Atmospherics is an example of a tangible attribute and has been used as a marketing tool for many years.

Atmospherics describes the physical elements in an operation's design that appeal to customers' emotions and encourages them to buy (Pride & Ferrell, 1997). Berry and Parasuraman (1991) stated that the principal responsibility for the service marketer is to manage tangibles to convey the proper signals about service.

The atmosphere of the exterior and interior of the operation may be friendly, exciting, quiet, or elegant. *Exterior atmospherics* is important to new customers who often judge a restaurant by its outside appearance. If windows are foggy or the grounds unkempt, customers might decide that service would be unacceptable, too. *Interior atmospherics* includes lighting, wall and floor coverings, furniture, and rest rooms. A pleasing and clean interior probably would indicate to the customer that the service would be impeccable. Sensory elements also contribute to atmosphere. *Color* can attract customers. Many limited-menu restaurants, for example, use bright colors, such as red and yellow, because they have been shown to make customers feel hungrier and eat faster, thus increasing turnover. *Sound* is important; a noisy restaurant probably would not be chosen by customers who are celebrating a wedding anniversary. *Odor* also might be relevant; the scent of freshly baked bread makes customers feel cared for and wanted. Again, these tangible sensory elements might reflect on the customer's perception of the intangible service (Pride & Ferrell, 1997).

Levitt (1981) stated that the most important thing to know about intangible service is that "customers don't know what they're getting until they don't get it." A customer is more precious than the tangible assets shown on a balance sheet, and companies that understand this concept continually tailor products and services to their customers. They look beyond the value of a single transaction to the customer's lifetime value to the company (Treacy & Wiersema, 1993).

Inseparability

Inseparability: Inability to separate production and service.

According to Pride and Ferrell (1997), **inseparability** of production and consumption is related to intangibility. Services are normally produced at the same time they are consumed. In a commercial foodservice operation, the waitstaff, bartender, and maître d'hôtel are producing services at the same time the customer is consuming them. The knowledge and efficiency of the waitstaff in taking the order and serving the meal, the desire of the bartender to mix a drink exactly the way the customer wants it, and the concern of the maître d'hôtel that the customer is satisfied are examples of inseparability of production and consumption. In hospitals, foodservice personnel deliver trays to patients who are either satisfied or dissatisfied immediately with the attitude or concern of the delivery person. Likewise, the warmth of a smile from a cook serving a child a school lunch is strongly associated with the acceptance of the meal.

Perishability

Perishability of services: Services cannot be stored for future sale.

The **perishability of services** means that those services cannot be stored for future sale (Evans & Berman, 1996). Unused capacity cannot be shifted from one time to another. Because service is produced and consumed simultaneously, it is perishable. The service supplier must try to regulate customer usage to develop consistent demand throughout various periods. The service operation must have the capacity and capability to produce when demand occurs; if demand does not occur, however, that capacity and capability are lost and wasted, resulting in losses in the bottom line (Lewis, Chacko, & Chambers, 1997). For example, if overstaffing occurs, the labor cost is too high; if understaffing occurs and demand increases, service becomes too slow.

One alternative is to charge prices high enough to permit overstaffing. Restaurant managers of operations known for a high level of service often use this scheme. Most foodservices cannot afford such a solution to the problem, and the result is irate customers. Reduction of staff is both a marketing and management decision, and the impact on the customer must be the first consideration. If service is being marketed, it becomes an expectation of the customer, and management must accept the risk of overstaffing and the higher cost to the customer. A customer, however, often makes a sacrifice beyond cost, which is time. Waiting for room service, for lunch in a restaurant, for a bottle of wine to be served, or for the check to come causes the customer to become irritated. An alternative is the limited-menu restaurant, which has been very successful because it capitalizes on the time saved. If marketing creates expectations, makes promises, offers value, and reduces risk, management needs to understand that the cost of keeping a customer is far less than that of creating a new one.

Heterogeneity

Heterogeneity of service:
Variation and lack of uniformity in the performance by different service employees.

Heterogeneity of service is concerned with the variation and lack of uniformity in the performance of people. This is different from the poor service caused by an insufficient number of staff; rather, it is fluctuations in service caused by unskilled employees, customer perceptions, and the customers themselves. Variations might occur between services within the same organization or in the service provided by one employee from day to day or from customer to customer. Most services are labor intensive, and the performance of each employee is different. Managers have difficulty in predicting how employees with different backgrounds and personalities will react in various circumstances.

Marketers of services who make promises to the customer never know how employees will handle a situation or how the customer will perceive a service. Lewis, Chacko, and Chambers (1997) stated that the consequence is that good service may equal bad service. One customer may be pleased that the waitstaff never permits the coffee cup to become empty, but another customer may be annoyed because the cup never becomes empty. Sometimes, less service is more service. An example is the popular salad bar. Many people like the idea that they can select what they want, although this is less service because they have to get their own food.

Components of Service Products

Customers are concerned with the components of goods, services, and environment when purchasing the hospitality product (Lewis, Chacko, & Chambers, 1997). *Goods* are mostly physical factors over which management has direct, or almost direct, control and are usually tangible. The manager's expertise determines the quality level of goods. Lewis, Chacko, and Chambers (1997) define price as being tangible, although it is a cost of services and goods. To the customer, however, price is tangible in any purchase decision.

Service includes nonphysical, intangible attributes that management should control. Personal elements provided by employees, such as friendliness, speed, attitude, and responsiveness, are very important components of service. In the environment category, items over which management may have some control may be included. These items may or may not be tangible but are something the customer feels. That feeling is what the manager is marketing. Décor, atmosphere, comfort, ambience, and architecture are attributes included in this category.

Service Marketing Mix

Managers desiring to market service must provide benefits that satisfy the needs of the customer. Target markets should be defined and the marketing mix identified before a marketing strategy can be finalized. The four elements required for a marketing mix for goods are applicable to service: product, distribution, promotion, and price.

Services are intangible products and thus difficult for customers to evaluate. If a limited-menu restaurant chain can standardize a service and market it more effectively than other chains can market the service, the chain generally will gain a greater share of the market. An example has been the serving of certain food items, such as baked-to-order pizza within 15 minutes of placing the order.

Distribution in the service context refers to making services available to prospective users. Instead of taking the goods to the customer, customers must come to the service. Pizza, hamburger, chicken, fish, and other specialty limited-menu restaurants distribute products that are the same in many locations.

Promotion: Use of communication to inform and influence consumers.

Lewis, Chacko, and Chambers (1997) define **promotion** as marketing communication that serves specifically as an incentive to stimulate sales on a short-term basis. Promotions are frequently used to stimulate business in off periods when normal business flow has decreased.

Establishing a price for service can be difficult because of its intangibility. The more standardized service becomes, the easier pricing is for the manager. Pricing service in a limited-menu restaurant with well-defined procedures for employees to follow is much easier than pricing in an upscale restaurant in which employees are encouraged to satisfy individual customer's desires.

STRATEGIC MARKETING

Marketing strategy pertains to the selection and analysis of a target market and the creation and maintenance of an appropriate marketing mix. Any strategic planning process begins with the organization's mission statement and objectives and ends with a marketing plan.

Strategic Planning Process

Evans and Berman (1996) identified seven interrelated steps in the strategic planning process for marketing:

- Define the organizational mission.
- Establish strategic business units.
- Set marketing objectives.
- Perform a situation analysis.
- Develop a marketing strategy.
- Implement tactical plans.
- Monitor results.

The organizational **mission statement** is a summation of the organization's purpose, competition, target market, product, and service and of the recipients of the service, including consumers, employees, owners, and the community. For example, the mission of a hospital could be to provide both inpatient and outpatient medical service to the people in the community within budgetary limitations. Each department would have a mission compatible with that of the organization. The mission of the foodservice department thus would be to provide food within the departmental budget to the patients, employees, and visitors.

After defining a mission, an organization should establish **strategic business units (SBUs).** Each SBU is a separate component of the organization and has a specific market focus and a manager with responsibility for placing all functions into a strategy. SBUs are the basis for a strategic marketing plan. In business terminology, the hospital is the corporate level, and the foodservice department is the strategic business unit. Every SBU has a clearly defined market segment with a strategy consistent with that of the corporation, its own mission, and its own competitors.

A **marketing objective** is a statement of what is to be accomplished through marketing activities. Each SBU in an organization needs to set its own objectives in clear, simple terms for marketing performance. Objectives generally are described in both quantitative terms (dollar sales, percentage profit growth, market share) and qualitative terms (image, uniqueness, customer service). Many restaurants and other food-service organizations combine quantitative and qualitative goals, such as dollar sales and uniqueness based on a new theme.

Situation analysis:
Identification of marketing opportunities and challenges.

Situation analysis is the identification of marketing opportunities and potential problems confronting an organization. The manager needs to know the current condition of the organization and the direction in which it is going.

A technique often used in situation analysis is a **SWOT analysis.** A SWOT analysis focuses on identifying the Strengths, Weaknesses, Opportunities and Threats to an organization. When using a SWOT analysis for marketing, the focus typically is on factors related to market share, customer loyalty, customer satisfaction, and previous marketing success. Strengths are defined as the unique resources that a company can provide. Weaknesses or constraints are those aspects of a company that limit the company's ability to achieve its goals. Opportunities are areas where competitive advantage exists or where new markets could be developed. Threats are those elements that might prevent accomplishment of objectives.

A **marketing strategy** encompasses selecting and analyzing a target market and creating and maintaining an appropriate marketing mix that will satisfy that market (Pride & Ferrell, 1997). A strategy should be as specific as possible. For example, to increase dessert sales, a poor strategy might be something imprecise like, "The addition of low-fat frozen yogurt to the menu will be advertised." A better strategy would provide more guidance: "Dessert sales will be increased by 10% within 3 months by adding low-fat frozen yogurt to the menu and increasing advertising to health-conscious consumers."

Tactic: Specific action.

The marketing strategy is implemented through a series of **tactics,** which are specific actions. According to Lewis, Chacko, and Chambers (1997), strategy is the way to gain and keep customers; tactics are the step-by-step procedures on how to do it. The objective could be "to be perceived as the restaurant of choice," and the strategy, "to give customers better value." Some of the tactics could include having a table ready for customers who have made reservations, calling customers by name, having the print on the menu large enough to read, and offering a selection for customers with special dietary needs. Tactics flow from strategy, which means the appropriate strategy must be developed first.

Monitoring results involves the comparison of performance standards against actual performance over a definite time. Budgets, timetables, sales, and cost analyses may be used to analyze results. If actual performance does not meet the standards, corrective action should be taken in problem areas. Many organizations have contingency plans if performance standards are not met.

Marketing Research

The foundation of a successful marketing plan is research (Yesawich, 1987). Only through research can proper judgments be made about the best combination of product, distribution, promotion, and price. Market research can help an establishment succeed, rather than merely survive, by attracting new customers, keeping up with trends, and tailoring menus to meet customer needs (Stern, 1990). Intuition and past experience, rather than scientific decision making, often govern marketing decisions, however.

The American Marketing Association defines **marketing research** as the function that links the consumer, customer, and public to the marketer through information that is used to identify and define marketing opportunities and problems; generate, refine, and evaluate marketing actions; monitor marketing performance; and improve understanding of marketing as a process (see www .marketingpower.com). To be effective, marketing research must be systematic and not haphazard or disjointed. Marketing research involves a series of steps including data collection, recording, and analysis (Evans & Berman, 1996). Data may be available from different sources: the organization itself, an impartial marketing research company, or a research specialist working for the organization.

Objectivity, accuracy, and thoroughness are important when conducting research.

- **Objectivity**—conducted in an unbiased, open-minded manner; conclusion based on data and analysis
- **Accuracy**—use of research tools that are carefully constructed and implemented
- **Thoroughness**—ensuring that the sample represents the population; a questionnaire, if used, is pretested; and the analysis of data is statistically correct.

The marketing research process, as shown in Figure 14.4, consists of five steps for logically solving a problem: problem definition, data collection, data analysis, recommendations, and preparation of the report. Foodservice managers conducting marketing research should think about each of these steps and tailor them to fit the problem.

The Marketing Plan

Marketing plan: Written document or blueprint governing an organization's marketing activities.

Pride and Ferrell (1997) define **marketing plan** as a written document or blueprint governing an organization's marketing activities, including the implementation and control of those activities. **Marketing planning** is a systematic process involving the assessment of marketing opportunities and resources, the determination of marketing objectives, the development of a marketing strategy, and planning for implementation and control. A marketing plan needs to be integrated and evaluated.

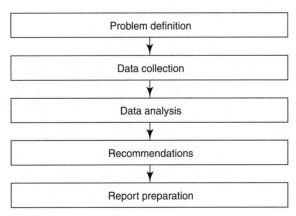

Figure 14.4. Marketing research process.

Development of Plan

Strategic planning should be done before a marketing plan is developed. The marketing should define the target market and marketing mix variables. The plan also should identify resources needed and objectives to be achieved.

A marketing plan should be real and workable and should be easy to execute (Lewis, Chacko, & Chambers, 1997). It also should be flexible but have a certain amount of stability. Specific responsibilities with times and dates for accomplishment should be designated in the plan. Finally, a marketing plan needs to be constantly reviewed and evaluated to keep it current.

Types of Plans

Marketing plans can be categorized according to duration, scope, and method of development (Evans & Berman, 1996). Marketing plans typically are developed for one year and are considered short range; medium-range plans from two to five years are sometimes used; and those over five years, long-range marketing plans, are seldom developed. Short- and medium-range plans are more detailed and more geared to the operation than long-range plans.

The scope of marketing plans varies tremendously. Separate marketing plans may be developed for individual menu items and special services.

Finally, the method of development of plans may be bottom-up, top-down, or a combination of the two. In the *bottom-up approach,* information from employees is used to establish objectives, budgets, forecasts, timetables, and marketing mixes. Bottom-up plans are realistic and good for morale. Coordination of each bottom-up plan into one integrated plan may be difficult to achieve because of conflicts, for example, in estimates of the impact of marketing a new menu item. In the *top-down approach,* top management directs and controls planning activities. Top-level managers understand the competition and environment and provide direction for marketing efforts. If input from lower-level managers is not sought, however, morale may diminish. A combination of these two approaches could be the best solution; top management could set the overall objectives and policy, and lower-level managers could establish the plans for implementing the policy (Evans & Berman, 1996).

Integration of Plans

Integration of marketing is necessary if the product, distribution, promotion, and price elements of the marketing mix are to be synchronized (Evans & Berman, 1996). An integrated marketing plan is one in which all the various components are unified, consistent, and coordinated. According to Evans and Berman (1996), a well-integrated marketing plan will include the following:

- Clear organizational mission
- Stability over time
- Coordination of the marketing mix
- Coordination among SBUs
- Compatible short-, medium-, and long-range plans
- Precisely defined target market(s)
- Long-term competitive advantages

A clear organizational mission defines an organization's type of business and place in the market. The mission is involved each time products or services are added or deleted or new target markets are sought or abandoned. A marketing plan must show stability over time to be implemented and evaluated correctly.

The product, distribution, promotion, and price components of the marketing mix need to be coordinated within each department (Evans & Berman, 1996). Co-ordination among individual departments or units is increased when the strategies and resources allocated to each are described in short-, medium-, and long-range plans. Compatible plans for each department or unit become the broad marketing plan for the organization. The target market needs to be identified in a marketing plan to guide marketing efforts and future direction. If two or more distinct target markets are present, each should be clearly defined. For example, a foodservice organization catering to children and parents probably will have separate strategies for each of these segments.

Customer expectations and quality of the product and service need to be emphasized in developing long-term plans for successful competition in the market. Internal customers, like the maître d', chef, waitperson, and cashier, all need to work together while keeping the external customer in focus.

Control and Evaluation

Control. Control is as necessary in marketing as in managing all facets of the foodservice organization. The manager should establish performance standards for marketing activities based on goals of the organization. Internal standards generally are expressed as profits, sales, or costs. Most organizations use external individuals or organizations, such as consultants or marketing research firms, for marketing assistance.

When foodservice managers attempt to control marketing activities, they frequently have problems because information is not always available. Even though controls should be flexible enough to allow for environmental changes, the frequency and intensity of changes may curtail effective control. Because marketing overlaps other activities, the precise costs of marketing are difficult to define.

Evaluation. Sales analysis can be used for evaluating the actual performance of marketing strategies (Pride & Ferrell, 1997). A *sales analysis* is the detailed study of sales data, either volume or market share. Dollar volume sales are frequently used because the dollar is the common denominator of profits, sales, and costs. Price increases and decreases, however, affect total sales figures and need to be considered in the analysis. For example, if a restaurant increases prices by 10% this year and its sales volume is 10% greater than last year's, it has not had any increase in unit sales. A restaurant marketing manager should factor out the effects of price changes.

Market share:
Percentage of industry sales for a product.

Market share is stated as the percentage of industry sales for a product. The rationale for using market share is to estimate if sales changes occurred because of the organization's marketing strategy or from uncontrollable environmental factors. The assumption is that industry sales decrease when restaurant sales decrease and market share remains constant. If a restaurant suffers a decrease in both sales and market share, however, the marketing strategy is not effective. Market share analysis should be interpreted with caution because it is based on uncontrollable factors, such as differing objectives among companies.

Professional Organization Profile

School Nutrition Services
Dietetic Practice Group
of the American Dietetic Association

MISSION

To be recognized leaders in "keeping nutrition in our schools"

WHO BELONGS TO THE ORGANIZATION

Members are also members of the American Dietetic Association engaged in the management of school food service and nutrition education programs at the local, state, and national levels or employed by companies providing products and services to these programs. Student membership available through the American Dietetic Association.

ADVANTAGES OF MEMBERSHIP

Members receive a quarterly newsletter, *The Nutrition Link;* earn continuing education credit by attendance at association sponsored seminars and workshops; have access to scholarships designated for members; and receive a membership directory for networking.

WEBSITE

www.eatright.org

MEET THE PRESIDENT

Linda Godfrey, RD; President 2005–2006; is an adjunct instructor at Samford University in Homewood, AL. Her career has included foodservice director positions in healthcare and schools, most recently as foodservice director for the Shelby County Schools in Alabama.

CHAPTER SUMMARY

This summary is organized by the learning objectives.

1. Marketing is a complex process that involves planning, promoting, and distributing goods, services, and ideas that satisfy customers and meet organizational goals. There are several terms that are used in marketing. Marketing mix is the combination of product, price, place, and promotion. Target market is a group of consumers with common characteristics. Market segmentation is the process of dividing a total market into groups based on consumer characteristics. Promotion is the use of various techniques to increase public awareness or renew interest in a product or service.

2. The marketing plan should define the target market, describe the marketing mix, and identify resources needed to execute the plan. The plan should be workable, easy to execute, and flexible, and it should clearly identify specific responsibilities and time/date deadlines for accomplishment.

3. There are many ways to segment a market. Segmentation by demographic characteristics would involve grouping consumers based on attributes such as age, gender, race, ethnicity, income, education, occupation, religion, social class, and so on. Segmentation by geographic characteristics would involve grouping consumers based on indicators such as city, state, region of the country or world, population of area, and so on. Psychographic segmentation would involve grouping of consumers based on factors such as lifestyle, motives, values, and so on.

TEST YOUR KNOWLEDGE

1. What is the marketing environment? How does it impact the development and execution of a marketing plan?
2. Define the term marketing concept and describe how it applies to a foodservice operation.
3. What are variables that influence the marketing mix and market segmentation?
4. Explain the four characteristics of services and describe how they impact marketing in foodservice operations.
5. Describe how strategic planning might be used to enhance foodservice marketing.

CLASS PROJECTS

1. Ask a manager from a local foodservice operation that has an active marketing program to speak to the class about his or her program; have the manager include description of target market, types of data collected, and how a marketing plan is developed and evaluated.
2. Divide into groups of two to three students. Develop a marketing plan for a local foodservice operation.

WEB SOURCES

www.bea.doc.gov	Bureau of Economic Analysis
www.marketingpower.com	American Marketing Association
www.hsmai.org	Hospitality Sales and Marketing Association International
www.demographics.com	American Demographics
www.sric-bi.com	SRI Consulting Business Intelligence
www.quirks.com	Quirk's Marketing Research Review
www.str-online.com	Smith Travel Research
www.census.gov	U.S. Census Bureau

BIBLIOGRAPHY

Albrecht, K. (1995). *At America's service: How your company can join the customer service revolution*. Homewood, IL: Dow Jones-Irwin.

Albrecht, K., & Zemke, R. (1995). *Service America! Doing business in the new economy*. Homewood, IL: Dow Jones-Irwin.

Allen, R. L. (1992). The world of target marketing. *Nation's Restaurant News, 26*(11), 25, 62.

Berry, L. L., & Parasuraman, A. (1991). *Marketing services: Competing through quality*. New York: Free Press.

Chaudhry, R. (1993). Food for tot. *Restaurants & Institutions, 103*(7), 131, 134.

Congram, C. A., & Friedman, M. L. (Eds.). (1991). *The AMA handbook of marketing for the service industries*. New York: AMACOM.

Davidow, W. H., & Uttal, B. (1989). Service companies: Focus or falter. *Harvard Business Review, 67*(4), 77–85.

Dodd, J. (1992). President's page: The fifth P. *Journal of the American Dietetic Association, 92,* 616–617.

Evans, J. R., & Berman, B. (1996). *Marketing* (7th ed.). Upper Saddle River, NJ: Prentice Hall.

Forgac, J. (1999). Marketing. In J. Martin & M. Conklin (eds.). *Managing child nutrition programs*. Gaithersburg, MO: Aspen, pp 611–626.

Gronroos, C. (1990). *Service management and marketing: Managing the moments of truth in service competition*. Lexington, MA: Lexington Books.

Hart, C. W., Casserly, G., & Lawless, M. J. (1984). The product life cycle: How useful? *Cornell Hotel and Restaurant Administration Quarterly, 25*(3), 54–63.

Harrell, G. B. (2002). *Marketing* (2nd ed.). Upper Saddle River, NJ: Prentice Hall.

Heskett, J. L. (1986). *Managing in the service economy*. Boston: Harvard Business School Press.

Houston, F. S. (1986). The marketing concept: What it is and what it is not. *Journal of Marketing, 50*(2), 81–87.

Hsu, C. H. C., & Powers, J. (2002). *Marketing hospitality* (3rd ed.). New York: John Wiley.

Jacobs, P. (1993). Staying focused: Strategic plans need constant care. *Nation's Restaurant News, 27*(20), 22.

Kanter, R. M. (1992). Think like the customer: The global business logic. *Harvard Business Review, 70*(4), 9–10.

Kashani, K. (1989). Beware the pitfalls of global marketing. *Harvard Business Review, 67*(5), 91–98.

Kotler, P. (1977). From sales obsession to marketing effectiveness. *Harvard Business Review, 55*(6), 67–75.

Kotler, P. (1996). *Marketing management: Analysis, planning and control* (9th ed.). Englewood Cliffs, NJ: Prentice Hall.

Kotler, P., Bowen, J., & Makens, J. (1999). *Marketing for hospitality and tourism* (2nd ed.). Upper Saddle River, NJ: Prentice Hall.

Levitt, T. (1981). Marketing intangible products and product intangibles. *Harvard Business Review, 59*(3), 94–102.

Lewis, R. C. (1984). Theoretical and practical considerations in research design. *Cornell Hotel and Restaurant Administration Quarterly, 24*(4), 25–35.

Lewis, R. C. (1989). Hospitality marketing: The internal approach. *Cornell Hotel and Restaurant Administration Quarterly, 30*(3), 41–45.

Lewis, R. C., Chacko, H. E., & Chambers, R. E. (1997). *Marketing leadership in hospitality: Foundations and practices* (2nd ed.). New York: Van Nostrand Reinhold.

Lovelock, C. H. (1980). Why marketing management needs to be different for services. In J. H. Donnelly & W. R. George (Eds.), *Marketing of services* (pp. 708–719). Chicago: American Marketing Association.

Lovelock, C. H. (1983). Classifying services to gain strategic marketing insights. *Journal of Marketing, 47*(3), 9–20.

Lovelock, C. H. (1996). *Services marketing* (3rd ed.). Englewood Cliffs, NJ: Prentice Hall.

McKenna, R. (1988). Marketing in an age of diversity. *Harvard Business Review, 66*(5), 88–95.

McKenna, R. (1991). Marketing is everything. *Harvard Business Review, 69*(1), 65–79.

National income and product accounts. (1992). *Survey of Current Business, 72*(9), 5–47.

Pine, B. J., II. (1993). *Mass customization: The new frontier in business competition.* Boston: Harvard Business School Press.

Powers, T. (1995). *Introduction to management in the hospitality industry* (5th ed.). New York: John Wiley.

Pride, W. M. & Ferrell, O. C. (1997). *Marketing: Concepts and strategies* (10th ed.). Boston: Houghton Mifflin.

Solomon, J. (1993). Homemade marketing strategies. *Restaurants USA, 13*(1), 17–19.

Star, S. H. (1989). Marketing and its discontents. *Harvard Business Review, 67*(6), 148–154.

Stern, G. M. (1990). The case for marketing research. *Restaurants USA, 10*(7), 26–29.

Sullivan, J. (1991). Market your restaurant as you work the floor. *Nation's Restaurant News, 25*(16), 22.

Swinyard, W. R., & Struman, K. D. (1986). Market segmentation: Finding the heart of your restaurant's market. *Cornell Hotel and Restaurant Administration Quarterly, 27*(1), 89–96.

Treacy, M., & Wiersema, F. (1993). Customer intimacy and other value disciplines. *Harvard Business Review, 71*(1), 84–93.

Uhl, K. P., & Upah, G. D. (1986). The marketing of services. In J. N. Sheth & D. E. Garrett (Eds.), *Marketing management: A comprehensive reader* (pp. 999–1026). Cincinnati: South-Western Publishing.

Vance, D. E. (1992). Capture your market—then work to keep it. *Nation's Restaurant News, 26*(6), 52.

West, J. J., & Olsen, M. D. (1989). Competitive tactics in foodservice: Are high performers different? *Cornell Hotel and Restaurant Administration Quarterly, 30*(1), 68–71.

Yesawich, P. C. (1987). Hospitality marketing for the '90s: Effective marketing research. *Cornell Hotel and Restaurant Administration Quarterly, 28*(1), 49–57.

Yesawich, P. C. (1988). Planning: The second step in market development. *Cornell Hotel and Restaurant Administration Quarterly, 28*(4), 71–81.

Yesawich, P. C. (1989). The final steps in market development: Execution and measurement of programs. *Cornell Hotel and Restaurant Administration Quarterly, 29*(4), 83–91.

Zeithaml, V. A., Parasuraman, A., & Berry, L. L. (1985). Problems and strategies in services marketing. *Journal of Marketing, 49*(2), 33–46.

Zeithaml, V. A., Parasuraman, A., & Berry, L. L. (1990). *Delivering quality service: Balancing customer perceptions and expectations.* New York: Free Press.

Chapter 14: Marketing Foodservice

CHECKING YOUR READING STRATEGIES
DISCUSSION AND CRITICAL THINKING QUESTIONS

1. **Preview the chapter** as you have been instructed. *Without reading the chapter itself*, write up an outline of the chapter. Leave room to fill in the details later. Use your typographical cues to help you. (Do not include the chapter summary or "Test Your Knowledge" questions in your outline.)

2. **Preview the chapter again**, this time focusing on all the graphic illustrations. Read all the captions and information in tables; look carefully at all photographs and drawings. Next, let your eyes scan over the columns of text. See if you can find where in the paragraphs the illustrated material is explained. What cues are given in the text to tie the illustrations to the words?

3. *Circle the best answer for each of the following questions.*

   1. According to the learning objectives listed at the beginning of the chapter, this chapter will cover how many points?
      a. Three
      b. Six
      c. Not enough information to answer the question

   2. What is the *overall purpose* of the chapter's introduction about marketing?
      a. To demonstrate how marketing affects philosophy
      b. To set up a framework for the chapter
      c. To emphasize foodservice

   3. How many types of graphic illustrations are used in this chapter? Look through the entire chapter. Select all that apply.
      a. Photographs
      b. Charts
      c. Graphs
      d. Organizational charts
      e. Shaded boxes (of formulas, theories, etc.)
      f. Process diagrams
      g. Margin notes
      h. Diagrams
      i. Tables
      j. Flow charts
      k. Pie charts
      l. Maps
      m. Branching/tree diagrams
      n. In-chapter exercises

   4. What typographical cues are used in the chapter to highlight important information for you? Select all that apply.
      a. Boldface print
      b. Font size
      c. Bulleted lists
      g. Italicized print
      h. Font style
      i. Underlining

    d. Color of print   j. Boxes

    e. Shading   k. Symbols (light bulb, question mark,

    f. Arrows to show direction/order   star, etc.)

4. **Preview all of the end-of-chapter questions.** Read over the chapter summary and the questions. These are the key points the authors feel you should draw from the chapter. How do the authors tie the concepts back to the text so you would know where to find the information? Go back and look for it. Make a checkmark in the margin so you will remember this is a key point when you read the chapter.

5. This text makes extensive use of **margin notes. Preview these notes as well.** Consider how they tie in with the paragraphs they are next to. Do they simply repeat key ideas, or do they add additional information? How helpful are they? Are they distracting? If so, what will you have to do to work around them?

6. Now go back to the first page of the chapter and **read the chapter**. Move through the chapter section by section. Read first, then decide what information is important for you to know and what is explanatory to illustrate the point. Next, return to the outline you drafted for question 1. Fill in the outline with the information you have determined to be important for you to remember. Consider your method as well. **How** did you determine which information was important enough to record?

7. Consider the "Professional Organization Profile" box. Why do you think the authors have included it? Of what benefit is this information to you? How can you begin to use it this semester?

8. Review Table 14.1, "Major Segmentation Variables for Consumer Markets." What data is this table compiling? How would it help you in your marketing?

9. Finally, **after reading** the chapter, answer the questions at the end. How well did you do?

GROUP PROJECTS

1. Compare your outline with that of your classmates. Are they all the same? If not, how do they differ? Why do you think that may be? Next, compare how well you and your classmates did when answering the questions at the end of the text's chapter. Did those of you with the more detailed outline do better? Why or why not?

2. With your group, discuss the benefits of previewing the illustrations in the text before reading, as opposed to waiting to explore them as they come up in the reading.

3. As a group, consider what the authors do to make this chapter interesting and appealing to you. Consider both the visual components and the information itself. How do page layout and writing style make assigned reading more enjoyable?

4. Discuss with your group how helpful the advice is for marketing. Is there anything the authors do not consider?

5. As a group, compare this text chapter with others in this textbook. What impact does the use of color have on your processing of the text material? How does this compare to the black and white presentation of the foodservice chapter?

6. As a group, compare the graphics, margin notations, other visual cues of this chapter with those in other text chapters in this book. Do the other chapters look crowded and this one more streamlined? Do you like having more room to annotate the text? Or do you prefer the author to highlight the information for you?

Unit III
Reading Strategies for Humanities

The humanities explain or explore what it means to be human. This discipline includes literature, philosophy, religion, the performing arts, the visual arts, and, often, history courses. The artists, composers, historians, philosophers, sculptors, theologians, and writers are so moved by what they have learned about the human condition that they try to explain us to us, if you will. Their approach is often so creative, abstract, insightful, thought-provoking, esoteric—in short, subjective—that the study of these disciplines often involves far more than comprehending and applying factual knowledge; it involves interpretation and evaluation. Reading textbooks for philosophy and religion courses is much like the reading you would do for a history text. In fact, your art history or theater appreciation classes will also work much like the history class. It is when you get to the arts themselves that the texts take a major departure from the trusty outline format most other disciplines' texts use. Again, knowing what to look for will help.

HISTORY
Civilization: Past and Present
Eleventh Edition

by

Palmira Brummett, Robert R. Edgar, Neil J. Hackett,

George F. Jewsbury, and Barbara Molony

While history is a form of social science since it is the study of human beings through the course of time, it is often housed in the school of humanities at many institutions instead of under social sciences. Perhaps this is because history is not studied with the same scientific method approach as, for example, sociology is. (It is also possible that anthropology, archaeology, or political science could be housed in the humanities at your school as well.) The primary focus of the humanities is to study the human condition, and here the field of study becomes more subjective than the more objective approach the scientists take. While these disciplines are quite factual, the humanities often consider the motives behind events, not just the factual evidence. History, then, combines both the facts of what happened, when, where, and to whom, but it also strives to figure out why and how things happened, and then looks to consider the long-term effects or results of peoples' actions. History is a particularly challenging course because the introductory courses cover anywhere from a couple of hundred years' worth of developments to thousands of years' worth. Also, the text is usually set up in a more simplified outline format than the detailed outline format seen in the texts used in the sciences. The chapters often appear to be topical or thematic, with longer passages between headings, and this often makes them appear quite daunting. Again, knowing what to look for and how to break the material into manageable chunks helps lighten the load.

Previewing the history chapter will help you to see what is in the chapter, review the graphics, and look for break points so that you can pause with the least interruption of the flow of thought. Be sure to make note of time lines and maps. The time lines will help you get a grasp on the time period to help you set it in your mind, and maps give you a sense of place. If your text comes with a study guide, in paperback or on-line, do use it. Oftentimes the professors turn to the study guides to help them generate test questions, so these guides could help in numerous ways.

Be prepared to take many pages of notes in your history class. If you read before the class meets, as your professor expects you to, this will help you separate out what is essential and what is not in order to help you take notes more efficiently.

LITERATURE
American 24-Karat Gold: 24 Classic American Short Stories
Second Edition

by

Yvonne Collioud Sisko

POETRY
An Introduction to Literature
Fourteenth Edition

by

Sylvan Barnet, William Burto, and William E. Cain

Often students think that because they have been reading stories throughout their lives, they know how to read literature. Well, if the goal is simply to understand the plot, or storyline, they may be correct. However, that is not the only goal in a literature class. As with all of the other disciplines, your professor will be expecting you to dig deeper and look for more. The professor wants to know what insight you have gained from the literature. In order to dig deeper, you need to start digging at the surface, at the literal level, and then work deeper to the interpretive level. For all of the arts, when you get to the interpretation stage, begin with the title. The title of the work, whether it is a novel, a painting, a sculpture, a symphony, or a ballet, is often a quick synopsis of the theme. By considering how the title relates to the work, you can already start looking for meaning. You can begin by considering what associations come to mind when you read the title. Make note of them. Then, after examining the work, consider how the title fits the work. Consider also what you know about the author, composer, or artist. How does that person's biography or time period relate to the work? Keeping in mind that people are the products of their upbringing and the society and era in which they live, their work usually reflects their life experiences. Sometimes this is an important consideration, particularly with autobiographical works, and other times it is insignificant. Regardless of what element you are working to interpret, *be sure you find supporting evidence within the work itself*, not in the editor's comments.

Additionally, most literature textbooks generally begin a work with some introductory material about the work's author. Read this section! It will not only tell you the person's name, but it will also give you a brief summary of key aspects of the person's life, time period, what he or she is known for, and—this is the *really* helpful part—a statement about the work under consideration. This can save you some time in trying to discern the theme, or message, the work is trying to convey to you. The same can be said for any other study aids the text's editor has included for you.

For the works of *non-fiction* you will read, whether they are essays or articles, after you have considered the work's title and the opening comments about the author and the work that the text's editor has provided, also preview the work as you would any other textbook. Look at the layout of the work. Notice that the editor often numbers the paragraphs in the margin. This is for easy reference so that if your professor guides you to, for example, paragraph eleven, you do not have to count the paragraphs yourself to find paragraph eleven. You will just scan over the margin until you see 11. There may also be some pre-reading questions or activities to get you started thinking about the work, as well as some post-reading questions or writing activities. Do read these in your preview; they will help you determine the significant elements of the work or the author's writing style more quickly and better prepare you for class discussion. This is because an author's thesis may be *explicit*, or stated, or it can be *implicit*, which means implied. If you have a stated thesis, then the author's point is relatively easy to determine. If you have an implied thesis, that means you have to "read between the lines," or infer, the author's point. If you have difficulty with inferring meaning, the editor's questions will be particularly helpful.

When reading *literature*, if you begin with six key elements, you can discern a great deal on your own before going to class. The first element is *plot*, which is the series of events that transpire in the work. This covers who does what to whom, and when and where things happen. You will also need to consider the how and why behind the development of the events. The second element is *characterization*. The *characters* in your story are the participants in the story. They may be humans, animals, or objects, even forces of nature. The story will include a *protagonist*, which is your main, or most important, character. (The protagonist is not to be confused with the hero since a hero has to have some key traits in order to be considered as such.) In addition to the protagonist is the *antagonist*, which is the force opposing the protagonist. For example, in *The Wizard of Oz*, Dorothy is the protagonist and the Wicked Witch of the West is the antagonist.

The third element is *setting*, which is where and when a story takes place. The setting may be very specific, such as at "high noon" in Dodge City, or it could be vague, such as in a house on a dark and stormy night. The setting may also have symbolic significance, depending on the location, time of day, month, or season. Another aspect to consider with setting is the social conventions of the time period in which the story is set. The characters need to behave according to their era in order for them to be credible to the reader. One thing to keep in mind: characters, regardless of whether or not they are human, need to behave as humans do so their human readers will be able to identify with them.

The fourth element is *point of view*, which is the perspective from which the story is told. Point of view is determined by how many of the character minds you are permitted to enter. If the story is told in the *first person*, the character telling the story refers to him- or herself as "I," and everything that happens is filtered through the mind of that character. The reader sees what the character sees, hears what the characters hears, and knows what only that character thinks or feels. This character is to be treated warily; it is often not the most reliable witness. Consider the narrator in Edgar Allan Poe's story "The Tell-Tale Heart." Not the most stable guy, right? Now compare that character with Nick Carraway of *The Great Gatsby*. Nick is a far more stable and reliable narrator. If a story is told from the perspective of one character, but the character is referred to as "he" or "she," then the author is using *third person limited*, which is a bit more reliable than first person since the perspective is filtered through the narrator. The most reliable point of view, though, is *third person omniscient*, which enables the reader to get into the minds of several characters. This is the most reliable viewpoint because the reader gets to know more, gets a fuller perspective, and understands more of the motivations behind the characters than one can when only knowing what one character thinks and feels.

The fifth element is the *atmosphere*, which considers the emotional feeling of a story. In an Edgar Allan Poe story, for example, the creepy feeling established by Poe's descriptions of the setting set up a sense of dread, leading the reader to anticipate a spooky, creepy tale. The *style*, or approach the author takes when setting up the story, enhances the atmosphere. The sixth element is the *theme*, or the message the author is trying to convey, which is what all of the other elements are leading up to. The author is trying to share some insight about the human condition, and we are expected to be able to discern that message. Sometimes we receive a nice, neat message, such as when Dorothy of *The Wizard of Oz* learns there's no place like home, and other times there are multiple lessons to learn or insights we really have to think about for a while before trying to sum up a theme. Be prepared to think about how all the elements work together to lead up to the theme to help you discern one.

There are other devices authors use to help convey meaning. In the genres of drama and poetry, devises such as rhyme, rhythm, alliteration, assonance, and other devices which emphasize the sounds of words are also important to consider, so reading those works aloud will help you. One device significant to all genres is the use of symbols. *Symbols* are things that represent something beyond themselves. For example, a circle is a symbol for something eternal or unending. A *conventional symbol* is a symbol which, over time, has come to represent something specific. For example, in our culture a red rose is a symbol for love. The red petals represent the passion of love, the soft petals and sweet scent represent the pleasant aspects of love, and the thorns represent the pain love can bring; therefore, the concrete flower represents the bittersweet aspects of something as abstract as the concept of love. A *symbolic gesture* or *act* is when an action represents something greater, such as when Lady MacBeth is wringing her hands while she sleepwalks in Shakespeare's drama *The Tragedy of MacBeth*. Lady MacBeth is trying to wash the bloodstains off her hands as well as wash away her guilt. When looking for symbols, the main thing to consider is anything specifically named. For example, if a character is standing under a tree, that is not as important as if the character is standing under an *oak* tree. Oak trees represent strength and wisdom, so we are to infer the character is strong and wise or is gaining strength and wisdom. Therefore, look for specific colors, times of day, seasons, months, types of animals or plants, character names, and so on. If you think something specific could be symbolic, it possibly is, so be sure to consider what it symbolizes as well so you are ready for class discussion. Remember, a writer revises the work several times before publishing it, so nothing is in there by accident. If you think something could be meaningful, it probably is.

While all of these elements apply to all literature, the different *genres*, or types, of literature may have elements unique to them. In *poetry*, for example, and *verse drama*, such as Shakespeare's plays, many people are put off by a poem's format, or layout, on the page. Do not be intimidated by this. When we read *prose*, such as an essay or work of fiction, we read from margin to margin, left to right, pausing as the punctuation indicates. The same premise works for poetry, except the lines will be arranged vertically on top of each other instead of horizontally as in prose. Just read the poem following the punctuation marks, instead of line breaks. Ignore the fact that the work is vertical instead of horizontal. What it all amounts to basically is the difference between $2 + 2 = 4$ versus

$$\begin{array}{r} 2 \\ + \ 2 \\ \hline 4. \end{array}$$

VISUAL ARTS

When reading for the *visual* or *performing* arts, you may need to use a combination of the history text strategies and the literature strategies. The textbooks are often arranged similarly to history texts. You will encounter the historic developments of the arts, so you will be exposed to artists, composers, and playwrights, their time periods, and their artistic eras. You will also study their works. When trying to evaluate their work, use some of the literary strategies to help you. You will also need to consider the physical qualities of the work and the aesthetic qualities.

In considering the physical qualities of works in the visual arts, you have plenty to choose from. There is the size of the piece itself: is it a small or large sculpture? Is it made from marble, metal, wood, or clay? Is it a painting? Oil or watercolor? The *medium*, or the material(s) used for the work, is important. So is the use of color, light, perspective, proportion, placement of objects, and so on. Considering the spatial organization of the piece is a good place to begin an interpretation. For music, the style of the piece is important. An opera has different traits than a symphony does. You would also consider the instruments used, how loudly or softly the music is played, the speed at which it is played, and the like. For the performance arts, you need to consider how voice and movement are incorporated and used. Song has different considerations than dance does. For song, use some of the poetry strategies to help interpret the words, then consider how the singer uses the voice and music to express the emotion conveyed through the words. Dance uses movement to convey emotion, so gestures, including symbolic gestures, are important to consider. Costume and music also help convey meaning in the performing arts, as do lighting, set design, and sounds. Again, everything is important, so take your time so you can try to take it all in.

European Cultural and Religious Transformations

The Renaissance and the Reformation 1300–1600

CHAPTER CONTENTS

ach of the world's civilizations has had a moment when a combination of stability, wealth, and confidence allowed its thinkers, artists, and artisans to create expressions of that civilization's values which not only pleased their contemporaries, but served as models for future generations. These moments are sometimes called "Golden Ages." The two parts of the Han dynasty in China (206 B.C.E.–8 C.E. and 23 C.E.–228 C.E.); the Classical Mayan civilization in Mexico and Central America in the first millennium of the Common Era; the early part of the Tokugawa Shogunate in Japan in the sixteenth through the early eighteenth centuries; and in Africa Great Zimbabwe (1290–1410), the Swahili city-states on the east coast of the continent (fourteenth century), and Benin and Mali in the fourteen and fifteenth centuries: All set standards of excellence for their citizens.

In the Mediterranean world the Hellenic accomplishments in the middle part of the fifth century B.C.E., the Hellenistic variations on Hellenic themes to the end of the first century B.C.E., and the Roman and Byzantine consolidation and transmission of those intellectual and artistic qualities formed the classical basis of European civilization. That precious legacy was enriched by the magnificent accomplishments of the Islamic world from 900–1100. The work of Arab thinkers, artists, and scientists was transmitted through Spain and into Italy in translations to become part of the Western heritage.

In each of the Golden Ages cited above, there was a certain well-being in which philosophical and artistic creation took place. Yet this was not the case for the Italian and Northern Renaissance during the fifteenth and sixteenth century. This period of European history began in crisis: recession, famine, plague, and war; it ended amid similar crises: war, revolutionary economic change, and religious ferment. In spite of, but in part because of these crises, Europe during the centuries of Renaissance and Reformation developed the individualism that marked this Golden Age of European history.

SOCIAL UPHEAVAL

■ *What were the most significant reasons for the great social crises in European society in the fourteen and fifteenth centuries?*

The period from 1300 to 1600 in Europe was one of the most disruptive in its history. Among the most significant challenges to European stability were economic depression and the devastation caused by the **Bubonic Plague.** The combination of these two forces provoked an upheaval that changed European society.

Economic Depression and Bubonic Plague

In the three centuries preceding 1300, European agricultural methods had improved, crops were more productive, arable land increased, and the population probably doubled between 1000 and 1300. But the beginning of the fourteenth century saw changing weather patterns bringing drought, famine, and widespread starvation and unemployment. Overpopulation and unsanitary lifestyles contributed to the factors that rendered Europe more vulnerable to the plague which killed probably one-third of Europe's population—around 25 million people—between 1347 to 1350 and continued to reappear sporadically until the seventeenth century.

Called the Black Death because of the discoloring effects it had on the body (especially the lymph nodes), the plague was carried by fleas on infected rats and had worked its way through the trade routes of Asia and India to Europe. Cities were particularly devastated; Florence's population fell from 114,000 to 50,000, London's from 60,000 to 40,000. The outbreak of the Hundred Years' War between France and England in 1337 (see Chapter 15) added to the destruction in both those nations. The Black Death had a very significant formative effect on the development of European history.

Many looked for spiritual explanations for the plague's devastation: that God was punishing a sinful humanity, or perhaps that there was no God at all. Many blamed the Jews for the plague and sought their expulsion from cities throughout Europe. Others found their scapegoats for problems—ranging from the plague, crop failures, economic crises, and religious upheaval—in their searches for witches in the next two centuries. Over 100,000 of these unfor-

tunates were prosecuted during this period, and many were executed by strangling, drowning, burning, or beheading. Seventy percent of those killed were women, nearly half of whom were older single women or widows.

The Plague's Effect on European Society

By devastating the population of Europe, the Plague fundamentally changed the social patterns in Europe. A lack of rural workers effectively ended the remnants of the feudal structure in many places on the continent. Wage payments replaced the centuries-old payments in kind. In the cities in the late fourteenth and early fifteenth century, urban skilled craftsmen and the guilds that gave them security in an earlier age now became beneficiaries of higher prices paid for their goods, and their economic good fortune resulted in increased power and participation in urban politics. The church was also an economic beneficiary of the era; despite the decline of its revenues from its agricultural holdings, its wealth was vastly increased from donations and bequests from those wishing to increase their chances of a heavenly reward. But for those not in the guilds, life in the cities became increasingly difficult as the social problems of urban growth outran the resources of the Catholic Church to deal with them.

The beginning of the sixteenth century marked the beginning of another economic downturn that spread suffering throughout Europe. Economic dislocation accompanying the early development of capitalism added to the strains of transitioning between medieval and modern times, especially for the peasantry. The sixteenth century also marked the end of the relatively favorable situation women had enjoyed in the Middle Ages. The new emphasis on wage labor and competition from men limited their opportunities for outside work. Although women could find some part-time employment as field laborers, this paid very little.

A new global economy brought high rates of inflation and shifting trade routes. The decline of the importance of the Hanseatic League in the Baltic and North Seas, the Mediterranean, and the routes connecting the two hurt the economy of central Europe. Later, the shifting of work to laborers in the surrounding villages—the cottage industry—ruined many old guild industries while swelling the ranks of the urban unemployed. Large-market agriculture weakened the peasants' traditional rights, subjected them to rents beyond their resources, and drove them from the land into the towns, where they joined the idle and the impoverished.

Bubonic Plague—An infectious and usually fatal disease caused by the bacterium *Yersinia pestis*, which is carried and spread by the rat flea. Characteristics include high fever and swollen lymph nodes (buboes).

The poor and out-of-work often increasingly directed their anger against the Church because it was a visible source of authority, and it was rich. For society at large the profit motive overshadowed the church's canon law, which stressed compassion for the weak and the poor and a **"just price."**

In the midst of all of this economic and social upheaval, there began in Italy a cultural movement that touched only the elites but had consequences that would affect the development of Western civilization: It would come to be called the Renaissance, or the "rebirth."

"just price"—A medieval theory of economics supported by the Christian church. The church maintained that a just price should set the standards of fairness in all financial transactions. According to this theory, making interest on any loans was considered improper and labeled as *usury*.

THE ITALIAN RENAISSANCE

■ *Why is this period in Europe's history called a Renaissance—a "rebirth"?*

This cultural rebirth or Renaissance did not take place in a vacuum. Prior to the twelfth century, almost all learning in Europe was under the control of the church, and medieval art and literature reflected the church's influence. Latin was the European language of diplomacy, scholarship, and serious literature. But in the later medieval period the number of literate men and women in secular society began to increase, and the popularity of literature written in the vernacular, or commonly spoken languages of Europe, gained more and more popularity and acceptance, especially in the forms of poetry and song.

This map illustrates Europe in the time of the Italian and Northern Renaissance, as well as some of the cities that served as centers for artistic and humanist activities during the period.

Literary Precedents

Dante, *Divine Comedy*

Dante and Chaucer provided a bridge between the medieval and Renaissance worlds. Dante Alighieri (DAHN-teh ah-lig-hi-EH-ree; 1265–1321) was the author of the *Divine Comedy*, one of the great masterpieces of world literature. Combining a deep religious impulse with classical and medieval literature, Dante composed an allegory of medieval man (Dante) journeying through earthly existence (hell) through conversion (purgatory) to a spiritual union with God (paradise). Dante's work is regarded both as a culmination of the medieval intellectual tradition and at the same time as a composition of such unique brilliance that it should be considered one of the first creative works of the Renaissance.

Geoffrey Chaucer (c. 1340–1400), the author of *Canterbury Tales*, wrote an English vernacular account of the journey of 29 pilgrims to the shrine of St. Thomas á Becket at Canterbury. His personality profiles and stories satirized contemporary English customs and lifestyles, and his work solidly established the vernacular as a legitimate literary form of expression in England.

Another voice of the transition was one of the most gifted vernacular poets of the fourteenth century was a woman—Christine de Pizan (pi-ZAHN; 1365–c. 1430), who wrote to support her children after her husband's death. She authored more than ten volumes of poetry and prose, and her allegorical work—*The Book of the City of Ladies*—presented a defense of women's significance in society and a plea for greater compassion to their burdens.

The Italian Setting for the Development of Humanism

In Italy during the fourteenth century, a growing number of literate and artistic individuals began to call themselves *humanists*—citizens of a modern world that would perfect itself through the recovery, study, and transmission of the cultural heritage of Greece and Rome. They believed themselves to be the initiators of a new era—a renaissance (rebirth) of the culture and values of classical antiquity. But this culture historians call the Italian Renaissance did not come into being without tremendous influence from its medieval past—in fact, many historians consider the Renaissance to be more of a natural maturation of medieval society than a radical break with traditional culture. Yet most students of the period agree that the heritage of the past, in combination with a newly found passionate concern with Greece and Rome and emerging political and economic patterns, produced a distinctly different culture.

During the fourteenth and fifteenth centuries, after recovering from the effects of the Black Plague, the city-states of northern and central Italy experienced a tremendous growth in population and expanded to become small territorial states. Eventually five such states emerged: the duchy of Milan; the Papal States, in which the restored authority of the popes crushed the independence of many smaller city-states in central Italy; the republics of Florence and Venice; and the kingdom of Naples. Selling or leasing their country holdings, Italian nobles moved to the cities and joined with the rich merchants to form an urban ruling class. By 1300 nearly all the land of northern and central Italy was owned by profit-seeking urban citizens who produced their goods for city markets. In the large export industries, such as woolen cloth (the industry employed 30,000 in Florence), a capitalistic system of production, in which the merchants retained ownership of the raw material and paid others to finish the product, brought great profits. More great wealth was gained from commerce, particularly the import-export trade in luxury goods from the East.

So much wealth was accumulated by these merchant-capitalists that they turned to money-lending and banking. From the thirteenth to the fifteenth centuries, Italians monopolized European banking (Florence alone had 80 banking houses by 1300). These economic and political successes made the Italian upper-class groups strongly assertive, self-confident, and passionately attached to their city-states. Even literature and art reflected their self-confidence.

Political leaders and the wealthy merchants, bankers, and manufacturers conspicuously displayed their wealth and that of their cities by patronizing the arts and literature. Artists and scholars were provided with governmental, academic, and tutorial positions and enjoyed the security and protection offered by their patrons and the advantage of working exclusively on commission. Among the most famous patrons were members of the Medici family, who ruled Florence for 60 years (1434–1494). Renaissance popes were lavish patrons who made Rome the foremost center of art and learning by 1500.

Humanism and the Classical Revival: Petrarch and Boccacio

Historians are not able to agree on an exact meaning of the Renaissance term known as *humanism*. But they generally agree that humanism consisted of the study and popularization of the Greek and Latin classics and the culture those classics described. The humanists, students of the classics as well as advocates of the Roman concept of a liberal education (or *studia humanitatis*), promoted an education in "humanistic studies," but also advocated civic patriotism and social betterment.

Discovery Through Maps

The Lagoon of Venice

Maps can be designed to illustrate much more than merely the physical features of a geographical area. They may also be designed to serve as vehicles to enhance the image of a particular state—to serve as propaganda. For instance, examine this cartographic rendering of the Lagoon of Venice and the neighboring regions of Friulli and Istria, one of a series of magnificently designed maps painted by Ignazio Danti (1536–1586), a mathematician, astronomer, geographer, and Dominican priest and bishop—another example of the idealized "Renaissance man." Danti was commissioned by Pope Gregory XIII to make a number of maps of ancient and modern Italy, many of which are presently on display in the Vatican Museum in Rome. Danti's map of the Lagoon of Venice depicts an idealized land and seascape that features a bustling harbor, replete with sailing vessels both mythical and contemporary to the sixteenth century. Over the harbor the sun radiates its glory on the land and sea, and a formal inscription in Latin gives testimony to the ancient significance of the harbor and past glories.

The primary purpose of this map was certainly not to provide geographical assistance, but rather to promote the power and glory of the Republic of Venice. Such a map provided its observers with a sense of the historic significance of the Lagoon, its almost mythical role in the history of the Italian peninsula, and the opulence and splendor of one of the most significant republics of Renaissance Italy.

Questions to Consider

1. What seem to be the most significant features emphasized in this map of the Lagoon of Venice? Why does the artist appear to focus most of his attention on the sea rather than the land itself?

2. What effects do you think this map would have had on its viewers in the sixteenth century? What impressions do you believe Danti wanted to impart to his contemporaries who studied this map?

3. Why do you think Danti portrayed such a variety of vessels from different eras and subjects drawn from both pagan mythology and Christian tradition in the harbor?

The classic example of the Renaissance nobleman, statesman, and patron of the arts was the Florentine Lorenzo de' Medici, known as Lorenzo the Magnificent. Under his patronage and guidance, Florence became the leading city of the Italian Renaissance, renowned for the splendor of its buildings and lavish support for the arts.

The humanists were also the founders of modern historical research and linguistics. Humanism was not an anti-Christian movement, and most humanists remained religious, but the church bureaucracy and the extreme authority claimed by the popes received their strongest criticism.

"Father of humanism" is a title given to Francesco Petrarca (frahn-CHEHS-koh peh-TRAHR-kah), better known as Petrarch (1304–1374), by later Italian humanists because he was the first to play a major role in making people conscious of the attractions of classical literature. He wrote Latin epic poetry and biography in addition to his famous and innovative love sonnets to a married woman named Laura, whom Petrarch admired romantically. Petrarch's works held to his Christian values, but displayed much more of a secular orientation and an involvement with the society and social issues of the day.

DOCUMENT

Petrarch, Letter to Cicero

Another celebrated early humanist was the Florentine Giovanni Boccaccio (gee-oh-VAH-nee boh-KAH-chee-oh; 1313–1375), a student and friend of Petrarch's who began his career as a writer of poetry and romances. But his masterpiece was the *Decameron*, a collection of one hundred stories told by three young men and seven young women, as they sought to avoid the Black Plague in the seclusion of a country villa. The *Decameron* offers a wealth of anecdotes, portraits of flesh-and-blood characters, and vivid glimpses of Renaissance life.

The *Decameron* was both the high point and the end of Boccaccio's career as a creative artist. Largely through the influence of Petrarch, whom he met in 1350, Boccaccio gave up writing in Italian and turned to the study of antiquity. He began to learn Greek, composed an encyclopedia of classical mythology, and visited monasteries in search of manuscripts. By the time Petrarch and Boccaccio died, the study of the literature and learning of antiquity was growing throughout Italy.

Classical Revival and Philosophy

The recovery and assimilation of Greek and Roman learning was a consuming passion of the humanists. The search for manuscripts became a mania, and before the middle of the fifteenth century, original works, unedited by the church, of most of the important Latin authors had been found. In addition to these Latin works, precious Greek manuscripts were brought to Italy from Constantinople after it fell to the Turks in 1453, and many Greek scholars were welcomed to Italy, in particular to Florence, where the Medici gave their support to a gathering of Florentine

A miniature portrait of Petrarch from his illuminated manuscript of Remedies Against Fortune. *In keeping with a classical tradition, Petrarch composed many letters—which he edited for publication—that were in effect literary essays expressing his own attitudes and humanistic concerns.*

humanists which came to be called the Academy. Under the leadership of the humanists Marsilio Ficino (mar-SEE-lee-oh fee-CHEE-noh) (1433–1499) and Pico della Mirandola (PEE-koh de-lah mee-RAHN-doh-lah; 1463–1494), the Academy focused its study on the works of Plato, and placed particular emphasis on Plato's admiration of human reason and free will. The influence of Aristotle still remained strong among Scholastic thinkers during the Renaissance, especially at the University of Padua, where the study of natural science, logic, and metaphysics continued to be emphasized. Scholasticism was the dominant school of thought in the West from the ninth through seventeenth centuries, drawing its inspiration from Aristotle, St. Augustine, and the declared truths of the church (see Chapter 9).

A growing number of women were well educated, read the classics, and wrote during the Renaissance.

Document   Machiavelli, *The Prince:* On Cruelty and Mercy

Niccoló Machiavelli, born into an impoverished branch of a noble family of Florence, began his pubic life as a diplomat in the service of the Florentine republic. When the Medici family returned to dominate Florence in 1512, Machiavelli was imprisoned and tortured for his supposed plot against the Medici family. He then retired to the countryside to write his most famous works. Machiavelli's best known work is *The Prince* (1532), which presents a description of how a prince might best gain control and maintain power. His ideal prince is calculating and ruthless in his quest to best those who would destroy him in his effort to establish a unified Italian state. The following excerpts from this famous work describe how a prince must decide how, when, and if a prince should use cruelty or mercy to accomplish his aims:

From this arises an argument: whether it is better to be loved than to be feared, or the contrary. I reply that one should like to be both one and the other: but since it is difficult to join them together, it is much safer to be feared than to be loved when one of the two must be lacking. For one can generally say that about men: that they are ungrateful, fickle, simulators and deceivers, avoiders of danger, greedy for gain; and while you work for their good they are completely yours, offering you their blood, their property, their lives, and their sons, as I said earlier, when danger is far away; but when it comes nearer to you they turn away. And that prince who bases his power entirely on their works, finding himself stripped of other preparations, comes to ruin; for friendships that are acquired by a price and not by greatness and nobility of character are purchases but are not owned, and at the proper moment they cannot be spent. And men are less hesitant about harming someone who makes himself loved than one who makes himself feared because love is held together by a chain of obligation which, since men are a sorry lot, is broken on every occasion in which their own self-interest is concerned; but fear is held together by a dread of punishment which will never abandon you.

A prince must nevertheless make himself feared in such a manner that he will avoid hatred, even if he does not acquire love: since to be feared and not hated can very well be combined; and this will always be so when he keeps his hands off the property and the women of his citizens and his subjects. And if he must take someone's life, he should do so when there is proper justification and manifest cause; but, above all, he should avoid the property of others; for men forget more quickly the death of their father than the loss of their patrimony. Moreover, the reasons for seizing their property are never lacking; and he who begins to live by stealing always finds a reason for taking what belongs to others; on the contrary, reasons for taking a life are rarer and disappear sooner. . . . I conclude, therefore, returning to the problem of being feared and loved, that since men love at their own pleasure and fear at the pleasure of the prince, a wise prince should build his foundation upon that which belongs to him, and not upon that which belongs to others: he must strive only to avoid hatred, as has been said.

Questions to Consider

1. Comment on Machiavelli's speculations about the nature of man, and the ways in which a prince should capitalize on the reality of human character as he analyses it. Is he overly cynical, or is he a realist?

2. Does Machiavelli's advice seem out of date given the realities of politics and the quest for power in the modern world?

3. What principles of conduct does Machiavelli advise a prince to cultivate? Is his prince a complete despot, or a more crafty and manipulative, yet ethical, student of man's nature?

From Peter Bondanella and Mark Musa, eds., *The Portable Machiavelli* (New York: Viking Press, 1979), pp. 135–136.

Most of these women were daughters or wives of wealthy aristocrats who could afford private tutoring in liberal studies, since the universities were for the most part still inaccessible to females. But in the works of most humanists—echoing their classical precedents—there is little that supports the participation of women on equal footing with males in scholarly or civic activities. Some historians even maintain that Renaissance women were more restricted in their intellectual pursuits than they had been in the late Middle Ages. Still, some noble women gained great reputation and respect for their political wisdom and intelligence. Battista Sforza (SFOHR-zah), wife of the Duke of Urbino in the fifteenth century, was well known for her knowledge of Greek and Latin and admired for her ability to govern in the absence of her husband. Her contemporary, Isabella d'Este, wife of the Duke of Mantua, was renowned for her education and support of the arts, and for assembling one of the finest libraries in Italy.

ITALIAN RENAISSANCE ART

- *How did Italian Renaissance artists differ from their medieval predecessors?*

Fourteenth- and fifteenth-century Italy produced innovations in art that culminated in the classic High Renaissance artistic style of the early sixteenth century. These innovations were the products of a new

Giotto, St. Francis Receiving the Stigmata *(c. 1295). Both a painter and architect, Giotto is credited as the first great genius of Italian Renaissance art. Like his medieval predecessors, his subjects were mainly religious, but his human subjects were portrayed as full of life and emotion. One of his favorite subjects was St. Francis of Assisi, who here receives the wounds of Jesus's crucifixion—the stigmata.*

society centered in rich cities, the humanistic and more secular spirit of the times, a revived interest in the classical art of Greece and Rome, and the creativity of some of the world's most gifted artists.

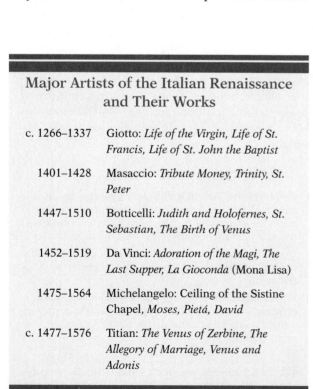

Major Artists of the Italian Renaissance and Their Works	
c. 1266–1337	Giotto: *Life of the Virgin, Life of St. Francis, Life of St. John the Baptist*
1401–1428	Masaccio: *Tribute Money, Trinity, St. Peter*
1447–1510	Botticelli: *Judith and Holofernes, St. Sebastian, The Birth of Venus*
1452–1519	Da Vinci: *Adoration of the Magi, The Last Supper, La Gioconda* (Mona Lisa)
1475–1564	Michelangelo: Ceiling of the Sistine Chapel, *Moses, Pietá, David*
c. 1477–1576	Titian: *The Venus of Zerbine, The Allegory of Marriage, Venus and Adonis*

From Giotto to Donatello

The new approach in painting was first evident in the work of the Florentine painter Giotto (JOT-toh; c. 1266–1337). Earlier Italian painters had copied the stylized, flat, and rigid images of Byzantine paintings and mosaics, Giotto observed from life and painted a three-dimensional world peopled with believable human beings moved by deep emotion. He humanized painting much as Petrarch humanized thought and St. Francis, whose life was one of his favorite subjects, humanized religion. Giotto initiated a new epoch in the history of painting, one that expressed the religious piety of his lay patrons, but also their delight in the images of everyday life.

Masaccio, Expulsion from Eden. *Masaccio's mastery of perspective creates the illusion of movement as the angel drives Adam and Eve from Paradise.*

In his brief lifetime the Florentine Masaccio (mah-SAH-chee-oh; 1401–1428) completed the revolution in technique begun by Giotto. As can be seen in his few surviving paintings, Masaccio was concerned with the problems of perspective, and the modeling of figures in light and shade (*chiaroscuro;* CHAH-roh-SKOO-roh). He was also the first Renaissance artist to paint nude figures (Adam and Eve, in his *Expulsion from Eden*), reversing the tradition of earlier Christian art.

Inspired by Masaccio's achievement, most *quattrocento* (quah-troh-CHEN-toh; Italian for "the 1400s" or "fifteenth century") painters constantly sought to improve technique. But the Florentine Sandro Botticelli (sahn-DROH boh-tah-CHEH-lee; 1447–1510) proceeded in a different direction, abandoning the techniques of straightforward representation of people and objects and trying instead to inspire the viewer's imagination and emotion through close attention to strikingly beautiful portraiture and decorative backdrop landscapes.

New directions were also being taken in sculpture, and it, like painting, reached stylistic maturity at the beginning of the *quattrocento*. The Florentine Donatello (1386–1466) produced truly freestanding statues based on the realization of the human body as a coordinated mechanism of bones and muscles; his *David* was the first bronze nude made since antiquity.

Botticelli, The Birth of Venus. *The last great Florentine painter of the early Renaissance, Botticelli did most of his best work for Lorenzo de' Medici and his court. In* The Birth of Venus, *Botticelli blends ancient mythology, Christian faith, and voluptuous representation.*

The High Renaissance, 1500–1530: Leonardo da Vinci, Raphael, and Michelangelo

The painters of the High Renaissance had learned the solutions to such technical problems as perspective space from the *quattrocento* artists. The artists of the earlier period had been concerned with movement, color, and narrative detail, but painters in the High Renaissance attempted to eliminate nonessentials and concentrated on the central theme of a picture and its basic human implications.

The three greatest High Renaissance painters were Leonardo da Vinci, Raphael, and Michelangelo. Leonardo da Vinci (1452–1519) was brilliant in a variety of fields: engineering, mathematics, architecture, geology, botany, physiology, anatomy, sculpture, painting, music, and poetry. Because he loved the process of experimentation more than seeing all his projects through to completion, few of the projects da Vinci started were ever finished. He was a master of soft modeling in light and shade and of creating groups of figures perfectly balanced in a given space. One of his most famous paintings is *La Gioconda*, known as the Mona Lisa, a portrait of a woman whose enigmatic smile captures an air of tenderness and humility. Another is *The Last Supper,* which he painted on the walls of the refectory of Santa Maria delle Grazie in Milan. In this painting da Vinci experimented with the use of an oil medium combined with plaster, which unfortunately was unsuccessful. The painting quickly began to disintegrate and has been restored several times.

Raphael (1483–1520) was summoned to Rome in 1508 by Pope Julius II to aid in the decoration of the Vatican. His **frescos** there display a magnificent blending of classical and Christian subject matter and are the fruit of careful planning and immense artistic

---

fresco—A type of wall painting in which water-based pigments are applied to wet, freshly laid lime plaster. The dry-powder colors, when mixed with water, penetrate the surface and become a permanent part of the wall. The Italian Renaissance was the greatest period of fresco painting.

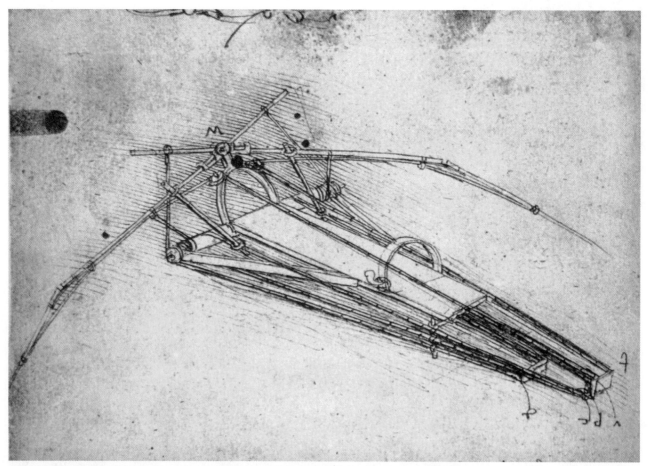

Leonardo da Vinci, Drawing of a Flying Machine. *One of the artist's later designs for a flying machine, which modern engineers speculate could have worked, although it was much too heavy. Da Vinci was convinced that a successful flying machine had to be modeled after the wings of bats and birds, as his numerous sketches of these animals show.*

knowledge. Critics consider him the master of perfect design and balanced composition.

The individualism and idealism of the High Renaissance have no greater representative than Michelangelo Buonarroti (MEE-kel-AHN-je-loh boo-na-ROH-ti; 1475–1564). Stories of this stormy and temperamental personality have helped shape our definition of a genius. His great energy enabled him to paint for Julius II in four years the entire ceiling of the Vatican's Sistine Chapel, an area of several thousand square yards, and his art embodies a superhuman ideal. With his unrivaled genius for rendering the

Raphael, Madonna of the Meadow *(c. 1505/1506). Raphael's painting in oil on canvas is a classic example of a composition based on the figure of a pyramid. The scene is formally balanced yet features the interaction of the figures. The infants portrayed are John the Baptist (left) and Jesus.*

Michelangelo, David. *To Michelangelo, the Florentine painter, sculptor, poet, and architect, sculpture was the noblest of the arts. The large marble statue of the biblical David was commissioned in 1501 to stand in Florence as a symbol of the city, its government, and its culture.*

human form, he devised a wealth of expressive positions and attitudes for his figures in scenes from Genesis. Michelangelo also excelled as poet, engineer, and architect and was undoubtedly the greatest sculptor of the Renaissance. The glorification of the human body was Michelangelo's great achievement. His statue of *David*, commissioned in 1501 when he was 26, expressed his idealized view of human dignity and majesty. He also became chief architect of St. Peter's in 1546, designed the great dome, and was still actively creative as a sculptor when he died, almost in his ninetieth year, in 1564.

From about 1530 to the end of the sixteenth century, Italian artists responded to the stresses of the age in a new style called *Mannerism.* Consciously revolting against the classical balance and simplicity of High Renaissance art, Mannerist artists sought to express their own inner vision in a manner that evoked shock in the viewer. Typical are the paintings of Parmigianino (par-me-zhian-NI-no), whose *Madonna with the Long Neck* (1535) purposely shows no logic of structure.

THE NORTHERN RENAISSANCE

■ *How did the Northern Renaissance differ from the Italian Renaissance?*

The Italian Renaissance, by seeking meaning in the classical world, had placed human beings once more in the center of life's stage and infused thought and art with humanistic values. These stimulating ideas spread north to inspire other humanists, who absorbed and adapted the Italian achievement to their own particular national circumstances.

Throughout the fifteenth century, hundreds of northern European students studied in Italy. Though their chief interest was the study of law and medicine, many were influenced by the intellectual climate of Italy with its new enthusiasm for the classics. When these students returned home, they often carried manuscripts—and later printed editions—produced by classical and humanist writers. Both literate laymen and devout clergy in the north were ready to welcome the new outlook of humanism, although these north-

Cellini, Saltcellar of Francis I. *The utilitarian purpose of the condiment dish is subordinate to its lavish decoration. Neptune, god of the sea, guards the boat-shaped salt container while a personification of Earth watches over the pepper. Figures around the base represent the four seasons and the four parts of the day. The intricacy of the design is a showcase for the sculptor's virtuosity.*

and new ideas reached a thousand times more people in a relatively short span of time. In the quickening of Europe's intellectual life, it is difficult to overestimate the effects of the printing press.

Humanism in France, Germany, Spain, and England

One of the best-known French humanists was François Rabelais (frahn-SWAH RAH-be-lay; c. 1483–1553), who is best remembered for his novel *Gargantua and Pantagruel*. Centering on figures from French folklore, this work relates the adventures of Gargantua and his son Pantagruel, genial giants of tremendous stature and appetite. Rabelais satirized his society while putting forth his humanist views on educational reform and inherent human goodness. He made powerful attacks on the abuses of the church and the

---

Major Figures in the Northern Renaissance and Their Works

c. 1395–1441	Jan van Eyck (painter): *Man with the Red Turban, Wedding Portrait*
c. 1466–1536	Desiderius Erasmus (humanist and scholar): *The Praise of Folly, Handbook of the Christian Knight*
1471–1528	Albrecht Dürer (painter): *Adam and Eve, The Four Apostles, Self-Portrait*
1478–1535	Sir Thomas More (humanist and diplomat): *Utopia*
c. 1483–1553	François Rabelais (writer): *Gargantua and Pantagruel*
1488–1523	Ulrich von Hutten (humanist and poet)
1547–1616	Miguel de Cervantes (writer): *Don Quixote*
1564–1616	William Shakespeare (playwright and poet): *Julius Caesar, Romeo and Juliet, King Lear*

---

ern humanists were more interested in religious reform than their Italian counterparts.

The Influence of Printing

Very important in the diffusion of the Renaissance and later in the success of the Reformation was the invention of printing with movable type in Europe. The essential elements—paper and block printing—had been known in China since the eighth century. During the twelfth century, the Spanish Muslims introduced papermaking to Europe; in the thirteenth, Europeans, in close contact with China (see Chapter 10), brought knowledge of block printing to the West. The crucial step was taken in the 1440s at Mainz, Germany, where Johann Gutenberg (YOH-hahn GOOT-en-berg) and other printers invented movable type by cutting up old printing blocks to form individual letters. Gutenberg used movable type for papal documents and for the first printed version of the Bible (1454).

Soon all the major countries of Europe possessed the means for printing books. Throughout Europe, the price of books sank to one-eighth of their former cost and came within the reach of many people who formerly had been unable to buy them. In addition, pamphlets and controversial tracts soon began to circulate,

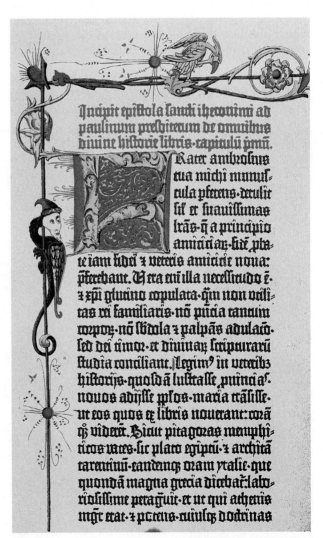

Facsimile copy of a page from the Gutenberg Bible, the Book of Genesis. With the development of printing, learning was no longer the private domain of the church and those few persons wealthy enough to own hand-copied volumes.

hypocrisy and repression he found in contemporary political and religious practice.

Another notable northern humanist was the French skeptic Michel de Montaigne (mee-SHEL de mohn-TANYE; 1533–1592). At age 38, he gave up the practice of law and retired to his country estate and well-stocked library, where he studied and wrote. Montaigne developed a new literary form and gave it its name—the *essay*. In 94 essays he set forth his personal views on many subjects: leisure, friendship, education, philosophy, religion, old age, death. He advocated open-mindedness and tolerance—rare qualities in the sixteenth century, when France was racked by religious and civil strife.

DOCUMENT

Montaigne, *Essays*

One of the most outstanding German humanists was Ulrich von Hutten (HOO-ten; 1488–1523). His idealism combined a zeal for religious reform and German nationalist feelings. This member of an aristocratic family, who wanted to unite Germany under the emperor, supported Martin Luther as a rallying point for German unity against the papacy, to which he attributed most of his country's ills.

In the national literatures that matured during the northern Renaissance, the transition from feudal knight to Renaissance courtier finds its greatest literary expression in a masterpiece of Spanish satire, *Don Quixote de la Mancha*, the work of Miguel de Cervantes (1547–1616). By Cervantes's time, knighthood and ideals of chivalry had become archaic in a world of practical concerns. Cervantes describes the adventures of Don Quixote (ki-HOH-te), a knight who is a representative of an earlier age. Don Quixote appears to be ridiculous old man who desires the great days of the past and has a series of misadventures in his attempts to recapture past glories. But Cervantes's real objective was to expose the inadequacies of chivalric idealism in a world that had acquired new and intensely practical aims. He did so by creating a sad but appealing character to serve as the personification of an outmoded way of life.

The reign of Queen Elizabeth I (1558–1603) was the high point of the English Renaissance and produced an astonishing number of gifted writers. Strongly influenced by the royal court, which served as the busy center of intellectual and artistic life, these writers produced works that were intensely emotional, richly romantic, and often wildly creative in combination with traditional poetic allusions to classical times.

The dominant figure in Elizabethan literature is William Shakespeare (1564–1616). His rich vocabulary and poetic imagery were matched by his turbulent imagination. He was a superb lyric poet, and numerous critics have judged him the foremost sonnet writer in the English language.

Shakespeare wrote 37 plays—comedies, histories, tragedies, and romances. His historical plays reflected the patriotic upsurge experienced by the English after the defeat of the Spanish Armada in 1588. For his comedies, tragedies, and romances, Shakespeare was content, in a great majority of cases, to borrow plots from earlier works. His great strength lay in his creation of characters and in his ability to translate his knowledge of human nature into dramatic speech and action. Today his comedies still play to enthusiastic audiences, but it is in his

Michel de Montaigne, author of the Essays. *Montaigne retired from the business world while in his thirties to reflect on and write about humanity's problems.*

tragedies that the poet-dramatist runs the gamut of human emotion and experience.

Shakespeare possessed in abundance the Renaissance concern for human beings and the world around them. His plays deal first and foremost with the human personality, passions, and problems.

Northern Painting

Before the Italian Renaissance began to influence the artistic circles of northern Europe, the painters of the Low Countries—modern Belgium, Luxembourg, and the Netherlands—had been making significant advances on their own. Outstanding was the Fleming Jan van Eyck (YAHN van AIK; c. 1395–1441), who painted in the realistic manner developed by medieval miniaturists. Van Eyck also perfected the technique of oil painting, which enabled him to paint with greater realism and attention to detail. In his painting of the merchant Arnolfini and his wife, for example, he painstakingly gives extraordinary reality to every detail, from his own image reflected in the mirror in the background to individual hairs on the little dog in the foreground.

The first German painter to be influenced deeply by Italian art was Albrecht Dürer (1471–1528) of Nuremberg. Dürer made several journeys to Italy, where he was impressed both with the painting of the Renaissance Italians and with the artists' high social status— a contrast with northern Europe, where artists were still treated as craftsmen, not men of genius. His own work is a blend of the old and the new and fuses the realism and symbolism of Gothic art with the style and passion of the Italian artists. In his own lifetime and after, Dürer became better known for his numerous engravings and woodcuts, produced for a mass market, than for his paintings.

Another famous German painter, Hans Holbein the Younger (1497–1543), chiefly painted portraits and worked abroad, especially in England. His memorable portraits blend the realism and concern for detail characteristic of all northern painting with Italian dignity.

Two northern painters who remained completely isolated from Italian influences were Hieronymus Bosch (hai-ROH-ni-muhs BAHSH; 1480–1516) and Pieter Brueghel (BROI-gel) the Elder (c. 1525–1569).

Jan van Eyck, Wedding Portrait. *The painting of a merchant named Arnolfini and his pregnant bride is extraordinary for its meticulously rendered realistic detail. Van Eyck painted exactly what he saw— he "was there," as his signature on the painting says (Johannes de Eyck fuit hic). The painting is also filled with symbolism; the dog, for instance, stands for marital fidelity.*

Jan van Eyck, *The Wedding Portrait,* 1434.

Hieronymous Bosch, Hell, *from* The Garden of Earthly Delights *(1503/1504). Part of a three-paneled altarpiece (a triptych) depicting the dreams that affect people in a pleasure-seeking world. The panel pictured here displays the horrors that await those sent to hell, where they spend their days tortured by half-human monsters, devils, and demons in a fantastic landscape.*

Brueghel retained a strong Flemish flavor in his portrayal of the faces and scenes of his native land. He painted village squares, landscapes, skating scenes, and peasants at work and at leisure just as he saw them, with an expert eye for detail.

Very little is known about the Dutch master Bosch other than that he belonged to one of the many puritanical religious sects that were becoming popular at the time. This accounts for his most famous painting, *The Garden of Delights*, a triptych whose main panel is filled with large numbers of naked men and women partaking in the sins of the flesh. The smaller left panel, by contrast, depicts an idealized Garden of Eden, while the right panel portrays a nightmarish hell filled with desperate sinners undergoing punishment. Bosch was a stern moralist whose obsession with sin and hell reflects the fears of many of his contemporaries—concerns that contributed to the religious movement known as the Reformation.

Erasmus, Thomas More, and Northern Humanism

The most influential of the northern humanists was Desiderius Erasmus (c. 1466–1536). Dutch by birth, he passed most of his long life elsewhere—in Germany, France, England, Italy, and especially Switzerland. He corresponded with nearly every prominent writer and thinker in Europe and personally knew popes, emperors, and kings. He was *the* scholar of Europe, and his writings and translations of the classics, and the works of the church fathers, as well as a new Latin translation of the New Testament, were eagerly read everywhere.

Perhaps the most famous and influential work by Erasmus was *The Praise of Folly*, a satire written in 1511 at the house of the English humanist Sir Thomas More. This influential work poked fun at and ridiculed a broad range of political, social, economic and religious evils of the day. Erasmus' scholarship and the objects of his literary attention typify the central concerns of the northern humanists. They were interested not only in the classics, but in the Bible and early Christian writings. Their primary focus of reform was not civil society and the state, but morality and a return to the simplicity of early Christianity.

The most significant figure in English humanism was Sir Thomas More (1478–1535), a good friend of Erasmus. More is best known for his *Utopia*, the first important description of an ideal state since Plato's *Republic*. In this work, More criticized his age through his portrayal of a fictitious sailor who contrasts the ideal

DOCUMENT

More, *Utopia*

Portrait of Erasmus *by Hans Holbein the Younger. Erasmus's scholarly achievements include a Greek edition of the New Testament and editions of the writings of St. Jerome and other early church fathers. Erasmus is best known, however, for his popular works, especially* The Praise of Folly.

the Complutensian Bible between 1502–1517, under the supervision of Cardinal Ximenes (HE-men-es). Similar texts in Greek, Latin, and Hebrew were printed on the same page for most of the books of the Bible to assure a proper translation of scripture. In other places, humanism's questioning of authoritative documents, such as Lorenzo da Valla's linguistic research that indicated that the Donation of Constantine was a forgery, emboldened critics of the church to press their case for change. Unfortunately for the church, it went through one of its most stormy periods between 1300 and 1500, and there was much to criticize.

THE CRISIS IN THE CATHOLIC CHURCH: 1300–1517

■ *What factors led to the erosion of church authority from 1300 to 1517?*

The power of the medieval papacy reached its height during the pontificate of Innocent III (1198–1216), who exerted his influence over kings and princes without serious challenge. The church seemed unrivaled in its prestige, dignity, and power. Yet that dominance was challenged on several fronts, and over the next two centuries, the power of the medieval church was diminished and transformed.

MAP

Religious Diversity in the Western World

Boniface VIII

Papal power was threatened by the growth of nation-states, whose monarchs challenged the church's temporal power, the papal bureaucracy's maintenance of a separate judicial structure for those under the pope's authority, and the privilege to collect **tithes** destined for Rome. In addition, the papacy became regularly criticized by reformers who questioned the legitimacy of papal authority and its secular power in place of the biblical example of simplicity and otherworldliness in matters of belief. The bourgeoisie, the middle-class workers and craftsmen of the towns whose attitudes were much more pragmatic than those of the rural peasantry of an earlier age, fostered an outlook of growing skepticism, national patriotism, and religious self-reliance.

life he has seen in Utopia (the "Land of Nowhere") with the harsh conditions of life in England. In Utopia, the evils brought on by political and social injustice were overcome by the holding of all property and goods in common. More's economic outlook was a legacy from the Middle Ages, and his preference for medieval collectivism over modern economic individualism was consistent with his preference for a church headed, in medieval style, by popes rather than by kings. This view prompted Henry VIII, who had appropriated the pope's position as head of the Church of England, to execute More, who had been one of Henry's most trusted advisers and officials, for treason.

Erasmus and More transmitted humanist values and research skills throughout Northern Europe. Through their writings they contributed to the increasing demand for reform of the Catholic Church: However, neither man sought the breakup of the church. In some places, such as Spain, the new humanistic linguistic and research skills were used to produce

---

tithes—Contribution of a tenth of one's income to the Church. Tithing dates to the Old Testament and was adopted by the Western Christian church in the sixth century and enforced in Europe by secular law from the eighth century.

Pope Boniface VIII (1294–1303) was an outspoken advocate of papal authority and a strident opponent of any monarch who dared to attempt to tax the church without papal consent. The powerful and popular kings of England, Edward I, and France, Philip IV the Fair, attempted to tax the church and limit the authority of papal courts, and in response Boniface boldly declared in the papal bull *Unam Sanctam* (OO-nam SANK-tam; 1302) that all temporal matters, and even rulers, were ultimately subject to the spiritual power wielded by the pope. Philip demanded that the pope be brought to trial by a general church council. In 1303 French officials and their allies broke into Boniface's summer home at Anagni, roughed the old man up, and attempted to arrest him and take him to France to stand trial, but the pope was rescued by his supporters. Boniface died a month later, perhaps from the shock and physical abuse he suffered during the attack.

DOCUMENT

Boniface VIII,
*Unam
Sanctum*

CASE STUDY

Role and
Authority of
the Pope

The Avignon Papacy

Philip's success was as complete as if Boniface had actually been dragged before the king to stand trial. Two years after Boniface's death, a French archbishop was chosen pope; he never went to Rome but instead moved the papal headquarters to Avignon (AH-vin-yahn), a city on the southern border of France, on land technically owned by the papacy, but where the popes and the papal court remained under strong French influence from 1305 to 1377. During this Avignon papacy, also called the Babylonian Captivity of the church, papal prestige suffered enormously. Most Europeans believed that Rome was the only proper capital for the church. Moreover, the English, Germans, and Italians accused the popes and the cardinals, the majority of whom now were also French, of being instruments of the French king.

The Avignon papacy also gave credence to critics who attacked the fiscal and moral corruption of the church bureaucracy and the very obvious lack of spiritual dedication of the Avignon popes. Increasing their demands for income from England, Germany, and Italy and living in splendor in a newly built fortress-palace, the Avignon popes expanded the papal bureaucracy, added new church taxes, and collected the old taxes more efficiently. These actions provoked denunciation of the wealth of the church and a demand for its reform.

Wycliffe and Hus

With the abuses of the church at Avignon all too obvious, reformers began to call for not only an end to corruption, but change in church teaching and structure. In England, a professor of philosophy and theology at Oxford, John Wycliffe (WIK-lif; c. 1320–1384), attacked not only church abuses but also certain of the church's doctrines. He also worked for the English royal government of Richard II as a cleric attached to foreign missions and was employed to write pamphlets justifying the Crown's seizure of Church property.

Wycliffe was strongly influenced by the writings of St. Augustine and emphasized the primacy of the Bible in the life of a Christian. He believed that God directly touched each person and that the role of the popes was of minor importance. In fact, he asserted, the kings had a higher claim on their subjects' loyalty, and the monarchs themselves were accountable only to God, not the pope. Wycliffe believed that the church is the community of believers, and not the Catholic hierarchy. He even went so far as to question the validity of some of the sacraments. Toward the end of his life, the Roman Church launched a counterattack, and after his death he was declared a heretic. In 1428 his remains were taken from consecrated ground and burned, and his ashes were thrown into a river. In the church's eyes, this act condemned his soul to perpetual wandering and suffering and destroyed the possibility that Wycliffe's followers could preserve any parts of his body as relics. But the influence of his writings took root in England through a group he helped organize called the "poor priests," later known as the Lollards, who were likewise condemned and outlawed, but they continued an underground church that surfaced in the sixteenth century.

In Bohemia, where a strong reform movement linked with the resentment of the Czechs toward their German overlords was under way, Wycliffe's opinions were popularized by Czech students who had studied with him at Oxford. In particular, his beliefs influenced John Hus (c. 1369–1415), a teacher in Prague and later rector of the university there. Hus's attacks on the abuses of clerical power led him to conclude that the true church was composed of a universal priesthood of believers and that Christ alone was its head. In 1402, after becoming the dominant figure at his university, he started to give sermons in the Czech language that soon attracted congregations as large as 3000 people. He preached that the Bible is the only source of faith and that every person has the right to read it in his own language. Like Wycliffe, Hus preached against clerical abuses and the claim of the church to guarantee salvation. This message became more explosive because it was linked with his criticism of the excesses of the German-dominated church at a time of a growing Czech nationalist movement.

In his preaching he openly acknowledged his debt to Wycliffe and refused to join in condemning him in

1410. Hus was later excommunicated and called to account for himself at the Council of Constance in 1415. Even though he had been given the assurance of safe passage, he was seized and burned at the stake as a heretic, and his ashes were thrown into the Rhine. His death led to the Hussite wars (1419–1437), in which the Czechs withstood a series of crusades against them. They maintained their religious reforms until their defeat by the Habsburgs in the Thirty Years' War.

The Great Schism of the Roman Catholic Church

In response to pressure from churchmen, rulers, scholars, and commoners throughout Europe, the papacy returned to Rome in 1377, it seemed for a time that its credibility would be regained. However, the reverse proved true. In the papal election held the following year, the **College of Cardinals** elected an Italian pope. A few months later the French cardinals declared the election invalid and elected a French pope, who returned to Avignon. During the Great **Schism** (1378–1417), as the split of the church into two allegiances was called, there were two popes, each with his college of cardinals and capital city, each claiming complete authority, each sending out papal administrators and collecting taxes, and each excommunicating the other. The nations of Europe gave allegiance as their individual political interests influenced them.

The Great Schism continued after the original rival popes died, and each group elected a replacement. Doubt and confusion caused many Europeans to question the legitimacy and holiness of the church as an institution.

The Conciliar Movement

Positive action came in the form of the Conciliar Movement. In 1395 the professors at the University of Paris proposed that a general council, representing the entire church, should meet to heal the schism. A majority of the cardinals of both factions accepted this solution, and in 1409 they met at the Council of Pisa,

deposed both popes, and elected a new one. But neither of the two deposed popes would give up his office, and the papal throne now had three claimants.

The intolerable situation necessitated another church council. In 1414 the Holy Roman Emperor assembled at Constance the most impressive church gathering of the period. By deposing the various papal claimants and electing Martin V as pope in 1417, the Great Schism was ended and a single papacy was restored at Rome.

The Conciliar Movement represented a reforming and democratizing influence in the church. But the movement was not to endure, even though the Council of Constance had decreed that general councils were superior to popes and that they should meet at regular intervals in the future. Taking steps to preserve his authority, the pope announced that to appeal to a church council without having first obtained papal consent was heretical. Together with the inability of later councils to bring about much-needed reform and with lack of support for such councils by secular

---

College of Cardinals—Cardinals are the highest-ranking churchmen serving under the pope in the Catholic Church. Collectively, they constitute the Sacred College of Cardinals, and their duties include electing the pope, acting as his principal counselors, and aiding in governing the church.

Schism—Literally a split or division (from the Greek *schizein* = to split). The word is usually used in reference to the Great Schism (1378–1417), when there were two, and later three, rival popes, each with his own College of Cardinals.

Religious Reforms and Reactions

1415	John Hus, Bohemian reformer, burned at the stake
1437–1517	Cardinal Ximenes carried out reforms of Spanish Catholic Church
c. 1450	Revival of witchcraft mania in Europe
1452–1498	Savonarola attempted religious purification of Florence
1483–1546	Martin Luther
1484–1531	Ulrich Zwingli, leader of Swiss Reformation
1491–1556	Ignatius Loyola, founder of Society of Jesus (Jesuits)
1509–1564	John Calvin, leader of Reformation in Geneva
1515–1582	St. Teresa of Avila, founder of Carmelite religious order
1517	Luther issues Ninety-Five Theses
1521	Luther declared an outcast by the Imperial Diet at Worms
1534–1549	Pontificate of Paul III
1545–1563	Council of Trent
1561–1593	Religious wars in France

rulers, the restoration of a single head of the church enabled the popes to discredit the Conciliar Movement by 1450. Not until almost a century later, when the Council of Trent convened in 1545, did a great council meet to reform the church. But by that time the church had already irreparably lost many countries to Protestantism.

While the popes refused to call councils to effect reform, they failed to bring about reform themselves. The popes busied themselves not with internal problems but with Italian politics and patronage of the arts. The issues of church reform and revitalization were largely ignored.

Political Challenges

During the fifteenth century major issues of contention between Rome and the various leaders of Europe dealt with the control of taxes and fees, the courts, the law, and trade. The Catholic Church owned vast properties and collected fortunes in tithes, fees, and religious gifts, controlling, by some estimates, between a fifth and a fourth of Europe's wealth. Impoverished secular rulers looked enviously at the church's wealth. Because the Atlantic states of England, France and Spain were more unified, they were better able to deal with Rome than states of the fragmented Holy Roman Empire.

No longer able to prevail over secular rulers by its religious authority alone after 1300, the papacy fared badly in an era of power politics in foreign relations. Free Italian cities, such as Venice and Florence, had helped build a new balance-of-power diplomacy after the 1450s. But the French invasion at the end of the fifteenth century made the peninsula an arena for desperate struggle between the Habsburg and French Valois (Val-WAH) dynasties that would last until 1559. The Papal States became a political pawn. The papacy's weaknesses were exploited by the troops of Charles V when they sacked Rome in 1527.

Spiritual and Intellectual Developments

The Roman Catholic Church faced more than just social and political challenges by 1500. At the lowest level, popular religion remained based on illiterate believers who worshiped for the magical or practical earthly benefits of the sacraments and the cults of the saints. In their short and grim lives they were far from the political intrigue and sophisticated theological disputes that would trigger the Reformations and much closer to beliefs in the existence of witches, ghosts, phantom grunting swine, and demons who might lurk around the next corner. Arguments between Augustinian and Dominican monks meant little, and dedi-

cation to the opinions of the pope in faraway Rome was weak. Of much greater concern was how to avoid going to Hell, a possibility that was constantly in evidence during this time of fragile life and early death.

At the elite levels, during the fifteenth century, humanist reformers believed that abuses in the Catholic Church resulted largely from misinterpretation of Scripture by late medieval Scholastic philosophers and theologians (see p. 274). Northern humanists like Erasmus and Sir Thomas More ridiculed later Scholastics as pedantic (see p. 412).

Intellectual conflict was not new in Europe. But the means of communicating the nature and extent of the disagreements after the 1450s was new. The printing presses, after their European introduction in the 1350s, produced 6 million publications in more than 200 European towns by 1500. There were better-educated people with a thirst to read these books, which dealt largely with religious themes, and the result was the force of mobilized public opinion.

Some of these readers responded to critics, such as the Augustinian monks, who saw the Scholastics as presumptuous and worldly. Following the teachings of St. Augustine, they believed humans to be such depraved sinners that there could be saved not through "good works," as the Church taught, but only through personal repentance and faith in God's mercy. **Augustinians** accepted only Scripture as religious truth; they believed that faith was more important than the Scholastics' manipulated power of reason. And it was to the Augustinians that Martin Luther would turn to pursue his search for understanding.

LUTHER AND THE GERMAN REFORMATION

■ *Why did the most important fracture in Christendom occur in Germany?*

Martin Luther had no intention of striking the spark that launched more than a century of European conflict. Born in 1483, the son of an ambitious and tough Thuringian peasant turned miner and small businessman, he was raised by his parents under a contradictory regime of Christian love and the attendant harsh physical discipline that would affect his way of dealing with the world after 1521. Like many young boys of his time, he enjoyed the sometimes earthy and profane humor of his peasant society. Unlike many of his friends, he, as did St. Augustine 1200 years earlier, distrusted his own passionate

Martin Luther

Augustinians—Founded in 1256, a religious order dedicated to following of St. Augustine's life and teaching.

nature and became obsessed with fear of the devil and an eternity in hell. Until 1517 Luther's pursuit of his salvation was an intensely personal one, with little regard to the larger context of upheaval in which he lived.

The Search for Salvation

Martin Luther found great comfort in the teachings of the humanists and the Augustinians. After four years of studying the law, he disappointed his father by entering an Augustinian monastery at age 22, following what was to him a miraculous survival in a violent thunderstorm. As a monk, however, Luther was tormented by what he saw as his sinful nature and the fear of damnation. Then, in his mid-thirties, he read St. Paul's Epistle to the Romans and found freedom from despair in the notion of justification by faith: "Then I grasped that the justice of God is that righteousness by which through grace and sheer mercy God justifies us through faith. Thereupon, I felt myself to be reborn and to have gone through open doors into paradise."[1]

As an Augustinian, Luther entered into abstract religious debates that became more spirited because of the widespread problems of the church in central Europe. The buying and selling of church offices and charging fees to give comfort through a variety of theologically questionable ceremonies to superstitious parishioners disturbed him. But the practice that outraged Luther and brought him openly to oppose the Roman Catholic Church was the sale of indulgences. Theologically, these were shares of surplus grace, earned by Christ and the saints and available for papal dispensation to worthy souls after death. Originally, indulgences were not sold or described as tickets to heaven. By the sixteenth century, however, papal salesmen regularly peddled them as guarantees of early release from purgatory.

Luther's immediate adversary in 1517 was a **Dominican** monk named Johan Tetzel (TET-zel), commissioned by the Pope Leo X and Archbishop Albert of Mainz to sell indulgences. At the papal level, this was part of a large undertaking by which Pope Leo X hoped to finance completion of St. Peter's Basilica in Rome: The Archbishop of Mainz received 50 percent of the money for his own purposes. Tetzel used every appeal to crowds of the country people around Wittenberg (vit-en-BERG), begging them to aid their deceased loved ones and repeating the slogan "A penny in the box, a soul out of purgatory."[2] Luther and many other Germans detested Tetzel's methods and his Roman connections. He also rejected Tetzel's Dominican theology, which differed from Augustinian beliefs.

Lucas Cranach, Martin Luther and His Friends. *That Martin Luther (left) and other Protestant reformers did not suffer the same fate as John Hus a century earlier was largely due to the political support of rulers such as the Elector Frederick of Saxony (center).*

There are moments in history when the actions of a single person will link all of the prevailing and contrasting currents of an era into an explosive mixture. In Wittenberg on October 31, 1517, Martin Luther issued his Ninety-Five Theses, calling for public debate—mainly with the Dominicans—on issues involving indulgences and basic church doctrines.

Dominicans—St. Dominic established this religious order in 1215 to go out into the world to teach and preach the word of God.

This document was soon translated from Latin into German and published in all major German cities. The Theses denied the pope's power to give salvation and declared that indulgences were not necessary for a contrite and repentant Christian. Number 62, for example, stated that the "true treasure" of the Church was the "Holy Gospel of the Glory and Grace of God," and number 36 indicated that Christians truly desiring forgiveness could gain it without "letters of pardon." The resulting popular outcry forced Tetzel to leave Saxony, and Luther was almost immediately hailed as a prophet, directed by God to expose the pope and a grasping clergy.

His message was so well received because it satisfied those who wanted a return to simple faith; it also appealed to those, like the humanists, who fought church abuses and irrational authority. Luther's message provided an outlet for German resentment against Rome, and it gave encouragement to princes seeking political independence. The ensuing controversy, which soon raged far beyond Wittenberg, split all of western Christendom and focused and strengthened the social, economic, and political contradictions of the time.

Luther was soon in trouble. Although Rome was not immediately alarmed, the Dominicans levied charges of heresy against their Augustinian competitor. Having already begun his defense in a series of pamphlets, Luther continued in 1519 by debating the eminent theologian John Eck (1486–1543) at Leipzig (LEIP-zig). There Luther denied the **infallibility of the pope** and church councils, declared the Scriptures to be the sole legitimate doctrinal authority, and proclaimed that salvation could be gained only by faith. That same year a last effort at reconciliation failed completely, and in June 1520 Luther was excommunicated by the pope.

Charles V, only recently crowned emperor and aware of Luther's increased following among the princes, afforded the rebellious monk an audience before the **Imperial Diet** at Worms in 1521 to hear his defense of statements against church teachings and papal authority. If Luther recanted, he could perhaps escape his excommunication and execution. After much discussion, when the Orator of the Empire finally asked if he was prepared to recant, Luther responded:

Your Lordships demand a simple answer. Here it is, plain and unvarnished. Unless I am convicted of error by the testimony of Scripture or (since I put no trust in the unsupported authority of Pope or of councils, since it is plain that they have often erred and often contradicted themselves) by manifest reasoning I stand convicted by the Scriptures to which I have appealed, and my conscience is taken captive by God's word, I cannot and will not recant anything, for to act against our conscience is neither safe for us, nor open to us. On this I take my stand, I can do no other. God help me. Amen."[3]

The Diet finally declared him an outcast. Soon afterward, as he left Worms, Luther was secretly detained for his own protection in Wartburg (VART-burg) Castle by Elector Frederick of Saxony, his secular lord. He would not burn at the stake, as did John Hus, because he enjoyed substantial political and popular support. His message had been spread by the 300,000 copies of his 30 works printed between 1517 and 1520, and he was a German hero.

The Two Kingdoms: God and the State

At Wartburg Luther set his course for the rest of his life as he began organizing an evangelical church distinct from Rome. Although he denounced much of the structure, formality, and ritual of the Catholic Church, Luther spent much of his time after the Diet of Worms building a new church for his followers. It reflected his main theological differences with Rome but kept many traditional ideas and practices. The fundamental principle of the Lutheran creed was that salvation occurred through faith that Christ's sacrifice alone could wash away sin. This departed from the Catholic doctrine of salvation by faith and good works, which required conformance to prescribed dogma and participation in rituals. The Catholic Mass became the Lutheran Communion, involving all who attended services and requiring no priestly blessing to transform the bread and wine into Christ's body and blood, which in Lutheran theory automatically "coexisted" with the wafer and the wine. Other changes included church services in German instead of Latin, an emphasis on preaching, the abolition of monasteries, and the curtailment of formal ceremonies foreign to the personal experiences of ordinary people. The Lutheran Church claimed to be a "priesthood of all believers" in which each person could receive God directly or through the Scriptures. To that end, Luther translated the Bible from Latin into German and composed the sermons that would be repeated in hundreds of Lutheran pulpits all over Germany and Scandinavia.

He took off his clerical habit in 1523 and two years later married a former nun, Katherine von Bora, who bore him six children, raised his nieces and nephews, managed his household, secured his income, entertained his colleagues, and served as his supportive companion. Luther's ideas on marriage and Christian equality promised women new opportunities, which

---

infallibility of the pope—The belief that popes cannot be wrong in matters of faith and doctrine.

Imperial Diet—A meeting of the political and religious leaders of the various member states of the Holy Roman Empire.

were only partly realized. He stressed the importance of wives as marriage partners for both the clergy and the **laity.** Contrary to Catholic doctrine, he even condoned divorce in cases of adultery and desertion. During the 1520s, his views drew numerous women to Wittenberg, where they found refuge from monasteries or their Catholic husbands. Some Lutheran women became wandering preachers, but they evoked protests from male ministers and legal prohibitions from many German municipal councils, including those of Nuremberg and Augsburg. Although first teaching that women were equal to men in opportunities for salvation and in their family roles, in his later writings, Luther described them as subordinate to their husbands and not meant for the pulpit.

DOCUMENT

Sermon at the Castle Pleissenberg

Lutheranism recognized two main human spheres of human obligation: The first and highest was to God; the other involved a subordinate loyalty to earthly governments, which also existed in accordance with God's will. Luther's idea of "two kingdoms," one of God and one of the world, fit well with contemporary political conditions, winning him support from German and Scandinavian rulers while connecting his movement to dynastic nationalism. Luther's political orientation was clearly revealed in 1522 and 1523 during a rebellion of German knights. When Lutheran support was not forthcoming, the rebellion was quickly crushed. Luther took no part in the struggle but was embarrassed by opponents who claimed his religion threatened law and order.

Another example of Luther's political and social conservatism was provided by a general revolt of peasants and discontented townsmen in 1524 and 1525. Encouraged by Lutheran appeals for Christian freedom, the rebels drew up petitions asking for religious autonomy. At first Luther expressed sympathy for the requests, particularly for each congregation's right to select its own pastor. Then, as violence erupted throughout central Germany in April and May 1525, imperial and princely troops crushed the rebel armies, killing an estimated 90,000 insurgents. Luther had advised rebel leaders to obey the law as God's will; when they turned to war, he penned a virulent pamphlet, *Against the Thievish and Murderous . . . Peasants.* In it he called on the princes to "knock down, strangle, . . . stab, . . . and think nothing so venomous, pernicious, or Satanic as an insurgent."[4]

There was soon a struggle for religious control in Germany between the emperor and the Lutheran princes. When Catholics sought to impose conformity in Imperial Diets during the late 1520s, Lutheran leaders drew up a formal protest (hence the appellation *protestant*). After this Augsburg Confession (1530) was

rejected, the Lutheran princes organized for defense in the Schmalkaldic League. Because Charles V was preoccupied with the French and the Turks, open hostilities were minimized, but a sporadic civil war dragged on until after Luther's death in 1546. It ended with the Peace of Augsburg in 1555, when the imperial princes were permitted to choose between Lutheranism and Catholicism in their state churches, thus increasing their independence of the emperor. In addition, Catholic properties confiscated before 1552 were retained by Lutheran principalities, which provided a means for financing their policies. Although no concessions were made to other protestant groups, such as the Calvinists, this treaty shifted the European political balance against the Empire and the church.

Outside Germany, Lutheranism furnished a religious stimulus for developing national monarchies in Scandinavia. There, as in Germany, rulers welcomed not only Lutheran religious ideas but also the chance to acquire confiscated Catholic properties. They appreciated having ministers who preached obedience to constituted secular authority. In Sweden, Gustavus Vasa (goos-TA-vus VAH-sah; 1523–1560) used Lutheranism to lead a successful struggle for Swedish independence from Denmark. In turn, the Danish king, who also ruled Norway, issued an ordinance in 1537 establishing the national Lutheran Church, with its bishops as salaried officials of the state. Throughout Eastern Europe, wherever there was a German community, the Lutheran church spread—for a brief time even threatening the supremacy of the Catholic Church in Poland and Lithuania.

HENRY VIII AND THE ANGLICAN REFORMATION

■ *What were the political considerations impelling Henry VIII to create the Anglican Church?*

England was affected by the same economic and social crises and changes of the fourteenth and fifteenth centuries as the rest of Europe. But unlike central Europe, England was one of the new Atlantic states characterized by national monarchies, centralized authority, and greater independence from the papacy. The Tudor dynasty adapted itself to the new conditions after the Hundred Years' War with France and the devastating War of the Roses, which destroyed much of the traditional nobility.

Legitimate Heirs and the True Church

During this time of difficult transition, it was necessary that each monarch raise a strong and healthy heir

---

laity—The community of believers in the Christian Church, served by the clergy, the trained and specialized leaders of the community.

to ensure the continuity of the dynasty and the strength of England. Henry VIII (1509–1547) became the heir to the English throne when his older brother Arthur died in 1502. It had not been expected that he would be king, and his education ran to that of a true Renaissance man. He showed talent in music, literature, philosophy, jousting, hunting, and theology. Not only did he become the king of England on his father's death in 1509, but he also soon married the woman who had been his brother's wife, Catherine of Aragon (1485–1536), thus continuing the dynastic alliance with Spain. Catherine was a cultured, strong, respected woman and devoted wife: she successfully conducted a war against Scotland when Henry was campaigning in France.

Henry was a devout Roman Catholic, who gained the title "Defender of the Faith" from the pope for a pamphlet he wrote denouncing Luther and his theology. However, his immediate problem in the 1520s was the lack of a male heir. After 11 years of marriage, he had only a sickly daughter and an illegitimate son. His queen, after four earlier pregnancies, gave birth to a stillborn son in 1518, and by 1527, when she was 42, Henry had concluded that she would have no more children. His only hope for the future of his dynasty seemed to be a new marriage and a new queen. This, of course, would require an annulment of his marriage to Catherine. In 1527 he appealed to the pope, asking for the annulment.

Normally, the request would probably have been granted; the situation, however, was not normal. Because she had been the wife of Henry's brother, Catherine's marriage to Henry had necessitated a papal dispensation, based on her oath that the first marriage had never been consummated. Now Henry professed concern for his soul, tainted by "living in sin" with Catherine. He also claimed that he was being punished, citing a passage in the Book of Leviticus that predicted childlessness for the man who married his dead brother's wife. The pope was sympathetic and

Holbein's portrait of Henry VIII, painted in 1542, shows a man sure of himself in his royal setting. He had by this time broken with Rome, married six times in pursuit of a legitimate male heir, and turned England into a major naval power. What the portrait does not show is all of the suffering and discord he left in his wake.

certainly aware of an obligation to the king, who had strongly supported the church. However, granting the annulment would have been admission of papal error, perhaps even corruption, in issuing the earlier dispensation. Added to the Lutheran problem, this would have doubly damaged the papacy. A more immediate concern for Henry was Catherine's nephew. As the aunt of Charles V, whose armies occupied Rome in 1527, she was able to exert considerable pressure on the pope to refuse an **annulment.**

When the pope delayed a decision, Henry began to rally his support at home. During the three years after 1531, when Catherine saw him for the last time, Henry took control of affairs. Sequestering his daughter Mary (1516–1558) and his banished wife in separate castles, he forbade them from seeing each other. The king forced the clergy into proclaiming him head of a separate, English church "as far as the law of Christ allows," extracted from Parliament the authority to appoint bishops, and designated his willing tool Thomas Cranmer (1489–1556) as archbishop of Canterbury. In 1533 Cranmer pronounced Henry's marriage to Catherine invalid; at the same time, he legalized his union with Anne Boleyn (bo-LIN), a lady of the court who was carrying his unborn child, the future Elizabeth I. Henry even forced his daughter Mary to accept him as head of the church and to admit the illegality of her mother's marriage—by implication acknowledging her own illegitimacy. Parliament also ended all payment of revenues to Rome.

Now, having little other choice, the pope excommunicated Henry, making the breach official on both sides. On his side, Henry divided up the Church's properties—some 25 percent of the wealth of the realm—to distribute to the gentry to consolidate his domestic support. In 1539 Parliament completed its

---

annulment—A religious or political judgment that a marriage was/is not valid, and hence no longer existed/exists.

seizure of monastery lands and the wealth of pilgrimage sites such as Canterbury Cathedral. Meanwhile, Catholics such as the former chancellor and humanist Sir Thomas More (see p. 412), who refused to swear allegiance to the new order, were executed.

There had already been a strong underground resistance movement present in England even before Henry came to power. English theologians, beginning with John Wycliffe and his followers, played an active role in the intellectual and theological debates of the High Middle Age. During the fifteenth and first part of the sixteenth centuries there was an active underground church, the Lollards, in which lay people—especially women—played an important role. William Tyndale's (1494–1536) skillful translation of the New Testament, a work marked by Lutheran influences, served as the basis for the English Bible published in 1537, which made scripture available to all literate English-speaking people. This popular Protestantism was not at all close to the new Anglican Church, which brought about little change in doctrine or ritual. The Six Articles, Parliament's declaration of the new creed and ceremonies in 1539, reaffirmed most Catholic theology except papal supremacy.

Radical Protestants and Renewed Catholics

In his later years, after the decapitation of Anne Boleyn on charges of adultery in 1536 (the year that Catherine of Aragon also died), Henry grew increasingly suspicious of popular Protestantism, which was buttressed by reformist movements spreading into England and Scotland from the Continent. Further, he refused to legalize clerical marriage, which caused great hardships among many Anglican clergymen, including some bishops, and their wives and lashed out indiscriminately at those people such as the protestant Anne Ayscough who dared to question him.

In the decade after Henry's death in 1547, religious fanaticism brought social and political upheaval. For six years, during growing political corruption, extreme protestants ruled the country and dominated the frail young king, Edward VI (1547–1553), born of Henry's third wife Jane Seymour—who died in childbirth. His government was controlled by the Regency Council, dominated first by the duke of Somerset and then, after 1549, by his rival, the duke of Northumberland. The same mix of political opportunism and religious change continued as the council members enriched themselves and pursued their ambitions. At the same time, a radical form of Protestantism swept through many parishes. The government sought political support by courting the religious radicals: it repealed the Six Articles, permit-

ted priests to marry, replaced the Latin service with Cranmer's English version, and adopted the Forty-Two Articles, the expression of extreme Protestantism.

When Edward died in 1553, Mary Tudor came to the throne and tried to restore Catholicism through harsh persecutions, which earned her the name "Bloody Mary" from Protestant historians. The new queen possessed many of the same admirable qualities of her mother, Catherine of Aragon: dignity, intelligence, compassion, and a strong moral sense. Her religious obsession, however, eventually cost her the support of a substantial number of her subjects. Her hopeless love for her Catholic husband, Philip II of Spain—who married her in 1554—led to her being seen as a puppet of Spanish diplomacy. She restored the Catholic Church service, proclaimed papal authority in her realm, and forged an alliance with Spain. In putting down the protestants, she burned 300 of them at the stake—among whom were Cranmer, two other bishops, and 55 women. Mary died pitifully, rejected by her husband and people, but steadfast in her hope to save English Catholicism. Leaving no heir, she was compelled to name Elizabeth, her half-sister, as her successor.

PROTESTANTISM FROM SWITZERLAND TO HOLLAND: ZWINGLI AND CALVIN

■ *Why were the protestants in the Rhine Valley so much more radical in their approaches than Luther or the Anglicans?*

A very different variety of church reforms took place in Switzerland and France. The leaders of these reforms were conscious of the state but not dominated by it, as the Anglicans were. Like the Lutherans, they were also concerned for the salvation of their souls, but in a much more doctrinal and often vindictive way. Calvinism was the most popular and the most conservative of the reforms, but there were many others, including multiple forms of **Anabaptism**. These movements went farther than Lutheranism and Anglicanism in rejecting Catholic dogma and ritual. Generally, they were opposed to monarchy, but their position did not become very apparent until they were deeply involved in religious wars after 1560, when they often found themselves under attack by both the Catholics and the Lutherans.

Anabaptism—A Protestant faith that holds that baptism and church membership come only when one is an adult. Anabaptists also tend to believe in a strict separation of church and state.

Document   Anne Ayscough (Mrs. Thomas Kyme), English Protestant Martyr

Anne Ayscough, the daughter of Sir William Ayscough, received a good education and became remarkably independent at a time when the normal expectation was that a woman's role was to look after the house and be able to entertain guests. She read voraciously, especially Tyndale's version of the New Testament, and participated vigorously in the theological controversies of her time. She did not like the papacy, nor did she much like Henry's VIII's pet theologians and their version of English Catholicism—the Anglican Church. Duty to her family forced her to marry a Catholic husband, but soon he was not pleased when she set out to spread the Gospels by reading from the Bible to the peasants—a practice later forbidden by the law of 1543. For Anne the issues were quite clear: "[T]he papists were the agents of Antichrist and would always be opposed to the Saints of God. . . . " In standing upon her own righteousness and excluding from her heart all love of her enemies, Anne Ayscough was very much a child of her age. In 1545 she was called to London to face charges of heresy. She was then tortured—the only woman in English history put on the rack, tried, and found guilty for her refusal to believe that the wafer literally becomes the body of Christ in the communion, a process called transubstantiation.

On the eve of her execution, she wrote: "O friend most dearly beloved in God, I marvel not a little what should move you to judge in me so slender a faith as to fear death, which is the end of all misery. In the Lord I desire you not believe of me such weakness. For I doubt it not but God will perform his work in me, like as he hath begun. I understand the Council is not a little displeased, that it should be reported abroad that I was racked in the Tower. They say now that what they did there was but to frighten me; whereby I perceive they are ashamed of their uncomely doings and fear much lest the King's majesty should have information thereof. Wherefore they do not want any man to tell it abroad. Well, their cruelty God forgive them."

At the same time, she wrote Henry VIII: "I Anne Ayscough, of good memory, although God hath given me the bread of adversity and the water of trouble (yet not so much as my sins have deserved), desire this to be known unto your Grace. Forasmuch as I am by the law condemned for an evil-doer, here I take heaven and earth to record that I shall die in my innocence. And according to what I have said first and will say last, I utterly abhor and detest all heresies. And as concerning the Supper of the Lord, I believe so much as Christ hath said, therein, which he confirmed with his most blessed blood, I believe so much as he willed me to follow, and I believe so much as the Catholic church of him doth teach. For I will not forsake the commandment of his holy lips. . . ."

And as she was taken out to be executed, her final prayer was written down: "O Lord, I have more enemies now than there be hairs on my head. Yet, Lord, let them never overcome me with vain words, but fight thus, Lord, in my stead, for on thee cast I my care. With all the spite they can imagine they fall upon me, which am thy poor creature. Yet, sweet Lord, let me pay no heed to them which are against me, for in thee is my whole delight. And, Lord, I heartily desire of thee, that thou wilt of thy most merciful goodness forgive them that violence which they do and have done unto me. Open also thou their blind hearts, that they may hereafter do that thing in thy sight, which is only acceptable before thee, and to set forth thy verity aright, without all vain fantasy of sinful men. So be it, O Lord, so be it."

Anne Ayscough was burned at the stake with four companions on July 16 1546. Already viewed as a heroine by many in England, she became the best known English martyr.

Questions to Consider

1. What was there in Anne Ayscough's views that provoked such a harsh response from the leaders of the English Church, such as putting her on the rack?

2. Why were heretics burned at the stake and not, for example, hanged, or decapitated?

3. What qualities earn a person such as Anne Ayscough the accolade of being a "martyr?" What is a martyr? Whom would you consider to be martyrs during the twentieth century?

From Derek Wilson, *A Tudor Tapestry: Men, Women and Society in Reformation England* (London: Heinemann, 1972), pp. 164, 229–232.

Ulrich Zwingli

Popular Protestantism arose early in Switzerland, where many of the same difficult conditions found in the German states favored its growth. During the late medieval period, the country prospered in the growing trade between Italy and Northern Europe. Busy Swiss craftsmen and merchants in Zurich, Bern, Basel, and Geneva suffered under their Habsburg overlords and by papal policies, particularly the sale of indulgences. In 1499 the Confederation of Swiss Cantons won independence from the Holy Roman Empire and the Habsburgs. To many Swiss, this was also the first step in repudiating outside authority.

The Swiss Reformation began in Zurich, shortly after Luther published his Theses at Wittenberg. It was led by Ulrich Zwingli (OOL-rikh ZWING-lee; 1484–1531), a scholar, priest, and former military chaplain, who persuaded the city council to create a regime of clergymen and magistrates to supervise government, religion, and individual morality. Zwingli agreed with Luther in repudiating papal in favor of scriptural authority. He simplified services, preached justification by faith, attacked monasticism, and opposed clerical celibacy. More rational than Luther, he was also more interested in practical reforms, going beyond Luther in advocating additional grounds for divorce and in denying any mystical conveyance of grace by baptism or communion; both, to Zwingli, were only symbols. These differences proved irreconcilable when Luther and Zwingli met to consider merging their movements in 1529.

As Zwingli's influence spread rapidly among the northern cantons, religious controversy separated north from south, rural from urban, and feudal overlords—both lay and ecclesiastical—from towns within their dominions. When, in the 1520s, Geneva repudiated its ancient obligations and declared its independence from the local bishop and the count of Savoy, the city became a hotbed of Protestantism, with preachers streaming in from Zurich. Zwingli was killed in the religious war of 1531, after which it was decided in the Second Peace of Kappel that each Swiss canton could choose its own religion.

John Calvin

Hoping to ensure the dominance of Protestantism in Geneva after the religious wars, local reformers invited John Calvin (1509–1564) to Geneva. Calvin arrived from Basel in 1536. He was an uncompromising French reformer and a formidable foe of the ungodly, but a caring colleague and minister to humble believers. His preaching, based on his study of theology in Paris and law in Orleans, ultimately won enough followers to make his church the official religion. From Geneva, the faith spread to Scotland, Hungary, France, Italy, and other parts of Europe after the early 1540s.

In Basel he had published the first edition of his *Institutes of the Christian Religion* (1536), a theological work that transformed the general Lutheran doctrines into a rational legal system based around the concept of predestination. It also earned Calvin his invitation to Geneva. His original plan for a city government there called for domination by the clergy and banishment of all dissidents. This aroused a storm of opposition from Anabaptists—who believed in adult baptism and separation of church and state—and from the more worldly portion of the population, and Calvin was forced into exile. He moved on to Strasbourg where he associated with other reformers who helped him refine his ideas. Calvin's second regime at Geneva after 1541 involved a long struggle with the city council. His proposed ordinances for the Genevan Church gave the clergy full control over moral and religious behavior, but the council modified the docu-

Margaret of Navarre, a supporter of Protestantism, was the author of the Heptameron, *a collection of tales modeled on Boccacio's* Decameron.

ment, placing all appointments and enforcement of law under its jurisdiction.

Although recognizing the Bible as supreme law and the *Institutes* as a model for behavior, the Geneva city council did not always act on recommendations from the Consistory, Calvin's supreme church committee. For the next 14 years Calvin fought against public criticism and opposition in the council. He gradually increased his power, however, through support from the protestant refugees who poured into the city. His influence climaxed after a failed "revolt of the godless" in 1555. From that year until his death in 1564, he dominated the council, ruling Geneva with an iron hand, within the letter, but not the spirit, of the original ordinances.

Particularly in the later period, the Consistory apprehended violators of religious and moral law, sending its members into households to check every detail of private life. Offenders were reported to secular magistrates for punishment. Relatively light penalties were imposed for missing church, laughing during the service, wearing bright colors, dancing, playing cards, or swearing. Religious dissent, blasphemy, mild heresies, and adultery received heavier punishments, including banishment. Witchcraft and serious cases of heresy led to torture, and then execution—sometimes as many as a dozen or more a year. Michael Servetus (SEHR-vee-tus; 1511–1553), a Spanish theologian-philosopher and refugee from the Catholic Inquisition, was burned for heresy in Calvin's Geneva because he had denied the doctrine of the trinity.

Calvin accepted Luther's insistence on justification by faith; like Luther, he saw Christian life as a constant struggle against the devil, and he expected a coming divine retribution, an end-time, when God would redress the evils that were increasing on every side. Calvin also agreed with Luther in seeing God's power as a relief for human anxiety and a source of inner peace. Both reformers believed man to be totally depraved, but Calvin placed greater emphasis on this point, at the same time emphasizing God's immutable will and purpose. If Calvinism, to human minds, seemed contradictory in affirming man's sinful nature and his creation in God's image, this connection only proved that God's purposes were absolutely beyond human understanding. For depraved humans, God required faith and obedience, not understanding.

God's omnipotence was Calvin's cardinal principle. He saw all of nature as governed by a divinely ordained order, discernible to man but governed by laws that God could set aside in effecting miracles as he willed. Carried to its logical conclusion, such ideas produced Calvin's doctrine of predestination.

DOCUMENT

Calvin on
Predestination

By predestination we mean the eternal decree of God, by which he determined with himself whatever he wished to happen with regard to every man. All are not created on equal terms, but some are preordained to eternal life, others to eternal damnation; and, accordingly, as each has been created for one or other of these ends, we say that he has been predestined to life or to death. . . .[5]

In Calvin's grand scheme, as laid out precisely in the *Institutes,* his church served to aid the elect in honoring God. The human purpose was not to win salvation—for this had already been determined—but to honor God and prepare the elect for salvation. As communities of believers, congregations were committed to constant war against Satan. They also functioned to spread the Word (Scripture), educate youth, and alleviate suffering among the destitute.

Calvin was particularly ambivalent in his views on government. Ministers of the church were responsible for advising secular authorities on religious policies and resisting governments that violated God's laws. He believed that all rulers were responsible to God and subject to God's vengeance. But throughout the1540s, when he was hoping to gain the support of monarchs, he emphasized the Christian duty of obedience to secular authorities. Even then, however, he advised rulers to seek counsel from church leaders, and he ordered the faithful, among both the clergy and the laity, to disregard any government that denied them freedom in following Christ. Although willing to support any political system that furthered the true faith, Calvin always preferred representative government.

Another ambiguity in Calvin's social thought involved his attitude toward women. Unlike Catholic theologians, he did not cast women in an inferior light. In his mind, men and women were equally full of sin, but they were also equal in their chance for salvation. As he sought recruits, he stressed women's right to read the Bible and participate in church services. At the same time he saw women as naturally subordinate to their husbands in practical affairs, including the conduct of church business.

Before the Peace of Augsburg, Calvinism was strongest in France, the reformer's own homeland, where the believers were known as *Huguenots.* Calvinism made gains elsewhere but did not win political power. In Italy, the duchess of Ferrara installed the Calvinist church service in her private chapel and protected Calvinist refugees. Strasbourg in the 1530s was a free center for protestant reformers such as Matthew Zell and his wife Katherine, who befriended many Calvinist preachers, including Martin Bucer (BOOT-sur), a missionary to England during the reign of Edward VI. In the same period, John Knox spread the Calvinist message in Scotland.

More extreme than Calvinism were many divergent protestant splinter groups, each pursuing its own "inner lights." Some saw visions of the world's end, some advocated a Christian community of shared wealth, some opposed social distinctions and economic inequalities, some—these Anabaptists—repudiated infant baptism as a violation of Christian responsibility, and some denied the need for any clergy. Most of the sects emphasized biblical literalism and direct, emotional communion between the individual and God. The majority of them were indifferent or antagonistic to secular government, many favored pacifism and substitution of the church for the state.

Women were prominent among the sects, although they were usually outnumbered by men. These women were known for their biblical knowledge, faith, courage, and independence. They helped found religious communities, wrote hymns and religious tracts, debated theology, and publicly challenged the authorities. Some preached and delivered prophecies, although such activities were suppressed by male ministers by the end of the century. More women than men endured torture and suffered martyrdom. Their leadership opportunities and relative freedoms in marriage, compared to women of other religions, were bought at the high price of hardship and danger.

Persecution of the sects arose largely because of their radical ideas. But Catholics and other protestants who opposed them usually cited two revolutionary actions. The first came when some radical preachers took part in the German peasants' revolt of the 1520s and shared in the savage punishments that followed. The second came in 1534 when a Catholic army besieged Münster (MIUN-ster).

Thousands of recently arrived Anabaptist extremists had seized control and expelled dissenters from this German city near the southern Netherlands. Following their radical theology, the "regime of saints" took private property, allowed polygamy, and planned to convert the world. John of Leyden (LI-den), a former Dutch tailor who claimed divine authority, headed a terrorist regime during the final weeks before the city fell. Those who survived the fall of the city suffered horrible tortures and then execution.

Among the most damaging charges against the Münster rebels were their alleged sexual excesses and the dominant role played by women in this immorality. Such charges were mostly distortions. The initiation of **polygamy,** justified by references

---

polygamy—A type of marriage in which a husband has more than one wife.

to the Old Testament, was a response to problems arising from a shortage of men, hundreds of whom had fled the city. Many other men were killed or injured in the fighting. Thus, the city leaders required women to marry so that they could be protected and controlled by husbands. Most Anabaptist women accepted the requirement as a religious duty. Although some paraded through the streets, shouting religious slogans, the majority prepared meals, did manual labor on the defenses, fought beside their men, and died in the fighting or at the stake. Most of the original, Catholic, Münster women, however, fiercely resisted forced marriage, choosing instead jail or execution.

Like Calvin later in Geneva, the Anabaptist regime of John of Leyden closely monitored and controlled private life and public behavior. Their theocratic state found its laws in Scripture. In looking at the laws of the city, capital punishment was applied in the following cases:

> *Whoever curses God and his holy Name or his Word shall be killed (Lev. 24).*
> *No one shall curse governmental authority (Ex. 22, Deut. 17), on pain of death.*
> *Both parties who commit adultery shall die (Ex. 20, Lev. 20, Matt. 5).*
> *. . . Whoever disobeys these commandments and does not truly repent, shall be rooted out of the people of God, with ban and sword, through the divinely ordained governmental authority.*[6]

For more than a century, memories of Münster plagued the protestant sects in general. Although most did not go to the extremes of "the saints," they were almost immediately driven underground throughout Europe, and their persecution continued long after they had abandoned violence. In time, they dispersed over the Continent and to North America as Mennonites, Quakers, and Baptists, to name only a few denominations. Given their suffering and oppression, voices of the radicals were among the first raised for religious liberty. Their negative experience with governments made them even more suspicious of authority than the Calvinists were. In both the Netherlands and England, they participated in political revolutions and helped frame the earliest demands for constitutional government, representative institutions, and civil liberties.

With the exception of Henry VIII's political reformation, the reformers, going back to Wycliffe and Hus and moving on through Luther and Calvin and the Anabaptists, did not believe that they were creating something new. Instead, they were trying to reclaim the purity of the early church.

REFORM IN THE CATHOLIC CHURCH

■ *How successful was the Catholic Church in dealing with the problems that faced it?*

The era of the Protestant Reformation was also a time of rejuvenation for the Roman Catholic Church. This revival was largely caused by the same conditions that had sparked Protestantism. Throughout the fifteenth century, many sincere and devout Catholics had recognized a need for reform, and they had begun responding to the abuses in their church long before Luther acted at Wittenberg. Almost every variety of reform opinion developed within the Catholic Church. Erasmus, More, and other Christian humanists provided precedents for Luther, but none followed him out of the Catholic Church. In a category of his own was Savonarola (sa-vo-na-RO-la; 1452–1498), a Dominican friar, puritan, and mystic who ruled Florence during the last four years before his death. This "Catholic Calvin" consistently railed against the worldly living and sinful luxuries he found: His criticisms of the pope and the clergy were

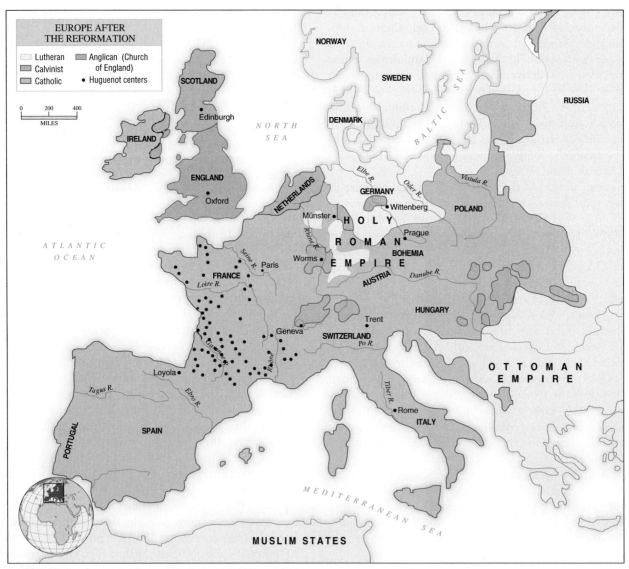

This map illustrates the geographical patterns of the Protestant Reformation. Lutheranism spread through German-speaking areas along the Baltic Sea but rarely crossed the Rhine River. The spread of Calvinism defies linguistic explanation.

much more severe than Luther's. At the other extreme of the Church was Cardinal Ximenes (1437–1517) in Spain, who carried out his own Reformation by disciplining the clergy, compiling the Complutensian Bible—eliminating many of the errors made by medieval copyists and instilling a new spirit of dedication into the monastic orders.

After the protestant revolt began, the primary Catholic reformer was Alessandro Farnese (far-NAY-se), Pope Paul III (1534–1549). Coming into office at a time when the church appeared ready to collapse, Paul struggled to overcome the troubled legacy of his Renaissance predecessors and restore integrity to the papacy. Realizing that issues raised by the protestants would have to be resolved and problems within the church corrected, he attacked the indifference, corruption, and vested interests of the clerical organization. In pursuing these reforms he appointed a commission, which reported the need for correcting such abuses as the worldliness of bishops, the traffic in benefices (church appointments with guaranteed incomes), and the transgressions of some cardinals. Their recommendations led Paul to call a church council, an idea that he continued to press against stubborn opposition for more than ten years.

When Paul died in 1549, he had already set the Roman Church on a new path, although his proposed church council, the Council of Trent, had only begun its deliberations. Perhaps his greatest contribution was his appointment of worthy members to the College of Cardinals, filling that body with eminent scholars and devout stewards of the church. As a result of his labors, the cardinals elected a succession of later popes who were prepared, intellectually and spiritually, to continue the process of regeneration.

The spirit of reform was reflected in a number of new Catholic clerical orders that sprang up in the early sixteenth century. Some of these worked with the poor, ministered to the sick, and taught. Among the better known were the Carmelites founded by St. Teresa of Avila (1515–1582) whose determination and selfless devotion became legendary. She inspired mystical faith and reforming zeal in written works such as *Interior Castle* and *The Ladder of Perfection*.

DOCUMENT

Rules for Thinking with the Church

The most significant of the new orders was the Society of Jesus, whose members are known as Jesuits. Organized along military lines, with their founder, the Spaniard Ignatius Loyola (1491–1556) as general and the pope as commander in chief, the Jesuits were an army of soldiers, sworn to follow orders and defend the faith. As preachers, teachers, confessors,

IMAGE

Ignatius of Loyola

organizers, diplomats, and spies, they took the field everywhere, founding schools and colleges, serving as missionaries on every continent, and working their way into government wherever possible. Their efforts were probably most responsible for the decided check that Protestantism received after the 1560s, as they zealously defended Catholicism in France, pushed the protestants out of Poland, and reclaimed southern Germany. Jesuit missions also helped Spain and Portugal develop their global empires.

Pope Paul's reform initiatives were given form by the great multinational church council, the first since 1415, which met in three sessions between 1545 and 1563 in the northern Italian city of Trent. Devoting much attention to the external struggle against Protestantism, the council also sought to eliminate internal abuses by ordering changes in church discipline and administration. It strictly forbade absenteeism, false indulgences, selling church offices, and secular pursuits by the clergy. Bishops were ordered to supervise their clergies—priests as well as monks and nuns—and to fill church positions with competent people. The Council of Trent also provided that more seminaries be established for educating priests while instructing the clergy to set examples and preach frequently to their flocks.

Rejecting all compromise, the Council of Trent retained the basic tenets of Catholic doctrine, including the necessity of good works as well as faith for salvation, the authority of church law and traditions, the sanctity of all seven sacraments, the use of only Latin in the Mass, and the spiritual value of indulgences, pilgrimages, veneration of saints, and the cult of the Virgin. The council also strengthened the power of the papacy. It defeated all attempts to place supreme church authority in any general council. When the final session voted that none of its decrees were valid without papal approval, the church became more than ever an absolute monarchy.

The full significance of Trent became evident after the 1560s when the Catholic reaction to Protestantism acquired a new vigor and militancy. Having steeled itself from within, the church and its shock troops, the Jesuits, went to war against protestants and other heretics. The new crusade was both open and secret. In Spain, Italy, and the Netherlands, the Inquisition more than ever before became the dreaded scourge of protestants and other heretics. Jesuit universities, armed with the Index of Forbidden Works, trained scholars and missionaries who would serve as priests and organizers in protestant countries such as England. Many died as martyrs, condemned by protestant tribunals, while others suffered similar fates meted out by pagans whom they sought to convert in America and Asia. But

The devotional works and personal example of St. Teresa of Avila, mystic and visionary, inspired the rebirth of Spanish Catholicism. In 1970 she was proclaimed a doctor of the church, the first woman to be so honored. The sculpture here, The Ecstasy of St. Teresa *(1645–1652), is by the Italian baroque artist Giovanni Bernini.*

Protestantism made no more significant gains in Catholic lands after Trent. Indeed, after Trent, the Catholic Church became a global church.

CONCLUSION

In could be argued that Europe's Golden Age of the Renaissance was no more than a recapitulation of that which had gone before. By resurrecting the gifts of the Greeks and Romans and learning from the sci-ence and history of the Arabs, the elites who partici-pated in the movement were, in fact, reactionaries. But in looking back, they invented new and demand-ing methods of research, and the most important legacy they revived was the old Greek message that "Man Can Know." This individual liberation could be seen immediately in the artistic and architectural works as well as in the writings of Lorenzo da Valla and Machiavelli. The new humanism was not neces-sarily intellectually superior to the best of the scholas-tic thinking. However, it allowed new questions to be posed in critical ways.

Christianity had always been a religion in ferment, and the authorities in Rome and Constantinople after the Seventh Ecumenical Council had sought to stamp out those who were not in accord with orthodoxy. Luther, in many ways, echoed the thoughts of John Wycliffe and John Hus. He succeeded where they failed because of the more favorable political context he found himself in.

In many ways, the Protestant Reformation and Catholic Counter-Reformation helped create the modern world. By breaking the religious monopoly of European Catholicism, Lutheranism and Anglicanism assisted the growth of northern European national monarchies. Later, the Puritan values and "work ethic" of Calvinism helped justify the profit-seeking activities of the middle classes. Even the Catholic Church itself was transformed by the various protestant challenges. After the Council of Trent, the Catholic Counter-Reformation checked the spread of Protestantism, and the Roman Church emerged strengthened to protect and advance itself. Because the Reformation and Counter-Reformation occurred at the same time of the development of the state system (see Chapter 16), faith came to play an integral, and often dangerous, role in politics until 1648.

Because these momentous changes coincided with the beginnings of the European explorations around the world (see Chapter 15), and the construction of Portuguese, Dutch, Spanish, French, and English empires, protestant and Catholic missionaries were able to spread their messages around the globe. Political and economic imperialism were accompanied by a religious imperialism. The Christians had no doubt they were saving the heathen from hell, but this well-intentioned zealousness had mixed, and sometimes destructive, results to the peoples of Asia, Africa, and the Americas touched by European expansion.

Suggestions for Web Browsing

You can obtain more information about topics included in this chapter at the websites listed below. See also the companion website that accompanies this text, **http://www.ablongman.com/ brummett**, which contains an online study guide and additional resources.

Italian Renaissance Art Project
http://www.italian-art.org

One of the very best and most comprehensive sites for reproductions of the major paintings, works of sculpture, and architecture from the Renaissance. An amazing resource of the study of Renaissance art.

Web Museum, Paris: Italian Renaissance (1420–1600)
http://www.ibiblio.org/wm/paint/tl/it-ren/

A useful site for anyone interested in the art of the Italian Renaissance, especially the work of Leonardo da Vinci, Raphael, and Michelangelo.

Florence in the Renaissance
http://www.mega.it/eng/egui/epo/secrepu.htm

A history of the Florentine Republic, with details about the city's influence on Renaissance culture.

Sistine Chapel
http://www.christusrex.org/www1/sistine/0-Tour.html

Photo collection depicting all facets of the Sistine Chapel, including images of Michelangelo's ceiling.

Michelangelo
http://www.michelangelo.com/buonarroti.html

Featuring the works of the artist beautifully illustrated and annotated. An outstanding site.

The Louvre
http://www.paris.org/Musees/Louvre

Website for one of the world's greatest museums offers many paths to some of the most beautiful Renaissance art in existence.

Medieval and Renaissance Women's History
http://womenshistory.about.com/od/medieval/

Site serves as a directory for a wide variety of discussions and references about Renaissance women painters, writers, and women of social standing.

Creative Impulse: Renaissance
http://history.evansville.net/renaissa.html

The University of Evansville's outstanding series of sites on Western civilization includes this compendium of art, history, and descriptions of daily life and culture. Includes one of the very best compilations of other sites dealing with the Renaissance.

Medieval and Renaissance Fact and Fiction
http://www.angelfire.com/mi/spanogle/medieval.html

A useful guide to Web resources for students interested in the history, culture, and literature of the Renaissance.

Northern Renaissance ArtWeb
http://www.msu.edu/~cloudsar/nrweb.htm

A collection of links for exploring the artists and literature of the Northern Renaissance.

Internet Medieval History Sourcebook: Protestant and Catholic Reformations
http://www.fordham.edu/halsall/sbook1y.html

Extensive online source for links about the Protestant and Catholic Reformations, including primary documents by or about precursors and papal critics, Luther, and Calvin and details about the Reformations themselves.

Martin Luther
http://www.wittenberg.de/e/seiten/personen/luther.html

This brief biography of Martin Luther includes links to his Ninety-Five Theses and images of related historical sites.

Tudor England
http://englishhistory.net/tudor.html/

Site detailing life in Tudor England includes biographies, maps, important dates, architecture, and music, including sound files.

Lady Jane Grey
http://www.ladyjanegrey.org/

A biography of the woman who would be queen of England for nine days, and a general history of the time.

Literature and Film

One of the best novels dealing with the Renaissance is Irving Stone, *The Agony and the Ecstasy: A Biographical Novel of Michelangelo* (New American Library, 1996). An outstanding account of the past and present of Florence is given by Mary McCarthy in *The Stones of Florence* (Harvest Books, 2002). There are also many excellent videos available on the art and architecture of the Renaissance. Some of the more notable are *The Art of the Western World: Early and High Renaissance: Realms of Light* (Kultur Video, 1994); *Leonardo Da Vinci: Renaissance Man to the World* (Madacy Entertainment, 1997); *The Art of Renaissance Science: Galileo and Perspective,* by Joseph W. Dauben for Science Television (1991); and *Florence: Cradle of the Renaissance* (Museum City Video, 1992).

The politics of the time provide a rich resource for novels. The activities of this time attracted the best attentions of Alexandre Dumas. Writing about events in France, he published *The Two Dianas,* (dealing with the time of Francis I), *The Page of the Duke of Savoy* (touching the time of the Emperor Charles V), *Ascanio* (France in the middle of the century), and *Marguerite de Valois* (touching the civil wars)—and this is only an incomplete list. Mark Twain wrote about the time of Edward VI in *The Prince and the Pauper.* More recently, Robin Maxwell sheds some light on the reign of Henry VIII in *The Secret Diary of Anne Boleyn: A Novel* (Scribner, 1998).

Filmmakers have been equally attracted to the period, especially the English scene. *A Man for All Seasons* (Columbia/Tristar, 1966), directed by Fred Zinnemann, is a fine telling of the story of Sir Thomas More. Queen Elizabeth has been the subject of films throughout the twentieth century, including *Elizabeth* (Umvd, 1998), directed by Shekhar Kapur, and indirectly in Academy Award winner *Shakespeare in Love* (Miramax, 1998), directed by John Madden. A film dealing with the period after Henry VIII is *Lady Jane* (Paramount, 1985), directed by Trevor Nunn. The 1933 film, *The Private Life of Henry VIII* (AAE Films), directed by Alexander Korda, is worth seeing. From the continent, *The Return of Martin Guerre* (Fox Lorber, 1982), directed by Daniel Vigne, does justice to Natalie Zemon Davis's fine monograph. The film of the life of *Martin Luther* (VCI Home Video, 1953) is a revealing look at the reformer.

Suggestions for Reading

Johnathan Zophy, *A Short History of Renaissance and Reformation Europe,* 2nd ed. (Prentice Hall, 1998) and John Hale, *The Civilization of Europe in the Renaissance* (Scribner, 1994) are both excellent introductions to the period. Jacob Burckhardt, *The Civilization of the Renaissance in Italy,* 2 Vols. (Torchbooks, 1958), first published in 1860, inaugurated the view that the Italian Renaissance of the fourteenth and fifteenth centuries was a momentous turning point in the history of Western civilization. The editors of this edition maintain that Burckhardt's major interpretations remain valid. Donald R. Kelley, *Renaissance Humanism* (Twayne, 1991), and Brian P. Copenhaver, *Renaissance Philosophy* (Oxford University Press, 1992) are excellent surveys. Katharina M. Wilson, ed., *Women Writers of the Renaissance and Reformation* (University of Georgia Press, 1987), is an excellent study of a neglected subject. John White, *Art and Architecture in Italy, 1250–1400,* 3rd ed. (Yale University Press, 1993) is an excellent overview. See also Charles Seymour Jr., *Sculpture in Italy, 1400–1500* (Yale University Press, 1994). Ross King, *Brunelleschi's Dome* (Walker, 2000), is an excellent account of the construction of the famous Florentine's work. Also, Silvio Bedini, *The Pope's Elephant* (Penguin, 2000), is a delightful account of Pope Leo X and his court.

A fascinating study of the attitudes of the Christian laity during the Reformation period can be found in Keith Thomas, *Religion and the Decline of Magic: Studies in Popular Beliefs in Sixteenth and Seventeenth Century England* (Oxford University Press, 1997). A useful context to the religious upheavals of the time is given by John Bossy, *Christianity in the West, 1400–1700* (Oxford University Press, 1985). On the impact of John Hus, see Thomas A. Fudge, *The Magnificent Ride: The First Reformation in Hussite Bohemia* (Ashgate Publishing, 1998). The general background of the Reformation is covered well in Steven E. Ozment, *Protestants: The Birth of a Revolution* (Doubleday, 1992). Brad S. Gregory, *Salvation at Stake: Christian Martyrdom in Early Modern Europe* (Harvard University Press, 2000), is a distinguished work of scholarship that takes the martyrs of the time at their word. Richard Marius, *Martin Luther: The Christian Between God and Death* (Belknap Press of Harvard University Press, 1999), is a superb new study of Luther to 1526. The context for the English Reformation is provided by Richard H. Britnell in *The Closing of the Middle Ages: England, 1471–1529* (Blackwell, 1997). Ulrich Gabler gives a thorough background of Ulrich Zwingli's place in history in his *Huldrych Zwingli: His Life and Work* (Clark, 1995).

William J. Bouwsma, *John Calvin* (Oxford University Press, 1988), is a scholarly portrayal of Calvin's human side, emphasizing his inner conflict against the humanistic trend of his time. On the "left wing" of Protestantism, Anthony Arthur's *The Tailor-King: The Rise and Fall of the Anabaptist Kingdom of Münster* (St. Martin's Press, 1999) is a first-rate history of the radical Reformation city-state in northern Germany. John C.

Olin places the Catholic response in perspective in *The Catholic Reformation: From Savonarola to Ignatius Loyola* (Fordham University Press, 1993). R. Po-chia Hsia, *The World of Catholic Renewal 1540–1770* (Cambridge University Press, 1998), is an innovative study of the history of the Catholic Church from the run up to the Council of Trent to the suppression of the Jesuits.

Chapter 14: European Cultural and Religious Transformations

CHECKING YOUR READING STRATEGIES

DISCUSSION AND CRITICAL THINKING QUESTIONS

1. **Preview the chapter** as you have been instructed. *Without reading the chapter itself*, write an outline of the chapter. Leave room to fill in the details later. Use your typographical cues to help you. What is different about this outline as compared to, for example, the biology or the psychology chapter's outline? Why do you think that is?

2. **Preview the chapter again**, this time focusing on all the graphic illustrations. Read all the captions and information in tables; look carefully at all photographs and drawings. Next, let your eyes scan over the columns of text. See if you can find where in the paragraphs the illustrated material is explained. What cues are given in the text to tie the illustrations to the words?

3. *Circle the best answer for each of the following questions.*

    1. According to the outline listed at the beginning of the chapter, this chapter will cover how many points?
       a. Three   c. Eight
       b. Five   d. Nine

    2. What is the *overall purpose* of the chapter's introduction?
       a. To set up the overall focus for the chapter
       b. To explain European expansion
       c. To explain European religions
       d. To demonstrate European supremacy through the Church

    3. How many types of graphic illustrations are used in this chapter? Look through the entire chapter. Select all that apply.
       a. Photographs   f. Works of art
       b. Charts   g. Diagrams
       c. Graphs   h. Tables
       d. Shaded boxes (of formulas,   i. Time lines
          theories, articles, etc.)   j. Margin notes
       e. Maps

    4. What typographical cues are used in the chapter to highlight important information for you? Select all that apply.
       a. Boldface print   g. Italicized print
       b. Font size   h. Font style
       c. Bulleted lists   i. Underlining
       d. Color of print   j. Boxes
       e. Arrows to show direction/order k. Shading
       f. Symbols (light bulb, question mark, star, etc.)

4. **Preview** the "Conclusion." It is as close to a summary as you will get with this chapter. This is essentially a summation of the key points the authors feel you should draw from the chapter.

How easily can you find the information in the chapter to tie the concepts back to the text? Go back and look for them. Make a checkmark in the margin so you will remember this is a key point when you read the chapter. Is this as easy to do as in the texts with a summary? Or is it more challenging? Why?

5. Now **go back to the first page of the chapter and read the chapter**. Move through the chapter section by section. Read first, then decide what information is important for you to know and what is explanatory to illustrate the point. Next, return to the outline you drafted for question 1. Fill in the outline with the information you have determined to be important for you to re- member. Consider your method as well. **How** did you determine which information was im- portant enough to record?

6. Did you **answer the "Questions to Consider"** at the end of the boxed articles? If not, go back and do them. These are the only review questions in the text. It would be a good idea to have these answers in your notes. Why do you think these questions are included in the text? Of what benefit are they to you and your understanding of the chapter?

7. There are three of the **boxed articles** in this chapter. Why do you think the authors have in- cluded them? How do they help you learn the material in the chapter?

8. Finally, **after reading the chapter**, thoroughly review your notes. Since this chapter does not include a summary, list of key terms, review questions, etc., it will be up to you to create your own study guide. In addition, this chapter uses only headings and subheadings, so you will have to do more work to fill out your outline as well. Therefore, consider how you determine which information is important enough to record. It would also be helpful to make a time line in your notes, compiling all the time lines in the chapter. You may also want to make notes on the map in the chapter, compiling visual and verbal information into one graphic.

GROUP PROJECTS

1. Compare your outline with that of your classmates. Are they all the same? If not, how do they differ? Why? Next, compare how well you and your classmates did with pulling the informa- tion out of the chapter. Do some of you have more detailed outlines than others? Why do you think that may be?

2. Within your group, discuss the benefits of previewing the illustrations in the text before reading, as opposed to waiting to explore them as they come up in the reading.

3. As a group, consider what the authors do to make this chapter interesting and appealing to you. Consider both the visual components and the information itself. How do page layout and writing style make assigned reading more enjoyable?

4. Discuss with your group which sections you found interesting and why.

5. Discuss with your group how helpful the chapter's information is for you to understand how religion has evolved into what it is today. Have the authors left out any factors you would like to have had covered? What additional issues do you think should have been included?

6. As a group, consider the boxed articles supplied in the text. Why are they included? How do they aid your understanding of the material?

Literature

from

Sisko: American 24-Karat Gold: 24 Classic American Short Stories

Second Edition

Non-fiction

Salvation

LANGSTON HUGHES

Langston Hughes was born in Joplin, Missouri in 1902. After his parents' separation, he spent his early childhood with his grandmother in Lawrence, Kansas. His grandmother gave him a positive outlook on his African American heritage and on life through her stories filled with characters who triumphed over life's problems with zeal and determination. At twelve, he moved back with his mother and lived in Lincoln, Illinois. Later, he served as a crewman on freighters and traveled to Africa, Holland, and Paris. He returned to Washington, D. C. and then moved to New York City. Sharing the same patron with Zora Neale Hurston, he attended Columbia University and eventually became a central figure in the Harlem Renaissance. He died in 1967.

Hughes enjoyed a fruitful writing career. His writings reflect the rhythms of Harlem and the positive attitudes of his grandmother. His poems and short stories are available in many collections.

Illustration by John Seymour

I was saved from sin when I was going on thirteen. But not really saved. It happened like this. There was a big revival at my Auntie Reed's church. Every night for weeks there had been much preaching, singing, praying, and shouting, some very hardened sinners had been brought to Christ, and the membership of the church had grown by leaps and bounds. Then just before the revival ended, they held a special meeting for children, "to bring the young lambs to the fold." My aunt spoke of it for days ahead. That night I was escorted to the front row and placed on the mourners' bench with all the other young sinners, who had not yet been brought to Jesus.

2   My aunt told me that when you were saved you saw a light, and something happened to you inside! And Jesus came into your life! And God was with you from then on! She said you could see and hear and feel Jesus in your soul. I believed her. I had heard a great many old people say the same thing and it seemed to me they ought to know. So I sat there calmly in the hot, crowded church, waiting for Jesus to come to me.

3   The preacher preached a wonderful rhythmical sermon, all moans and shouts and lonely cries and dire pictures of hell, and then he sang a song about the ninety and nine safe in the fold, but one little lamb was left out in the cold. Then he said: "Won't you come? Won't you come to Jesus? Young lambs, won't you come?" And he held out his arms to all us young sinners there on the mourners' bench. And the little girls cried. And some of them jumped up and went to Jesus right away. But most of us just sat there.

4   A great many old people came and knelt around us and prayed, old women with jet-black faces and braided hair, old men with work-gnarled hands. And the church sang a song about the lower lights are burning, some poor sinners to be saved. And the whole building rocked with prayer and song.

5   Still I kept waiting to *see* Jesus.

6   Finally all the young people had gone to the altar and were saved, but one boy and me. He was a rounder's son named Westley. Westley and I were surrounded by sisters and deacons praying. It was very hot in the church, and getting late now. Finally Westley said to me in a whisper: "God damn! I'm tired o' sitting here. Let's get up and be saved." So he got up and was saved.

7   Then I was left all alone on the mourners' bench. My aunt came and knelt at my knees and cried, while prayers and songs swirled all around me in the little church. The whole congregation prayed for me alone, in a mighty wail of moans and voices. And I kept waiting serenely for Jesus, waiting, waiting—but he didn't come. I wanted to see him, but nothing happened to me. Nothing! I wanted something to happen to me, but nothing happened.

8   I heard the songs and the minister saying: "Why don't you come? My dear child, why don't you come to Jesus? Jesus is waiting for you. He wants you. Why don't you come? Sister Reed, what is this child's name?"

9   "Langston," my aunt sobbed.

10   "Langston, why don't you come? Why don't you come and be saved? Oh, Lamb of God! Why don't you come?"

11   Now it was really getting late. I began to be ashamed of myself, holding everything up so long. I began to wonder what God thought about Westley, who certainly hadn't seen Jesus either, but who was now sitting proudly on the platform, swinging his knickerbockered legs and grinning down at me, surrounded by deacons and old women on their knees praying. God had not struck Westley dead for taking his name in vain or for lying in the temple. So I decided that maybe to save further trouble, I'd better lie, too, and say that Jesus had come, and get up and be saved.

12   So I got up.

13   Suddenly the whole room broke into a sea of shouting, as they saw me rise. Waves of rejoicing swept the place. Women leaped in the air. My aunt threw her arms around me. The minister took me by the hand and led me to the platform.

14   When things quieted down, in a hushed silence, punctuated by a few ecstatic "Amens," all the new young lambs were blessed in the name of God. Then joyous singing filled the room.

15   That night, for the last time in my life but one—for I was a big boy twelve years old—I cried. I cried, in bed alone, and couldn't stop. I buried my head under the quilts, but my aunt heard me. She woke up and told my uncle I was crying because the Holy Ghost had come into my life, and because I had seen Jesus. But I was really crying because I couldn't bear to tell her that I had lied, that I had deceived everybody in church, that I hadn't seen Jesus, and that now I didn't believe there was a Jesus any more, since he didn't come to help me.

Follow-up Questions

10 Short Questions

Select the best answer for each.

_____ 1. The narrator and the author
are probably
a. different people.
b. relatives.
c. the same person.

_____ 2. This occasion is probably
a. a religious ceremony.
b. a school graduation.
c. a birthday party.

_____ 3. The narrator probably
lives with
a. his parents.
b. Westley.
c. his aunt.

_____ 4. In this story, sinners need
a. to stay the same.
b. to change.
c. to sing.

_____ 5. The narrator feels he needs
a. to hear God.
b. to see God.
c. to feel God.

_____ 6. Compared to the girls,
the boys
a. take longer.
b. take less time.
c. take the same amount
of time.

_____ 7. "Lambs" refers to
a. the children to be saved.
b. the older people.
c. the minister.

_____ 8. The ceremony is generally
a. very quiet.
b. very active.
c. very reserved.

_____ 9. In the end, Westley
a. does see God.
b. does feel God.
c. lies about seeing God.

_____ 10. In the end, the narrator
a. does see God.
b. does feel God.
c. lies about seeing God.

5 Significant Quotations

Explain the importance of each of these quotations.

1. "That night I was escorted to the front row and placed on the
mourners' bench with all the other young sinners, who had not yet
been brought to Jesus."

2. "She said you could see and hear and feel Jesus in your soul.
I believed her."

3. "Westley and I were surrounded by sisters and deacons praying."

4. "Suddenly the whole room broke into a sea of shouting, as they saw
me rise."

5. "That night, for the last time in my life but one—for I was a big boy
twelve years old—I cried."

2 COMPREHENSION ESSAY QUESTIONS

Use specific details and information from the story to answer these questions as completely as possible.

1. How would you describe the narrator's experience? Use specific details and information from the story to support your answer.

2. What significant roles do the setting and the supporting characters play? Use specific details and information from the story to support your answer.

DISCUSSION QUESTIONS

Be prepared to discuss these questions in class.

1. When have you told a lie to get yourself out of a difficult position? How is your experience similar to or different from the narrator's experience?

2. What are the ironies in this story? Use specific details from the story to support your thinking.

WRITING

Use each of these ideas for writing an essay.

1. Discuss a time when you have been expected to do more—or less—than you could do, and discuss the results of that unmet expectation.

2. Discuss a spiritual experience you have had or someone you know has had, and discuss the results of that experience.

Further Writing

1. Research evangelistic religions and the impact of congregations and rituals on their members' conduct and beliefs.

2. Research religious passage rites among either mainstream and/or tribal religions.

An Essay: "Salvation" by Langston Hughes

CHECKING YOUR READING STRATEGIES
DISCUSSION AND CRITICAL THINKING QUESTIONS

1. **Preview the chapter** as you have been instructed. You should notice right away that this looks different from the other textbooks. Review how to read literature. Begin with the title. What associations come to your mind when you read the word "salvation"? Jot them down so you can remember them after you finish reading. **Preview the questions** at the end of the story as well.

2. **Read the biographical information** about the author. What information do you think might be helpful to know as you read the story? Why?

3. *Circle the best answer for each of the following questions.*

   1. According to the biographical information at the beginning of the story, which aspects of Hughes' life might be most relevant to your understanding of the piece?
      a. Where he was born
      b. Where he was living when this story is set
      c. The lessons he learned from his grandmother
      d. None of the above

   2. What is the *overall purpose* of the biographical introduction?
      a. To set up the overall focus for the story
      b. To explain the story you are about to read
      c. To give you some background information about the author

   3. How many types of graphic illustrations are used in this chapter? Look through the entire chapter. Select all that apply.
      a. Drawings
      b. Shaded boxes (of formulas, theories, articles, etc.)
      c. Photographs
      d. Margin notations
      e. Works of art

   4. What typographical cues are used in the chapter to highlight important information for you? Select all that apply.
      a. Boldface print
      b. Italicized print
      c. Font size
      d. Boxes
      e. Numbered paragraphs

4. **After reading** the story, how do you feel? What emotions does Hughes stir in you? How do you think he causes you to feel something? Why does he?

5. **Answer the questions at the end of the story.** These are the only review questions in the text. It would be a good idea to have these answers in your notes. Why do you think these questions are included in the text? Of what benefit are they to you and your understanding of the chapter?

6. Finally, **after reading** the chapter, thoroughly review your notes. Since this chapter does not include a summary, list of key terms, review questions, etc., it will be up to you to create your own study guide. Therefore, consider how you determine which information is important enough to record. What do you think is important to remember and why?

GROUP PROJECTS

1. Compare your notes with those of your classmates. Are they all the same? If not, how do they differ? Why? Next, compare how well you and your classmates did with pulling the information out of the chapter. Do some of you have more details than others? Why do you think that may be?

2. Within your group, discuss the benefits of previewing the aids in the text before reading, as opposed to waiting to explore them after reading.

3. As a group, consider what the author does to make this story interesting and appealing to you. How does his writing style make the assigned reading more enjoyable?

4. Discuss with your groups which passages you found interesting and why. Discuss with your group how the humor affects the story.

5. As a group, consider the emotional impact of the story. How did Hughes make you feel about this experience? How do emotions affect your understanding of the material?

6. This "story" is actually not fiction. It is an autobiographical essay by Hughes. How does knowing this affect your interpretation of the story?

7. What is Hughes' theme, or thesis? How are you able to determine it? What lesson do you think he wants you to learn from his experience?

The Masque of the Red Death

Edgar Allan Poe

Edgar Allan Poe was born in 1809 and orphaned at a young age. He was adopted by John Allan, a rather militaristic businessman from Richmond, Virginia. Adoption by a person of means was not uncommon and would have been fortunate for the young Poe, except that his free spirit and his father's precision clashed. John Allan provided Poe with study at the University of Virginia—but Poe withdrew, due to drinking problems—and then at West Point—but Poe was dismissed, due to a disciplinary problem. Poe later married his very young cousin, Virginia Clemm, but the probable nonconsummation of this marriage and the early death of young Virginia contributed to Poe's idealization of both real and imagined women. His life, in fact, was one of continual disappointments. After Virginia's death, Poe sank into intermittent depressions, suffered bouts of insanity, and experienced hallucinations. Writing for many others, he wanted to publish his own magazine, but this dissolved in financial failure. He eventually died in Baltimore in 1849.

However, it is from these very problems that Poe's genius soars. He envelops the reader with his perceived worlds of the sane and insane, the rational and macabre, with equal ease. Credited with developing the modern mystery form, Poe's every word and every action draw the reader in, mixing reality with irreality, sane with insane. His other works include "The Pit and the Pendulum" and "The Fall of the House of Usher."

Illustration by John Seymour

The "Red Death" had long devastated the country. No pestilence had ever been so fatal, or so hideous. Blood was its Avatar and its seal—the redness and the horror of blood. There were sharp pains, and sudden dizziness, and then profuse bleeding at the pores, with dissolution. The scarlet stains upon the body and especially upon the face of the victim, were the pest ban which shut him out from the aid and from the sympathy of his fellow-men. And the whole seizure, progress, and termination of the disease, were the incidents of half an hour.

2   But the Prince Prospero was happy and dauntless and sagacious. When his dominions were half depopulated, he summoned to his presence a thousand hale and light-hearted friends from among the knights and dames of his court, and with these retired to the deep seclusion of one of his castellated abbeys. This was an extensive and magnificent structure, the creation of the prince's own eccentric yet august taste. A strong and lofty wall girdled it in. This wall had gates of iron. The courtiers, having entered, brought furnaces and massy hammers and welded the bolts. They resolved to leave means neither of ingress nor egress to the sudden impulses of despair or of frenzy from within. The abbey was amply provisioned. With such precautions the courtiers might bid defiance to contagion. The external world could take care of itself. In the meantime it was folly to grieve, or to think. The prince had provided all the appliances of pleasure. There were buffoons, there were improvisatori, there were ballet-dancers, there were musicians, there was Beauty, there was wine. All these and security were within. Without was the "Red Death."

3   It was toward the close of the fifth or sixth month of his seclusion, and while the pestilence raged most furiously abroad, that the Prince Prospero entertained his thousand friends at a masked ball of the most unusual magnificence.

4   It was a voluptuous scene, that masquerade. But first let me tell of the rooms in which it was held. There were seven—an imperial suite. In many palaces, however, such suites form a long and straight vista, while the folding doors slide back nearly to the walls on either hand, so that the view of the whole extent is scarcely impeded. Here the case was very different; as might have been expected from the duke's love of the *bizarre*. The apartments were so irregularly disposed that the vision embraced but little more than one at a time. There was a sharp turn at every twenty or thirty yards, and at each turn a novel effect. To the right and left, in the middle of each wall, a tall and narrow Gothic window looked out upon a closed corridor which pursued the windings of the suite. These windows were of stained glass whose color varied in accordance with the prevailing hue of the decorations of the chamber into which it opened. That at the eastern extremity was hung, for

example, in blue—and vividly blue were its windows. The second chamber was purple in its ornaments and tapestries, and here the panes were purple. The third was green throughout, and so were the casements. The fourth was furnished and lighted with orange—the fifth with white—the sixth with violet. The seventh apartment was closely shrouded in black velvet tapestries that hung all over the ceiling and down the walls, falling in heavy folds upon a carpet of the same material and hue. But in this chamber only, the color of the windows failed to correspond with the decorations. The panes here were scarlet—a deep blood color. Now in no one of the seven apartments was there any lamp or candelabrum, amid the profusion of golden ornaments that lay scattered to and fro or depended from the roof. There was no light of any kind emanating from lamp or candle within the suite of chambers. But in the corridors that followed the suite, there stood, opposite to each window, a heavy tripod, bearing a brazier of fire, that projected its rays through the tinted glass and so glaringly illumined the room. And thus were produced a multitude of gaudy and fantastic appearances. But in the western or black chamber the effect of the fire-light that streamed upon the dark hangings through the blood-tinted panes was ghastly in the extreme, and produced so wild a look upon the countenances of those who entered, that there were few of the company bold enough to set foot within its precincts at all.

5   It was in this apartment, also, that there stood against the western wall, a gigantic clock of ebony. Its pendulum swung to and fro with a dull, heavy, monotonous clang; and when the minute-hand made the circuit of the face, and the hour was to be stricken, there came from the brazen lungs of the clock a sound which was clear and loud and deep and exceedingly musical, but of so peculiar a note and emphasis that, at each lapse of an hour, the musicians of the orchestra were constrained to pause, momentarily, in their performance, to hearken to the sound; and thus the waltzers perforce ceased their evolutions; and there was a brief disconcert of the whole gay company; and, while the chimes of the clock yet rang, it was observed that the giddiest grew pale, and the more aged and sedate passed their hands over their brows as if in confused revery or meditation. But when the echoes had fully ceased, a light laughter at once pervaded the assembly; the musicians looked at each other and smiled as if at their own nervousness and folly, and made whispering vows, each to the other, that the next chiming of the clock should produce in them no similar emotion; and then, after the lapse of sixty minutes (which embrace three thousand and six hundred seconds of the Time that flies), there came yet another chiming of the clock, and then were the same disconcert and tremulousness and meditation as before.

6   But, in spite of these things, it was a gay and magnificent revel. The tastes of the duke were peculiar. He had a fine eye for colors and effects. He disregarded the *decora* of mere fashion. His plans were bold and fiery, and his conceptions glowed with barbaric lustre. There are some who would have thought him mad. His followers felt that he was not. It was necessary to hear and see and touch him to be *sure* that he was not.

7   He had directed, in great part, the movable embellishments of the seven chambers, upon occasion of this great *fête*; and it was his own guiding taste which had given character to the masqueraders. Be sure they were grotesque. There were much glare and glitter and piquancy and phantasm—much of what has been since seen in "Hernani." There were arabesque figures with unsuited limbs and appointments. There were delirious fancies such as the madman fashions. There were much of the beautiful, much of the wanton, much of the *bizarre*, something of the terrible, and not a little of that which might have excited disgust. To and fro in the seven chambers there stalked, in fact, a multitude of dreams. And these—the dreams—writhed in and about, taking hue from the rooms, and causing the wild music of the orchestra to seem as the echo of their steps. And, anon, there strikes the ebony clock which stands in the hall of the velvet. And then, for a moment, all is still, and all is silent save the voice of the clock. The dreams are stiff-frozen as they stand. But the echoes of the chime die away—they have endured but an instant—and a light, half-subdued laughter floats after them as they depart. And now again the music swells, and the dreams live, and writhe to and fro more merrily than ever, taking hue from the many-tinted windows through which stream the rays from the tripods. But to the chamber which lies most westwardly of the seven there are now none of the maskers who venture; for the night is waning away; and there flows a ruddier light through the blood-colored panes; and the blackness of the sable drapery appals; and to him whose foot falls upon the sable carpet, there comes from the near clock of ebony a muffled peal more solemnly emphatic than any which reaches *their* ears who indulge in the more remote gaieties of the other apartments.

8   But these other apartments were densely crowded, and in them beat feverishly the heart of life. And the revel went whirlingly on, until at length there commenced the sounding of midnight upon the clock. And then the music ceased, as I have told; and the evolutions of the waltzers were quieted, and there was an uneasy cessation of all things as before. But now there were twelve strokes to be sounded by the bell of the clock; and thus it happened, perhaps, that more of thought crept, with more of time, into the meditations of the thoughtful among those who revelled. And thus too, it happened, perhaps, that before the last

echoes of the last chime had utterly sunk into silence, there were many individuals in the crowd who had found leisure to become aware of the presence of a masked figure which had arrested the attention of no single individual before. And the rumor of this new presence having spread itself whisperingly around, there arose at length from the whole company a buzz, or murmur, expressive of disapprobation and surprise—then, finally, of terror, of horror, and of disgust.

9   In an assembly of phantasms such as I have painted, it may well be supposed that no ordinary appearance could have excited such sensation. In truth the masquerade license of the night was nearly unlimited; but the figure in question had out-Heroded Herod, and gone beyond the bounds of even the prince's indefinite decorum. There are chords in the hearts of the most reckless which cannot be touched without emotion. Even with the utterly lost, to whom life and death are equally jests, there are matters of which no jest can be made. The whole company, indeed, seemed now deeply to feel that in the costume and bearing of the stranger neither wit nor propriety existed. The figure was tall and gaunt, and shrouded from head to foot in the habiliments of the grave. The mask which concealed the visage was made so nearly to resemble the countenance of a stiffened corpse that the closest scrutiny must have had difficulty in detecting the cheat. And yet all this might have been endured, if not approved, by the mad revellers around. But the mummer had gone so far as to assume the type of the Red Death. His vesture was dabbled in *blood*—and his broad brow, with all the features of the face, was besprinkled with the scarlet horror.

10   When the eyes of Prince Prospero fell upon this spectral image (which, with a slow and solemn movement, as if more fully to sustain its *rôle*, stalked to and fro among the waltzers) he was seen to be convulsed, in the first moment with a strong shudder either of terror or distaste; but, in the next, his brow reddened with rage.

11   "Who dares"—he demanded hoarsely of the courtiers who stood near him—"who dares insult us with this blasphemous mockery? Seize him and unmask him—that we may know whom we have to hang, at sunrise, from the battlements!"

12   It was in the eastern or blue chamber in which stood the Prince Prospero as he uttered these words. They rang throughout the seven rooms loudly and clearly, for the prince was a bold and robust man, and the music had become hushed at the waving of his hand.

13   It was in the blue room where stood the prince, with a group of pale courtiers by his side. At first, as he spoke, there was a slight rushing movement of this group in the direction of the intruder, who, at the moment was also near at hand, and now, with deliberate and stately step, made closer approach to the speaker. But from a certain nameless

awe with which the mad assumptions of the mummer had inspired the whole party, there were found none who put forth hand to seize him; so that, unimpeded, he passed within a yard of the prince's person; and, while the vast assembly, as if with one impulse, shrank from the centres of the rooms to the walls, he made his way uninterruptedly, but with the same solemn and measured step which had distinguished him from the first, through the blue chamber to the purple—through the purple to the green—through the green to the orange—through this again to the white—and even thence to the violet, ere a decided movement had been made to arrest him. It was then, however, that the Prince Prospero, maddening with rage and the shame of his own momentary cowardice, rushed hurriedly through the six chambers, while none followed him on account of a deadly terror that had seized upon all. He bore aloft a drawn dagger, and had approached, in rapid impetuosity, to within three or four feet of the retreating figure, when the latter, having attained the extremity of the velvet apartment, turned suddenly and confronted his pursuer. There was a sharp cry— and the dagger dropped gleaming upon the sable carpet, upon which, instantly afterward, fell prostrate in death the Prince Prospero. Then, summoning the wild courage of despair, a throng of the revellers at once threw themselves into the black apartment, and, seizing the mummer, whose tall figure stood erect and motionless within the shadow of the ebony clock, gasped in unutterable horror at finding the grave cerements and corpse-like mask, which they handled with so violent a rudeness, untenanted by any tangible form.

14   And now was acknowledged the presence of the Red Death. He had come like a thief in the night. And one by one dropped the revellers in the blood-bedewed halls of their revel, and died each in the despairing posture of his fall. And the life of the ebony clock went out with that of the last of the gay. And the flames of the tripods expired. And Darkness and Decay and the Red Death held illimitable dominion over all.

FOLLOW-UP QUESTIONS

10 SHORT QUESTIONS

Select the <u>best</u> answer for each.

____ 1. As a victim of the Red Death bleeds, one
    a. has the help and support of friends.
    b. does not have the help and support of friends.
    c. gets better rapidly.

____ 2. Prince Prospero
    a. cares about the general population.
    b. is kind to the general population.
    c. shows little concern for the general population.

____ 3. Prince Prospero
    a. thinks he can escape the Red Death.
    b. thinks he cannot escape the Red Death.
    c. does not know about the Red Death.

____ 4. He and his court
    a. think they will be infected with the disease.
    b. think they will not be infected with the disease.
    c. do not know about the disease.

____ 5. The castle rooms are
    a. all the same.
    b. one big room.
    c. separated and different.

____ 6. The black room's only other color is
    a. white.
    b. blue.
    c. blood red.

____ 7. The clock has
    a. an unsettling chime.
    b. a pleasant chime.
    c. a sweet, musical chime.

____ 8. The mummer enters
    a. an afternoon party.
    b. a formal ball.
    c. a masked ball.

____ 9. The mummer
    a. is wearing a mask.
    b. is not wearing a mask.
    c. is wearing heavy makeup.

____ 10. The prince and his guests
    a. escape the Red Death.
    b. never see the Red Death.
    c. die from the Red Death.

5 SIGNIFICANT QUOTATIONS

Explain the importance of each of these quotations.

1. "No pestilence had ever been so fatal, or so hideous."

2. "When his dominions were half depopulated, he summoned to his presence a thousand hale and light-hearted friends [. . .] and with these retired to the deep seclusion of one of his castellated abbeys."

3. "It was toward the close of [. . .] his seclusion, and while the pestilence raged most furiously abroad, that the Prince Prospero entertained his thousand friends at a masked ball of the most unusual magnificence."

4. "It was in this apartment, also, that there stood against the western wall, a gigantic clock of ebony."

5. "Then, summoning the wild courage of despair, a throng of revellers at once threw themselves into the black apartment, and, seizing the mummer [. . .] gasped in unutterable horror at finding the grave cerements and corpse-like mask [. . .] untenanted by any tangible form."

2 COMPREHENSION ESSAY QUESTIONS

Use specific details and information from the story to answer these questions as completely as possible.

1. How does the black chamber prepare you for the figure's appearance? Use specific details and information from the story to support your explanation.

2. What happens to Prince Prospero? Use specific details and information from the story to support your explanation.

DISCUSSION QUESTIONS

Be prepared to discuss these questions in class.

1. To what current concerns might you compare the masked character? Use specific details from the story to support your ideas.

2. How does the illustration demonstrate this story? Use specific details from the story to support your thinking.

WRITING

Use each of these ideas for writing an essay.

1. We have all been to strange places. Describe a place you have been to that seemed to reek of disease or evil.

2. We have all met scary or gloomy people. Describe your encounter with a scary person and how you handled the situation.

Further Writing

1. Read literary analyses of "The Masque of the Red Death" (available in a library). Then discuss whom or what beyond biological disease the figure of Red Death might represent in this story.

2. Research the AIDS/HIV virus, and use this story in your introduction to your research.

A Short Story: "The Masque of the Red Death"
by Edgar Allan Poe

CHECKING YOUR READING STRATEGIES

DISCUSSION AND CRITICAL THINKING QUESTIONS

1. **Preview the chapter** as you have been instructed. You should notice right away that this looks different from the other textbooks. Review how to read literature. Begin with the title. What associations come to your mind when you read the words "masque" or "red death"? Jot them down so you can remember them after you finish reading. **Preview the questions** at the end of the story as well.

2. **Read the biographical information** about the author. What information do you think might be helpful to know as you read the story? Why?

3. *Circle the best answer for each of the following questions.*

   1. According to the biographical information at the beginning of the story, which aspects of Poe's life might be most relevant to your understanding of the piece?
      a. Where he was born
      b. Where he was living when this story is set
      c. The information about his writing
      d. None of the above

   2. What is the *overall purpose* of the biographical introduction?
      a. To set up the overall focus for the story
      b. To explain the story you are about to read
      c. To give you some background information about the author
      d. To explain the significance of the symbols

   3. How many types of graphic illustrations are used in this chapter? Look through the entire chapter. Select all that apply.
      a. Drawings
      b. Shaded boxes (of formulas, theories, articles, etc.)
      c. Photographs
      d. Margin notations
      e. Works of art

   4. What typographical cues are used in the chapter to highlight important information for you? Select all that apply.
      a. Boldface print   d. Font style
      b. Italicized print   e. Numbered paragraphs
      c. Font size   f. Boxes

   5. What is the correct order of the rooms?
      a. White, blue, violet, purple, orange, green, and black
      b. Blue, purple, green, orange, white, violet, and black
      c. Orange, green, blue, violet, purple, black, and white
      d. Green, blue, orange, purple, black, violet, and white

4. **After reading the story**, how do you feel? What emotions does Poe stir in you? How do you think he causes you to feel something? Why does he?

5. Poe believed that fiction and poetry should strive to create a "single effect," which means that the work should stir one emotion in the reader, such as sadness or terror. What single effect does Poe try to maintain in this story? How does he do it? (Note: consider atmosphere.)

6. Explain how **the title** relates to the story.

7. Consider the **symbols** used in the story. Why do you think the rooms are colored as they are? What do the colors represent? Why do the rooms flow from east to west? Why is Death red? How does Prince Prospero's name fit with the story?

8. **Answer the questions at the end** of the story. These are the only review questions in the text. It would be a good idea to have these answers in your notes. Why do you think these questions are included in the text? Of what benefit are they to you and your understanding of the chapter?

9. Finally, **after reading** the chapter, thoroughly review your notes. Since this chapter does not include a summary, list of key terms, review questions, etc., it will be up to you to create your own study guide. Therefore, consider how you determine which information is important enough to record. What do you think is important to remember and why?

GROUP PROJECTS

1. Compare your notes with those of your classmates. Are they all the same? If not, how do they differ? Why? Next, compare how well you and your classmates did with pulling the information out of the chapter. Do some of you have more details than others? Why do you think that may be?

2. Within your group, discuss the benefits of previewing the aids in the text before reading, as opposed to waiting to explore them after reading.

3. As a group, consider what the author does to make this story interesting and appealing to you. How does his writing style make the assigned reading more enjoyable? Less enjoyable?

4. Discuss with your group which passages you found interesting and why. Discuss with your group how the description of the setting affects the story.

5. As a group, consider the emotional impact of the story. How did Poe make you feel about this experience? How do emotions affect your understanding of the material?

6. What is the theme of this story? How did you determine it? How do the symbols help you with determining theme?

Poetry

from

Barnet, Burto, and Cain: *An Introduction to Literature*
Fourteenth Edition

EDWIN ARLINGTON ROBINSON

Edward Arlington Robinson (1869-1935) grew up in Gardiner, Maine, spent two years at Harvard, and then returned to Maine, where he published his first book of poetry in 1896. Though he received encouragement from neighbors, his finances were precarious, even after President Theodore Roosevelt, having been made aware of the book, secured for him an appointment as customs inspector in New York from 1905 to 1909. Additional books won fame for Robinson, and in 1922 he was awarded the first of the three Pulitzer Prizes for poetry that he would win.

Richard Cory   [1896]

Whenever Richard Cory went down town,
We people on the pavement looked at him:
He was a gentleman from sole to crown,
Clean favored, and imperially slim.   4

And he was always quietly arrayed,
And he was always human when he talked;
But still he fluttered pulses when he said,
"Good-morning," and he glittered when he walked.   8

And he was rich—yes, richer than a king—
And admirably schooled in every grace:
In fine,° we thought that he was everything
To make us wish that we were in his place.   12

So on we worked, and waited for the light,
And went without the meat, and cursed the bread;
And Richard Cory, one calm summer night,
Went home and put a bullet through his head.   16

---

[11] *In fine* *in short.*

❖ TOPICS FOR CRITICAL THINKING AND WRITING

1. Consult the entry on irony in the glossary. Then read the pages referred to in the entry. Finally, write an essay of 500 words on irony in "Richard Cory."
2. What do you think were Richard Cory's thoughts shortly before he "put a bullet through his head"? In 500 words, set forth his thoughts and actions (what he sees and does). If you wish, you can write in the first person, from Cory's point of view. Further, if you wish, your essay can be in the form of a suicide note.
3. Write a sketch (250-350 words) setting forth your early impression or understanding of someone whose later actions revealed you had not understood the person.

A Poem: "Richard Cory," by Edwin Arlington Robinson

CHECKING YOUR READING STRATEGIES

DISCUSSION AND CRITICAL THINKING QUESTIONS

1. **Preview the poem** as you have been instructed. You should notice right away that this looks different from the other textbooks. Review how to read literature. Begin with the title. What associations come to your mind when you read the name "Richard Cory"? Jot them down so you can remember them after you finish reading. **Preview the questions** at the end of the poem as well.

2. **Read the biographical information** about the author. What information do you think might be helpful to know as you read the poem? Why?

3. *Circle the best answer for each of the following questions.*

    1. According to the biographical information at the beginning of the story, which aspects of Robinson's life might be most relevant to your understanding of the piece?
       a. Where he was born
       b. The information about his writing
       c. Where he was living when this poem is set
       d. None of the above

    2. What is the *overall purpose* of the biographical introduction?
       a. To set up the overall focus for the poem
       b. To explain the poem you are about to read
       c. To give you some background information about the author
       d. To explain the significance of the symbols

    3. How many types of graphic elements are used with this poem? Look over the entire page. Select all that apply.
       a. Drawings
       b. Photographs
       c. Shaded boxes (of formulas, theories, articles, etc.)
       d. Margin notations
       e. Works of art
       f. None of the above

    4. What typographical cues are used in the chapter to highlight important information for you? Select all that apply.
       a. Boldface print
       b. Italicized print
       c. Font size
       d. Font style
       e. Numbered lines
       f. Boxes

4. **After reading** the poem, how do you feel? What emotions does Robinson stir in you? How do you think he causes you to feel something? Why does he?

5. Explain how the **title** relates to the poem.

6. Consider the **symbols** used in the poem. The poem is described as having "imperial imagery," which means there are symbols which suggest royalty. What imperial images can you find? What kind of an image do they create about Cory?

7. In poetry, the sound of the words is very important. How would you describe the sound, or rhythm, of the poem?

8. How do the last two lines of the poem affect you? When compared with the language used in the majority of the poem, what impact do the words "put a bullet through his head" have?

9. **Answer the questions** at the end of the poem. These are the only review questions in the text. It would be a good idea to have these answers in your notes. Why do you think these questions are included in the text? Of what benefit are they to you and your understanding of the poem?

10. Finally, **after reading** the chapter, thoroughly review your notes. Since this poem does not include a summary, list of key terms, review questions, etc., it will be up to you to create your own study guide. Therefore, consider how you determine which information is important enough to record. What do you think is important to remember and why?

GROUP PROJECTS

1. Compare your notes with those of your classmates. Are they all the same? If not, how do they differ? Why? Next, compare how well you and your classmates did with pulling the information out of the poem. Do some of you have more details than others? Why do you think that may be?

2. Within your group, discuss the benefits of previewing the aids in the text before reading, as opposed to waiting to explore them after reading.

3. As a group, consider what the author does to make this poem interesting and appealing to you. How does his writing style make the assigned reading more enjoyable? Less enjoyable?

4. Discuss with your group which passages you found interesting and why. Discuss with your group how the description of the character affects the poem.

5. As a group, consider the emotional impact of the poem. How did Robinson make you feel about this experience? How do emotions affect your understanding of the material?

6. What is the theme of this poem? How did you determine it? How do the symbols help you with determining theme?

PAUL LAURENCE DUNBAR

Paul Laurence Dunbar (1872–1906), born in Ohio to parents who had been slaves in Kentucky, achieved fame for his dialect poetry. He published early—even while in high school—and by 1896, with the publication of Lyrics of Lowly Life, *had three books to his credit. Because he often used black speech patterns and pronunciation, Dunbar's work was sometimes thought to present demeaning racial stereotypes, but in recent years critics have seen the protest beneath the quaint surface. In the following poem, however, he works entirely within a traditional white idiom, although the subject is distinctively African-American.*

Sympathy
[1899]

I know what the caged bird feels, alas!
   When the sun is bright on the upland slopes;
When the wind stirs soft through the spring grass,
And the river flows like a stream of glass.
   When the first bird sings and the first bud opes,   5
And the faint perfume from its chalice steals—
I know what the caged bird feels!

I know why the caged bird beats his wing
   Till its blood is red on the cruel bars;
For he must fly back to his perch and cling   10
When he fain would be on the bough a-swing;
   And a pain still throbs in the old, old scars
And they pulse again with a keener sting—
I know why he beats his wing!

I know why the caged bird sings, ah me,   15
   When his wing is bruised and his bosom sore,—
When he beats his bars and he would be free;
It is not a carol of joy or glee,
   But a prayer that he sends from his heart's deep core,
But a plea, that upward to Heaven he flings—   20
   I know why the caged bird sings

▨ TOPICS FOR CRITICAL THINKING AND WRITING

1. Pay careful attention to Dunbar's use of language. Describe, for example, what the comparison "like a stream of glass" in the first stanza expresses about the river, and comment on the implications of the word "chalice."

2. Some readers have felt that the second stanza is the weakest in the poem, and that the poem improves if this stanza is omitted. Why do you suppose they hold this view? Do you agree with it? Explain. Should Dunbar have dropped this stanza?

3. After reading and rereading the poem, try to summarize its overall effect. Explain why the speaker sees such an intimate connection between himself and the "caged bird."

A Poem: "Sympathy," by Paul Laurence Dunbar

CHECKING YOUR READING STRATEGIES

DISCUSSION AND CRITICAL THINKING QUESTIONS

1. **Preview the poem** as you have been instructed. You should notice right away that this looks different from the other textbooks. Review how to read literature. Begin with the title. What associations come to your mind when you read the word "Sympathy"? Jot them down so you can remember them after you finish reading. **Preview the questions** at the end of the poem as well.

2. **Read the biographical information** about the author. What information do you think might be helpful to know as you read the poem? Why?

3. *Circle the best answer for each of the following questions.*

   1. According to the biographical information at the beginning of the poem, which aspects of Robinson's life might be most relevant to your understanding of the piece?
      a. Where he was born
      b. Where he was living when this poem is set
      c. The information about his writing
      d. None of the above

   2. What is the *overall purpose* of the biographical introduction?
      a. To set up the overall focus for the poem
      b. To explain the poem you are about to read
      c. To give you some background information about the author
      d. To explain the significance of the symbols

   3. How many types of graphic elements are used with this poem? Look over the entire page. Select all that apply.
      a. Drawings
      b. Photographs
      c. Shaded boxes (of formulas, theories, articles, etc.)
      d. Margin notations
      e. Works of art
      f. None of the above

   4. What typographical cues are used in the chapter to highlight important information for you? Select all that apply.
      a. Boldface print
      b. Italicized print
      c. Font size
      d. Font style
      e. Numbered lines
      f. Boxes

4. **After reading the poem,** how do you feel? What emotions does Dunbar stir in you? How do you think he causes you to feel something? Why does he?

5. Explain how the **title** relates to the poem.

6. Consider the **symbols** used in the poem. Why do you think Dunbar repeats the image of "the caged bird"? What kind of an image does it create about the speaker?

7. In poetry, the sound of the words is very important. How would you describe the sound, or rhythm, of the poem?

8. **Answer the questions at the end** of the poem. These are the only review questions in the text. It would be a good idea to have these answers in your notes. Why do you think these questions are included in the text? Of what benefit are they to you and your understanding of the poem?

9. Finally, **after reading** the chapter, thoroughly review your notes. Since this poem does not include a summary, list of key terms, review questions, etc., it will be up to you to create your own study guide. Therefore, consider how you determine which information is important enough to record. What do you think is important to remember and why?

GROUP PROJECTS

1. Compare your notes with those of your classmates. Are they all the same? If not, how do they differ? Why? Next, compare how well you and your classmates did with pulling the information out of the poem. Do some of you have more details than others? Why do you think that may be?

2. Within your group, discuss the benefits of previewing the aids in the text before reading, as opposed to waiting to explore them after reading.

3. As a group, consider what the author does to make this poem interesting and appealing to you. How does his writing style make the assigned reading more enjoyable? Less enjoyable?

4. Discuss with your groups which passages you found interesting and why. Discuss with your group how the description of the character affects the poem.

5. As a group, consider the emotional impact of the poem. How did Dunbar make you feel about this experience? How do emotions affect your understanding of the material?

6. What is the theme of this poem? How did you determine it? How do the symbols help you with determining theme?

Visual Arts *(found in the History text chapter)*

Paintings: page 60, 65–66, 68–69, 71, 74–77, 81, 84, 87
Drawings and Etchings: page 70, 73
Multi-dimensional art: page 72, 92

CHECKING YOUR READING STRATEGIES
DISCUSSION AND CRITICAL THINKING QUESTIONS

1. **Preview and reading** are probably going to occur simultaneously when evaluating works of art. You should notice right away that this assignment will need to be handled differently than reading paragraphs of text. Review how to "read" art. **Begin with the title.** How does the title, if one is provided, fit with the work? Write your connections in your notes so you can remember them after you finish.

2. What sort of information is provided for you in the caption? Which information do you think might be helpful to you as you assess the work? Why?

3. *Circle the best answer for each of the following questions.*

   1. According to the information at the beginning of this text, what elements of art might be most relevant to your understanding of the aesthetic aspect of the works?
      a. Where the work was designed
      b. When the work was designed
      c. The medium used for the work
      d. None of the above

   2. What is the *primary purpose* of the caption?
      a. To set up the overall historical focus for the work
      b. To explain the facts you are about to read
      c. To give you some background information about who or what is being portrayed in the work
      d. To explain the significance of the materials used to create the work

   3. How many types of artistic elements could you consider with these works? Select all that apply.
      a. Color
      b. Light
      c. Perspective
      d. Materials used
      e. Size
      f. Shape
      g. Texture
      h. Border/Frame
      i. Condition the work is in
      j. Realism
      k. Details
      l. Spatial design

   4. What organizational patterns could you use to evaluate the works? Select all that apply.
      a. Chronological
      b. Spatial
      c. Thematic
      d. None of these

4. **After** carefully scrutinizing each work, consider your reactions to the piece. How does it make you feel? Does the work or the accompanying information cause you to feel anything? How and why might these feelings be relevant?

5. Artists create their works for many reasons and purposes. Some are functional, like furniture or pottery; other works are used to provide a record of a person or an event. Select one work of art from each of the three categories. For what purpose or reason do you think it was created, and why?

6. Select one work of art from each category. For each work, which artistic element strikes you as being the most significant, and why?

GROUP PROJECTS

1. Compare your observations with those of your classmates. Are they all the same? If not, how do they differ? Why? Next, compare how well you and your classmates did with finding the details in the works of art. Do some of you have more details than others? Why do you think that may be?

2. Within your group, discuss the benefits of previewing the art and the accompanying captions before attempting to evaluate the piece.

3. As a group, consider what the artist does to make the work interesting and appealing to you. How does the artist's style make the artwork more enjoyable? Less enjoyable?

4. Discuss with your groups which pieces you found interesting and why. Discuss with your group how the title of the piece affects the evaluation of it.

5. As a group, consider the emotional impact of the art. How do the artists make you feel about their work? What do they do to help you connect to the people, the events, or the objects of their time? How do emotions affect your understanding of the material?

6. Does the multi-dimensional art cause any additional reactions on your part? How does the artist engage your tactile sense?

Unit IV
Reading Strategies for Mathematics and Automotives

from

Automotive Technology: Principles, Diagnosis, and Service

Third Edition

by

James D. Halderman

Mathematics is a discipline which is tied to so many other disciplines that it is important to study the subject regardless of what you plan to major in or what career you plan to pursue. Mathematics does not cover mathematical operations alone; it also trains you in logical, orderly thinking and in problem solving, two sets of skills which are essential life skills. However, a math text is not read like most other college texts. In math texts, the shaded or boxed bits of information, such as definitions, theorems, formulas, or sample problem solutions, are your friends. While you might skip over these set-off sections in another text, you *cannot* overlook them in math texts. These boxes are essential. Reading what they say and practicing the sample problems will save you time in the long-run.

In addition, you will want to pay particular attention to the graphics used to illustrate concepts in a math text. In many texts, you will read a description and may have to search around the page for the graphic or exercise used to help reinforce the point. In a math text, each point comes with its written and illustrative example. This way you can read what is explained and see the illustration immediately following the description so you can "see" what the author is saying. Also pay attention to charts and graphs, as they also help to reinforce the material at hand.

When you are provided with sample problems, it would be helpful for you to practice the samples yourself before tackling your assigned problems. Copy the sample equation onto a sheet of paper and close the text. Next, work the problem yourself. When you have finished, re-open the text to check your work. If your work is correct, move on to the next set. If it is not, then look to see where you made your error. Recopy the equation, close the book, and work the problem again. Check your work again. Repeat this until you can solve the problem correctly. Practicing and mastering the method now will save you more time and errors when working on your assignment. When you do work on your assignment, make note of any problems that are particularly difficult for you and ask the professor about them in class. Do not be afraid to ask questions or to seek out extra help. Math is *not* a spectator event; it takes a lot of practice.

In the chapter here, "Math, Charts, and Calculations," math strategies are applied to an automotive course, illustrating how prevalent math is in other disciplines. This chapter explains how to convert measurements from our measuring system to metric, which is a valuable skill for anyone to have.

OBJECTIVES: **After studying Chapter 14, the reader will be able to:** Add and subtract decimal numbers. • Read a chart and graph. • Calculate percentages.

KEY TERMS: chart • decimal point • diagram • direct drive • drive gear • driven gear • fractions • gear reduction • graph • overdrive • percentage • scientific notation • variable

DECIMALS

Decimals are commonly used by service technicians. The placement of the decimal point indicates the value of the number. The naming of decimals includes tenths, hundredths, thousandths, and higher. Decimals are used to represent fractions of a unit by using a dot called a **decimal point** to indicate that the number is a decimal.

Tenths A decimal with one number to the right of the decimal point indicates an accuracy of 1/10 or 0.1. For example, 0.7 is the same as 7/10 and is pronounced "seven tenths" or "zero point seven." A decimal can also include numbers larger than zero, but has a resolution or accuracy measured in tenths, such as in 14.7.

Hundredth Decimals with two numbers to the right of the decimal point indicate an accuracy to 1/100 or 0.01. For example, 0.47 is pronounced "forty-seven hundredth" or "zero point four seven."

Thousandth A decimal with three numbers to the right of the decimal point indicates an accuracy to 1/1000 or 0.001. For example, 0.867 is pronounced "eight hundred sixty-seven thousandth" or "zero point eight six seven."

Adding and Subtracting Decimals When adding or subtracting decimals, the decimal point has to be aligned. This ensures that the numbers are placed into the correct position of tenth, hundredth, and thousandth. For example:

$$\begin{array}{r} 0.147 \\ + \ 0.02 \\ \hline 0.167 \end{array}$$

Notice that the top number is expressed in thousandths and the lower number is expressed in hundredths. The final figure is also shown in thousandths.

> **NOTE:** If these numbers were measurements, the first result cannot be more accurate than the least accurate measurement. This means that the final result should be expressed in hundredths instead of thousandths.

When subtracting or multiplying decimals, keep the decimal points aligned or use a calculator making certain to include the decimal point.

PERCENTAGE

Percentage is the relationship of a value or number out of 100. Using money as an example, three quarters (25 cents each) equals 75 cents ($0.75) or 75% of a dollar ($1.00). Many examples are not that easy, for example, 70 is what percentage of 120? To determine the percentage, divide the first number (70) by the second number (120).

$$70 \div 120 = 0.58$$

To convert this number to a percentage, multiply the number by 100 or move the decimal point two places to the right (58) and then add a percentage symbol to indicate that the number is a percentage (58%).

SCIENTIFIC NOTATION

Very large and very small decimal numbers are frequently expressed using scientific notation. **Scientific notation** is written as a number multiplied by the number of zeros to the right or left of the decimal point. For example, 68,000 could be written as 6.8×10^4, indicating that the number shown has 3 zeros plus the 8 to the right of the decimal point. Small numbers, such as 0.00068, would use a negative sign beside the number over the 10 to represent that the decimal point needs to be moved toward the left (6.8×10^{-4}).

ADDING AND SUBTRACTING

Technicians are often required to add or subtract measurements when working on vehicles. For example, adding and subtracting is needed to select shims (thin pieces of steel) for adjusting valve clearance or differential preload measurements.

For example, if the valve clearance specification is 0.012 in. and the clearance is actually 0.016 in., and the shim that is in place between the camshaft lobe and the valve bucket is 0.080 in. thick, what size (thickness) of shim needs to be installed to achieve the correct valve clearance?

Solution: The shim thickness of 0.080 in. results in a valve clearance of 0.016 in. The specification requires that the shim needs to be thicker to reduce the valve clearance. See Figure 14–1.

To determine the thickness of a shim, the amount of clearance needed to be corrected needs to be calculated. The original clearance is 0.016 in. and the specification is 0.012 in. The difference is determined by subtracting the actual clearance from the specified clearance:

$$0.016 - 0.012 = 0.004 \text{ in.}$$

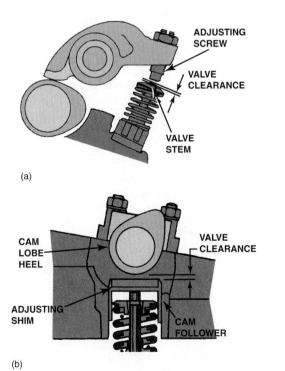

(a)

(b)

Figure 14–1 Valve clearance allows the metal parts to expand and maintain proper operation, both when the engine is cold or at normal operating temperature. (a) Adjustment is achieved by turning the adjusting screw. (b) Adjustment is achieved by changing the thickness of the adjusting shim.

The result (0.004 in.) then needs to be added to the thickness of the existing shim to determine the thickness of the replacement shim needed to achieve the correct valve clearance.

Existing shim thickness =	0.080 in.
Additional thickness needed =	+ 0.004 in.
Thickness of new shim =	0.084 in.

FRACTIONS

Fractions, such as 1/2, 1/4, or 5/8 are commonly found in specifications for hose inside diameter measurements. A tape measure or machinists rule can be used to measure the fitting or the original part. Sometimes, fractions need to be converted to decimal units if the replacement parts are offered by that measurement method. When comparing fractions to decimal units, think about the number of cents in a dollar.

1/2 dollar = 50 cents

Quarter = 25 cents

1/10 (dime) = 10 cents

1/20 (nickel) = 5 cents

Other fractions, such as 3/8, 5/8, and 5/16 are harder to determine. If a chart is not available, divide the bottom number, called the denominator into the top number, called the numerator.

3/8 = 3.0 divided by 8 = 0.375

5/8 = 5.0 divided by 8 = 0.625

5/16 = 5.0 divided by 16 = 0.3125

MULTIPLYING AND DIVIDING

Multiplying by a service technician is usually done to determine gear ratios and to determine the total of many of the same items. For example, the final overall gear ratio is determined by multiplying the transmission gear ratio by the final drive ratio and is covered later in this chapter.

Dividing is commonly done when calculating total resistance of many resistances connected in parallel. In this situation, the value of the resistance is divided by the number of equal resistances. For example, if four bulbs with a resistance of 0.4 ohm were connected in parallel, the total resistance would be just 0.1 ohm ($0.4 \div 4 = 0.1$).

MATHEMATICAL FORMULAS

A formula uses letters to represent values or measurements and indicates how these numbers are to be multiplied, divided, added, or subtracted. To use a formula, the technician needs to replace the letters with the actual number and perform the indicated math functions.

For example, a formula used to determine engine speed in revolutions per minute (RPM) and is represented by the following formula:

$$\text{RPM} = \frac{\text{mph} \times \text{gear ratio} \times 336}{\text{tire diameter (inches)}}$$

This formula is used to determine the speed of the engine compared to the gear ratio and tire size. Sometimes, wheel and tire sizes are changed and knowing this is helpful.

To calculate the engine speed, the actual information needs to be placed into the formula.

$$Mph = 70\ mph$$
$$Gear\ ratio = 2{:}41{:}1$$
$$Tire\ diameter = 26\ inches$$

Replacing the terms with the actual numbers results in the following:

$$RPM = \frac{70 \times 2.41 \times 336}{26} = \frac{5668}{26} = 2180\ RPM$$

FUEL ECONOMY CALCULATOR

To calculate fuel economy in miles per gallons, two factors must be known:

1. How far was the vehicle driven.
2. How many gallons of fuel were needed.

This calculation requires that the fuel tank be filled two times; first at the start of the test and then at the end of the test distance. For example:

Step #1 Fill the tank until the nozzle clicks off.

> **NOTE:** Try to use the same station and pump, if possible, to achieve the most accurate results.

Step #2 Drive a reasonable distance. For the example, we drove 220 miles.

Step #3 Fill the fuel tank and record the number of gallons used. For this example, exactly 10.0 gallons.

Step #4 Calculate fuel economy: MPG = Miles driven divided by the number of gallons used.

$$MPG = 220\ divided\ by\ 10.0 = 22.0\ miles\ per\ gallon$$

FREQUENTLY ASKED QUESTION ???

How Is Metric Fuel Economy Measured?

In the United States fuel economy is expressed in miles per gallon. Outside of the United States, fuel economy is measured in the number of liters of fuel needed to travel 100 kilometers (62 miles), abbreviated L/100 km. This means that as the number increases, the fuel economy decreases. For example:

MPG	L/100 km
5	47.0
10	23.5
15	15.7
20	11.8
25	9.4
30	7.8
35	6.7
40	5.9
45	5.2
50	4.7

In the metric system, the fuel is measured; in the United States, the miles are measured.

GEAR RATIOS

When one gear turns another, the speed that the two gears turn in relation to each other is the gear ratio. Gear ratio is expressed as the number of rotations the **drive gear** must make in order to rotate the **driven gear** through one revolution. To obtain a gear ratio, simply divide the number of teeth on the driven gear by the number of teeth on the drive gear. Gear ratios, which are expressed relative to the number one, fall into three categories:

- Direct drive
- Gear reduction
- Overdrive

Direct Drive If two meshed gears are the same size and have the same number of teeth, they will turn at the same speed. Since the drive gear turns once for each revolution of the driven gear, the gear ratio is 1:1; this is called a **direct drive.** When a transmission is in direct drive, the engine and transmission turn at the same speed.

Gear Reduction If one gear drives a second gear that has three times the number of teeth, the smaller drive gear must travel three complete revolutions in order to drive the larger gear through one rotation. See Figure 14–2. Divide the number of teeth on the driven gear by the number of teeth on the drive gear and you get a 3:1 gear ratio (pronounced three to one). This type of gear arrangement, where driven gear speed is slower than drive gear speed, provides **gear reduction.** Gear reduction may also be called underdrive as drive speed is less than, or under, driven speed. Both terms mean the same thing and use is a matter of preference.

Gear reduction is used for the lower gears in a transmission. First gear in a transmission is called "low" gear because output speed, not gear ratio, is low. Low gears have numerically high gear ratios. That is, a 3:1 gear ratio is a lower gear than those with a 2:1 or 1:1 gear ratio. These three ratios taken in order represent a typical upshift pattern from low gear (3:1), to second gear (2:1), to drive gear (1:1).

Overdrive **Overdrive** is the opposite of a gear reduction condition and occurs when a driven gear turns faster than its drive gear. For the gears shown in Figure 14–3, the driven gear turns three times for each turn of the drive gear. The driven gear is said to overdrive the drive gear. For this example, the gear ratio is 0.33:1. Overdrive ratios of 0.65:1 and 0.70:1 are typical of those used in automotive applications.

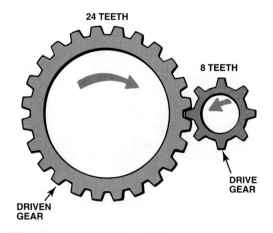

Figure 14–2 The drive gear is attached or is closer to the power source and rotates or drives the driven gear.

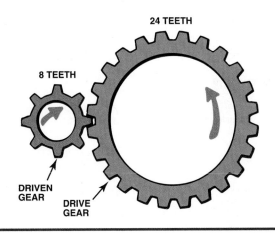

Figure 14–3 If the driven gear is rotating faster than the drive gear, it is called an overdrive ratio.

> **NOTE:** Ratios always end in 1 with a colon in between. Therefore, the first number is less than 1 if it is an overdrive ratio and greater than 1 if it is a gear reduction ratio.

GRAPHS, CHARTS, AND DIAGRAMS

Graph Reading A **graph** is a visual display of information. Graphs are commonly used in the automotive service industry to illustrate trends or specifications along with time or some other variable. A **variable** is a measurement of something that changes, such as engine speed or time. A graph has two variables displayed. One variable changes from left to right on the horizontal axis. This is called the X axis. The other variable is displayed on the vertical axis, called the Y axis.

A graph is created by making a series of dots at various locations and then connecting the dots with a line. See Figure 14–4.

Interpreting a Graph To interpret a graph, select a point along the horizontal axis (X axis) and then look directly above the point

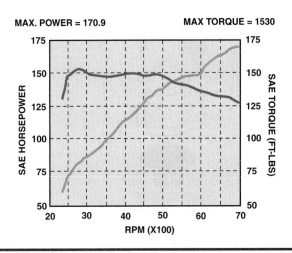

Figure 14–4 A graph showing horsepower and torque. Notice that the curves cross at 5252 RPM or a little bit to the right of the 50, which is expressed in hundreds times 10 (thousands) of RPM.

where the line appears. Mark this spot and then look directly to the left along the vertical axis (Y axis) to see what value is represented by the points on the graph.

Chart Reading A **chart** is used to represent data, such as numbers or specifications, along with another variable, such as model or year of vehicle. A chart is very useful for showing many different specifications or other facts in an easy-to-read format. See Figure 14–5 for an example of a transmission specifications chart, which shows the transmission parts listed along the horizontal axis (X axis) and gear of the automatic transmission along the vertical or Y axis.

Interpreting a Chart A chart can look complicated but if studied, it is easy to interpret. Start by looking along the horizontal or vertical axis for the information, such as model year of the vehicle. Then, look directly above the model year to determine the specification for that particular model year.

RANGE	GEAR	2–4 BAND	REVERSE INPUT CLUTCH	OVERRUN CLUTCH	FORWARD CLUTCH	FORWARD SPRAG CL. ASSEMBLY	3–4 CLUTCH	LO-ROLLER CLUTCH	LO-REV. CLUTCH
PARK-NEUTRAL									
OVERDRIVE	FIRST GEAR				APPLIED	HOLDING		HOLDING	
	SECOND GEAR	APPLIED			APPLIED	HOLDING			
	THIRD GEAR				APPLIED	HOLDING	APPLIED		
	FOURTH GEAR	APPLIED			APPLIED		APPLIED		
DRIVE	FIRST GEAR			APPLIED	APPLIED	HOLDING		HOLDING	
	SECOND GEAR	APPLIED		APPLIED	APPLIED	HOLDING			
	THIRD GEAR			APPLIED	APPLIED	HOLDING	APPLIED		
MANUAL 2ND	FIRST GEAR			APPLIED	APPLIED	HOLDING		HOLDING	
	SECOND GEAR	APPLIED		APPLIED	APPLIED	HOLDING			
MANUAL 1ST	FIRST GEAR			APPLIED		HOLDING		HOLDING	APPLIED
REVERSE	REVERSE		APPLIED						APPLIED

Figure 14–5 A typical chart showing what is applied in what gear in an automatic transmission.

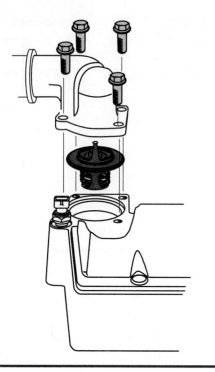

Figure 14–6 An exploded view showing how the thermostat is placed in the engine.

Diagram Reading   A **diagram** is a graphic design that explains or shows the arrangement of parts. Diagrams are commonly used in the automotive service industry to show how a component is assembled and in which order the parts are placed together. See Figure 14–6 for an example.

Interpreting a Diagram   A diagram usually shows the relationship of many parts. Lines are used to show the centerline of the part and the identity of the part is often shown as a number or letter. A separate chart or area of the diagram needs to be looked at to determine the name of the part. Diagrams are most helpful when disassembling or assembling a component, such as a transmission. For best results, use electronic information and print out the diagram so it can be written on and can be thrown away when the repair has been completed. This process also helps prevent getting grease on the pages of a service manual.

SUMMARY

1. Decimals are used in many automotive applications and specifications.
2. Adding and subtracting decimal numbers are needed for many automotive service procedures.
3. A formula is used to determine the volume of something if other values are known.
4. A gear ratio is determined by dividing the number of teeth on the driven gear by the number of teeth on the drive gear.

REVIEW QUESTIONS

1. What is the formula for determining fuel economy?
2. Why are the torque and horsepower of an engine equal at 5252 RPM?
3. What service operation may require the technician to add and subtract?
4. What service operation may require the technician to multiply or divide?

5. How is fuel economy expressed in the metric system?
6. What math function is needed to calculate the overall gear ratio if the transmission and differential ratios are both known?

CHAPTER QUIZ

1. Ten of 30 vehicles checked during a safety inspection had at least one tire that was under inflated. This represents what percentage of the vehicles?
   a. 25%
   b. 33%
   c. 43%
   d. 67%

2. Which of the following shows the relationship of parts?
   a. Chart
   b. Graph
   c. Diagram
   d. Schematic

3. Add 0.102 in. and 0.080 inch. The answer is _____.
   a. 0.182 inch
   b. 0.1082 inch
   c. 0.0082 inch
   d. 0.8200 inch

4. Which is the largest?
   a. 1/10
   b. .25
   c. .375
   d. 1/50

5. What is 26 out of 87 in percentage?
   a. 33.5%
   b. 11.3%
   c. 29.97%
   d. 61.0%

6. What number is being represented by the scientific notation 6.28×10^3?
   a. 6.28
   b. 628
   c. 6,280
   d. 62,800

7. 3/16 is what number in decimal form?
   a. 0.1875
   b. 1.875
   c. 0.5333
   d. 5.333

8. How is 0.183 pronounced?
   a. One hundred eighty-three thousandth
   b. One thousand eighty-three
   c. Zero dot one hundred and eighty-three hundredths
   d. One tenth and 83 hundredths

9. Metric fuel economy is measured in what units?
   a. Miles per gallon
   b. Miles per kilometer
   c. Liters per 100 kilometers
   d. Kilometers per liter

10. Which number is the smallest?
    a. 1/16
    b. .25
    c. 3/8
    d. .33

Chapter 14: Math, Charts, and Calculations

CHECKING YOUR READING STRATEGIES

DISCUSSION AND CRITICAL THINKING QUESTIONS

1. **Preview** the chapter as you have been instructed. *Without reading the chapter itself*, write an outline of the chapter. Leave room to fill in the details later. Use your typographical cues to help you. (Do not include the "Summary" in your outline.) How detailed is it? What do you discover about trying to outline a math chapter that is different from the previous chapters we have considered? Will an outline also work for this discipline, or do you need another organization plan? What other methods might be helpful? Mind maps? Flash cards? Chart? Table? Get creative and explore options that would work best for you.

2. **Preview** the chapter again, this time focusing on all the graphic illustrations. Read all the captions and information in tables, then look carefully at all graphs, tables, and drawings. Next, let your eyes scan over the columns of text. See if you can find where in the paragraphs the illustrated material is explained. What cues are given in the text to tie the illustrations to the words?

3. *Circle the best answer for each of the following questions:*

   1. According to the objectives listed at the beginning of the chapter, this chapter will cover how many points?
      a. Four
      b. One hundred and four
      c. Three
      d. Not enough information to answer the question

   2. How many types of graphic illustrations are used in this chapter? Look through the entire chapter. Select all that apply.
      a. Photographs
      b. Diagrams
      c. Charts
      d. Tables
      e. Graphs
      f. Flow charts
      g. Process diagrams
      h. Pie charts
      i. Shaded boxes (of formulas, theories, sample problems, etc.)

   3. What typographical cues are used in the chapter to highlight important information for you? Select all that apply.
      a. Boldface print
      b. Italicized print
      c. Font size
      d. Font style
      e. Bulleted lists
      f. Underlining
      g. Color of print
      h. Boxes
      i. Shading
      j. Symbols (light bulb, question mark, star, etc.)
      k. Arrows to show direction/order

4. **Preview** the "Summary," the review questions, and the chapter quiz. Read over the review of the concepts and the questions. These are the key points the authors feel you should draw from the chapter. How do the authors tie the concepts back to the text so you would know where

to find the information? Go back and look for it. Make a checkmark in the margin so you will remember this is a key point when you read the chapter.

5. Now go back to the first page of the chapter and **read** the chapter. Move through the chapter section by section. Read first, then decide what information is important for you to know and what is explanatory to illustrate the point. Then, return to the outline you drafted for question 1. Fill in the outline with the information you have determined to be important for you to remember. If you have ruled out the outline, still take notes. Rework sample problems or formulas in your notebook. Make flash cards of formulas. This is a discipline that requires practice, practice, practice! Consider your method as well. **How** did you determine which information was important enough to record?

6. What is more helpful to you in this text—the descriptions in-text or the examples? Why?

7. Look over the tables and graphs. Which one is easier for you to remember? Why?

8. Next, consider the drawings in Figure 14-1 and 14-3. What have the authors done to help you remember their explanation? How effective are these graphics, and why? Make note of other such graphics used in the text and compare them as well, considering which are more helpful for remembering information.

9. Finally, **after reading** the chapter, answer the review questions at the end of the chapter. Take the chapter quiz as well. How well did you do? Which of the strategies used by the authors, or you, helped you the most? Remember these for the future.

GROUP PROJECTS

1. Compare your outline, notes, or flash cards with those of your classmates. Are they all the same? If not, how do they differ? Why do you think that may be? Did someone develop a strategy that you think could work well for you? Ask that person to show you how to use it. Don't be afraid to share strategies; it is not cheating. Next, compare how well you and your classmates did when answering the questions at the end of the text's chapter. Did those of you with the more detailed outline or notes do better? Or were other strategies more helpful? Why or why not?

2. As a group, discuss the benefits of previewing the illustrations in the text before reading, as opposed to waiting to explore them as they come up in the reading.

3. Discuss how helpful it was to practice the example problems before tackling the homework exercises.

4. With the group, consider what the authors do to make this chapter interesting and appealing to you. Consider both the visual components and the information itself. How do page layout and writing style make assigned reading more enjoyable?

5. Discuss with your group what you have learned about the importance of knowing how to convert measurements. Why will it be important for you to understand how and when these conversions are used?

Unit V
Reading Strategies for Natural Sciences

from

Life on Earth

Fifth Edition

by

Teresa Audesirk, Gerald Audesirk, and Bruce E. Byers

The natural sciences comprise the physical sciences and the life sciences. The physical sciences include astronomy, chemistry, geology, physical geography, and physics. The life sciences cover all forms of biology: biology, botany, physiology, and zoology. The purpose of the disciplines is in their name: the root, *sci,* means "to know." Thus, the sciences set out to help us understand, or know, our universe by means of empirical evidence, which is evidence collected through our five senses, allowing us to observe and study the world around us and the life systems within it. Studying the sciences helps you understand the world in which you live and the life circulating within you.

The scientific method was developed to provide a systematic means for observing, recording, and analyzing data. This methodical approach is also evident in the explanation of the accumulated knowledge, as you will see in your textbooks. Therefore, it would be helpful for you to try to think like a scientist as you read and when you experiment. Scientists begin with a question they wish to answer. They then observe their subject to discern as much as they can from the available data. Next, they will experiment with the materials to see how things react to different conditions, such as light or temperature. Experiments are often replicated in order to gain enough data to establish a pattern in order to reach a conclusion. Keep asking yourself the questions *how* and *why.* In order to seek answers, you must question, so do not read science passively.

As with any discipline, understanding the thought processes of the individuals who work in the field will help you understand how they, and you, will approach material. Given the massive quantities of knowledge scientists have accumulated, it is helpful to categorize evidence based on similarities, so look for a good deal of *cataloguing* or *categorizing* of information. You will need to learn the terminology in order to understand the categories, but reviewing word roots, prefixes, and suffixes will help. In the sciences, most names come from Latin and Greek. You will also see that some ordinary words will take on specialized meanings in subjects, and that applies to science. Learning symbols and abbreviations will be important to understanding scientific notation, as will algebra. (Math is definitely used in the sciences, so many schools require that you successfully complete algebra before taking your science courses.)

As with any text, after previewing the science text, you would do well to read the chapter section by section, moving from heading to heading. Expect the reading to go slowly. This is definitely an "information-dense" discipline. This is not easy reading, but it is interesting. Expect to be exposed to many new terms and ideas. Draw diagrams if they will help you remember information, practice sample problems, work with a study group, or meet with the professor if you need to. Do what you need to do and use the methods that work for you to master this important material.

The structure of sciences texts is probably the most organized of all texts given the amount of information to be conveyed and learned. Use the layout of the chapter and the graphic elements to help you sort through the material. Begin with the chapter goals or objectives. These are the important points to be discussed. Pay attention to font sizes, ink color, lists, margin notes, and graphic symbols used to highlight ideas (such as a light bulb or a question mark). The illustrations are great to combine with your notes. Cut-away diagrams enable you to see what the inside and outside of something looks like. Enlargements can help you envision what is invisible to the human eye. If you have the visual image, plus your annotations (notes) with the picture, you can study terms and see the corresponding object together. Pay attention to descriptions of procedures because you may need to use them in the lab or a clinical setting. Tables are great for compiling information or data you need to know, and the fact that they are in the text saves you time so you don't have to construct the table, so use it to your advantage. As you work your way through the chapter, use the chapter summary or review questions as a way to get more out of your reading. By reading either or both of them before reading the chapter itself, you will already be aware of which are the most important points to look for.

The chapter here combines biology with a current topical issue, obesity, to stimulate interest and relevance. In one chapter, everyone learns information that can be readily applied to oneself. You have a body, so refer to your own anatomy and physiology as you read this material. By applying material to yourself, you will make it meaningful and remember it far better than if you try to use rote memorization. The goal is to apply your knowledge, and this chapter is a good one to try out that technique.

chapter 21

Nutrition, Digestion, and Excretion

Now free from anorexia, former supermodel Carré Otis still walks the runways, but no longer in the top fashion shows. Instead, she travels a path to a healthier life.

Case Study   Dying to Be Thin

Ana Carolina Reston at the peak of her modeling career—glamorous, but dying.

ormer supermodel Carré Otis explains, "The sacrifices I made were life threatening. I had entered a world that seemed to support a 'whatever it takes' mentality to maintain abnormal thinness." For many models, performers, and others in the public eye, meeting expectations for thinness is a continuing battle that can lead to eating disorders. At 5 feet 10 inches, Otis once weighed only 100 pounds, giving her a body mass index (BMI) of 14.3. (The World Health Organization considers a BMI below 16 as "starvation.") Now maintaining a healthy weight—at the expense of her modeling career—Otis has become a spokesperson for the National Eating Disorders Association, hoping that she can help others avoid the damage her body suffered.

Otis suffered from two eating disorders, anorexia and bulimia. People with anorexia typically eat very little, and often exercise almost nonstop in an effort to lose still more weight. About half of all anorexics also develop bulimia—binge eating of relatively large amounts of food, followed by self-induced vomiting or overdosing with laxatives to purge the food from their bodies. Anorexics lose muscle mass and often damage their digestive, cardiac, endocrine, and reproductive systems.

Sometimes, the damage proves fatal. In October 2006, Ana Carolina Reston (photo at left), one of Brazil's leading models, was hospitalized for a kidney malfunction. After three weeks in intensive care, she died from multiple organ failure and septicemia (massive infection throughout the bloodstream). At 5 feet 8 inches and 88 pounds, her BMI was only 13.4. Two other extremely thin models, the Uruguayan sisters Luisel and Eliana Ramos, died in 2006 and 2007, respectively, from heart failure probably brought on by anorexia.

Anorexia and bulimia typically strike teenage girls and women in their 20s, who often feel pressured to conform to unrealistic ideals of body size and shape. Because many people with anorexia or bulimia never consult a physician, no one really knows how common these disorders might be. In the United States, health authorities estimate that between 200,000 and a few million people, mostly young women, suffer from anorexia, bulimia, or other eating disorders.

In this chapter, you will learn about the processes of nutrition, digestion, and excretion. As you do, think about how anorexia and bulimia affect the structures and functions of the digestive and urinary tracts. Besides not enough Calories, what specific nutrients might be missing from a "starvation" diet? Why would anorexia and bulimia damage many organs throughout the body? Why are anorexics at risk for heart attacks? ■

21.1 How Do Animals Regulate the Composition of Their Bodies?

In Chapter 19, we introduced the concept of homeostasis—keeping an organism's body within the narrow range of conditions that allows it to survive and reproduce. Nutrition, digestion, and excretion play crucial roles in homeostasis.

A **nutrient** is any substance that an animal needs but cannot synthesize in its own body, and hence must acquire from its environment as it eats or drinks. Nutrients provide animals with both the materials with which to construct their bodies and the energy to fuel their life processes. An animal may obtain nutrients directly in usable form (for example, water, sodium, or glucose); combined into large, complex molecules such as fats or proteins; or as parts of the bodies of plants or other animals that they eat. **Digestion** is the process whereby an animal physically grinds up and chemically breaks down its food, producing small, simple molecules that can be absorbed into the circulatory system. **Nutrition** is a more comprehensive term that includes taking food into the body, converting it into usable forms, absorbing the resulting molecules from the digestive tract into the circulatory system, and using the nutrients in the animal's own metabolism.

When an animal eats or drinks, it never obtains precisely the right mixture of water, minerals, carbohydrates, fats, and proteins that it needs to build and sustain itself. Some components of its food may be indigestible—hair, bone, and cellulose, for example, cannot be digested by most animals. Other substances in food may be harmful, including toxins produced by many plants. An animal's own metabolism produces carbon dioxide and some highly toxic molecules, such as ammonia, that must be eliminated. Finally, an animal may simply consume too much of otherwise useful substances, such as water, sodium, or potassium. **Excretion** is the disposal of these indigestible, toxic, or surplus materials. There is a great diversity of excretory structures and functions in the animal kingdom. As a general rule, however, indigestible food is expelled from the digestive tract as feces (see section 21.5). Carbon dioxide and, in some animals, ammonia and some other toxic molecules are excreted by the respiratory tract (lungs or gills) or the skin. Surplus minerals and most toxic substances, whether eaten or produced by the animal's own metabolism, are excreted by the urinary tract (see sections 21.6, 21.7, and 21.8).

21.2 What Nutrients Do Animals Need?

Animal nutrients fall into six major categories: lipids, carbohydrates, proteins, minerals, vitamins, and water.

The Primary Sources of Energy Are Lipids and Carbohydrates

Cells require a continuous supply of energy to stay alive and perform their functions. In animals, energy is provided mostly by three kinds of nutrients: lipids, carbohydrates and, to a lesser extent, proteins. These molecules, or parts of them, are used in glycolysis and cellular respiration, and the energy derived from them is used to produce ATP (see pp. 100–105).

Energy in food can be measured in **calories,** defined as the energy required to raise the temperature of 1 gram of water by 1 degree Celsius. However, this unit is so small—a single Big Mac with cheese contains 700,000 calories—that it is customary to use **Calories** (with a capital *C*) instead; a Calorie contains 1,000 calories (lowercase *c*). The unit that you see in the "Nutritional Information" tables on cereal boxes and in fast-food restaurants is the Calorie; a Big Mac, for example, contains 700 Calories. The average human body at rest burns about 1,550 Calories per day (usually somewhat more if you're young and/or male; less if you're older and/or female), and people burn more Calories when exercising than when resting (Table 21-1). In a really fit athlete, vigorous exercise can raise energy consumption from a resting rate of about 1 Calorie per minute to nearly 20 Calories per minute.

Lipids Include Fats, Phospholipids, and Cholesterol

Lipids are a diverse group of molecules that includes triglycerides (fats and oils), phospholipids, and cholesterol (see pp. 30–33). Fats and oils are used primarily as a source of energy. Phospholipids are important components of all cellular membranes. Cholesterol is used to manufacture cellular membranes, several hormones including estrogen and testosterone, and bile (which aids in fat digestion).

Table 21-1	Approximate Energy Consumed by a 150-Pound Person Performing Different Activities				
		Time to "Work Off"			
Activity	**Calories/Hour**	**500 Calories (Cheeseburger)**	**300 Calories (Ice Cream Cone)**	**70 Calories (Apple)**	**40 Calories (1 Cup Broccoli)**
Running (6 mph)	700	43 min	26 min	6 min	3 min
Cross-country skiing (moderate)	560	54 min	32 min	7.5 min	4 min
Roller skating	490	1 hr 1 min	37 min	8.6 min	5 min
Bicycling (11 mph)	420	1 hr 11 min	43 min	10 min	6 min
Walking (3 mph)	250	2 hr	1 hr 12 min	17 min	10 min
Frisbee® playing	210	2 hr 23 min	1 hr 26 min	20 min	11 min
Studying	100	5 hr	3 hr	42 min	24 min

Dying to Be Thin

Continued

In her efforts to lose weight, Ana Reston ate almost nothing but tomatoes and apples for several months. These foods contain virtually no fat, so she would have lacked essential fatty acids, damaging her cell membranes.

▲ Figure 21-1 **Fat provides lightweight energy storage** Although their diet consists mostly of sugar (in the nectar of flowers), ruby-throated hummingbirds convert sugars to fat for energy storage prior to migrating in the fall.

Animals of some species can synthesize all of the types of lipids they need. Others must acquire specific lipid building blocks, called **essential fatty acids,** from their food. For example, humans are unable to synthesize linoleic acid, which is required for the synthesis of certain phospholipids. Therefore, we must obtain this essential fatty acid from our diet, mainly from vegetable oils such as safflower or sunflower oil. In most developed nations, obesity is an increasingly serious health problem, so many people rightly try to limit the amount of fat in their diets. However, a truly fat-free diet would be lethal.

Fats Store Energy in Concentrated Form

Humans and most other animals store energy primarily as fat. When an animal eats more Calories than it uses, most of the excess carbohydrates, fats, or proteins are converted to fat for storage. Fats have two major advantages as energy-storage molecules. First, they contain more than twice as much energy per unit weight as either carbohydrates or protein (about 9 Calories per gram for fats compared with about 4 Calories per gram for carbohydrates and proteins). Second, lipids are hydrophobic; that is, they do not dissolve in water. Fat deposits, therefore, do not cause water to accumulate in the body. For both these reasons, fats store more calories with less weight than do other molecules.

Minimizing weight allows an animal to move faster and farther (important for escaping predators, hunting prey, and migrating) and to use less energy for movement (important when food supplies are limited). For example, ruby-throated hummingbirds (Fig. 21-1) migrate across the Gulf of Mexico in the fall. Obviously, the open ocean doesn't provide anything for a hummingbird to eat. Therefore, a ruby-throat that weighs 2 to 3 grams in early summer puts on about 2 grams of fat before migrating. If it stored carbohydrate or protein instead, it would have to gain almost 6 grams to provide the same amount of energy. It probably could barely fly, and certainly couldn't make it across the Gulf before collapsing from exhaustion.

Because people evolved under the same food constraints as other animals did, we have a strong tendency to eat when food is available, even if we aren't really hungry. In addition, foods that are high in fat and sugar usually taste the best. Many people now have access to almost unlimited, high-calorie food, and have jobs that do not require much exercise. Under these circumstances, we often need considerable willpower to avoid becoming overweight.

Carbohydrates Are a Source of Quick Energy

Carbohydrates include simple sugars, as well as longer chains of sugars called polysaccharides (see p. 29). The simple sugar glucose is the primary source of energy for most cells, but the typical diet contains little glucose. During digestion, glucose is derived from the breakdown of more complex carbohydrates, such as sucrose and starch.

Animals, including humans, store the carbohydrate **glycogen**—a large, highly branched chain of glucose molecules—in the liver and muscles. Glycogen provides much of the energy used during exercise, but people typically store less than a pound of it, the equivalent of less than 2,000 Calories. Therefore, marathon runners can go about 20 miles before their glycogen is used up. The expression "hitting the wall" describes the extreme fatigue that long-distance runners experience when their supply of glycogen is gone.

Proteins Provide Amino Acids for Building New Proteins

Protein in the diet serves mainly as a source of amino acids to make the body's own proteins. Dietary protein is broken down in the digestive tract to yield amino acids. In your cells, the amino acids are linked in specific sequences to form the many different proteins specific to your body. Any excess protein in the diet is broken down to extract energy for immediate use or for storage as fat.

Humans can synthesize only 12 of the 20 amino acids commonly used in proteins. The other eight, called **essential amino acids,** must be supplied in the diet. Two additional amino acids are usually synthesized in fairly small amounts, and so are essential for growing children but usually not for adults. Although animal proteins almost always contain sufficient amounts of all of the essential amino acids, many plant proteins are deficient in some, so vegetarians must take steps to avoid protein deficiency. Generally, they need to make sure their diet includes a variety of plants (for example, legumes, grains, and corn) whose proteins collectively provide all of the essential amino acids. Protein deficiency can cause a variety of debilitating conditions, including kwashiorkor, which is seen in some impoverished countries (**Fig. 21-2**).

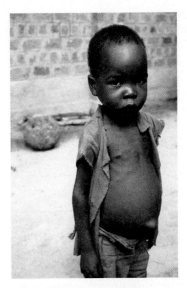

▲ **Figure 21-2 Kwashiorkor** Symptoms of kwashiorkor, caused by protein deficiency, include a swollen abdomen and emaciated arms and legs.

Minerals Are Elements Required by the Body

The term "mineral" has very different meanings in geology and in nutrition. In geology, a mineral is a homogeneous, usually crystalline, element or compound, such as the beautiful crystals often displayed in natural history museums. In nutrition, a **mineral** is specifically a chemical element (not a compound) required for proper bodily function (**Table 21-2**). Because animals cannot manufacture elements, minerals must be obtained through the diet, either from food or dissolved in drinking water. Essential minerals include calcium, magnesium, and phosphorus, which are major constituents of bones and teeth. Others, such as sodium and potassium, are essential for muscle contraction and the conduction of nerve impulses. Iron is used in the production of hemoglobin, and iodine is found in hormones produced by the thyroid gland. In addition, trace amounts of several other minerals, including zinc, copper, and selenium, are required, typically as parts of enzymes.

Vitamins Play Many Roles in Metabolism

Vitamins are a diverse group of organic compounds that animals require in very small amounts. The body cannot synthesize most vitamins (or cannot synthesize them in adequate amounts), so they are normally obtained from food. Convenience foods—doughnuts, soda, and French fries, for example—usually contain lots of Calories but not many vitamins. The vitamins considered essential in human nutrition are listed in **Table 21-3**. These vitamins are often grouped into two categories: water soluble and fat soluble.

Water-Soluble Vitamins

Water-soluble vitamins include vitamin C and the eight compounds that make up the B-vitamin complex. These substances dissolve in the water of

Table 21-2	Minerals, Sources, and Functions in Humans		
Mineral	**Dietary Sources**	**Major Functions in Body**	**Deficiency Symptoms**
Calcium	Milk, cheese, green vegetables, legumes	Bone and tooth formation Blood clotting Nerve impulse transmission	Stunted growth Rickets, osteoporosis Convulsions
Phosphorus	Milk, cheese, meat, poultry, grains	Bone and tooth formation Acid-base balance	Weakness Demineralization of bone Loss of calcium
Potassium	Meats, milk, fruits	Acid-base balance Body water balance Nerve function	Muscular weakness Paralysis
Chlorine	Table salt	Formation of gastric juice Acid-base balance	Muscle cramps Apathy Reduced appetite
Sodium	Table salt	Acid-base balance Body water balance Nerve function	Muscle cramps Apathy Reduced appetite
Magnesium	Whole grains, green leafy vegetables	Activation of enzymes in protein synthesis	Growth failure Behavioral disturbances Weakness, spasms
Iron	Eggs, meats, legumes, whole grains, green vegetables	Constituent of hemoglobin and enzymes involved in energy metabolism	Iron-deficiency anemia (weakness, reduced resistance to infection)
Fluorine	Fluoridated water, tea, seafood	Strengthening teeth and probably bone	High frequency of tooth decay
Zinc	Widely distributed in foods	Constituent of enzymes involved in digestion	Reduced growth rate Small sex glands
Iodine	Seafish and shellfish, dairy products, many vegetables, iodized salt	Constituent of thyroid hormones	Goiter (enlarged thyroid)
Chromium	Fruits, vegetables, whole grains	Metabolism of sugar and fats	Reduced glucose tolerance Elevated insulin in blood

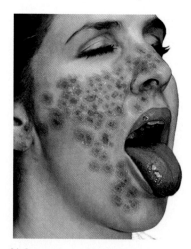

▲ **Figure 21-3 Pellagra** Scaly, reddish brown skin lesions and a red and swollen tongue are caused by a deficiency of niacin, a B vitamin.

the blood plasma and are excreted by the kidneys, so they are not stored in the body in any appreciable amounts. Water-soluble vitamins generally work together with enzymes to promote essential chemical reactions in the body's cells.

Because each vitamin participates in several metabolic processes, a deficiency of a single vitamin can have wide-ranging effects (see Table 21-3). For example, deficiency of niacin, a B vitamin, causes pellagra, associated with cracked, scaly skin as well as digestive and nervous system disorders (Fig. 21-3). In 1996, the U.S. Food and Drug Administration (FDA) ordered folic acid, another B vitamin, to be added to grain foods such as bread, pasta, and rice. The addition of folic acid has reduced the incidence of neural tube defects (serious birth defects of the brain and spinal cord linked to folic acid deficiency in pregnant women) by about 20%. Researchers believe that supplementing food with folic acid has also contributed to a decline in both stroke and heart disease.

Fat-Soluble Vitamins

The fat-soluble vitamins are A, D, E, and K. Vitamin A is used to produce the light-capturing molecule in the retina of the eye, and vitamin A deficiency can cause poor night vision or, in severe cases, blindness. Vitamin D is important for bone formation. Several recent studies have found a high incidence of vitamin D deficiency in the United States, including in urban adolescents, postmenopausal

Table 21-3 **Vitamins, Sources, and Functions in Humans**

Vitamin	Dietary Sources	Functions in Body	Deficiency Symptoms
Water soluble			
B-complex			
Vitamin B$_1$ (thiamin)	Milk, meat, bread	Coenzyme in metabolic reactions	Beriberi (muscle weakness, peripheral nerve changes, edema, heart failure)
Vitamin B$_2$ (riboflavin)	Widely distributed in foods	Constituent of coenzymes in energy metabolism	Reddened lips, cracks at corner of mouth, lesions of eye
Niacin	Liver, lean meats, grains, legumes	Constituent of two coenzymes in energy metabolism	Pellagra (skin and gastrointestinal lesions; nervous mental disorders)
Vitamin B$_6$ (pyridoxine)	Meats, vegetables, whole-grain cereals	Coenzyme in amino acid metabolism	Irritability, convulsions, muscular twitching, dermatitis, kidney stones
Pantothenic acid	Milk, meat	Constituent of coenzyme A, with a role in energy metabolism	Fatigue, sleep disturbances, impaired coordination
Folic acid	Legumes, green vegetables, whole wheat	Coenzyme involved in nucleic and amino acid metabolism	Anemia, gastrointestinal disturbances, diarrhea, retarded growth, birth defects
Vitamin B$_{12}$	Meats, eggs, dairy products	Coenzyme in nucleic acid metabolism	Pernicious anemia, neurological disorders
Biotin	Legumes, vegetables, meats	Coenzymes required for fat synthesis, amino acid metabolism, and glycogen formation	Fatigue, depression, nausea, dermatitis, muscular pains
Others			
Choline	Egg yolk, liver, grains, legumes	Constituent of phospholipids, precursor of the neurotransmitter acetylcholine	None reported in humans
Vitamin C (ascorbic acid)	Citrus fruits, tomatoes, green peppers	Maintenance of cartilage, bone, and dentin (hard tissue of teeth); collagen synthesis	Scurvy (degeneration of skin, teeth, gums, blood vessels; epithelial hemorrhages)
Fat soluble			
Vitamin A (retinol)	Beta-carotene in green, yellow, and red vegetables; retinol added to dairy products	Constituent of visual pigment; maintenance of epithelial tissues	Night blindness, permanent blindness
Vitamin D	Cod-liver oil, eggs, dairy products	Promotes bone growth and mineralization; increases calcium absorption	Rickets (bone deformities) in children; skeletal deterioration
Vitamin E (tocopherol)	Seeds, green leafy vegetables, margarines, shortenings	Antioxidant, prevents cellular damage	Possibly anemia
Vitamin K	Green leafy vegetables; product of intestinal bacteria	Important in blood clotting	Bleeding, internal hemorrhages

women (who may suffer more bone fractures as a result), and African Americans. People with dark skin are at particular risk because vitamin D is synthesized in skin exposed to sunlight, and dark pigmentation reduces the penetration of sunlight to the cells beneath that synthesize vitamin D. Pediatricians are seeing an alarming increase in rickets (Fig. 21-4), particularly in African American children, as a consequence of vitamin D deficiency. Vitamin E is an *antioxidant*, which may help to protect the body against damaging substances that are formed as cells use oxygen to produce high-energy molecules such as ATP. Vitamin K helps regulate blood clotting.

Fat-soluble vitamins can be stored in body fat and may accumulate in the body over time. For this reason, some fat-soluble vitamins (vitamin A, for example) may be toxic if excessive amounts are eaten.

Dying to Be Thin

Continued

People with anorexia usually don't eat a nutritionally balanced diet. Vitamin deficiencies are very common. If their diets lack the essential amino acids, they will suffer from deficiencies of protein metabolism. If anorexics fail to ingest enough of the right minerals, they can develop severe imbalances of sodium, potassium, calcium, and magnesium in their blood and extracellular fluid, which can result in nervous and cardiac disorders.

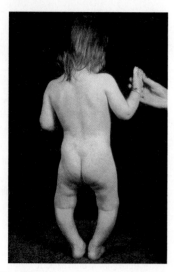

▲ Figure 21-4 **Rickets** The bone deformities (particularly bow legs) that are characteristic of rickets result from vitamin D deficiency.

▲ Figure 21-5 **Food labeling** The U.S. government requires quite complete nutritional labeling of foods, such as in this sample. **QUESTION:** Does this food seem to be a good nutritional choice? Explain.

Web Animation Mechanical and Chemical Breakdown of Food

The Human Body Is About Two-Thirds Water

Water is a crucial part of both the structure and physiology of all animals. For example, water is the principal component of saliva, blood, lymph, extracellular fluid, and the cytoplasm within each cell. Most metabolic reactions occur in a watery solution, and water directly participates in the hydrolysis reactions that break down proteins, carbohydrates, and fats into simpler molecules (see p. 27). As we will see later in this chapter, the kidneys excrete wastes dissolved in the water of urine.

The average adult human requires about 10 cups (2.5 liters) of water per day, but this need can increase dramatically with exercise, high temperatures, or low humidity, as water evaporates from sweat and from our lungs when we breathe. Although people can often survive for weeks without food, death occurs in a few days without water, because we lose so much every day. Water intake occurs mostly through eating and drinking. There is enough water in the typical diet for about half of the usual daily requirement, with the rest obtained by drinking fluids.

Nutritional Guidelines Help People Obtain a Balanced Diet

Most people in the United States are fortunate to live amidst an abundance of food. However, the amazing diversity of foods in a typical U.S. supermarket and the easy availability of fast food can lead to poor nutritional choices. To help people make informed choices, the U.S. government has recently placed nutritional guidelines called "My Pyramid" on an interactive Web site. Another source of information is the nutritional labeling required on commercially packaged foods. These labels provide complete information about Calorie, fiber, fat, sugar, and vitamin content (Fig. 21-5). Also, most fast-food chains provide nutritional information about their products.

Are You Too Heavy?

A simple way to determine whether your weight is likely to pose a health risk is to calculate your body mass index (BMI). The BMI takes into account your weight and height to arrive at an estimate of body fat. This simple calculation assumes that you have an average amount of muscle, so it does not apply to bodybuilders or marathon runners. The formula is as follows: weight (in kilograms)/height^2 (in meters), but you can calculate your BMI by multiplying your weight (in pounds) by 703, then dividing by your height^2 (in inches). Or, simply type "BMI" on your favorite Internet search engine, and you will find many sites that calculate it for you. A BMI between 18.5 and 25 is considered healthy. People with anorexia usually have a BMI of 17.5 or lower. Unless you are a bodybuilder and have far more muscle than average, a BMI between 25 and 30 indicates that you are probably overweight and a BMI over 30 indicates that you are probably obese. "Health Watch: Obesity and the Brain–Gut Connection" on p. 408 explores some potential future treatments for obesity.

21.3 What Are the Major Processes of Digestion?

Animals eat the bodies of other organisms, but these organisms may resist becoming food. Plants, for example, support each cell with a wall of indigestible cellulose. Animals may be covered with indigestible fur, scales, or feathers. In addition, the complex lipids, proteins, and carbohydrates in food cannot be used directly. These nutrients must be broken down before they can be used by the cells of the animal that has consumed them; after being broken down, they are recombined into new molecules. Animals have various types of digestive tracts, each finely tuned for a unique diet and lifestyle. Amid this diversity, however, all digestive systems must accomplish certain tasks:

- **Ingestion.** The food must be brought into the digestive tract through an opening, usually called a mouth.
- **Mechanical breakdown.** In most animals, food must be physically broken down into smaller pieces. The particles produced by mechanical breakdown provide a large surface area for attack by digestive enzymes.
- **Chemical breakdown.** The particles of food must be exposed to digestive enzymes that break down large molecules into smaller subunits.
- **Absorption.** The small molecules must be transported out of the digestive tract and into the body cells. In a few animals, the small molecules may be absorbed directly into the body cells.
- **Elimination.** Indigestible materials must be expelled from the body.

21.4 What Types of Digestive Systems Are Found in Non-Human Animals?

The animal kingdom displays a remarkable diversity of digestive systems, ranging from digestion inside single cells in sponges, to relatively simple sacs in jellyfish and anemones, through an array of tubular digestive systems with two openings in animals as different as earthworms, insects, and humans.

In Sponges, Digestion Occurs Within Individual Cells

Sponges are the only animals that rely exclusively on individual cells to digest their food (Fig. 21-6). As you might suspect, this limits their food to microscopic organisms or particles. Sponges circulate seawater through pores in their bodies.

▼ Figure 21-6 **Intracellular digestion in a sponge** *(a)* Tube sponges in the Virgin Islands. *(b)* Single-celled microorganisms are filtered from the water, and *(c)* are trapped on the outside of the fringed collar of a collar cell, engulfed by phagocytosis, and digested inside the cytoplasm of the collar cell.

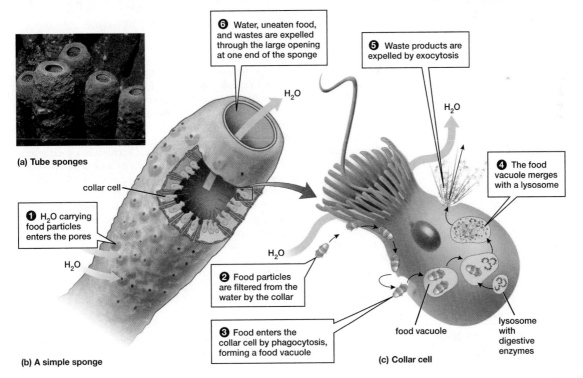

6 Water, uneaten food, and wastes are expelled through the large opening at one end of the sponge

5 Waste products are expelled by exocytosis

H_2O

H_2O

(a) Tube sponges

collar cell

4 The food vacuole merges with a lysosome

1 H_2O carrying food particles enters the pores

H_2O

H_2O

2 Food particles are filtered from the water by the collar

3 Food enters the collar cell by phagocytosis, forming a food vacuole

food vacuole

lysosome with digestive enzymes

(b) A simple sponge

(c) Collar cell

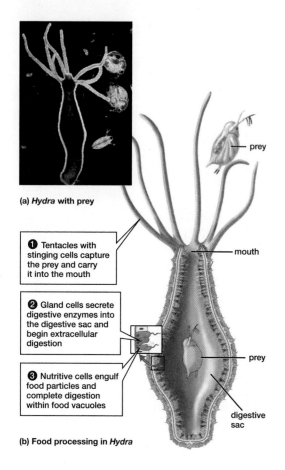

(a) Hydra with prey

❶ Tentacles with stinging cells capture the prey and carry it into the mouth

❷ Gland cells secrete digestive enzymes into the digestive sac and begin extracellular digestion

❸ Nutritive cells engulf food particles and complete digestion within food vacuoles

mouth

prey

digestive sac

(b) Food processing in Hydra

◀ Figure 21-7 **Digestion in a sac** *(a)* A *Hydra* (a cnidarian) has just captured and ingested a waterflea (*Daphnia*, a microscopic crustacean). *(b)* Within the digestive cavity of *Hydra*, enzymes digest the prey into smaller particles and nutrients.

Fringes of plasma membrane on specialized *collar cells* filter microscopic organisms from the water and ingest the prey by phagocytosis (see p. 50). Because the food is so small, mechanical breakdown, which is essential in most digestive systems, is unnecessary. Rather, phagocytosis encloses the food in a small sac called a food vacuole, which basically serves as a temporary, miniature stomach. The vacuole fuses with other sacs called lysosomes, which contain digestive enzymes, and the food is then digested within the vacuole into smaller molecules that can be absorbed into the cell cytoplasm. Undigested remnants of food remain in the vacuole, which eventually expels its contents back into the seawater.

Jellyfish and Their Relatives Have Digestive Systems Consisting of a Sac with a Single Opening

In most other animals, digestion takes place in a chamber within the body where enzymes break down chunks of food. One of the simplest of these chambers is found in cnidarians, such as sea anemones, *Hydra,* and jellyfish. These animals possess a digestive sac with a single opening for ingesting food and ejecting wastes (Fig. 21-7). This opening is generally referred to as the mouth, but it also serves as the anus. The animal's stinging tentacles capture its prey, which is then moved into the digestive sac where enzymes break it down. Cells lining the cavity absorb the nutrients and engulf small food particles. The undigested remains are eventually expelled through the mouth.

Most Animals Have Digestive Systems Consisting of a Tube with Several Specialized Compartments

Most animal species, including worms, mollusks, arthropods, and vertebrates, have a digestive system that is principally a one-way tube through the body. It begins with a mouth and ends with an anus. Such digestive systems usually consist of a series of specialized regions that process food in an orderly sequence, first grinding it up, then breaking it down with enzymes, absorbing the nutrient molecules into the circulatory system, and finally excreting the undigested wastes. This orderly processing in a tube allows the animal to eat more frequent meals than does a saclike digestive system.

The earthworm, which continuously ingests soil as it burrows, is a good example (Fig. 21-8). A tubular digestive system is essential to its way of life. Soil and bits of vegetation enter the mouth and pass through the pharynx and the esophagus to the crop, a thin-walled storage organ. The crop collects the food and gradually passes it to the gizzard. There, bits of sand and muscular contractions grind the food into smaller particles. The food then travels to the intestine, where enzymes digest it into simple molecules that can be absorbed by the cells lining the intestine and, ultimately, into the circulatory system. Indigestible material passes out through the anus.

Different species of animals show a remarkable diversity of digestive tracts. There are specializations for capturing and ingesting food, such as the slender bills and long tongues of hummingbirds, the sharp canines and meat-slicing molars of

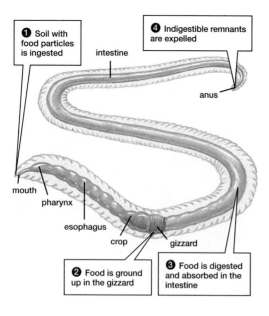

❶ Soil with food particles is ingested

intestine

❹ Indigestible remnants are expelled

anus

mouth

pharynx

esophagus

crop

gizzard

❷ Food is ground up in the gizzard

❸ Food is digested and absorbed in the intestine

◀ Figure 21-8 **Tubular digestive systems** The earthworm has a one-way digestive system that passes food through a series of compartments, each specialized to play a specific role in breaking down food and absorbing it.

tigers, and the pincers of lobsters and ants. The digestive tracts of carnivores tend to be short and simple, because meat is fairly easy to digest. Herbivores, however, often have chambers housing bacteria that digest the abundant cellulose found in plants, because the herbivores themselves cannot produce cellulose-digesting enzymes. Some animals, such as spiders, inject enzymes into their prey, so that the prey is actually digested outside of the spider's body and the spider slurps up the resulting liquid diet.

21.5 How Do Humans Digest Food?

Like most other animals, humans have a tubular digestive tract with several compartments in which food is broken down—first physically and then chemically (Fig. 21-9). Nearly everything of nutritional value is extracted and absorbed into

◄ **Figure 21-9 The human digestive system** The digestive system includes both the digestive tube, consisting of the oral cavity, pharynx, esophagus, stomach, small intestine, and large intestine; and organs such as the salivary glands, liver, gallbladder, and pancreas, which produce and store digestive secretions. **QUESTION:** Why is the stomach both muscular and expandable?

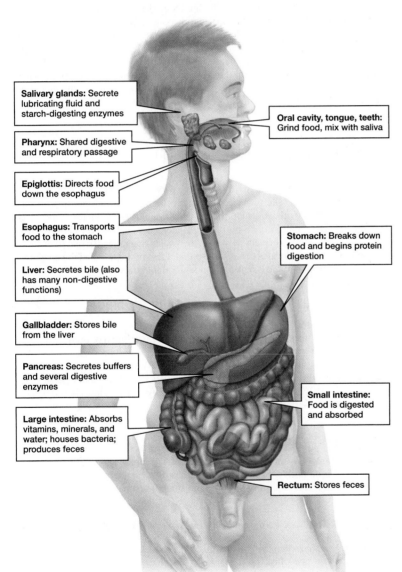

Salivary glands: Secrete lubricating fluid and starch-digesting enzymes

Pharynx: Shared digestive and respiratory passage

Epiglottis: Directs food down the esophagus

Esophagus: Transports food to the stomach

Liver: Secretes bile (also has many non-digestive functions)

Gallbladder: Stores bile from the liver

Pancreas: Secretes buffers and several digestive enzymes

Large intestine: Absorbs vitamins, minerals, and water; houses bacteria; produces feces

Oral cavity, tongue, teeth: Grind food, mix with saliva

Stomach: Breaks down food and begins protein digestion

Small intestine: Food is digested and absorbed

Rectum: Stores feces

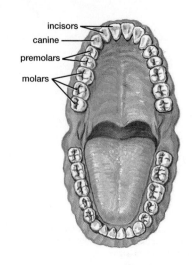

incisors
canine
premolars
molars

◀ **Figure 21-10 Teeth begin the mechanical breakdown of food** Human teeth allow us to process a wide range of foods. The human mouth contains teeth specialized for a variety of functions: flat incisors for biting, pointed canines for tearing, and premolars and molars for crushing and grinding.

the circulatory system. Digesting and absorbing food requires coordinated action from the various structures of the digestive system.

Breakdown of Food Begins in the Mouth

You take a bite, you salivate, and you begin chewing. This begins both the mechanical and chemical breakdown of food. In humans and other mammals, the mechanical work is done mostly by teeth. In adult humans, 32 teeth of varying shapes and sizes tear, cut, and grind food into small pieces (Fig. 21-10).

While the food is being pulverized by the teeth, the first phase of chemical digestion begins as three pairs of salivary glands pour saliva into the mouth. Saliva has many functions. It contains the digestive enzyme amylase, which begins the breakdown of starches into sugar. Saliva also contains a bacteria-killing enzyme and antibodies that help to guard against infection. It lubricates food to facilitate swallowing and dissolves some food molecules, such as acids and sugars, carrying them to taste buds on the tongue. The taste buds bear sensory receptors that help to identify the type and the quality of the food.

The Pharynx Connects the Mouth to the Rest of the Digestive System

With the help of the muscular tongue, the food is manipulated into a mass and pressed backward into the **pharynx,** a muscular cavity connecting the mouth with the esophagus (Fig. 21-11a). The pharynx also connects the nose and mouth with the larynx, which leads to the trachea, the tube that conducts air to the lungs. This arrangement occasionally causes problems, as anyone who has ever choked on a piece of food can attest. Normally, however, the swallowing reflex (triggered by food entering the pharynx) elevates the larynx, so that a flap of tissue called the epiglottis blocks off the opening to the larynx and guides food into the esophagus (Fig. 21-11b).

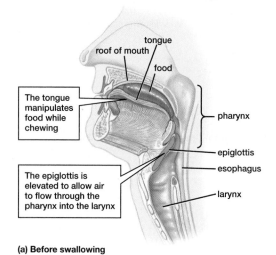

tongue
roof of mouth
food

The tongue manipulates food while chewing

The epiglottis is elevated to allow air to flow through the pharynx into the larynx

pharynx
epiglottis
esophagus
larynx

(a) Before swallowing

The Esophagus Conducts Food to the Stomach

Swallowing forces food into the **esophagus,** a muscular tube that propels the food from the mouth to the stomach. Muscles surrounding the esophagus produce a wave of contraction that begins just above the swallowed food and progresses down the esophagus, forcing the food toward the stomach. This muscular action, called **peristalsis,** occurs throughout the digestive tract, and is so effective that a person can actually swallow while upside-down. Mucus secreted by cells that line the esophagus helps to protect the lining from abrasion and lubricates the food during its passage.

The Stomach Stores and Breaks Down Food

The human **stomach** is an expandable muscular sac capable of holding as much as a gallon of food and liquids. The stomach has three primary functions. First, it stores food and releases it gradually into the small intestine at a rate suitable for

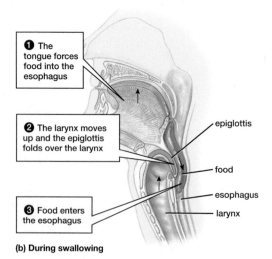

❶ The tongue forces food into the esophagus

❷ The larynx moves up and the epiglottis folds over the larynx

❸ Food enters the esophagus

epiglottis
food
esophagus
larynx

(b) During swallowing

◀ **Figure 21-11 The challenge of swallowing (a)** Swallowing is complicated by the fact that both the esophagus (part of the digestive system) and the larynx (part of the respiratory system) open into the pharynx. **(b)** During swallowing, the larynx moves upward beneath the epiglottis. The epiglottis folds down over the larynx, sealing off the opening to the respiratory system and directing food down the esophagus instead.

proper digestion and absorption. Second, the stomach assists in the mechanical breakdown of food. Its muscular walls produce a variety of churning movements that break up large pieces of food. The third function of the stomach is to break food down chemically.

Glands in the stomach lining secrete hydrochloric acid, a protein called pepsinogen, and mucus. The hydrochloric acid gives the fluid in the stomach a pH of 1 to 3 (about the same as lemon juice). This kills many microbes that are inevitably swallowed along with food. Pepsinogen is the inactive precursor of a protein-digesting enzyme called pepsin. The stomach's acidity converts pepsinogen to pepsin, which then begins digesting the proteins in food. Why not just secrete pepsin in the first place? The glands secrete pepsinogen because pepsin would digest the very cells that manufacture it before it ever got into the stomach. Finally, mucus coats the stomach lining and serves as a barrier to self-digestion. The protection, however, is not perfect, so the cells lining the stomach must be replaced every few days.

Food in the stomach is gradually converted to a thick, acidic liquid called **chyme,** which consists of partially digested food and digestive secretions. Peristaltic waves (about three per minute) propel the chyme toward the small intestine. A ring of muscle at the lower end of the stomach allows only about a teaspoon of chyme to enter the small intestine with each contraction. It takes 2 to 6 hours, depending on the size of the meal, to empty the stomach completely.

Although digestion begins in the stomach, almost no absorption of nutrients occurs there. Only a few substances, including water, alcohol, and some other drugs, can enter the bloodstream through the stomach wall.

Most Digestion Occurs in the Small Intestine

The **small intestine** is about 1 inch in diameter and 10 feet long in a living human adult. The small intestine digests food into small molecules and absorbs these molecules into the bloodstream. The first role of the small intestine—digestion—is accomplished with the aid of secretions from three sources: the liver, the pancreas, and the cells of the small intestine itself.

The Liver and Gallbladder Provide Bile

The **liver** has many functions, including storing glycogen and detoxifying many poisonous substances. Its role in digestion is to produce **bile,** a complex mixture of bile salts, other salts, water, and cholesterol. Bile is stored in the **gallbladder** (see Fig. 21-9) and released into the small intestine through a tube called the bile duct. Although they help in the digestion of lipids, bile salts are not enzymes. Rather, much like dish detergent, bile salts have a hydrophobic part that interacts with fats and a hydrophilic part that dissolves in water. As a result, bile salts disperse chunks of fat into microscopic particles, exposing a large surface area to attack by lipid-digesting enzymes produced by the pancreas.

The Pancreas Secretes Digestive Substances

The **pancreas** consists of two major types of cells. One type produces hormones that help to regulate blood sugar (as we shall see in Chapter 23), and the other produces a digestive secretion called **pancreatic juice.** About a quart of pancreatic juice is released into the small intestine each day. This secretion contains water, sodium bicarbonate, and several digestive enzymes that break down carbohydrates, lipids, and proteins. Sodium bicarbonate (the active ingredient in baking soda) neutralizes the acidic chyme in the small intestine, producing a slightly basic pH. In contrast to the stomach's digestive enzymes, which require an acidic pH, pancreatic digestive enzymes require a slightly basic pH to function properly.

The Intestinal Wall Completes Digestion and Absorbs Nutrients

The wall of the small intestine contains cells that complete the digestive process and absorb the small molecules that result. Digestive enzymes are actually

---

Dying to Be Thin

Continued

When someone with bulimia vomits, the contents of the stomach erupt back through the esophagus, pharynx, and mouth. These structures do not have the thick mucous layer that protects the stomach, so the stomach acid burns away the cells of their linings. Further, the acid dissolves the enamel of the teeth, so that prolonged bulimia can lead to significant tooth loss.

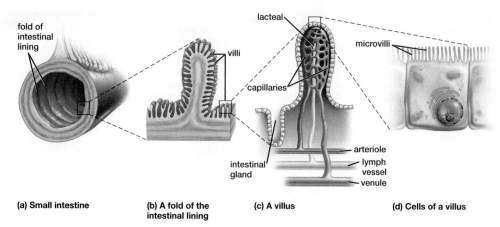

(a) Small intestine

(b) A fold of the intestinal lining

(c) A villus

(d) Cells of a villus

▲ Figure 21-12 **The small intestine** *(a)* The folds of the small intestine maximize the surface area available to absorb nutrients. *(b)* Large folds in the intestinal lining are themselves carpeted with tiny, finger-like projections called villi, *(c)* which enclose a network of capillaries and a lymph vessel, or lacteal. *(d)* If we use a microscope to zoom in on one villus, we see that the epithelial cells on its surface are sheathed in plasma membranes that have yet another level of microscopic projections, microvilli. **QUESTION:** What might the anatomy of the small intestine be like if its folds, villi, and microvilli had not evolved?

embedded in the plasma membranes of the cells that line the small intestine, so the final phase of digestion occurs as the nutrient is being absorbed into the cell. As in the stomach, the small intestine is protected from digesting itself by mucus, which is secreted by specialized cells in its lining.

Most Absorption Occurs in the Small Intestine

The small intestine is the major site of nutrient absorption into the blood. The small intestine has numerous folds and projections, giving it an internal surface area about 600 times greater than a smooth tube of the same length (Fig. 21-12a,b). Finger-like projections called **villi** (singular, villus) cover the entire surface of the intestinal wall (Fig. 21-12c). Villi, which range from 0.5 to 1.5 millimeters in length, give the intestinal lining a velvety appearance to the naked eye. Each individual cell of a villus bears a fringe of microscopic projections called **microvilli** (Fig. 21-12d). Collectively, these projections of the small intestine wall give it a surface area of more than 2,700 square feet (about 250 square meters)—almost the size of a tennis court.

Contractions of the circular muscles of the intestine slosh the chyme back and forth, bringing nutrients into contact with the absorptive surface of the small intestine. Within each villus is a network of blood capillaries and a single lymph capillary, called a *lacteal* (see Fig. 21-12c). Most nutrients, including water, simple sugars, amino acids, vitamins, and minerals, pass through the cells lining the small intestine and enter the capillaries. The breakdown products of fat (glycerol and fatty acids), however, take a different route. After diffusing into the cells lining the small intestine, they are resynthesized into fats, coated with protein, and then released as particles into the extracellular fluid within the villi. These particles are far too large to enter the blood capillaries, but they can pass through the lacteal wall. Suspended in lymph, the particles move from the lacteals through other lymph vessels, and are eventually delivered to the bloodstream when the lymph vessels empty into the veins (see pp. 382–384).

The Large Intestine Absorbs Water, Minerals, and Vitamins, and Forms Feces

The **large intestine** in a living human adult is about 5 feet long and 3 inches in diameter. The large intestine has two parts. For most of its length it is called the **colon;** its final 6-inch compartment is called the **rectum.** The leftovers of digestion flow from the small intestine into the colon: a mixture of water, minerals, indigestible fibers (mostly cellulose, from the cell walls of vegetables and fruits), and small amounts of undigested fats and proteins. The colon contains a flourishing bacterial population that lives on these nutrients. These bacteria synthesize vitamin B_{12}, thiamin, riboflavin, and, most importantly, vitamin K, which would otherwise be deficient in a typical diet. Cells lining the large intestine absorb these vitamins as well as water and minerals.

After absorption is complete, the result is the semisolid **feces,** consisting mostly of indigestible wastes and bacteria (about one-third of the dry weight of feces). The feces are transported by peristaltic movements until they reach the rectum, where expansion of this chamber stimulates the urge to defecate.

Digestion Is Controlled by the Nervous System and Hormones

When you eat, your body coordinates the events that convert food into nutrients circulating in your blood. The secretions and muscular activity of the digestive tract are regulated by both nerves and hormones.

Sensory Signals Initiate Digestion

The sight, smell, taste, and sometimes just the thought of food generate signals from the brain that act on many parts of the digestive tract. For example, nerve impulses stimulate the salivary glands and cause the stomach to begin secreting acid and mucus. As food moves through the digestive tract, its bulk stimulates local nervous reflexes that cause peristalsis.

Hormones Help Regulate Digestive Activity

There are at least a couple of dozen hormones that control appetite, satiation, and digestion. Here, we discuss only four major hormones, all secreted by the digestive system. These enter the bloodstream, circulate through the body, and act on specific receptors within the digestive tract. Like most hormones, they are regulated by negative feedback. For example, nutrients in chyme such as amino acids and peptides from protein digestion stimulate cells in the stomach lining to release the hormone *gastrin* into the bloodstream. Gastrin travels back to the stomach cells and stimulates further acid secretion, which promotes protein digestion. When the stomach contents become sufficiently acidic, gastrin secretion is inhibited, which in turn inhibits further acid secretion.

In response to chyme, the cells of the small intestine release *secretin* and *cholecystokinin*. These hormones stimulate the release of digestive fluids into the small intestine: bicarbonate and digestive enzymes from the pancreas and bile from the liver and gallbladder. *Gastric inhibitory peptide*, produced by cells of the small intestine in response to fatty acids and sugars in chyme, stimulates the pancreas to release insulin, which stimulates many body cells to absorb sugar. Gastric inhibitory peptide (as its name suggests) also inhibits both acid production and peristalsis in the stomach. As a result, it slows the rate at which chyme is pumped into the small intestine, providing additional time for digestion and absorption to occur.

A host of other hormones also regulate appetite, the sensation of fullness, and the rate at which food is metabolized. Some of these offer hope for controlling weight gain and obesity, as we discuss in the "Health Watch: Obesity and the Brain–Gut Connection" on p. 408.

21.6 What Are the Functions of Urinary Systems?

We may load our digestive tracts with pepperoni pizza, hot fudge sundaes, and coffee, but our cells must remain bathed in a precisely regulated solution of salts and nutrients. The digestive system is relatively unselective, so that any molecule that *can* be absorbed into the circulatory system through the small intestine *is* absorbed, whether the molecule is useful or toxic, needed immediately or already available in excess. How does the animal body, then, maintain homeostasis, fine-tuning and

health watch

Obesity and the Brain–Gut Connection

In 2006, medical experts estimated that about 65% of American adults were overweight; about half of these were obese (defined as a body mass index of more than 30—that's a 5-foot 6-inch woman weighing about 185 pounds, or a 5-foot 10-inch man weighing about 210 pounds). Overweight people have traditionally been told to eat less and exercise more. While that's good advice, it clearly isn't stemming the rise in obesity in the United States and many other countries around the world. And obesity isn't just a matter of personal health or fitting into airline seats. In the United States, every year, obesity is estimated to cost more than $100 billion in medical expenses and reduced productivity on the job, and to contribute to 300,000 deaths.

For at least the past half-century, diet books have appeared on bookshelves with depressing frequency, each claiming to be the answer to the prayers of the overweight. Diet pills have been around for decades, too, but most either have little long-term effect or are dangerous. Many overweight people diet strenuously for a few weeks, lose a few pounds, and find themselves a few months later just as heavy as before. Can anything really be done?

Maybe soon, something can be. Researchers have discovered a bewildering array of hormones that are produced by the digestive tract and act on the brain, influencing appetite, satiation, and metabolism. In 1994, Jeffrey Friedman of Rockefeller University discovered a hormone, synthesized by fat cells, that travels to the brain and suppresses appetite. Perhaps optimistically, Friedman called the hormone *leptin*, after a Greek word meaning thin. Many people hoped that a simple injection of leptin would suppress appetite in overweight people, so they could comfortably eat less and lose weight. No such

luck. It turns out that obese people make plenty of leptin, more than lean people do, but their brains don't respond to it.

Since then, researchers have found additional eating-related hormones, some of which look a lot more promising than leptin. Two of these hormones, with opposing effects on appetite and satiation, are ghrelin and peptide YY (often called PYY) (Fig. E21-1). When the stomach has been empty for a few hours, it churns out ghrelin, which travels to the brain and stimulates hunger. After a meal, ghrelin levels drop dramatically. Food in the intestines causes PYY to be produced, which travels to the brain to reduce hunger. Unfortunately, in dieters and overweight people, both ghrelin and PYY act in ways that make dieting hard and eating easy. Ghrelin levels increase when people diet and lose weight, which makes them feel hungrier and hungrier. Obese people also generally produce less PYY after a meal, so they don't feel full even though they've eaten enough food.

These two hormones are attractive targets for weight control. In 2006, researchers at the

Scripps Research Institute successfully vaccinated rats against ghrelin. The vaccines caused the rats to produce antibodies that bind ghrelin, so it can't get to the brain and stimulate hunger. The vaccinated rats ate normally, but gained less weight than control rats, indicating that their metabolism might have increased. Also in 2006, Nastech Pharmaceutical Company started clinical trials of a PYY nasal spray in people. When sprayed into the nose, PYY apparently penetrates to the brain and reduces appetite.

Will these new treatments help people to lose weight and keep it off? Or will other pathways in the body compensate for too much PYY or not enough ghrelin? Appetite, metabolism, and satiation are controlled by complex, interacting mechanisms, and it's too early to tell if treatments targeting ghrelin and PYY will work. Nevertheless, someday biomedical science may solve enough of the puzzle of weight gain and weight loss to produce effective treatments. For hundreds of millions of people around the world, that day can't come soon enough.

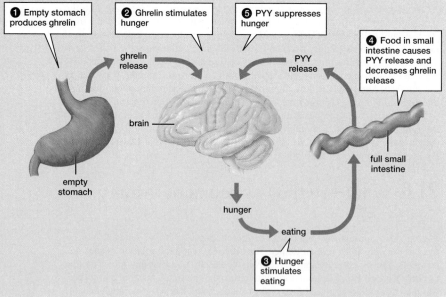

▶ Figure E21-1 **Hunger and satiation are regulated by hormones** The digestive tract produces ghrelin and PYY, which interact to regulate appetite, fullness, and probably metabolism.

❶ Empty stomach produces ghrelin

❷ Ghrelin stimulates hunger

❺ PYY suppresses hunger

❹ Food in small intestine causes PYY release and decreases ghrelin release

ghrelin release

PYY release

brain

empty stomach

full small intestine

hunger

eating

❸ Hunger stimulates eating

precisely regulating its internal environment? The skin, digestive tract, and respiratory system all play a role. However, eliminating harmful substances and excess nutrients while retaining useful substances is primarily the domain of the urinary system.

Whether we consider flatworms, fishes, or people, all urinary systems function similarly. First, the blood or other body fluids are filtered, with water and small dissolved molecules moving from the blood into the urinary system. Next, nutrients are selectively reabsorbed back into the blood. Often, highly toxic substances that must be removed very quickly are actively secreted from the blood into the urinary system. Finally, wastes and excess nutrients, dissolved in variable amounts of water, are excreted from the body.

21.7 What Types of Urinary Systems Are Found in Non-Human Animals?

There are nearly as many types of urinary systems (in invertebrates, these are usually called excretory systems) as there are phyla of animals. In a few, such as sponges, individual cells merely dump their wastes into the surrounding water. Most animals, however, have complex urinary systems, often under nervous and hormonal control, that precisely regulate which substances are excreted and which are kept in the body's fluids. These mechanisms ensure that the internal chemical composition of the animal remains fairly constant, despite enormous changes in its diet or living conditions. Here, we discuss only two of the many types of excretory systems in invertebrates.

Flame Cells Filter Fluids in Flatworms

The freshwater flatworm lives in streams. Because it constantly absorbs water by osmosis, it must excrete the water or else it will explode. Therefore, the major function of its excretory system is to regulate water balance. The flatworm's excretory system consists of a network of tubes that branch throughout the body (**Fig. 21-13**). At intervals, the branches end blindly in single-celled bulbs called flame cells. Water and dissolved substances are filtered from the body into the bulbs, where a cluster of beating cilia (that reminded their discoverers of the flickering flame of a candle) produces a current that forces the fluid through the tubes. Within the tubes, more wastes are added and some nutrients are reabsorbed. The resulting solution is expelled through pores in the body surface. Flatworms also have a large surface area through which many cellular wastes leave by diffusion.

Nephridia Filter Fluids in Earthworms

Earthworms, mollusks, and several other invertebrates have simple filtering structures called *nephridia* (singular, nephridium) that resemble the filtering structures that we will examine in vertebrate kidneys. The earthworm body is composed of repeating segments, and nearly every segment contains its own pair of nephridia. Fluid fills the body cavity that surrounds the earthworm's internal organs. This fluid collects both wastes and nutrients from the blood and tissues. The fluid is moved by cilia into a narrow, tubelike portion of the nephridium (**Fig. 21-14**). Here, salts and other dissolved nutrients are absorbed back into the blood, leaving water and wastes behind. The resulting urine is stored in an enlarged bladder-like portion of the nephridium and is excreted through an excretory pore in the body wall.

21.8 How Does the Human Urinary System Work?

Urinary systems of all vertebrates, including humans, face major challenges. Urine formation begins by filtering the blood. Size, however, is the only criterion for filtration—anything small enough to fit through the pores of the filter will leave the

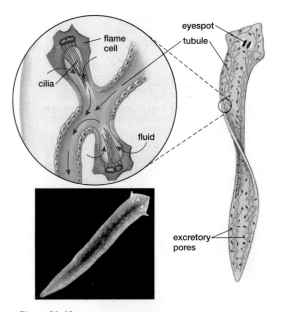

▲ **Figure 21-13 The simple excretory system of a flatworm** In the flatworm (inset), hollow flame cells direct excess water and dissolved wastes into a network of tubes. The beating cilia of the flame cells help move the fluid to excretory pores.

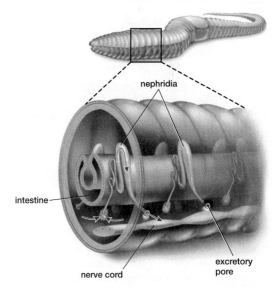

▲ **Figure 21-14 The excretory system of the earthworm** This system consists of structures called nephridia, one pair per segment. Fluid is drawn into one end of the nephridia, and urine is released at the other end through an excretory pore.

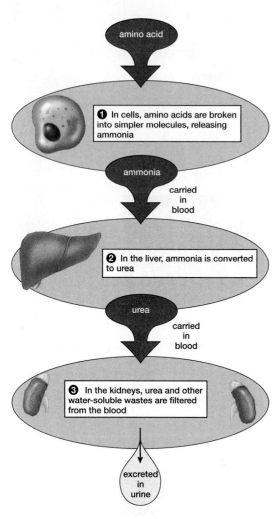

◀ Figure 21-15 **A flow diagram showing the formation and excretion of urea** QUESTION: In some animals, ammonia is not converted into urea but, instead, circulates in the blood until it is excreted. In what types of environments would you expect to find such animals?

blood and enter the urinary system. Therefore, not only wastes, but also water and nutrients that the body cannot afford to lose, are filtered out. In humans and many other vertebrates, the kidneys have evolved complex internal structures and metabolic abilities that eliminate wastes while retaining most of the water and nutrients.

The Human Urinary System Produces, Transports, and Excretes Urine

The **kidneys** are organs in which the fluid portion of the blood is collected and filtered. From this fluid, water and important nutrients are then reabsorbed into the blood. The remaining fluid, called **urine**—consisting of toxic substances, cellular waste products, excess vitamins, salts, some hormones, and water—stays behind to be excreted from the body. The rest of the urinary system channels and stores urine until it is eliminated from the body.

The Urinary System Is Crucial for Homeostasis

The urinary system of humans and other vertebrates helps maintain homeostasis in the body in several ways. These include:

- Regulating blood levels of minerals and other ions such as sodium, potassium, chloride, and calcium.
- Regulating the water content of the blood.
- Maintaining the proper pH of the blood.
- Retaining important nutrients such as glucose and amino acids in the blood.
- Eliminating cellular waste products such as urea. When amino acids are used in cells as a source of energy or for the synthesis of new molecules, ammonia (NH_3) is produced as a by-product. Ammonia is very toxic. In mammals, the liver converts ammonia to urea, a far less toxic substance (Fig. 21-15). In the kidneys, urea is filtered from the blood and ultimately excreted in the urine.

Web Animation Human Urinary System Anatomy

The Urinary System Consists of the Kidneys, Ureter, Urinary Bladder, and Urethra

Human kidneys are paired organs located on either side of the spinal column, slightly above the waist (Fig. 21-16). Each is approximately 5 inches long, 3 inches wide, and 1 inch thick. Blood enters each kidney through a renal artery. After the blood has been filtered, it exits through a renal vein. The kidneys produce urine that leaves each kidney through a narrow, muscular tube called the **ureter.** Using peristaltic contractions, the ureters transport urine to the **urinary bladder.** This hollow, muscular chamber collects and stores the urine. During urination, contraction of the bladder forces the urine out of the body through the **urethra,** a single narrow tube about 1.5 inches long in women and about 8 inches long in men.

Urine Is Formed in the Nephrons of the Kidneys

Each kidney contains a solid outer layer where urine forms and an inner chamber that collects urine and funnels it into the ureter (Fig. 21-17). The outer layer of each kidney contains about a million tiny individual tubes, called **nephrons,** which filter the blood, process the filtered fluid, and form urine. Each nephron

Dying to Be Thin

Continued

The malnutrition, vomiting, and laxative use that accompany anorexia and bulimia often wreak havoc with the body's absorption of minerals such as sodium, potassium, and calcium. Despite heroic efforts, the kidneys often cannot maintain the proper concentrations of these minerals in the bloodstream. When mineral homeostasis fails, nervous disorders, heart attacks, or multiple organ failure may result.

▶ Figure 21-16 **The human urinary system** Diagrammatic view of the human urinary system and its blood supply. **QUESTION:** Why is there such an extensive blood supply to the kidneys and the individual nephrons?

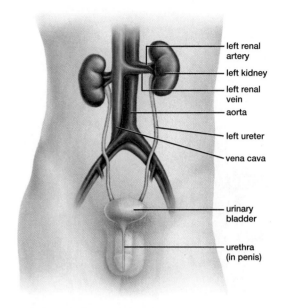

has three major parts (Fig. 21-18): (1) the **glomerulus,** a dense knot of capillaries from which fluid is filtered from the blood and collected into (2) a surrounding cuplike structure, called **Bowman's capsule,** which funnels the fluid into (3) a long, twisted **tubule.** The Bowman's capsule channels fluid into the **proximal tubule.** The fluid then moves through the **loop of Henle** and the **distal tubule.** Different portions of the tubule selectively modify the fluid as it travels through them. In the tubule, nutrients are selectively reabsorbed from the fluid back into the blood, while wastes and some of the water are left behind to form urine. Additional wastes are also secreted into the tubule from the blood. Finally, the distal tubules of multiple nephrons drain into a **collecting duct,** which conducts urine into the renal pelvis, a hollow, funnel-like structure in the center of the kidney that connects with the ureter.

Blood Is Filtered by the Glomerulus

Urine formation starts with the process of **filtration** (Fig. 21-19, step **❶**). Blood enters each nephron by an arteriole that branches from the renal artery. Within the cup-shaped portion of the nephron—Bowman's capsule—the arteriole branches into numerous capillaries that form the mass of the glomerulus (see Fig. 21-18). The walls of these capillaries are extremely permeable to water and small dissolved molecules, but blood cells and most proteins are too large to be filtered out, so they remain in the blood. Blood pressure within the capillaries drives water and dissolved substances from the blood out through the capillary walls. The resulting watery fluid, called the **filtrate,** is collected in Bowman's capsule, beginning its journey through the rest of the nephron.

Web Animation Urine Formation

The Filtrate Is Converted to Urine in the Tubules of the Nephron

The filtrate collected in Bowman's capsule contains a mixture of wastes, essential nutrients, and a lot of water. In fact, in the average adult human, 8 quarts (about 7.5 liters) of fluid are filtered into the nephrons *every hour*. When you consider that a human has only a little over 5 quarts (about 5 liters) of blood, and only a little over 3 quarts (about 3 liters) of that is water, you can appreciate how important it is for the kidneys to reclaim almost all of the water that is filtered. Normally, a person produces only about 1.5 quarts (1.5 liters) of urine each day, so more than 99% of the water is returned to the blood.

Overall, therefore, the nephrons must restore the nutrients and most of the water to the blood while retaining wastes for elimination. This task is accomplished by two processes: tubular reabsorption and tubular secretion.

Tubular Reabsorption Moves Water and Nutrients from the Nephron to the Blood   From Bowman's capsule, the filtrate passes through the proximal tubule, which is surrounded by capillaries. Most of the water and nutrients in the filtrate move from the proximal tubule into the capillaries in a process called **tubular reabsorption** (Fig. 21-19, step **❷**). The cells of the proximal tubule actively transport salts and other nutrients, such as amino acids and glucose, out of the tubule and into the surrounding extracellular fluid. The nutrient molecules then diffuse from the extracellular fluid into the adjacent capillaries. Water follows the nutrients

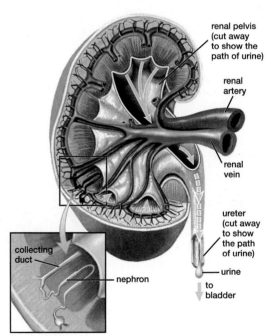

▶ Figure 21-17 **Cross section of a kidney** The cross section shows the blood supply and internal structure of a kidney. A single nephron (inset), considerably enlarged, is drawn to show the orientation of nephrons in the kidney and their connection to a collecting duct. Collecting ducts empty urine into the renal pelvis, which drains into the ureter. Yellow arrows show the pathway of urine flow.

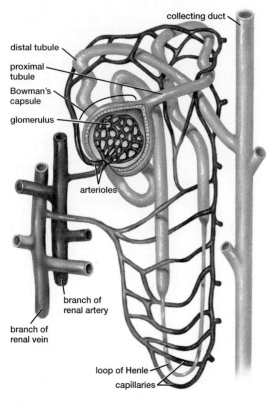

▲ Figure 21-18 **An individual nephron and its blood supply**

out of the tubule and into the capillaries by osmosis. Wastes such as urea remain in the tubule and become more concentrated as water leaves.

Tubular Secretion Moves Wastes from the Blood into the Nephron   In **tubular secretion,** wastes such as hydrogen ions, potassium, ammonia, and many drugs are moved from the capillaries into the nephron (**Fig. 21-19**, step ❸). Typically, the cells of the distal tubule actively transport wastes from the surrounding extracellular fluid into the tubule. Lowering the concentration of wastes in the extracellular fluid produces a concentration gradient so that the wastes passively diffuse out of the capillaries.

Why bother with tubular secretion, when these wastes are mostly small molecules that can enter the nephron by filtration anyway? Because many of these wastes, such as acid and ammonia, are extremely toxic, even the rapid filtration of the blood into Bowman's capsule cannot remove them from the blood fast enough. Tubular secretion speeds up the process of ridding the body of these dangerous substances.

Urine Becomes Concentrated in the Collecting Ducts

Finally, in the collecting ducts, **concentration** of urine may occur through the removal of water (**Fig. 21-19**, step ❹). When mammals (including humans) and birds need to conserve water, they can produce urine that has a higher concentration of dissolved materials than their blood has.

Urine can become concentrated because there is a concentration gradient of salts and urea in the extracellular fluid that surrounds the nephrons and the collecting ducts. (The concentration gradient is created and maintained by the loops of Henle.) As filtrate travels through the collecting ducts to the renal pelvis, it passes through areas of increasingly concentrated extracellular fluid. As the difference in concentration between the filtrate and the surrounding fluid increases, water leaves the filtrate by osmosis and is carried off by the surrounding capillaries. The filtrate in the collecting duct, now called urine, can become as concentrated as the surrounding fluid, which may be four times as concentrated as blood. The urine remains concentrated because the rest of the excretory system is fairly impermeable to water, salts, and urea.

▶ Figure 21-19 **Urine formation in the nephron and collecting duct**

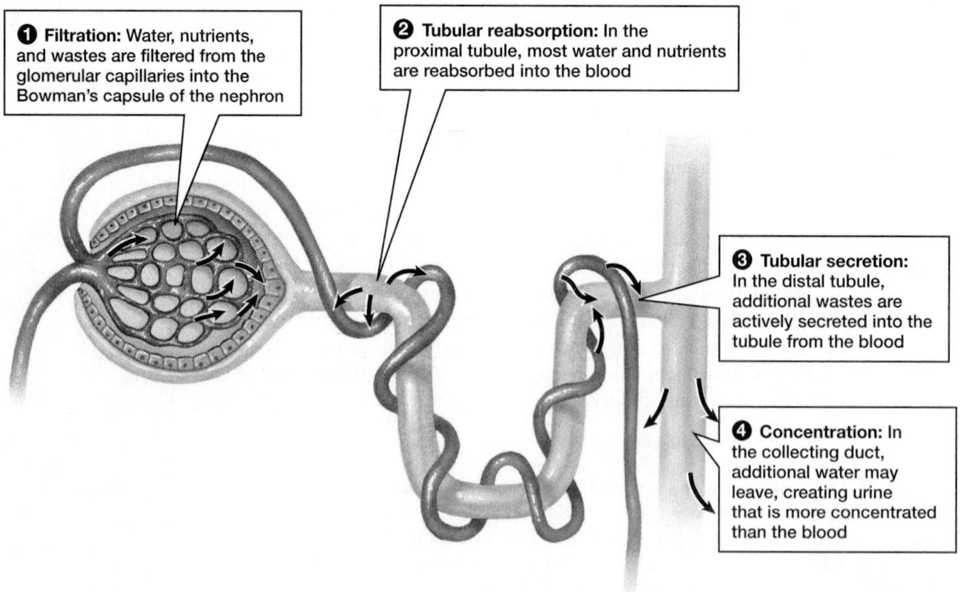

❶ **Filtration:** Water, nutrients, and wastes are filtered from the glomerular capillaries into the Bowman's capsule of the nephron

❷ **Tubular reabsorption:** In the proximal tubule, most water and nutrients are reabsorbed into the blood

❸ **Tubular secretion:** In the distal tubule, additional wastes are actively secreted into the tubule from the blood

❹ **Concentration:** In the collecting duct, additional water may leave, creating urine that is more concentrated than the blood

Negative Feedback Regulates the Water Content of the Blood

Maintaining the proper volume of water in the body is a key function of the urinary system, as we have seen, but the appropriate amount of water to retain changes continually as conditions change. The kidneys, therefore, must reabsorb more water when a person is perspiring heavily and less water when the person has just drunk a lot of water.

The amount of water reabsorbed into the blood is controlled by negative feedback (see pp. 365–366). One of these feedback mechanisms is based on the amount of *antidiuretic hormone (ADH)* circulating in the blood. This hormone (secreted by the pituitary gland) allows more water to be reabsorbed from the urine. It does so by increasing the permeability of the distal tubule and the collecting duct to water. The release of ADH is regulated by receptor cells in the brain that monitor the concentration of the blood and by receptors in the heart that monitor blood volume.

Let's look at an example. A lost traveler staggers through the hot desert, perspiring heavily and losing water with every breath. As he becomes dehydrated, his blood volume falls, and the osmotic concentration of his blood rises, triggering release of ADH by the pituitary gland (Fig. 21-20). The ADH increases the permeability of the distal tubule and the collecting duct, thereby increasing the reabsorption of water. Water is returned to the blood, leaving urine that is more concentrated than the blood.

Eventually, our traveler finds an oasis and overindulges in the cool, clear water of a spring. His blood volume rises and its osmotic concentration falls, triggering a decrease in his ADH output. Reduced ADH makes his distal tubules and collecting ducts less permeable to water, so less water is reabsorbed from them. He will now produce urine that is more dilute than the blood. In extreme cases, urine flow may exceed 1 quart (about 1 liter) per hour. As the proper water level in his blood is restored, the increased osmotic concentration of the blood and decreased blood volume will again stimulate some ADH release, thus maintaining homeostasis by keeping the blood water content within narrow limits.

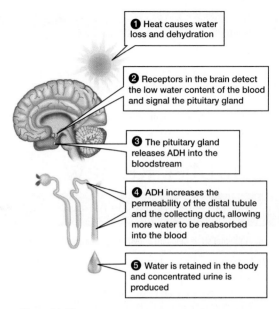

❶ Heat causes water loss and dehydration

❷ Receptors in the brain detect the low water content of the blood and signal the pituitary gland

❸ The pituitary gland releases ADH into the bloodstream

❹ ADH increases the permeability of the distal tubule and the collecting duct, allowing more water to be reabsorbed into the blood

❺ Water is retained in the body and concentrated urine is produced

▲ **Figure 21-20 Dehydration stimulates ADH release and water retention QUESTION:** Alcohol inhibits ADH release. How does alcohol consumption affect the body's water balance?

Dying to be Thin   Revisited

In the most extreme cases, eating disorders, as you might predict, can cause death from starvation. However, long before they literally starve to death, people with eating disorders seriously damage their bodies, and often die of other causes. According to Carré Otis, "It was common for the young girls I worked with to have a heart attack," probably brought about by massive imbalances in the concentrations of sodium and potassium in the blood, caused by malnutrition. At age 30, Otis herself required surgery to repair her damaged heart.

How do people develop eating disorders? Anorexia and bulimia usually arise from a faulty self-image or from the perceived demands of family, friends, or career. At her first foreign modeling assignment in 2004, Ana Reston was told that she was fat, even though she weighed only about 110 pounds. Friends and associates trace her descent to multiple organ failure from that time.

Genes apparently play a role, too. Women whose mother or sister suffers from anorexia are 12 times more likely to develop anorexia, and 4 times more likely to develop bulimia, than women without such a family history. Not surprisingly, if one member of a pair of identical twins develops an eating disorder, the other is highly likely to as well. However,

although genetic contributions to personality traits such as perfectionism, anxiety, or low self-esteem are suspected, no one has yet identified any specific genes that might predispose anyone to eating disorders.

Eating disorders are difficult to treat. Victims are usually given nutritional therapy to help them recover from malnutrition. Psychotherapy is often necessary, and antidepressant drugs are helpful in some cases. Because many victims hide or deny their problem, and because treatment is expensive, the majority of sufferers are inadequately treated. Successes do occur, however. The TV show *American Idol* may have saved the life of one of its stars, Katharine McPhee, who suffered from bulimia. Worried that repeated vomiting might eat away at her vocal cords and hurt her chances to win the *Idol* singing competition, McPhee spent 3 months, 6 days a week, at an eating disorder clinic. It worked: She is no longer bulimic, was the *Idol* runner-up, and released her first CD in January 2007.

Consider This

In 2006, the Madrid Fashion Week in Spain banned any models with a BMI below 18 (a 5-foot 8-inch model weighing about 120 pounds).

Among women who couldn't meet the new BMI requirements are Spain's most famous model, Esther Canadas, who has a BMI of about 14. In 2007, a fashion show in Milan mandated a minimum BMI of 18.5. Most modeling agencies, of course, strenuously object to the BMI rule.

Thousands of young women become anorexic, many of them because they think that society finds extreme thinness to be desirable. Is there any way to change this message? Are there any appropriate measures that a free society can or should take to reverse or limit this message?

Chapter Review

Summary of Key Concepts

For additional study help and activities, go to www.mybiology.com.

21.1 How Do Animals Regulate the Composition of Their Bodies?

Nutrition, digestion, and excretion are crucial to homeostasis, maintaining internal conditions that sustain life. Nutrients are substances that an animal requires in its diet, providing both energy and materials to construct its body. Digestion is the process of converting food into molecules that can be absorbed by the circulatory system. Through excretion by the digestive and respiratory tracts, the skin, and especially the urinary tract, animals retain needed nutrients and dispose of surplus nutrients, wastes, and toxic molecules in their food.

21.2 What Nutrients Do Animals Need?

Each animal species has specific nutritional requirements. These requirements include molecules that can be broken down to liberate energy, such as lipids, carbohydrates, and protein; chemical building blocks used to construct complex molecules; minerals; vitamins needed for the chemical reactions of metabolism; and water.

21.3 What Are the Major Processes of Digestion?

Digestive systems must accomplish five tasks: ingestion, mechanical and chemical breakdown of food, absorption, and elimination of wastes. Digestive systems convert the complex molecules of the bodies of ingested organisms into simpler molecules that can be used.

Web Animation   Mechanical and Chemical Breakdown of Food

21.4 What Types of Digestive Systems Are Found in Non-Human Animals?

In sponges, individual cells ingest and digest food. The simplest multicellular digestive system is a saclike cavity such as that of cnidarians, in which there is a single opening that serves as both mouth and anus. Most animals have a tubular digestive system with specialized parts where food is processed in an orderly sequence.

21.5 How Do Humans Digest Food?

In humans, digestion begins in the mouth, where food is mechanically broken down by chewing, and chemical digestion is initiated by saliva. Food is then conducted to the stomach by peristaltic waves of the esophagus. In the acidic environment of the stomach, food is churned into smaller particles, and protein digestion begins. Gradually, the liquefied food, now called chyme, is released to the small intestine. There, it is neutralized by sodium bicarbonate from

the pancreas. Secretions from the liver, pancreas, and the cells of the intestine complete the breakdown of proteins, fats, and carbohydrates. In the small intestine, the simple molecular products of digestion are absorbed into the bloodstream for distribution to the body cells. The large intestine absorbs water, minerals, and vitamins, and converts indigestible material to feces.

Digestion is regulated by the nervous system and hormones. The smell and taste of food and the action of chewing trigger the secretion of saliva in the mouth and the production of gastrin by the stomach. Gastrin stimulates stomach acid production. As chyme enters the small intestine, additional hormones are produced by intestinal cells, including secretin, which causes sodium bicarbonate production to neutralize the acidic chyme. Other hormones stimulate bile release and cause the pancreas to secrete digestive enzymes into the small intestine.

21.6 What Are the Functions of Urinary Systems?

The urinary system plays a crucial role in homeostasis, regulating the water and mineral content of the blood, as well as blood pH. The organs of the urinary system help retain nutrients and eliminate cellular wastes and toxic substances.

21.7 What Types of Urinary Systems Are Found in Non-Human Animals?

In the invertebrate flatworm, wastes and excess water are filtered from the body fluids into tubules. Cilia on flame cells move the fluids through the tubules and expel them through pores in the body surface. In the earthworm, nephridia (which resemble individual nephrons) filter fluid that bathes the organs and blood vessels, storing excess water and wastes, which are excreted through pores.

21.8 How Does the Human Urinary System Work?

The urinary system of vertebrates (including humans) helps maintain homeostasis in the body in several ways, including (1) regulating the blood levels of important minerals and other ions; (2) regulating the water content of the blood by negative feedback involving antidiuretic hormone (ADH), produced in the pituitary gland of the brain; (3) maintaining proper pH of the blood; (4) retaining important nutrients; and (5) eliminating cellular waste products such as urea.

The urinary system of humans and other vertebrates consists of kidneys, ureters, bladder, and urethra. Kidneys produce urine, which is conducted by the ureters to the bladder, a storage organ. Urine passes out of the body through the urethra.

Each kidney contains more than a million individual nephrons in its outer layer. Urine formed in the nephrons enters collecting ducts that empty into the renal pelvis, from which it is funneled into the ureter. Each nephron is served by an arteriole that branches from the renal artery. The arteriole further branches into a mass of capillaries called the glomerulus. There, water and dissolved substances are filtered from the blood by pressure. The filtrate is collected in the cup-shaped Bowman's capsule and conducted along the tubular portion of the nephron. During tubular reabsorption, nutrients are actively pumped out of the filtrate through the walls of the tubule. Nutrients then enter capillaries that surround the tubule, and water follows by osmosis. Some wastes remain in the filtrate; others are pumped into the tubule by tubular secretion. The tubule forms the loop of Henle, which creates a salt concentration gradient surrounding it. After completing its passage through the tubule, the filtrate enters the collecting duct, which passes through the concentration gradient. Final passage of the filtrate through this gradient via the collecting duct concentrates the urine.

Web Animation Human Urinary System Anatomy

Web Animation Urine Formation

Key Terms

bile *p. 145*
Bowman's capsule *p. 151*
calorie *p. 135*
Calorie *p. 135*
chyme *p. 145*
collecting duct *p. 151*
colon *p. 146*
concentration *p. 152*
digestion *p. 135*
distal tubule *p. 151*
esophagus *p. 144*
essential amino acid *p. 137*

essential fatty acid *p. 136*
excretion *p. 135*
feces *p. 147*
filtrate *p. 151*
filtration *p. 151*
gallbladder *p. 145*
glomerulus *p. 151*
glycogen *p. 137*
kidney *p. 150*
large intestine *p. 146*
liver *p. 145*
loop of Henle *p. 151*

microvillus (plural, microvilli) *p. 146*
mineral *p. 137*
nephron *p. 150*
nutrient *p. 134*
nutrition *p. 135*
pancreas *p. 145*
pancreatic juice *p. 145*
peristalsis *p. 144*
pharynx *p. 144*
proximal tubule *p. 151*
rectum *p. 146*

small intestine *p. 145*
stomach *p. 144*
tubular reabsorption *p. 151*
tubular secretion *p. 152*
tubule *p. 151*
ureter *p. 150*
urethra *p. 150*
urinary bladder *p. 150*
urine *p. 150*
villus (plural, villi) *p. 146*
vitamin *p. 137*

Thinking Through the Concepts

Suggested answers to end-of-chapter and figure-based questions can be found at the end of the text.

Fill-in-the-Blank

1. A substance that an animals needs to build or operate its body, but that it cannot synthesize itself, is called a(n) _____. _____ is the process of physically and chemically breaking down food into molecules that can be absorbed into the circulatory system. Indigestible material, waste products of cellular metabolism, toxic substances, and substances eaten in excess of the body's needs are eliminated through _____, which occurs in the _____, _____, _____, and _____ (major organs or organ systems of the body).

2. The primary sources of energy for animals are _____ and _____. Organic molecules needed in very small amounts that an animal cannot synthesize itself (in sufficient quantities) are called _____. _____ are important components of bone, teeth, and the dissolved materials in the blood and extracellular fluid.

3. Amino acids and fatty acids that the body requires but cannot synthesize are called _____.

4. Digestion includes five major processes: _____, _____, _____, _____, and _____.

5. Most animals have a tubular digestive tract. The major cavities of the human digestive tract are the _____, _____, _____, stomach, _____, and _____.

6. Glands in the stomach wall produce three major secretions: _____, _____, and _____.

7. Enzymes from the _____ empty into the small intestine; this gland also produces an acid-neutralizing buffer called _____. The small intestine also receives _____ from the liver and gallbladder; this secretion, although not an enzyme, is important in the digestion of _____ (type of nutrient).

8. In humans, urine is produced in tiny tubules of the kidney, called _____. Blood is first filtered into the beginning of the tubules, the _____. The filtrate is then processed through tubular absorption and secretion. Finally, it is concentrated in the _____. Urine is stored in the _____ and leaves the body through the _____.

9. If you begin to dehydrate, a gland called the _____ releases the hormone _____, which causes your kidneys to reabsorb water and produce concentrated urine.

Review Questions

1. List six general types of nutrients, and describe the role of each in nutrition.

2. List and describe the function of the three principal secretions of the stomach.

3. List the substances secreted into the small intestine, and describe the origin and function of each.

4. Describe the structural and functional adaptations of the human small intestine that ensure good digestion and absorption.

5. Control of the human digestive tract involves messages that coordinate activity in one chamber with those taking place in subsequent chambers. List the coordinating events you discovered in this chapter in the appropriate order, beginning with tasting, chewing, and swallowing a piece of meat and ending with residue that enters the large intestine. What initiates each process?

6. What are the major functions of the urinary system in any animal?

7. Describe the processes of filtration, tubular reabsorption, and tubular secretion.

Applying the Concepts

1. IS THIS SCIENCE? Humor writer Dave Barry described Calories as "tiny units of measurement that cause food to taste good." Is this pure humor, or is there some scientific truth to this statement? Use evolutionary concepts in your answer. How is this statement related to the current obesity problem in affluent countries such as the United States?

2. One of the common remedies for constipation (difficulty eliminating feces) is a laxative solution that contains magnesium salts. In the large intestine, magnesium salts are absorbed very slowly by the intestinal wall, remaining in the intestinal tract for long periods of time. Thus, the salts affect water movement in the large intestine. On the basis of this information, explain the laxative action of magnesium salts.

3. Some employers require their employees to submit to urine tests before they can be employed and at random intervals during their employment. Refusal to take the test or failure to "pass" the test could be grounds for termination. What is the purpose of a urine test? How would you feel if you had to undergo a urine test to obtain or keep a job? Explain your answers.

For additional resources, go to mybiology.com.

Chapter 21: Nutrition, Digestion, and Excretion

CHECKING YOUR READING STRATEGIES
DISCUSSION AND CRITICAL THINKING QUESTIONS

1. **Preview the chapter** as you have been instructed. *Without reading the chapter itself*, write an outline of the chapter. Leave room to fill in the details later. Use your typographical cues to help you. (Do not include the summary in your outline.)

2. **Preview the chapter again,** this time focusing on all the graphic illustrations. Read all the captions, information in tables, and look carefully at all drawings. Next, let your eyes scan over the columns of text. See if you can find where in the paragraphs the illustrated material is explained. What cues are given in the text to tie the illustrations to the words?

3. *Circle the best answer for each of the following questions.*

    1. According to the listing at the beginning of the chapter, this chapter will cover how many topics?
       a. Eight
       b. Nine
       c. Twenty-one
       d. Not enough information to answer the question

    2. What is the *overall purpose* of the chapter's introduction, "Dying to Be Thin"?
       a. To explain what fashion models do
       b. To explain how fashion models work
       c. To set up the focus for the chapter
       d. To demonstrate that catchy graphics help you remember information

    3. How many types of graphic illustrations are used in this chapter? Look through the entire chapter. Circle all that apply.
       a. Photographs
       b. Charts
       c. Graphs
       d. Organizational charts
       e. Shaded boxes (of formulas, theories, etc.)
       f. Process diagrams
       g. Margin notes
       h. Diagrams
       i. Tables
       j. Flow charts
       k. Maps
       l. Branching/tree diagrams
       m. Drawings

    4. What typographical cues are used in the chapter to highlight important information for you? Circle all that apply.
       a. Boldface print
       b. Font size
       c. Italicized print
       d. Font style
       e. Bulleted lists
       f. Color of print
       g. Shading
       h. Symbols (light bulb, question mark, star, etc.)
       i. Underlining
       j. Boxes
       k. Arrows to show direction/order

4. **Preview the summary.** Read over the "Chapter Review" of the concepts and the questions. These are the key points the authors feel you should draw from the chapter. How do the authors tie the concepts back to the text so you would know where to find the information? Go back and look for it. Make a checkmark in the margin so you will remember this is a key point when you read the chapter.

5. Now go back to the first page of the chapter and **read the chapter**. Move through the chapter section by section. Read first, then decide what information is important for you to know and what is explanatory to illustrate the point. Next, return to the outline you drafted for question 1. Fill in the outline with the information you have determined to be important for you to remember. Consider your method as well. **How** did you determine which information was important enough to record?

6. Of what benefit to you are tables 21.1, 21.2, and 21.3?

7. How helpful is "Health Watch" on the text's page 148 when related to the "Dying to Be Thin" boxes? Why do you think the authors included these sections and other practical advice, such as how to read packaging labels (Fig. 21-5), in a textbook?

8. Finally, **after reading** the chapter, answer the questions at the end of the chapter under "Thinking Through the Concepts." How well did you do?

GROUP PROJECTS

1. Compare your outline with that of your classmates. Are they all the same? If not, how do they differ? Why do you think that may be? Next, compare how well you and your classmates did when answering the questions at the end of the text's chapter. Did those of you with the more detailed outline do better? Why or why not?

2. As a group, discuss the benefits of previewing the illustrations in the text before reading, as opposed to waiting to explore them as they come up in the reading.

3. With your group, consider what the authors do to make this chapter interesting and appealing to you. Consider both the visual components and the information itself. How do page layout and writing style make assigned reading more enjoyable?

4. As a group, discuss why you think the authors have included practical advice in a textbook.

Unit VI
Reading Strategies for Social Sciences and Criminal Justice

from

Criminal Justice Today:
An Introductory Text for the 21st Century
Tenth Edition

by

Frank Schmalleger

As the natural sciences work to understand the workings of the universe, the social sciences work to understand human behavior. This discipline focuses on human beings as individuals, such as in psychology, and in groups, such as in sociology. This discipline includes anthropology, archaeology, education, political science, criminal justice, psychology, sociology, and history, although many schools often house history in the humanities. Social scientists also use the scientific method to study their subjects, but since human beings are so varied, they are much more difficult to predict than, for example, at what temperature water freezes. Therefore, social scientists use a great deal of observational, long-range experiments. Often human subjects must be observed over a period of years in order to enable scientists to draw conclusions.

Social scientists use many of the same strategies natural scientists use. Expect to read about theories, experiments, and case studies. The scientific method is also used here. You will read about the theorists in the field and the contributions they have made to the discipline, so expect to read some history in these texts as well.

The chapter included here from a criminal justice text pulls from several social science disciplines to discuss its topic. In considering "Terrorism and Multi-national Justice," the author draws on psychology, sociology, political science, criminology, and history—even computer science—all of which helps illustrate just how complex human issues are. There are many factors to consider when studying humans. Be sure to pay attention to the illustrative examples (called "exhibits" here) since they often give you real-world examples to illustrate how these social theories are practiced in reality.

CHAPTER 17

Terrorism and Multinational Criminal Justice

LEARNING OBJECTIVES

After reading this chapter, you should be able to

- Describe the principles that form the basis of Islamic law.
- Identify important international criminal justice organizations and explain their role in fighting international crime.
- Explain globalization and explicate its possible relationship to crime and terrorism.
- Define *terrorism,* and identify two major types of terrorism.

OUTLINE

America's response to globalization in the criminal justice arena will necessitate major changes in both law and policy, placing greater emphasis on the education and training of practitioners at all levels of government. In addition to culture and language, tomorrow's criminal justice practitioner must have a broader understanding of the legal systems of other countries and respect for the customs and practices of immigrants, as well as an increasing number of international visitors.

—Richard Ward, Dean and Director, Criminal Justice Center, Sam Houston State University[1]

In the 21st century, Americans have come to appreciate that they are part of a global society and that criminal transgressions within and beyond our Nation's borders have worldwide ramifications.

—Office for Victims of Crime[2]

Hear the author discuss this chapter at cjtoday.com

Introduction

On May 8, 2007, federal agents arrested a reputed Islamic terrorist who lived in Cherry Hill, New Jersey, and who went by the unlikely name of Elvis. Eljjvir Duka, 23, was one of six aspiring Islamic holy warriors who, the government said, were planning to attack the U.S. Army base at Fort Dix, which is near Cookstown, New Jersey.[3] The men apparently had trained out of a rented house in Pennsylvania's Pocono Mountains. They were arrested after a 15-month investigation that began when a store clerk saw them firing automatic weapons and shouting "God is great!" in Arabic on a videotape that they had asked to have transferred to DVD. The men were taken into custody after meeting with an undercover agent to purchase automatic weapons that they planned to use in the attack. The group had been infiltrated by Federal Bureau of Investigation (FBI) agents, and some of their conversations had been secretly recorded—including one in which the group's leader regretted having missed an opportunity to launch an attack at the Army-Navy football game in Philadelphia in 2006. Three of the men taken into custody are ethnic Albanian brothers who were born in the former Yugoslavia and were living in the United States illegally. One is a naturalized American citizen from Jordan, and another is a legal permanent resident from Turkey. The sixth is a legal permanent resident born in Yugoslavia. All are Muslim and in their mid-twenties, and one worked as a pizza delivery person with easy access to the targeted base.

The six men, some of whom had been living in the United States since childhood and had attended public schools here, held jobs ranging from roofer to cabdriver and seemed to have had no clear motivation other than a shared desire to kill U.S. soldiers in the name of Islam. Although they were not directly affiliated with any other known terrorist organization, the group had watched al-Qaeda videos posted on foreign websites and were apparently inspired by the idea of a worldwide Jihad, or holy war. "This is a new brand of terrorism where a small cell of people can bring enormous devastation," said Christopher J. Christie, the U.S. attorney for New Jersey.[4]

Although the link between small, independently organized terrorist groups, like the New Jersey cell, and larger, more formal organizations like al-Qaeda may be mostly ideological, it can still provide a powerful motivation for destructive criminal activities. Hence, it has become vitally important for American criminal justice and other government organizations to appreciate the ideology, culture, and means of communications linking criminal and terrorist groups in this country to those overseas and around the world.

comparative criminologist

One who studies crime and criminal justice on a cross-national level.

Criminologists who study crime and criminal justice on a cross-national level are referred to as **comparative criminologists**, and their field is called *comparative criminal justice, comparative criminology,* or *cross-national criminal justice.* Comparative criminal justice is becoming increasingly valued for the insights it provides. By contrasting native institutions of justice with similar institutions in other countries, procedures and problems in one system can be reevaluated in the light of world experience. As technological advances effectively "shrink" the world, we are able to learn firsthand about the criminal justice systems of other countries and to use that information to improve our own.

This chapter explains the value of comparative criminal justice, points to the problems that arise in comparing data from different nations, and explains international terrorism within the context of cross-national crime. By way of example, this chapter also briefly examines criminal justice systems based on Islamic principles. International police agencies are described, and the role of the United Nations (UN) in the worldwide fight against crime and terrorism is discussed. Additional information on the justice systems of many countries can be found in the *World Factbook of Criminal Justice Systems,* available at **Library Extra 17–1** at cjtoday.com. Another place to visit for international criminal justice information is the National Institute of Justice's (NIJ) International Center, which is accessible via **Web Extra 17–1** at cjtoday.com.

LIBRARY Extra ▪▪▪▪   **WEB** Extra ▪▪▪▪

Ethnocentrism and the Study of Criminal Justice

The study of criminal justice in the United States has been largely **ethnocentric.** Because people are socialized from birth into a particular culture, they tend to prefer their own culture's way of doing things over that of any other. Native patterns of behavior are seen as somehow "natural" and therefore better than foreign ones. The same is true for values, beliefs, and customs. People tend to think that their religion holds a spiritual edge over other religions, that their values and ethical sense are superior to those of others, and that the fashions they wear, the language they speak, and the rituals of daily life in which they participate are somehow better than comparable practices elsewhere. Ethnocentric individuals do not consider that people elsewhere in the world cling to their own values, beliefs, and standards of behavior with just as much fervor as they do.

Only in recent years have American students of criminal justice begun to examine the justice systems of other cultures. Unfortunately, not all societies are equally open, and it is not always easy to explore them. In some societies, even the *study* of criminal justice is taboo. As a result, data-gathering strategies taken for granted in Western societies may not be well received elsewhere. One author, for example, has observed that in China, "the seeking of criminal justice information through face-to-face questioning takes on a different meaning in Chinese officialdom than it does generally in the Western world. While we accept this method of inquiry because we prize thinking on our feet and quick answers, it is rather offensive in China because it shows lack of respect and appreciation for the information given through the preferred means of prepared questions and formal briefings."[5] Hence, most of the information available about Chinese criminal justice comes by way of bureaucracy, and routine Western social science practices like door-to-door interviews, participant observation, and random surveys would produce substantial problems for researchers who attempt to use these techniques in China.

ethnocentric

Holding a belief in the superiority of one's own social or ethnic group and culture.

Lecture Note

Explain ethnocentrism as culture-centeredness. Discuss how ethnocentrism can be a limiting factor in the study of international criminal justice.

Thematic Question

What is ethnocentrism? Why can ethnocentrism be problematic for the study of criminal justice? How can ethnocentrism be overcome?

Problems with Data

Similar difficulties arise in the comparison of crime rates from one country to another. The crime rates of different nations are difficult to compare because of (1) differences in the way a specific crime is defined, (2) diverse crime-reporting practices, and (3) political and other influences on the reporting of statistics to international agencies.[6]

Definitional differences create what may be the biggest problem. For cross-national comparisons of crime data to be meaningful, it is essential that the reported data share conceptual similarities. Unfortunately, that is rarely the case. Nations report offenses according to the legal criteria by which arrests are made and under which prosecution can occur. Switzerland, for example, includes bicycle thefts in its reported data on what we call "auto theft" because Swiss data gathering focuses more on the concept of personal transportation than it does on the type of vehicle stolen. The Netherlands has no crime category for robberies, counting them as thefts. Japan classifies an assault that results in death as an assault or an aggravated assault, not as a homicide. Greek rape statistics include crimes of sodomy, "lewdness," seduction of a child, incest, and prostitution. China reports only robberies and thefts that involve the property of citizens; crimes against state-owned property fall into a separate category.

Social, cultural, and economic differences among countries compound these difficulties. Auto theft statistics, for example, when compared between countries like the United States and China, need to be placed in an economic as well as demographic context. While the United States has two automobiles for every three people, China has only one car per every 100 of its citizens. For the Chinese auto theft rate to equal that of the United States, every automobile in the country would have to be stolen nearly twice each year!

Thematic Question

As you read about Islamic law, identify instances of your own ethnocentrism. What problems does ethnocentrism create for your own study of criminal justice?

Lecture Note

Describe the difficulties that arise in the comparison of crime rates from one country to another. Include definitional differences, diverse reporting practices, and political influences on the reporting of crime.

Thematic Question

Identify some of the problems associated with the international study of criminal justice. Why is it so difficult to compare crime rates between nations?

Reporting practices vary substantially between nations. The International Criminal Police Organization (Interpol) and the United Nations are the only international organizations that regularly collect crime statistics from a large number of countries.[7] Both agencies can only request data and have no way of checking on the accuracy of the data reported to them. Many countries do not disclose the requested information, and those that do often make only partial reports. In general, small countries are more likely to report than are large ones, and nonsocialist countries are more likely to report than are socialist countries.[8]

International reports of crime are often delayed. Complete up-to-date data are rare since the information made available to agencies like the United Nations and Interpol is reported at different times and according to schedules that vary from nation to nation. In addition, official United Nations world crime surveys are conducted infrequently. To date, only ten such surveys have been undertaken.[9]

Crime statistics also reflect political biases and national values. Some nations do not accurately admit to the frequency of certain kinds of culturally reprehensible crimes. Communist countries, for example, appear loathe to report crimes like theft, burglary, and robbery because the very existence of such offenses demonstrates felt inequities within the Communist system. After the breakup of the Soviet Union, Alexander Larin, a criminal justice scholar who worked as a Russian investigator during the 1950s and 1960s, revealed that "inside the state security bureaucracy, where statistics were collected and circulated, falsification of crime figures was the rule, not the exception. The practice was self-perpetuating," said Larin. "Supervisors in the provinces were under pressure to provide Moscow with declining crime rates. And no self-respecting investigator wanted to look worse than his neighbor. . . . From the top to the bottom, the bosses depended on their employees not to make them look bad with high crime statistics."[10]

On the other hand, observers in democratic societies showed similar biases in their interpretation of statistics following the end of the cold war. Some Western analysts, for example, reporting on declines in the prison populations of Eastern and Central Europe during that period, attributed the decline to lessened frustration and lowered crime rates brought about by democratization. In one country, Hungary, prison populations declined from 240 inmates per 100,000 residents in 1986 to 130 per 100,000 in 1993, with similar decreases in other nations.[11] The more likely explanation, however, is the wholesale post-Soviet release of political dissidents from prisons formerly run by Communist regimes. Learn more about world crime via the UN's *Global Report on Crime and Justice,* which is available at Library Extra 17–2 at cjtoday.com. View data from the UN Survey on Crime Trends via Web Extra 17–2, and access the *European Sourcebook of Crime and Criminal Justice Statistics* at Library Extra 17–3.

LIBRARY Extra

WEB Extra

An Iraqi man holding a picture of top Shiite cleric Ayatollah Ali Sistani during a protest in support of an Islamic constitution. The traditions and legal systems of many Middle Eastern countries are strongly influenced by Islamic law, which is based on the teachings of the Koran and the sayings of the Prophet Muhammad. How does Islamic law differ from the laws of most Western nations?

Islamic Criminal Justice

Islamic law has been the subject of much discussion in the United States since the September 11, 2001, terrorist attacks on the World Trade Center and the Pentagon. It is important for American students of criminal justice to recognize, however, that Islamic law refers to legal ideas (and sometimes entire legal systems) based on the teachings of Islam and that it bears no intrinsic relationship to acts of terrorism committed by misguided zealots with Islamic backgrounds. Similarly, Islamic law is by no means the same thing as Jihad (Islamic holy war) or Islamic fundamentalism. Although Americans are now much better informed about the concept of Islamic law than they were in the past, some may not be aware that various interpretations of Islam still form the basis of laws in many countries and that the entire legal systems of some nations are based on Islamic principles. Islamic law holds considerable sway in a large number of countries, including Syria, Iran, Iraq (where a new constitution was voted on and approved in 2005), Pakistan, Afghanistan, Yemen, Saudi Arabia, Kuwait, the United Arab Emirates, Bahrain, Algeria, Jordan, Lebanon, Libya, Ethiopia, Gambia, Nigeria, Oman, Qatar, Senegal, Tunisia, Tajikistan, Uzbekistan, and Turkey (which practices official separation of church and state).

Islamic law descends directly from the teachings of the Prophet Muhammad, whom the *Cambridge Encyclopedia of Islam* describes as a "prophet-lawyer."[12] Muhammad rose to fame in the city of Mecca (in what is now Saudi Arabia) as a religious reformer. Later, however, he traveled to Medina, where he became the ruler and lawgiver of a newly formed religious society. In his role as lawgiver, Muhammad enacted legislation whose aim was to teach men what to do and how to behave in order to achieve salvation. As a consequence, Islamic law today is a system of duties and rituals founded on legal and moral obligations—all of which are ultimately sanctioned by the authority of a religious leader (or leaders) who may issue commands (known as *fatwas* or *fatwahs*) that the faithful are bound to obey.

Criminal justice professor Sam Souryal and his coauthors describe four aspects of justice in Arab philosophy and religion. Islamic justice, they say, means the following:[13]

- A sacred trust, a duty imposed on humans to be discharged sincerely and honestly. As such, these authors say, "justice is the quality of being morally responsible and merciful in giving everyone his or her due."

- A mutual respect of one human being by another. From this perspective, a just society is one that offers equal respect for individuals through social arrangements made in the common interest of all members.

- An aspect of the social bond that holds society together and transforms it into a brotherhood in which everyone becomes a keeper of everyone else and each is held accountable for the welfare of all.

- A command from God. Whoever violates God's commands should be subject to strict punishments according to Islamic tradition and belief.

As Souryal and his coauthors observe, "The third and fourth meanings of justice are probably the ones most commonly invoked in Islamic jurisprudence" and form the basis of criminal justice practice in many Middle Eastern countries.

The *Hudud* Crimes

Islamic law (or *Shari'ah* in Arabic, which means "path of God") forms the basis of theocratic judicial systems in Kuwait, Saudi Arabia, the Sudan, Iran, and Algeria. Other Arabic nations, such as Egypt, Jordan, and Iraq, recognize substantial elements of Islamic law in their criminal justice systems but also make wide use of Western and nontheocratic legal principles. Islamic law is based on four sources. In order of importance, these sources are (1) the Koran (also spelled *Quran* and *Qur'an*), or Holy Book of Islam, which Muslims believe is the word of God, or Allah; (2) the teachings of the Prophet Muhammad; (3) a consensus of the clergy in cases where neither the Koran nor the prophet directly addresses an issue; and (4) reason or logic, which should be used when no solution can be found in the other three sources.[14]

Islamic law recognizes seven ***Hudud* crimes**—or crimes based on religious strictures. *Hudud* (sometimes called *Hodood* or *Huddud*) crimes are essentially violations of "natural law" as interpreted by Arab culture. Divine displeasure is thought to be the basis of crimes defined as *Hudud,* and *Hudud* crimes are often said to be crimes against God (or, more specifically, God's rights). The Koran specifies punishments for four of the seven *Hudud* crimes: (1) making war on

It may be only a matter of time before al-Qaeda or other groups attempt to use chemical, biological, radiological or nuclear weapons. We must focus on that.

—CIA Director Porter Goss[i]

Lecture Note

Introduce the concept of Islamic law (*Shari'ah*). Describe *Hudud* offenses as crimes against God and *Tazir* offenses as crimes against society. Describe how the Western distinction between *mala in se* offenses and *mala prohibita* offenses parallels the Islamic offense categories.

Islamic law

A system of laws, operative in some Arab countries, based on the Muslim religion and especially the holy book of Islam, the Koran.

***Hudud* crime**

A serious violation of Islamic law that is regarded as an offense against God. *Hudud* crimes include such behavior as theft, adultery, sodomy, alcohol consumption, and robbery.

Iraqi Shiite Muslims flagellating themselves during a procession in Karbala, Iraq, on March 20, 2006. Islamic law, which is based on the teachings of Islam, underpins the legal systems of many nations in the Middle East and elsewhere. What kinds of offenses does it prohibit? What punishments does it specify?

With criminals' ability to cross international borders in a few hours, and the advances of our modern age, such as the Internet and telecommunications, crime can no longer be viewed as just a national issue.

—Assistant U.S. Attorney General Laurie Robinson

Allah and His messengers, (2) theft, (3) adultery or fornication, and (4) false accusation of fornication or adultery. The three other *Hudud* offenses are mentioned by the Koran, but no punishment is specified: (1) "corruption on earth," (2) drinking alcohol, and (3) highway robbery—and the punishments for these crimes are determined by tradition.[15] The *Hudud* offenses and associated typical punishments are shown in Table 17–1. "Corruption on earth" is a general category of religious offense, not well understood in the West, which includes activities like embezzlement, revolution against lawful authority, fraud, and "weakening the society of God." In 2004, for example, Mehdi Hassan, a 36-year-old Pakistani was sentenced to life in prison by a court in Lahore for burning a copy of the Koran. Hassan was convicted and sentenced under Pakistan's laws covering offenses against Islam.[16]

Islamic law mandates strict punishment of moral failure. Sexual offenders, even those who engage in what would be considered essentially victimless crimes in Western societies, are subject to especially harsh treatment. The Islamic penalty for sexual intercourse outside of marriage, for example, is 100 lashes. Men are stripped to the waist, women have their clothes bound tightly, and flogging is carried out with a leather whip. Adultery carries a much more severe penalty: flogging and stoning to death.

TABLE 17–1 Crime and Punishment in Islamic Law: The Iranian Example

Islamic law looks to the Koran and to the teachings of the Prophet Muhammad to determine which acts should be classified as crimes. The Koran and tradition specify punishments to be applied to designated offenses, as the following verse from the Koran demonstrates: "The only reward of those who make war upon Allah and His messenger and strive after corruption in the land will be that they will be killed or crucified, or have their hands and feet on alternate sides cut off, or will be expelled out of the land" (*Surah* V, Verse 33). Other crimes and punishments include the following:

Offense	Punishment
Theft	Amputation of the hand
Adultery	Stoning to death
Fornication	One hundred lashes
False accusation (of fornication or adultery)	Eighty lashes
Corruption on earth	Death by the sword or by burning
Drinking alcohol	Eighty lashes; death if repeated three times
Robbery	Cutting off of hands and feet on alternate sides, exile, or execution

Note: For more information, see Sam S. Souryal, Dennis W. Potts, and Abdullah I. Alobied, "The Penalty of Hand Amputation for Theft in Islamic Justice," *Journal of Criminal Justice,* Vol. 22, No. 3 (1994), pp. 249–265; and Parviz Saney, "Iran," in Elmer H. Johnson, ed., *International Handbook of Contemporary Developments in Criminology* (Westport, CT: Greenwood Press, 1983), pp. 356–369.

Under Islamic law, even property crimes are firmly punished. Thieves who are undeterred by less serious punishments may eventually suffer amputation of the right hand. In a reputedly humane move, Iranian officials recently began to use an electric guillotine, specially made for the purpose, which can sever a hand at the wrist in one-tenth of a second. For amputation to be imposed, the item stolen must have value in Islam. Pork and alcohol, for example, are regarded as being without value, and their theft is not subject to punishment. Islamic legal codes also establish a minimum value for stolen items that could result in a sentence of amputation. Likewise, offenders who have stolen because they are hungry or are in need are exempt from the punishment of amputation and receive fines or prison terms.

The video *Divine Law* from the ABC News/Prentice Hall Video Library is recommended. Ask students why some punishments under Islamic law seem so extreme to Westerners.

Slander and the consumption of alcohol are both punished by 80 lashes. Legal codes in strict Islamic nations also specify whipping for the crimes of pimping, lesbianism, kissing by an unmarried couple, cursing, and failure of a woman to wear a veil. Islamic law provides for the execution, sometimes through crucifixion, of robbers. Laws stipulate that anyone who survives three days on the cross may be spared. Depending on the circumstances of the robbery, however, the offender may suffer the amputation of opposite hands and feet or may be exiled.

Rebellion, or revolt against a legitimate political leader or established economic order, which is considered an aspect of "corruption on earth," is punishable by death. The offender may be killed outright in a military or police action or, later, by sentence of the court. The last of the *Hudud* crimes is rejection of Islam. The penalty, once again, is death and can be imposed for denying the existence of God or angels, denying any of the prophets of Islam, or rejecting any part of the Koran.

Souryal and coauthors observe that *Hudud* crimes can be severely punished because "punishment serves a three-tiered obligation: (1) the fulfillment of worship, (2) the purification of society, and (3) the redemption of the individual." However, they add, the interests of the individual are the least valuable component of this triad and may have to be sacrificed "for the wholesomeness and integrity of the encompassing justice system."[17]

The *Tazir* Crimes

All crimes other than *Hudud* crimes fall into an offense category called *tazirat*. **Tazir crimes** are regarded as any actions not considered acceptable in a spiritual society. They include crimes against society and against individuals, but not against God. *Tazir* crimes may call for *quesas* (retribution) or *diya* (compensation or fines). Crimes requiring *quesas* are based on the Arabic principle of "an eye for an eye" and generally require physical punishments up to and including death. *Quesas* offenses may include murder, manslaughter, assault, and maiming. Under Islamic law, such crimes may require the victim or his representative to serve as prosecutor. The state plays a role only in providing the forum for the trial and in imposing punishment. Sometimes victims' representatives dole out punishment. In 1997, for example, 28-year-old taxi driver Ali Reza Khoshruy, nicknamed "The Vampire" because he stalked, raped, and killed women at night after picking them up in his cab, was hung from a yellow crane in the middle of Tehran, the Iranian capital.[18] Before the hanging, prison officials and male relatives of the victims cursed Khoshruy and whipped him with thick leather belts as he lay tied to a metal bed. The whipping was part of a 214-lash sentence.

Tazir crime

A minor violation of Islamic law that is regarded as an offense against society, not God.

Islamic Courts

Islamic courts typically exist on three levels.[19] The first level hears cases involving the potential for serious punishments, including death, amputation, and exile. The second level deals with relatively minor matters, such as traffic offenses and violations of city ordinances. Special courts, especially in Iran, may hear cases involving crimes against the government, narcotics offenses, state security, and corruption. Appeals within the Islamic court system are only possible under rare circumstances and are by no means routine. A decision rendered by second-level courts will generally stand without intervention by higher judicial authorities.

Under Islamic law, men and women are treated very differently. Testimony provided by a man, for example, can be heard in court. The same evidence, however, can only be provided by two virtuous women; one female witness is not sufficient.

While Islamic law may seem archaic or even barbaric to many Westerners, Islamic officials defend their system by pointing to low crime rates at home and by pointing to what they consider

Class Activity

Ask students to clip newspaper articles about crime and punishment in foreign countries or to find and print such articles from the Web. Discuss the stories in class, and have students decide which ones demonstrate a seemingly competent and equitable system of criminal justice.

near anarchy in Western nations. An early criticism of Islamic law was offered by Max Weber at the start of the twentieth century.[20] Weber said that Islamic justice is based more on the moral conceptions of individual judges than on any rational and predictable code of laws. He found that the personality of each judge, what he called "charisma," was more important in reaching a final legal result than was the written law. Weber's conclusion was that a modern society could not develop under Islamic law because enforcement of the law was too unpredictable. Complex social organizations, he argued, could only be based on a rational and codified law that is relatively unchanging from place to place and over time.[21]

More recent observers have agreed that "Islamic justice is based on philosophical principles that are considered alien, if not unconscionable, to the Western observer." However, these same writers note, strict punishments such as hand amputation "may not be inconsistent with the fundamentals of natural law or Judeo-Christian doctrine. The imposition of the penalty in specific cases and under rigorous rules of evidence—as the principle requires—may be indeed justifiable, and even necessary, in the Islamic context of sustaining a spiritual . . . society."[22]

International Criminal Justice Organizations

At the beginning of the third millennium, the criminal phenomenon not only does not care about borders, but it also participates in globalization.

—Andre Bossard, former Secretary General of Interpol[ii]

The first international conference on criminology and criminal justice met in London in 1872.[23] It evolved out of emerging humanitarian concerns about the treatment of prisoners. Human rights, the elimination of corporal punishment, and debates over capital punishment occupied the conference participants. Although other meetings were held from time to time, little agreement could be reached among the international community on criminal etiology, justice paradigms, or the philosophical and practical bases for criminal punishment and rehabilitation. Finally, in 1938, the International Society for Criminology (ISC) was formed to bring together people from diverse cultural backgrounds who shared an interest in social policies relating to crime and justice. In its early years, membership in the ISC consisted mostly of national officials and academics with close government ties.[24] As a consequence, many of the first conferences (called *international congresses*) sponsored by the ISC strongly supported the status quo and were devoid of any significant recommendations for change or growth.

Throughout the 1960s and 1970s, the ISC was strongly influenced by a growing worldwide awareness of human rights. About the same time, a number of international organizations began to press for an understanding of the political and legal processes through which deviance and crime come to be defined. Among them were the Scandinavian Research Council for Criminology (formed in 1962), the Criminological Research Council (created in 1962 by the Council of Europe), and other regional associations concerned with justice issues.

A number of contemporary organizations and publications continue to focus world attention on criminal justice issues. Perhaps the best-known modern center for the academic study of crossnational criminal justice is the International Center of Comparative Criminology at the University of Montreal. Established in 1969, the center serves as a locus of study for criminal justice professionals from around the world and maintains an excellent library of international criminal justice information. The International Police Executive Symposium (IPES) was founded in 1994 to bring international police researchers and practitioners together and to facilitate cross-cultural and international exchanges between criminal justice experts around the world. IPES, which is associated with the Human Rights and Law Enforcement Institute (HRALEI) at the State University of New York at Plattsburg, publishes *Police Practice and Research: An International Journal.* The Office of International Criminal Justice (OICJ), with offices in Illinois, Indiana, and Texas, has also become a well-known contributor to the study of comparative criminal justice. In conjunction with Sam Houston State University's Criminal Justice Center (in Huntsville, Texas), OICJ publishes the magazine *Crime and Justice International* and sponsors study tours of various nations. Visit OICJ via **Web Extra 17–3** at cjtoday.com.

In 1995, Mitre Corporation in McLean, Virginia, began an Internet service that provides information about the UN Crime Prevention Branch. The UN Crime and Justice Information Network (UNCJIN) holds much promise as an online provider of international criminal justice information. Visit UNCJIN via **Web Extra 17–4** at cjtoday.com. Similarly, the World Justice Information Network (WJIN), sponsored by the National Institute of Justice and the U.S. Department of State, provides a members-only forum for the discussion of justice issues around the globe. Apply for membership in WJIN via **Web Extra 17–5**. Finally, the UN Center for International Crime Prevention, in conjunction with the World Society of Victimology, sponsors the International Victimology website, available via **Web Extra 17–6**.

WEB
Extra
■ ■ ■ ■

The Role of the United Nations in Criminal Justice

The United Nations, composed of 185 member states and based in New York City, is the largest and most inclusive international body in the world. From its inception in 1945, the United Nations has been very interested in international crime prevention and world criminal justice systems. A UN resolution entitled the International Bill of Human Rights supports the rights and dignity of everyone who comes into contact with a criminal justice system.

One of the best-known specific UN recommendations on criminal justice is its Standard Minimum Rules for the Treatment of Prisoners. The rules call for the fair treatment of prisoners, including recognition of the basic humanity of all inmates, and set specific standards for housing, nutrition, exercise, and medical care. Follow-up surveys conducted by the United Nations have shown that the rules have had a considerable influence on national legislation and prison regulations throughout the world.[25] Although the rules do not have the weight of law unless adopted and enacted into local legislation, they carry the strong weight of tradition, and at least one expert claims that "there are indeed those who argue that the rules have entered the *corpus* of generally customary human rights law, or that they are binding . . . as an authoritative interpretation of the human rights provisions of the UN charter."[26]

A more recent and potentially significant set of recommendations can be found in the UN Code of Conduct for Law Enforcement Officials. The code calls on law enforcement officers throughout the world to be cognizant of human rights in the performance of their duties. It specifically proscribes the use of torture and other abuses.

The UN World Crime Surveys, which report official crime statistics from nearly 100 countries, provide a global portrait of criminal activity. Seen historically, the surveys have shown that crimes against property are most characteristic of nations with developed economies (where they constitute approximately 82% of all reported crime), while crimes against the person occur much more frequently in developing countries (where they account for 43% of all crime).[27] Complementing the official statistics of the World Crime Surveys are data from the International Victim Survey (IVS), which is conducted in approximately 50 countries. To date, three surveys have been conducted—in 1989, 1992, and 1996–1997.

Through its Office for Drug Control and Crime Prevention (ODCCP), the United Nations continues to advance the cause of crime prevention and to disseminate useful criminal justice information. The program provides forums for ongoing discussions of justice practices around the world. It has regional links throughout the world, sponsored by supportive national governments that have agreed to fund the program's work. The European Institute for Crime Prevention and Control (HEUNI), for example, provides the program's regional European link in a network of institutes operating throughout the world. Other network components include the UN Interregional Crime and Justice Research Institute (UNICRI) in Rome; an Asian regional institute (UNAFEI) in Tokyo; ILANUE, based in San Jose, Costa Rica, which focuses on crime problems in Latin America and the Caribbean; an African institute (UNAFRI) in Kampala, Uganda; Australia's AIC in Canberra; an Arabic institute (ASSTC) in Riyadh, Saudi Arabia; and other centers in Siracusa, Italy, and in Vancouver and Montreal, Canada.[28] Visit the UN Office for Drug Control and Crime Prevention via **Web Extra 17–7** at cjtoday.com.

In 1995, the United States signed an agreement with the UN Crime Prevention and Criminal Justice Branch that is intended to facilitate the international sharing of information and research findings.[29] Under the agreement, the National Institute of Justice joined 11 other criminal justice research organizations throughout the world as an associate UN institute.

Continuing a tradition begun in 1885 by the former International Penal and Penitentiary Commission, the United Nations holds an international congress on crime every five years. The first UN crime congress, the 1955 Congress on the Prevention of Crime and the Treatment of Offenders, met in Geneva, Switzerland. Crime congresses provide a forum through which member states can exchange information and experiences, compare criminal justice practices between countries, find solutions to crime, and take action at an international level. The Tenth UN crime congress was held in Vienna, Austria, in 2000. Topics discussed at the meeting included (1) promoting the rule of law and strengthening the criminal justice systems of various nations, (2) the need for international cooperation in combating transnational crime, and (3) the need for a fair, ethical, and effective system of criminal justice in the promotion of economic and social development. CJ Today Exhibit 17–1 contains the UN declaration on crime and justice that resulted from the Vienna meeting.

The meeting also led to passage of the 2000 UN Protocol to Prevent, Suppress and Punish Trafficking in Persons, Especially Women and Children, which supplements the UN Convention against Transnational Organized Crime.[30] Nations that are parties to the protocol must criminalize the offense of human trafficking, prevent trafficking, protect and assist victims of trafficking,

Thematic Question

What crime- and justice-related issues should the United Nations concentrate on? Why?

WEB
Extra
■■■■

CJ Today Exhibit 17–1

Vienna Declaration on Crime and Justice

We the Member States of the United Nations,

Concerned about the impact on our societies of the commission of serious crimes of a global nature and convinced of the need for bilateral, regional and international cooperation in crime prevention and criminal justice,

Concerned in particular about transnational organized crime and the relationships between its various forms,

Convinced that adequate prevention and rehabilitation programmes are fundamental to an effective crime control strategy, and that such programmes should take into account social and economic factors which may make people more vulnerable to, and likely to engage in criminal behaviour,

Stressing that a fair, responsible, ethical and efficient criminal justice system is an important factor in the promotion of economic and social development and of security,

Aware of the promise of restorative approaches to justice that aim to reduce and promote the healing of victims, offenders and communities,

Having assembled at the Tenth United Nations Congress on the Prevention of Crime and the Treatment of Offenders in Vienna from 10 to 17 April 2000 to decide to take effective concerted action, in a spirit of cooperation, to combat the world crime problem,

Declare as follows:

- We emphasize the responsibility of each State to establish and maintain a fair, responsible, ethical and efficient criminal justice system.

- We recognize the necessity of closer coordination and cooperation among States in combating the world crime problem, bearing in mind that action against it is a common and shared responsibility. . . .

- We undertake to strengthen international cooperation in order to create a conducive environment for the fight against organized crime, promoting growth and sustainable development and eradicating poverty and unemployment.

- We also commit ourselves to the development of action-oriented policy recommendations based on the special needs of women as criminal justice practitioners, victims, prisoners and offenders.

- We commit ourselves to the development of more effective ways of collaborating with one another with a view to eradicating the scourge of trafficking in persons, especially women and children, and the smuggling of migrants. . . .

- We also commit ourselves to the enhancement of international cooperation and mutual legal assistance to curb illicit manufacturing of and trafficking in firearms, their parts and components and ammunition, and we establish 2005 as the target year for achieving a significant decrease in their incidence worldwide.

- We reaffirm that combating money-laundering and the criminal economy constitutes a major element of the strategies against organized crime. . . .

- We decide to develop action-oriented policy recommendations on the prevention and control of computer-related crime. . . . We also commit ourselves to working towards enhancing our ability to prevent, investigate and prosecute high-technology and computer-related crime.

- We note that acts of violence and terrorism continue to be of grave concern. In conformity with the Charter of the United Nations and taking into account all the relevant General Assembly resolutions, we will together, in conjunction with our other efforts to prevent and to combat terrorism, take effective, resolute and speedy measures with respect to preventing and combating criminal activities carried out for the purpose of furthering terrorism in all its forms and manifestations. . . .

- We also note that racial discrimination, xenophobia and related forms of intolerance continue and we recognize the importance of taking steps to incorporate into international crime prevention strategies and norms measures to prevent and combat crime associated with racism, racial discrimination, xenophobia and related forms of intolerance.

- We affirm our determination to combat violence stemming from intolerance on the basis of ethnicity and resolve to make a strong contribution, in the area of crime prevention and criminal justice. . . .

- We also recognize the importance of prison reform, the independence of the judiciary and the prosecution authorities, and the International Code of Conduct for Public Officials. . . .

- We shall endeavour, as appropriate, to use and apply the United Nations standards and norms in crime prevention and criminal justice in national law and practice. . . .

- We further recognize with great concern that juveniles in difficult circumstances are often at risk of becoming delinquent or easy candidates for recruitment by criminal groups, including groups involved in transnational organized crime, and we commit ourselves to undertaking countermeasures to prevent this growing phenomenon. . . .

- We recognize that comprehensive crime prevention strategies at the international, national, regional and local levels must address the root causes and risk factors related to crime and victimization through social, economic, health, educational and justice policies. . . .

- We commit ourselves to according priority to containing the growth and overcrowding of pre-trial and detention prison populations, as appropriate, by promoting safe and effective alternatives to incarceration.

- We decide to introduce, where appropriate, national, regional and international action plans in support of victims of crime, such as mechanisms for mediation and restorative justice. . . .

- We encourage the development of restorative justice policies, procedures and programmes that are respectful of the rights, needs and interests of victims, offenders, communities and all other parties. . . .

Source: Excerpted from the Tenth United Nations Congress on the Prevention of Crime and the Treatment of Offenders, *Vienna Declaration on Crime and Justice: Meeting the Challenges of the Twenty-First Century*, Vienna, April 10–17, 2000.

Young girls working in a brothel in Thailand. The 2003 federal Trafficking Victims Protection Reauthorization Act focuses on the illegal practice of sex trafficking and on the illegal "obtaining of a person for labor services." How common is human trafficking? In what parts of the world is it most prevalent?

and promote international cooperation to combat the problem of trafficking.[31] Learn more about the crime of human trafficking via the Protection Project at Web Extra 17–8 at cjtoday.com, and read the U.S. Department of State's 2003 *Trafficking in Persons Report* at Library Extra 17–4 at cjtoday.com.

WEB Extra

LIBRARY Extra

Interpol and Europol

The **International Criminal Police Organization (Interpol)**, headquartered in Lyons, France, traces its origins back to the first International Criminal Police Congress of 1914, which met in Monaco.[32] The theme of that meeting was international cooperation in the investigation of crimes and the apprehension of fugitives. Interpol, however, did not officially begin operations until 1946, when the end of World War II brought about a new spirit of international harmony.

Today, 182 nations belong to Interpol.[33] The U.S. Interpol unit is called the U.S. National Central Bureau (USNCB) and is a separate agency within the U.S. Department of Justice. USNCB is staffed with personnel from 12 federal agencies, including the Drug Enforcement Administration, the Secret Service, and the Federal Bureau of Investigation. Through USNCB, Interpol is linked to all major U.S. computerized criminal records repositories, including the FBI's National Crime Information Index, the State Department's Advanced Visa Lookout System, and the Department of Homeland Security's Master Index.

Interpol's primary purpose is to act as a clearinghouse for information on offenses and suspects who are believed to operate across national boundaries. The organization is committed to promoting "the widest possible mutual assistance between all criminal police authorities within the limits of laws existing in . . . different countries and in the spirit of the Universal Declaration of Human Rights."[34] Historically, Interpol pledged itself not to intervene in religious, political, military, or racial disagreements in participant nations. As a consequence, a number of bombings and hostage situations that were related to these types of disagreements were not officially investigated until 1984, when Interpol officially entered the fight against international terrorism.

In late 2001, Interpol's Seventieth General Assembly unanimously adopted the Budapest Anti-Terrorism Resolution. The resolution calls for greater police cooperation in fighting international terrorism. In 2005, delegates attending Interpol's first Global Conference on Preventing Bio-Terrorism met in Lyon, France, and agreed on a series of measures aimed at preventing or effectively responding to bioterror attacks.[35] As this book goes to press, Interpol continues to expand its activities. It is in the process of developing a centralized international forensic DNA database and is creating an international framework for disaster victim identification.[36]

Interpol does not have its own field investigators. The agency has no powers of arrest or of search and seizure in member countries. Instead, Interpol's purpose is to facilitate, coordinate, and encourage police cooperation as a means of combating international crime. It draws on the willingness of local and national police forces to lend support to its activities. The headquarters

International Criminal Police Organization (Interpol)

An international law enforcement support organization that began operations in 1946 and today has 182 member nations.

Lecture Note

Describe the theme of international police cooperation that characterizes Interpol. Ask what role students envision for Interpol in the twenty-first century.

WEB
Extra
■ ■ ■ ■

LIBRARY
Extra
■ ■ ■ ■

European Police Office (Europol)

The integrated police–intelligence gathering and dissemination arm of the member nations of the European Union.

staff of Interpol consists of about 250 individuals, many with prior police experience, who direct data-gathering efforts around the world and who serve to alert law enforcement organizations to the movement of suspected offenders within their jurisdiction. Visit Interpol headquarters via Web Extra 17–9, and read the organization's latest annual activity report at Library Extra 17–5 at cjtoday.com.

The members of the European Union (EU) agreed to the establishment of the **European Police Office (Europol)** in the Maastricht Treaty of February 7, 1992. Based in The Hague, the Netherlands, Europol started limited operations in 1994 in the form of the Europol Drugs Unit. Over time, other important law enforcement activities were added to the Europol agenda. The Europol Convention was ratified by all member states in 1998, and Europol commenced full operations the next year. Europol's mission is to improve the effectiveness and cooperation of law enforcement agencies within the member states of the European Union with the ultimate goal of preventing and combating terrorism, illegal drug trafficking, illicit trafficking in radioactive and nuclear substances, illegal money laundering, trafficking in human beings, and other serious forms of international organized crime. Europol is sometimes described as the "European Union police clearing house."[37] Following the July 2005 London underground and bus bombings, in which more than 50 people died and hundreds were injured, German Interior Minister Otto Schily asked his European Union counterparts meeting in Brussels to give Europol executive powers to conduct EU-wide investigations.[38]

Europol and Interpol work together to develop information on international terrorism, drug trafficking, and trafficking in human beings.[39] Learn more about Europol via Web Extra 17–10 at cjtoday.com.

WEB
Extra
■ ■ ■ ■

The International Criminal Court

Unfortunately, the world is not yet ready for a transnational criminal justice system.

—Andre Bossard, former Secretary General of Interpol[iii]

On April 12, 2000, the International Criminal Court (ICC) was created under the auspices of the United Nations. The ICC, whose operations are only now beginning, is intended to be a permanent criminal court for trying individuals (not countries) who commit the most serious crimes of concern to the international community, such as genocide, war crimes, and crimes against humanity—including the wholesale murder of civilians, torture, and mass rape. The ICC intends to be a global judicial institution with international jurisdiction complementing national legal systems around the world. Support for the ICC was developed through the United Nations, where more than 90 countries approved the court's creation by ratifying what is known as the Rome Statute of the International Criminal Court. The ICC's first prosecutor, Luis Moreno Ocampo of Argentina, was elected in April 2003.[40]

The ICC initiative began after World War II, with unsuccessful efforts to establish an international tribunal to try individuals accused of genocide and other war crimes.[41] In lieu of such a court, military tribunals were held in Nuremberg, Germany, and Tokyo, Japan, to try those accused of war crimes. The 1948 UN Genocide Convention[42] called for the creation of an international criminal court to punish genocide-related offenses and identified the crimes (1) genocide, (2) conspiracy to commit genocide, (3) direct and public incitement to commit genocide, (4) attempt to commit genocide, and (5) complicity in genocide.

In December 1948, the UN General Assembly adopted the Universal Declaration of Human Rights and the Convention on the Prevention and Punishment of the Crime of Genocide. It also called for criminals to be tried "by such international penal tribunals as may have jurisdiction." A number of member states soon asked the United Nation's International Law Commission (ILC) to study the possibility of establishing an ICC.

Development of an ICC was delayed by the cold war that took place between the world's superpowers, who were not willing to subject their military personnel or commanders to international criminal jurisdiction in the event of a "hot" war. In 1981, however, the UN General Assembly asked the International Law Commission to consider creating an international Code of Crimes.

The 1992 war in Bosnia-Herzegovina, which involved clear violations of the Genocide and Geneva Conventions, heightened world interest in the establishment of a permanent ICC. A few years later, 160 countries participated in the Conference of Plenipotentiaries on the Establishment of an International Criminal Court,[43] which was held in Rome. At the end of that conference, member states voted overwhelmingly in favor of the Rome Statute,[44] calling for establishment of an ICC. Effective July 1, 2002, the Rome Statute criminalized trafficking in persons, categorizing it as a crime against humanity.

A few years ago, in what became a stumbling block on the road to the court's creation, the United States expressed concern about the ICC, saying that members of the American military could become subject to ICC jurisdiction. That concern led to U.S. efforts to delay the court's cre-

Kofi Annan, then secretary-general of the United Nations, speaking in Rome at opening ceremonies that marked the signing of the Treaty on Establishment of the International Criminal Court in 1998. What is the jurisdiction of the International Criminal Court?

ation. The issue was resolved in 2002 when the UN Security Council voted to exempt members of the American military from prosecution by the court's War Crimes Tribunal.[45] The Security Council resolution, however, must be renewed annually if it is to remain in force.[46]

In 2005, in one of the court's first official actions, a panel of ICC judges decided to allow independent Dutch investigators to carry out forensic tests in the Democratic Republic of Congo (DRC) as part of an ongoing investigation into the deaths of thousands of people in genocidal violence throughout central Africa.[47] In 2007, the court announced that it would hold its first trial; Thomas Lubanga is charged with kidnapping and forcibly recruiting child soldiers during the DRC civil war in violation of international law. Prosecutors claim that Lubanga kidnapped children as young as ten and forced them to fight—leaving many dead or injured.[48] Learn more about this case and other activities of the ICC by visiting the Coalition for an International Criminal Court via **Web Extra 17–11** at cjtoday.com.

Before the ICC came into existence, Belgium made its courts available to the rest of the world for the prosecution of alleged crimes against humanity.[49] The country's legal system, in essence, took on the role of global prosecutor for these kinds of crimes. Under a 1993 Belgian law, which is regarded by many as the world's most expansive statute against genocide and other crimes against humanity, Belgian justices were called on to enforce substantial portions of the country's criminal laws on a global scale. Belgian courts also focused on enforcing the 1949 Geneva Convention governing the conduct of war and the treatment of refugees. Belgian law specifically provides for the criminal prosecution of individuals who are not Belgian citizens, and it provides no immunity to prosecution for foreign leaders. In 2001, for example, a Brussels jury convicted four people, including two Catholic nuns, of contributing to ethnic violence in the central African nation of Rwanda in 1994.

Belgian authorities have investigated more than a dozen complaints involving current and former state officials, including Ariel Sharon (prime minister of Israel), Saddam Hussein (former Iraqi leader), Hissene Habre (former dictator of Chad), Hashemi Rafsanjani (former president of Iran), Driss Basri (former interior minister of Morocco), Denis Sassou Nguesso (president of Congo-Brazzaville), and Fidel Castro (leader of Cuba). In the case of the Cuban leader, Cuban exiles charged Castro in Brussels's criminal court in October 2001 with false imprisonment, murder, torture, and other crimes against humanity. As a result of such investigations, Belgium has experienced strained relationships with a number of countries, and some in the nation have questioned the wisdom of charging sitting heads of state with violations of the criminal law.

WEB
Extra
▪▪▪▪

The effects of globalization have created a growing phenomenon of globalized crime that is threatening the stability and values of the entire world community.

—Daniel Mabrey, Sam Houston State University[iv]

Globalization and Crime

Globalization refers to the internationalization of trade, services, investments, information, and other forms of human social activity, including crime. The process of globalization is fed by modern systems of transportation and communication, including air travel, television, and the Internet. Globalization contributes to growing similarities in the way people do things and in the beliefs and values that they hold. The lessening of differences brought about by globalization is highlighted by a definition from one authoritative source, which says that globalization is "a process of social homogenization by which the experiences of everyday life, marked by the diffusion of commodities and ideas, can foster a standardization of cultural expressions around the

globalization

The internationalization of trade, services, investment, information, and other forms of human social activity.

Globalization has given us cheap Chinese T-shirts and Indian software; it has also brought the international trade in atomic weapons design and al-Qaeda websites.

—Philip Stephens, in the Financial Times

world."[50] The adoption of English as the *de facto* standard language on the Internet and of the global software community, for example, has exposed many around the world to literature and ideas that they might not otherwise have encountered and has influenced the way they think. Consequently, globalization is opposed in many parts of the world by those who would hold to traditional ways of thinking and acting. Instead of inevitably uniting humanity, as some had hoped, globalization has also made people aware of differences—and has led many people to reject cultures and ideas dissimilar to their own.

The first steps toward globalization occurred long before the modern era and were taken by nation-states seeking to expand their spheres of influence. The banner of globalization today is carried by multinational corporations whose operations span the globe. The synergistic effects of rapid travel, instantaneous communication, and national economies that are tied closely to one another have led to an increasingly rapid pace of the globalization process, which some refer to as *hyperglobalization*. Criminal entrepreneurs and terrorists are among those with a global vision, and at least some of them think and plan like the CEOs of multinational businesses. Today's international criminal community consists of terrorists, drug traffickers, pornography peddlers, identity thieves, copyright violators, and those who traffic in human beings, body parts, genetic material, and military weapons.

Transnational Crime

In 2006, Cheng Chui Ping, known to her associates as the Snakehead Queen, was sentenced in U.S. District Court to 35 years in prison for having smuggled as many as 3,000 illegal immigrants into the United States from her native China. "Snakeheads" are human smugglers, and prior to her arrest Ping may have been the most active human trafficker in New York City. Her fees, which were partially determined by an immigrant's ability to pay, ranged up to $40,000 per person, and the FBI says that her illegal transnational activities may have netted her as much as $40 million.[51]

transnational crime

Unlawful activity undertaken and supported by organized criminal groups operating across national boundaries.

Transnational crime and the internationally organized criminal groups that support it are partly the result of an ongoing process of globalization. Transnational crime is unlawful activity undertaken and supported by organized criminal groups operating across national boundaries, and it promises to become one of the most pressing challenges of the twenty-first century for criminal justice professionals. In a recent conference in Seoul, Korea, Assistant U.S. Attorney General Laurie Robinson addressed the issue of transnational crime, saying, "The United States recognizes that we cannot confront crime in isolation. . . . It is clear crime does not respect international boundaries. It is clear crime is global. As recent economic trends demonstrate, what happens in one part of the world impacts all the rest. And crime problems and trends are no different."[52]

According to the United Nations, an offense can be considered transnational in nature if any of the following conditions are met:[53]

1. It is committed in more than one country.
2. It is committed in one country but a substantial part of its preparation, planning, direction, or control takes place in another country.
3. It is committed in one country but involves an organized criminal group that engages in criminal activities in more than one country.
4. It is committed in one country but has substantial effects in another country.

The post–cold war world is more dangerous and less stable than when power was balanced among superpowers. The power vacuum created in many parts of the world by the fall of the Soviet Union and the growing instability in the Middle East has led to a number of new threats. According to Robert Gelbard, U.S. assistant secretary for international narcotics and law enforcement affairs, "The main threat now is transnational organized crime. It comes in many forms: drug trafficking, money laundering, terrorism, alien smuggling, trafficking in weapons of mass destruction, [human trafficking, often involving forced prostitution], fraud and other forms of corruption. These problems all have one critical element in common," says Gelbard. "They threaten the national security of all states and governments—from our closest allies to those that we find most repugnant. No country is safe. International criminal organizations all seek to establish pliant governments that can be manipulated through bribery and intimidation. They respect no national boundaries and already act with virtual impunity in many parts of the world."[54]

According to the National Institute of Justice, transnational crime groups have profited more from globalization than have legitimate businesses, which are subject to domestic and host country laws and regulations. NIJ points out that transnational crime syndicates and networks, abetted by official corruption, blackmail, and intimidation, can use open markets and open societies to their full advantage.[55]

Worse still, entire nations may become rogue countries, or quasi-criminal regimes where criminal activity runs rampant and wields considerable influence over the national government. Russia, for example, appears to be approaching this status through an intertwining of the goals of organized criminal groups and official interests that run to the top levels of government. The number of organized criminal groups operating in Russia is estimated to be more than 12,000.[56] Emilio Viano, professor of criminology at American University and an expert on Russian organized crime, notes that "what we have is an immense country practically controlled by organized crime. These groups are getting stronger and stronger and using Russia as a base for their global ventures—taking over everything from drugs and prostitution to currency exchange and stealing World Bank and IMF [International Monetary Fund] loans."[57] In late 2006, for example, Russian organized crime hitmen shot and killed Andrei Kozlov, the top deputy chairman of the Russian Central Bank.[58] Kozlov, who was gunned down as he left a soccer match in Moscow, had worked for four years to fight criminality and money laundering in Russia's banking system in an effort to draw foreign investments into the country.

The recent globalization of crime and terrorism, which is sometimes termed the *globalization of insecurity,* has necessitated enhanced coordination of law enforcement efforts in different parts of the world as well as the expansion of American law enforcement activities beyond national borders. In 2003, for example, the U.S. Congress passed the Trafficking Victims Protection Reauthorization Act (TVPA)[59] to further protect victims of human trafficking, regardless of their country of origin. Trafficking offenses under the law, which is aimed primarily at international offenders, include (1) sex trafficking, in which a commercial sex act is induced by force, fraud, or coercion or in which the person induced to perform such act has not attained 18 years of age,[60] and (2) the recruitment, harboring, transportation, provision, or obtaining of a person for labor services, through the use of force, fraud, or coercion, for the purpose of subjection to involuntary servitude, peonage, debt bondage, or slavery. The TVPA also provides funds for training U.S. law enforcement personnel at international police academies, and U.S. police agencies routinely send agents to assist law enforcement officers in other countries who are involved in transnational investigations.

Another tool in the fight against transnational crime is **extradition**. Not all countries, however, are willing to extradite suspects wanted in the United States. Consequently, as Kevin Ryan of Vermont's Norwich University observes, "The globalization of United States law enforcement policy has also entailed the abduction of fugitives from abroad to stand trial when an asylum nation refuses an extradition request."[61] While certainly not a common practice, the forcible removal of criminal suspects from foreign jurisdictions appears more likely with suspected terrorists than with other types of criminals. A 2007 special report on transnational organized crime and its impact on the United States is available at **Library Extra 17–6** at cjtoday.com. For additional information on transnational organized crime and the globalization phenomenon, see **Web Extra 17–12** at cjtoday.com.

Terrorism

Terrorism as a criminal activity and the prevention of further acts of terrorism became primary concerns of American political leaders and justice system officials following the September 11, 2001, terrorist attacks on the United States. There is, however, no single uniformly accepted definition of terrorism that is applicable to all places and all circumstances. Some definitions are statutory in nature, while others were created for such practical purposes as gauging success in the fight against terrorism. Still others relate to specific forms of terrorism, such as cyberterrorism (discussed later in this section), and many legislative sources speak only of "acts of terrorism" or "terrorist activity" rather than terrorism itself because the nature of Western jurisprudence is to legislate against acts rather than against concepts.

The federal Foreign Relations Authorization Act[62] defines *terrorism* in terms of four primary elements. The act says that terrorism is (1) premeditated, (2) politically motivated (3) violence (4) committed against noncombatant targets.[63] The FBI offers a nonstatutory working definition of terrorism as "a violent act or an act dangerous to human life in violation of the criminal laws of the United States or of any state to intimidate or coerce a government, the civilian population, or any segment thereof, in furtherance of political or social objectives."[64] Among the laws that define certain forms of human *activity* as terrorism, the Immigration and Nationality Act provides one of the most comprehensive and widely used definitions. That definition is shown in CJ Today Exhibit 17–2.

CJ Today Exhibit 17–2

What Is Terrorist Activity?

Federal law enforcement efforts directed against agents of foreign terrorist organizations derive their primary authority from the Immigration and Nationality Act, found in Title 8 of the U.S. Code. The act defines *terrorist activity* as follows:

(ii) "Terrorist activity" defined

As used in this chapter, the term "terrorist activity" means any activity which is unlawful under the laws of the place where it is committed (or which, if committed in the United States, would be unlawful under the laws of the United States or any State) and which involves any of the following:

(I) The hijacking or sabotage of any conveyance (including an aircraft, vessel, or vehicle).

(II) The seizing or detaining, and threatening to kill, injure, or continue to detain, another individual in order to compel a third person (including a governmental organization) to do or abstain from doing any act as an explicit or implicit condition for the release of the individual seized or detained.

(III) A violent attack upon an internationally protected person (as defined in section 1116(b)(4) of title 18) or upon the liberty of such a person.

(IV) An assassination.

(V) The use of any—

(a) biological agent, chemical agent, or nuclear weapon or device, or

(b) explosive or firearm (other than for mere personal monetary gain), with intent to endanger, directly or indirectly, the safety of one or more individuals or to cause substantial damage to property.

(VI) A threat, attempt, or conspiracy to do any of the foregoing.

(iii) "Engage in terrorist activity" defined

As used in this chapter, the term "engage in terrorist activity" means to commit, in an individual capacity or as a member of an organization, an act of terrorist activity or an act which the actor knows, or reasonably should know, affords material support to any individual, organization, or government in conducting a terrorist activity at any time, including any of the following acts:

(I) The preparation or planning of a terrorist activity.

(II) The gathering of information on potential targets for terrorist activity.

(III) The providing of any type of material support, including a safe house, transportation, communications, funds, false documentation or identification, weapons, explosives, or training, to any individual the actor knows or has reason to believe has committed or plans to commit a terrorist activity.

(IV) The soliciting of funds or other things of value for terrorist activity or for any terrorist organization.

(V) The solicitation of any individual for membership in a terrorist organization, terrorist government, or to engage in a terrorist activity.

Thematic Question

Examine Gwynn Nettler's characteristics of terrorism. How are terrorists like other criminals? How do they differ?

domestic terrorism

The unlawful use of force or violence by an individual or a group that is based and operates entirely within the United States and its territories, acts without foreign direction, and directs its activities against elements of the U.S. government or population.[vi]

international terrorism

The unlawful use of force or violence by an individual or a group that has some connection to a foreign power, or whose activities transcend national boundaries, against people or property in order to intimidate or coerce a government, the civilian population, or any segment thereof, in furtherance of political or social objectives.[vii]

According to criminologist Gwynn Nettler, all forms of terrorism share six characteristics:[65]

- *No rules.* There are no moral limitations on the type or degree of violence that terrorists can use.
- *No innocents.* No distinctions are made between soldiers and civilians. Children can be killed as well as adults.
- *Economy.* Kill one, frighten 10,000.
- *Publicity.* Terrorists seek publicity, and publicity encourages terrorism.
- *Meaning.* Terrorist acts give meaning and significance to the lives of terrorists.
- *No clarity.* Beyond the immediate aim of destructive acts, the long-term goals of terrorists are likely to be poorly conceived or impossible to implement.

Moreover, notes Nettler, "Terrorism that succeeds escalates."[66]

Types of Terrorism

It is important to distinguish between two major forms of terrorism: domestic and international. Distinctions between the two forms are made in terms of the origin, base of operations, and objectives of a terrorist organization. In the United States, **domestic terrorism** refers to the unlawful use of force or violence by an individual or a group that is based and operates entirely within this country and its territories without foreign direction and whose acts are directed against elements of the U.S. government or population.[67] **International terrorism,** in contrast, is the unlawful use of force or violence by an individual or a group that has some connection to a foreign power, or whose activities transcend national boundaries, against people or property in order to intimidate or coerce a government, the civilian population, or any segment thereof, in furtherance of political or social objectives.[68] International terrorism is sometimes mistakenly called *foreign* *terrorism,* a term that, strictly speaking, refers only to acts of terrorism that occur outside of the United States.

DOMESTIC TERRORISM

Throughout the 1960s and 1970s, domestic terrorism in the United States required the expenditure of considerable criminal justice resources. The Weathermen, Students for a Democratic Society, the Symbionese Liberation Army, the Black Panthers, and other radical groups routinely challenged the authority of federal and local governments. Bombings, kidnappings, and shootouts peppered the national scene. As overt acts of domestic terrorism declined in frequency in the 1980s, international terrorism took their place. The war in Lebanon; terrorism in Israel; bombings in France, Italy, and Germany; and the many violent offshoots of the Iran-Iraq war and the first Gulf War occupied the attention of the media and of much of the rest of the world. Vigilance by the FBI, the Central Intelligence Agency (CIA), and other agencies largely prevented the spread of terrorism to the United States.

Worrisome today are domestic underground survivalist and separatist groups and potentially violent special-interest groups, each with its own vision of a future America. In 1993, for example, a confrontation between David Koresh's Branch Davidian followers and federal agents left 72 Davidians (including Koresh) and four federal agents dead in Waco, Texas.

Exactly two years to the day after the Davidian standoff ended in a horrific fire that destroyed the compound, a powerful truck bomb devastated the Alfred P. Murrah Federal Building in downtown Oklahoma City. One hundred sixty-eight people died, and hundreds more were wounded. The targeted nine-story building had housed offices of the Social Security Administration; the Drug Enforcement Administration; the Secret Service; the Bureau of Alcohol, Tobacco, Firearms, and Explosives; and a day-care center called America's Kids. The fertilizer-and-diesel-fuel device used in the terrorist attack was estimated to have weighed about 1,200 pounds and had been left in a rental truck on the Fifth Street side of the building. The blast, which left a crater 30 feet wide and 8 feet deep and spread debris over a ten-block area, demonstrated just how vulnerable the United States is to terrorist attack.

In 1997, a federal jury found 29-year-old Timothy McVeigh guilty of 11 counts, ranging from conspiracy to first-degree murder, in the Oklahoma City bombing. Jurors concluded that McVeigh had conspired with Terry Nichols, a friend he had met in the Army, and with unknown others to destroy the Murrah Building. Prosecutors made clear their belief that the attack was intended to revenge the 1993 assault on the Branch Davidian compound. McVeigh was sentenced to death and was executed by lethal injection at the U.S. penitentiary in Terre Haute, Indiana, in 2001.[69] McVeigh was the first person under federal jurisdiction to be put to death since 1963. In 2004, Terry Nichols was convicted of 161 counts of first-degree murder by an Oklahoma jury and was sentenced to 161 life terms for his role in the bombings.[70] He had previously been convicted of various federal charges.

Some experts believe that the Oklahoma City attack was modeled after a similar bombing described in the *Turner Diaries,* a novel used by extremist groups to map their rise to power.[71] Just as Hitler's biography *Mein Kampf* served as a call to arms for Nazis in Europe during the 1930s, the *Turner Diaries* describes an Aryan revolution that occurs in the United States during the 1990s in which Jews, blacks, and other minorities are removed from positions of influence in government and society.

> *No group or nation should mistake America's intentions: We will not rest until terrorist groups of global reach have been found, have been stopped, and have been defeated.*
>
> —President George W. Bush

Lecture Note

Highlight the growth of radical groups throughout America by pointing to the white supremacist and separatist organizations described in this chapter and in Chapter 2. Ask students whether they think such organizations will ever present a real threat to our nation's security.

Sport utility vehicles destroyed in a New Year's Day fire at a Ford Lincoln Mercury dealership in Girard, Pennsylvania. The Earth Liberation Front (ELF), a domestic terrorist organization, claimed responsibility for the fire. What are the goals of the ELF?

CJ News

Domestic Terrorism: New Trouble at Home

Since 9/11, the nation's attention has been focused on possible threats from Islamic terrorists. But home-grown terrorists have been steadily plotting and carrying out attacks in unrelated incidents across the nation, according to federal authorities and two organizations that monitor hate groups.

None of the incidents over the past few years matched the devastation of 9/11 or even the 1995 bombing of the Oklahoma City federal building, which killed 168 and remains the deadliest act of terrorism against the nation by a U.S. citizen.

But some of the alleged domestic terrorists who have been arrested had ambitious plans. The people and groups range from white supremacists, anti-government types and militia members to eco-terrorists and people who hate corporations. They include violent anti-abortionists and black and brown nationalists who envision a separate state for blacks and Latinos. And they have been busy.

"Not a lot of attention is being paid to this, because everybody is concerned about the guy in a turban. But there are still plenty of angry, Midwestern white guys out there," says U.S. Marshals Service chief inspector Geoff Shank.

Shank, who is based in the Chicago area, says the concerns about domestic terrorism range from anti-abortion extremists who threaten to attack clinics and doctors to some violent biker gangs that may be involved in organized crime. And the FBI said in June [2004] that eco-terrorism—acts of violence, sabotage or property damage motivated by concern for animals or the environment—was the nation's top domestic terrorism threat. The bureau said then that eco-terrorists had committed more than 1,100 criminal acts and caused property damage estimated [to be] at least $110 million since 1976.

Alleged terrorist plots by U.S. citizens are not new, but many of the recent conspiracies were overshadowed by 9/11 and the hunt for terrorists abroad. Most of the foiled plots didn't get very far. And few got much publicity. But there were some potentially close calls, such as the scheme by William Krar, an east Texas man who stockpiled enough sodium cyanide to gas everyone in a building the size of a high school basketball gymnasium before he was arrested in 2002.

Shank, whose unit mainly searches for fugitives, including some wanted on domestic terror-related charges, led the manhunt for Clayton Lee Waagner, 48, of Kennerdell, Pa. Waagner was convicted in December [2003] of mailing hundreds of threat letters containing bogus anthrax to abortion clinics in 24 states. During his trial in Philadelphia, prosecutors documented Waagner's ties to the Army of God, an extremist group that believes violence against abortion providers is an acceptable way to end abortion.

"There's been a very, very heavy focus nationally on foreign terrorism since 9/11," says Mark Potok of the Southern Poverty Law Center in Montgomery, Ala., which has tracked hate groups since 1971. "The reality is that, meanwhile, domestic terrorism has hummed along at quite a steady clip. It . . . still poses a very serious threat."

William Krar, 63, left, and his common-law wife, Judith Bruey, 55, being escorted by authorities following their sentencing at the U.S. courthouse in Tyler, Texas, on May 4, 2004, after pleading guilty to illegally stockpiling an array of dangerous chemical weapons and conspiracy to possess illegal chemical weapons. Krar received a sentence of 11 years in prison, while Bruey was ordered to serve five years. How can we protect ourselves against domestic terrorists?

Among the incidents since 9/11:

- In Tennessee, the FBI recently arrested a man who agents say hated the federal government and was attempting to acquire chemical weapons and explosives to blow up a government building. Demetrius "Van" Crocker, 39, of McKenzie, Tenn., pleaded not guilty on November 5, 2004. His attorney, public defender Stephen Shankman, did not return calls.

- In May [2004], Krar, 63, of Noonday, Texas, was sentenced to more than 11 years in prison after he stockpiled enough sodium cyanide to kill everyone inside a 30,000-square-foot building. Krar, described by federal prosecutors as a white supremacist, also had nine machine guns, 67 sticks of explosives and more than 100,000 rounds of ammunition. Investigators and the federal prosecutor said they didn't know what Krar intended to do with the potentially deadly chemicals. Krar's common-law wife, Judith Bruey, 55, pleaded guilty to conspiracy to possess illegal weapons and was sentenced to nearly five years.

- In 2004, two Utah men described by the U.S. attorney there as "domestic terrorists" pleaded guilty to setting separate arson fires related to eco-terrorism. Justus Ireland, 23, admitted start-

CJ News (continued)

ing a fire that caused $1.5 million damage at a West Jordan lumber company and spray-painting "ELF" at the site. The Earth Liberation Front has been connected to dozens of acts of vandalism and arson around the country since 1996. Joshua Demmitt, 18, of Provo, pleaded guilty to starting a fire at Brigham Young University's Ellsworth Farm, where animal experiments are conducted, in the name of the Animal Liberation Front. A third man, Harrison Burrows, 18, also of Provo, pleaded guilty earlier.

- In May 2004, the FBI's domestic terrorism unit charged seven members of an animal rights group with terrorism after investigating what they said was a marked increase in crimes to stop the use of animals for product testing. The activists, arrested in New York, New Jersey, California and Washington state, are members of Stop Huntingdon Animal Cruelty. The group seeks to shut down Huntingdon Life Sciences, a New Jersey product-testing company.

  Prosecutors allege that the activists set fire to Huntingdon employees' cars, vandalized shareholders' homes and threatened their families. They are charged with conspiring to commit terrorism against an enterprise that uses animals for research and could face up to three years in prison if convicted.

- In mid-2004, a Brookfield, Wisconsin, man labeled a domestic terrorist by federal prosecutors received an eight-year prison sentence for interfering with Madison police radio frequencies. Rajib Mitra, 26, had blocked police radio signals and later broadcast sex sounds over police radios. His attorney argued that the transmissions were an accident.

Mitra was one of the first defendants sentenced under guidelines changed after the Sept. 11 terrorist attacks. The changes, effective November 5, 2003, impose stiffer penalties for domestic terrorism. Under the previous sentencing guidelines, Mitra probably would have been sentenced to 18 to 24 months.

Mitra's attorney, Chris Van Wagner, says his client was not a terrorist and should have received a lesser punishment. "It's clear that (the guidelines) were put in place to punish those who seek to subvert our government and not intended to increase the punishment for people who simply engage in criminal mischief but had no terrorist angle or connection whatsoever," Van Wagner says. "He was just a dolphin caught in a tuna net."

Mitra was charged under provisions of the USA PATRIOT Act that make it a crime to cause such public-safety problems, even if there were no monetary damages. "This is a vivid example of how the PATRIOT Act has been used in cases that clearly have nothing to do with terrorism and that are far removed from what Congress was concerned about when it passed the PATRIOT Act," says Timothy Edgar of the American Civil Liberties Union.

During the 1990s, anti-government groups sprang up all over the country, according to the Southern Poverty Law Center and the Anti-Defamation League, which was founded in 1913 to combat anti-

Semitism and now monitors hate groups. Many formed militias to prepare for large-scale resistance to the government, which the groups blamed for the Randy Weaver siege at Ruby Ridge, Idaho, in 1992 and the Branch Davidian confrontation in Waco, Texas, in 1993.

Many of these group members believed the federal government was secretly setting up concentration camps for dissident Americans and was planning a takeover of the United States by United Nations troops as part of a "new world order." Many also said that mysterious black helicopters were conducting surveillance in the West, according to the ADL.

"The 'black helicopter' crowd is still out there," says Wisconsin federal prosecutor Tim O'Shea, referring to extremists who distrust and abhor the federal government.

Potok says the Southern Poverty Law Center identified 751 hate groups last year, a 6% increase over the 708 such organizations it counted in 2002.

Potok, director of the center's Intelligence Project, which monitors hate groups, says, "I don't mean to minimize the work of groups with ties to al-Qaeda. Obviously, there's a huge external threat as well. But there's a tendency to want to externalize the threat and say the people who want to hurt us don't look like us, they don't worship the same god and don't have the same skin color."

In 2004, the National District Attorneys Association, which has about 7,000 members, held a first-ever conference on domestic terrorism in Washington, D.C., to help local prosecutors identify potential terrorist groups.

"It was very well received," says the association's vice president, Robert Honecker, a prosecutor in Monmouth County, N.J. "They were appreciative of getting the information and the knowledge so they would be prepared should something happen in their jurisdiction."

Some of the alleged efforts by domestic terrorists are chilling.

According to an FBI affidavit in the Tennessee case, Crocker had inquired last spring about where he could obtain nuclear waste or nuclear materials. An informant told the FBI that Crocker, who had "absolute hatred" for the government, wanted "to build a bomb to be detonated at a government building, particularly a courthouse, either federal or state."

In September 2004, according to the affidavit, Crocker told an undercover FBI agent "it would be a good thing if somebody could detonate some sort of weapon of mass destruction in Washington, D.C.," while both houses of Congress "were in session." Crocker allegedly told the agent he admired Adolf Hitler and the Nazi Party. He said "establishing a concentration camp for Jewish insurance executives would be a desirable endeavor."

Crocker later bought what he thought was Sarin nerve gas and a block of C-4 explosive from the undercover agent, the affidavit says.

Authorities arrested Crocker in 2004.

For the latest in crime and justice news, visit the Talk Justice news feed at http://www.crimenews.info.

Source: Larry Copeland, "Domestic Terrorism: New Trouble at Home," USA TODAY, November 15, 2004. Reprinted with permission.

*Those who employ terrorism
. . . strive to subvert the rule
of law and effect change
through violence and fear.*

—National Strategy for Combating
Terrorism, 2003

In 2005, 38-year-old Eric Robert Rudolph pleaded guilty to a string of bombing attacks in Alabama and Georgia, including a blast at Atlanta's Centennial Park during the 1996 Olympics in which one person died and 111 were injured.[72] Rudolph, an antiabortion and antigay extremist, was sentenced to life in prison without the possibility of parole after having eluded law enforcement officers for years.

Active fringe groups include those espousing a nationwide "common law movement," under which the legitimacy of elected government officials is not recognized. An example is the Republic of Texas separatists who took neighbors hostage near Fort Davis, Texas, in 1997 to draw attention to their claims that Texas was illegally annexed by the United States in 1845. While not necessarily bent on terrorism, such special-interest groups may turn to violence if thwarted in attempts to reach their goals.

Sometimes individuals can be as dangerous as organized groups. In 1996, for example, 52-year-old Theodore Kaczynski, a Lincoln, Montana, antitechnology recluse, was arrested and charged in the Unabomber case. The Unabomber (so called because the bomber's original targets were universities and airlines) had led police and FBI agents on a 17-year-long manhunt through a series of incidents that involved as many as 16 bombings, resulting in three deaths and 23 injuries. Kaczynski pleaded guilty to federal charges in 1998 and was sentenced to life in prison without possibility of parole.

INTERNATIONAL TERRORISM

Class Activity

Ask students to assemble a list of international terrorist incidents that have taken place around the globe during the past year. The U.S. Department of State publication *Patterns of Global Terrorism* might be a good place to start. Which countries experienced the largest number of international incidents of terrorism? Which countries had the fewest? How do rates of international terrorism within the United States compare to rates elsewhere?

In 1988, Pan American's London–New York Flight 103 was destroyed over Scotland by a powerful two-stage bomb as it reached its cruising altitude of 30,000 feet, killing all of the 259 passengers and crew members aboard. Another 11 people on the ground were killed and many others injured as flaming debris from the airplane crashed down on the Scottish town of Lockerbie. It was the first time Americans were undeniably the target of international terrorism. Any doubts that terrorists were targeting U.S. citizens were dispelled by the 1996 truck bomb attack on U.S. military barracks in Dhahran, Saudi Arabia. Nineteen U.S. Air Force personnel were killed and more than 250 others were injured in the blast, which destroyed the Khobar Towers housing complex.

The 1993 bombing of the World Trade Center in New York City and the 1995 conviction of Sheik Omar Abdel-Rahman and eight other Islamic fundamentalists on charges of plotting to start a holy war and of conspiring to commit assassinations and bomb the United Nations[73] indicated to many that the threat of international terrorism could soon become a part of daily life in America. According to some terrorism experts, the 1993 explosion at the World Trade Center, which killed four people and created a 100-foot hole through four subfloors of concrete, ushered in an era of international terrorist activity in the United States. In 1999, the Second U.S. Circuit Court of Appeals upheld the convictions of the sheik and his coconspirators. They remain in federal prison.

In 2001, Islamic terrorist Osama bin Laden showed the world how terrorists can successfully strike at American interests on U.S. soil when members of his organization allegedly attacked the World Trade Center and the Pentagon using commandeered airliners, killing approximately 3,000 people. Earlier, in 1998, bin Laden's agents struck American embassies in Nairobi, Kenya, and Dares Salaam, Tanzania, killing 257 people, including 12 Americans. In 2003, a coordinated attack by Islamic extremists on a residential compound for foreigners in Riyadh, Saudi Arabia, killed 34 people (nine attackers died), including eight Americans, and wounded many more.[74] Similar attacks are continuing in the Middle East and elsewhere.

Some believe that the wars in Afghanistan and Iraq, as well as a coordinated international effort against al-Qaeda, may have substantially weakened that organization's ability to carry out future strikes outside of the Middle East. Those who study international terrorism, however, note that Jihadism, or the Islamic holy war movement, survives independent of any one organization and appears to be gaining strength around the world.[75] Jihadist principles continue to serve as the organizing rationale for extremist groups in much of the Muslim world. Learn more about the global threat from Islamic fundamentalism at Library Extra 17–7 at cjtoday.com.

LIBRARY
Extra
■ ■ ■ ■

CYBERTERRORISM

cyberterrorism

A form of terrorism that makes use of high technology, especially computers and the Internet, in the planning and carrying out of terrorist attacks.

A new kind of terrorism, called **cyberterrorism**, makes use of high technology, especially computers and the Internet, in the planning and carrying out of terrorist attacks. The term was coined in the 1980s by Barry Collin, a senior research fellow at the Institute for Security and Intelligence in California, who used it to refer to the convergence of cyberspace and terrorism.[76] It was later popularized by a 1996 RAND report that warned of an emerging "new terrorism" distinguished by how terrorist groups organize and by how they use technology. The report warned of a coming "netwar" or "infowar" consisting of coordinated cyberattacks on our nation's economic, busi-

A still frame taken from a security video camera that recorded the detonation of a bomb in Atocha railway station in Madrid, Spain, on March 11, 2004. The bomb was one in a series of terrorist explosions that went off within seconds of one other on Madrid's trains, killing 191 people. Hundreds more were injured by the blasts, which were blamed on Muslim extremists linked to al-Qaeda who were operating in Spain. Could such attacks happen here in the United States?

© Reuters/Corbis

ness, and military **infrastructure**.[77] A year later, FBI agent Mark Pollitt offered a working definition of *cyberterrorism,* saying that it is "the premeditated, politically motivated attack against information, computer systems, computer programs, and data which results in violence against noncombatant targets by subnational groups or clandestine agents."[78]

Scenarios describing cyberterrorism possibilities are imaginative and diverse. Some have suggested that a successful cyberterrorist attack on the nation's air traffic control system might cause airplanes to collide in midair or that an attack on food- and cereal-processing plants that drastically altered the levels of certain nutritional supplements might sicken or kill a large number of our nation's children. Other such attacks might cause the country's power grid to collapse or could muddle the records and transactions of banks and stock exchanges. Possible targets in such attacks are almost endless.

In 1998, the Critical Infrastructure Assurance Office (CIAO) was created by a presidential directive to coordinate the federal government's initiatives on critical infrastructure protection and to provide a national focus for cyberspace security. In 2001, the White House formed the President's Critical Infrastructure Protection Board (PCIPB) and tasked it with recommending policies in support of critical infrastructure protection.[79] In September 2002, the PCIPB released an important document entitled *The National Strategy to Secure Cyberspace,*[80] which is available at Library Extra 17–8 at cjtoday.com. In 2003, CIAO functions were transferred to the National Cyber Security Division (NCSD) of the Directorate of Information Analysis and Infrastructure Protection within the Department of Homeland Security. According to DHS, the creation of NCSD improved protection of critical cyberassets by "maximizing and leveraging the resources" of previously separate offices.[81] NCSD coordinates its activities with the U.S. Computer Emergency Response Team (US-CERT), which runs a National Cyber Alert System. Visit US-CERT, which is also a part of the Department of Homeland Security, at Web Extra 17–13 at cjtoday.com. Another group, the Secret Service National Threat Assessment Center (NTAC), is developing its Critical Systems Protection Initiative and will soon offer advanced cybersecurity prevention and response capabilities to the nation's business community. Visit NTAC at Web Extra 17–14 at cjtoday.com.

NARCOTERRORISM

Some authors have identified a link between major drug traffickers and terrorist groups.[82] In mid-2005, for example, Afghan drug lord Bashir Noorzai was arrested in New York and held without bond on charges that he tried to smuggle more than $50 million worth of heroin into the United

infrastructure

The basic facilities, services, and installations that a country needs to function. Transportation and communications systems, water and power lines, and institutions that serve the public, including banks, schools, post offices, and prisons, are all part of a country's infrastructure.[viii]

LIBRARY Extra

WEB Extra

WEB Extra

States.[83] Noorzai, who was on the Drug Enforcement Administration's list of most wanted drug kingpins, had apparently operated with impunity under the protection of the Taliban between 1990 and 2004. According to the DEA, Noorzai's organization "provided demolitions, weapons and manpower to the Taliban." In exchange, the Taliban were said to have protected Noorzai's opium crops and transit routes through Afghanistan and Pakistan.

narcoterrorism

A political alliance between terrorist organizations and drug-supplying cartels. The cartels provide financing for the terrorists, who in turn provide quasi-military protection to the drug dealers.

The link between drug traffickers and insurgents has been termed **narcoterrorism.**[84] Narcoterrorism, simply defined, is the involvement of terrorist organizations and insurgent groups in the trafficking of narcotics.[85] The relationship that exists between terrorist organizations and drug traffickers is mutually beneficial. Insurgents derive financial benefits from their supporting role in drug trafficking, while the traffickers receive protection and benefit from the use of terrorist tactics against foes and competitors.

The first documented instance of an insurgent force financed at least in part with drug money came to light during an investigation of the virulent anti-Castro Omega 7 group in the early 1980s.[86] Clear-cut evidence of modern narcoterrorism, however, is difficult to obtain. Contemporary insurgent organizations with links to drug dealers probably include the 19th of April Movement (M-19) operating in Colombia, Sendero Luminoso (Shining Path) of Peru, the Revolutionary Armed Forces of Colombia, and the large Farabundo Marti National Liberation Front, which has long sought to overthrow the elected government of El Salvador.[87]

Lecture Note

Define *narcoterrorism* as the political alliance between terrorist organizations and drug-supplying cartels. Ask students how narcoterrorism might directly affect the United States.

Narcoterrorism raises a number of questions. Drug researcher James Inciardi summarizes them as follows:[88]

- What is the full threat posed by narcoterrorism?
- How should narcoterrorism be dealt with?
- Is narcoterrorism a law enforcement problem or a military one?
- How might narcoterrorism be affected by changes in official U.S. policy toward drugs and drug use?
- Is the international drug trade being used as a tool by anti-U.S. and other interests to undermine Western democracies in a calculated way?

Unfortunately, in the opinion of some experts, the United States is ill prepared to combat this type of international organized crime. Testifying before the Senate's Foreign Relations Subcommittee on Terrorism, Narcotics, and International Operations, William J. Olson, a senior fellow at the National Strategy Information Center, told Congress that more than $1 trillion (equivalent to one-sixth of the U.S. gross national product) is generated yearly by organized criminal activities like those associated with narcoterrorism. "We must recognize that the rules of the crime game have changed," said Olson. "International criminal organizations are challenging governments, permeating societies. They're running roughshod over weak institutions and exploiting gaps in the U.S. and international response. They have the upper hand at the moment and they know it," he said.[89] Other experts testified that a comprehensive national strategy—one that goes far beyond law enforcement and criminal prosecution to include diplomacy and organized international efforts—is needed to combat international organized criminal enterprises before they can co-opt global markets and worldwide financial institutions.[90]

Even more potentially damaging are efforts being made by some criminal groups to wrest control of political institutions in various parts of the world. As transnational organized crime expert Emilio C. Viano points out, "powerful drug constituencies influence the electoral process more and more, seeking to gain actual political representation and consequently weaken the rule of law in a number of countries."[91]

Causes of Terrorism

According to the U.S. government,[92] international terrorist organizations build on a process shown in Figure 17–1. The federal government's *National Strategy for Combating Terrorism,*[93] from which this figure is derived, says that the *underlying conditions* that lead to terrorism include poverty, political corruption, religious and ideational conflict, and ethnic strife. Such conditions provide terrorists with the opportunity to legitimize their cause and to justify their actions. Feeding on the social disorganization fostered by these conditions, terrorists position themselves to demand political change.

The video *The Final Report* from the ABC News/Prentice Hall Video Library is recommended. Ask students what lessons might be learned from the report described in the video.

The second level in Figure 17–1, the *international environment,* refers to the geopolitical boundaries within which terrorist organizations form and through which they operate. If international borders are free and open, then terrorist groups can readily establish safe havens, hone their capabilities, practice their techniques, and provide support and funding to distant members

FIGURE 17–1

International terrorist organizations: the building process.

Source: National Strategy for Combating Terrorism (Washington, DC: The White House, 2003), p. 6.

and collaborators. Either knowingly or unwittingly, nations (*states*) can provide the physical assets and bases needed for the terrorist *organization* to grow and function. Finally, the terrorist *leadership,* at the top of the pyramid, provides the overall direction and strategy that give life to the organization's terror campaign.

Combating Terrorism

Terrorism represents a difficult challenge to all societies. The open societies of the Western world, however, are potentially more vulnerable than are totalitarian regimes like dictatorships. Western democratic ideals restrict police surveillance of likely terrorist groups and curtail luggage, vehicle, and airport searches. Press coverage of acts of terrorism encourage copycat activities by other fringe groups and communicate information on workable techniques. Laws designed to limit terrorist access to technology, information, and physical locations are stopgap measures at best. The federal Terrorist Firearms Detection Act of 1988 is an example. Designed to prevent the development of plastic firearms by requiring handguns to contain at least 3.7 ounces of detectable metal,[94] it applies only to weapons manufactured within U.S. borders.

In 1996, the Antiterrorism and Effective Death Penalty Act (AEDPA) became law. The act includes a number of provisions. It

- Bans fund-raising and financial support within the United States for international terrorist organizations
- Provides $1 billion for enhanced terrorism-fighting measures by federal and state authorities
- Allows foreign terrorism suspects to be deported or to be kept out of the United States without the disclosure of classified evidence against them
- Permits a death sentence to be imposed on anyone committing an international terrorist attack in the United States in which a death occurs
- Makes it a federal crime to use the United States as a base for planning terrorist attacks overseas
- Orders identifying chemical markers known as *taggants* to be added to plastic explosives during manufacture
- Orders a feasibility study on marking other explosives (except gunpowder)

More than a year before the events of September 11, 2001, the National Commission on Terrorism released a report titled *Countering the Changing Threat of International Terrorism.*[95] The commission, created by House and Senate leaders in 1998 in response to the bombings of the U.S. embassies in Kenya and Tanzania, was led by former U.S. Ambassador-at-Large for Counter-Terrorism L. Paul Bremer. The commission's report, which we now see presaged the 2001 attacks on the World Trade Center and the Pentagon, began with these words: "International terrorism poses an increasingly dangerous and difficult threat to America." The report identified Afghanistan, Iran, Iraq, Sudan, and Syria as among state sponsors of terrorism and concluded

Powerful international criminal groups now work outside national or international law. They include traffickers in drugs, money laundering, the illegal trade in arms— including trade in nuclear materials—and the smuggling of precious metals and other commodities. These criminal elements exploit both the new liberal international economic order and the different approaches and practices of States. They command vast sums of money, which they use to suborn State officials. Some criminal "empires" are richer than many poorer States. These problems demand a concerted, global response.

—Former United Nations Secretary-General Boutros Boutros-Ghali[ix]

In this kind of conflict, where the enemy is hard to identify, the increased interest in civil liberties can be a problem for the government.

—Lee Casey, Washington lawyer[x]

that "the government must immediately take steps to reinvigorate the collection of intelligence about terrorists' plans, use all available legal avenues to disrupt and prosecute terrorist activities and private sources of support, convince other nations to cease all support for terrorists, and ensure that federal, state, and local officials are prepared for attacks that may result in mass casualties." A number of the commission's recommendations were implemented only *after* the terrorist attacks of 2001.

Following the 2001 attacks, Congress enacted, and the president signed, the USA PATRIOT Act. The act, which is discussed in detail in other chapters and which was reauthorized in 2006 with some amendments, created a number of new crimes, such as terrorist attacks against mass transportation and harboring or concealing terrorists. Those crimes were set forth in Title VIII of the act, titled "Strengthening the Criminal Laws against Terrorism." Excerpts from Title VIII can be found in CJ Today Exhibit 17–3.

ANTITERRORISM COMMITTEES AND REPORTS

A number of important antiterrorism reports and studies have been released during the last seven or eight years by various groups, including the Advisory Panel to Assess Domestic Response Capabilities for Terrorism Involving Weapons of Mass Destruction (also known as the Gilmore Commission), the National Commission on Terrorism, the U.S. Commission on National Security in the Twenty-First Century, the New York–based Council on Foreign Relations (CFR), and the National Commission on Terrorist Attacks upon the United States (aka the 9/11 Commission).

Some pre–September 11, 2001, reports offered valuable suggestions that, if followed, might have helped prevent the events that took place on that day. Some of the subsequent reports have been voices of reason in the rush to strengthen the nation's antiterrorism defenses at potentially high costs to individual freedoms. The 2002 CFR report, for example, notes that "systems such as those used in the aviation sector, which start from the assumption that every passenger and every bag of luggage poses an equal risk, must give way to more intelligence-driven and layered security approaches that emphasize prescreening and monitoring based on risk criteria."

The report of the 9/11 Commission, released on July 22, 2004, which many saw as especially valuable, said that the September 11, 2001, attacks should have come as no surprise because the U.S. government had received clear warnings that Islamic terrorists were planning to strike at targets within the United States (see CJ Today Exhibit 17–4). The report also said that the United States is still not properly prepared to deal adequately with terrorist threats and called for the creation of a new federal intelligence-gathering center to unify the more than a dozen federal agencies currently gathering terrorism-related intelligence at home and abroad. In December 2005, members of the 9/11 Commission held a final news conference in which they lambasted the lack of progress made by federal officials charged with implementing safeguards to prevent future terrorist attacks

Palestinian boys holding toy rifles as a girl displays a poster of Osama bin Laden in Gaza City during a demonstration at Al Azhar University to honor suicide bombers. The school was organized by members of the Islamic Jihad. The 9/11 Commission report, released in 2004, pointed to the radical ideology underpinning international Islamic terrorism today and bemoaned the fact that too many Middle Eastern children are being socialized into a culture of terrorism. How can radical ideologies be combated?

CJ Today Exhibit 17–3

The USA PATRIOT Act of 2001 (as Amended and Reauthorized in 2006)

Title VIII of the USA PATRIOT Act created two new federal crimes of terrorist activity: (1) terrorist attacks against mass transportation systems and (2) harboring or concealing terrorists. The following excerpts from the act describe these offenses.

TITLE VIII—STRENGTHENING THE CRIMINAL LAWS AGAINST TERRORISM

Sec. 801. Terrorist Attacks and Other Acts of Violence against Mass Transportation Systems.

Chapter 97 of title 18, United States Code, is amended by adding at the end the following:

§ 1993. Terrorist attacks and other acts of violence against mass transportation systems

(a) GENERAL PROHIBITIONS.—Whoever willfully—

(1) wrecks, derails, sets fire to, or disables a mass transportation vehicle or ferry;

(2) places or causes to be placed any biological agent or toxin for use as a weapon, destructive substance, or destructive device in, upon, or near a mass transportation vehicle or ferry, without previously obtaining the permission of the mass transportation provider, and with intent to endanger the safety of any passenger or employee of the mass transportation provider, or with a reckless disregard for the safety of human life;

(3) sets fire to, or places any biological agent or toxin for use as a weapon, destructive substance, or destructive device in, upon, or near any garage, terminal, structure, supply, or facility used in the operation of, or in support of the operation of, a mass transportation vehicle or ferry, without previously obtaining the permission of the mass transportation provider, and knowing or having reason to know such activity would likely derail, disable, or wreck a mass transportation vehicle or ferry used, operated, or employed by the mass transportation provider;

(4) removes appurtenances from, damages, or otherwise impairs the operation of a mass transportation signal system, including a train control system, centralized dispatching system, or rail grade crossing warning signal without authorization from the mass transportation provider;

(5) interferes with, disables, or incapacitates any dispatcher, driver, captain, or person while they are employed in dispatching, operating, or maintaining a mass transportation vehicle or ferry, with intent to endanger the safety of any passenger or employee of the mass transportation provider, or with a reckless disregard for the safety of human life;

(6) commits an act, including the use of a dangerous weapon, with the intent to cause death or serious bodily injury to an employee or passenger of a mass transportation provider or any other person

while any of the foregoing are on the property of a mass transportation provider;

(7) conveys or causes to be conveyed false information, knowing the information to be false, concerning an attempt or alleged attempt being made or to be made, to do any act which would be a crime prohibited by this subsection; or

(8) attempts, threatens, or conspires to do any of the aforesaid acts,

shall be fined under this title or imprisoned not more than twenty years, or both, if such act is committed, or in the case of a threat or conspiracy such act would be committed, on, against, or affecting a mass transportation provider engaged in or affecting interstate or foreign commerce, or if in the course of committing such act, that person travels or communicates across a State line in order to commit such act, or transports materials across a State line in aid of the commission of such act.

(b) AGGRAVATED OFFENSE.—Whoever commits an offense under subsection (a) in a circumstance in which—

(1) the mass transportation vehicle or ferry was carrying a passenger at the time of the offense; or

(2) the offense has resulted in the death of any person, shall be guilty of an aggravated form of the offense and shall be fined under this title or imprisoned for a term of years or for life, or both.

Sec. 803. Prohibition against Harboring Terrorists.

(a) In General.—Chapter 113B of title 18, United States Code, is amended by adding after section 2338 the following new section:

§ 2339. Harboring or concealing terrorists

(a) Whoever harbors or conceals any person who he knows, or has reasonable grounds to believe, has committed, or is about to commit, an offense under section 32 (relating to destruction of aircraft or aircraft facilities), section 175 (relating to biological weapons), section 229 (relating to chemical weapons), section 831 (relating to nuclear materials), paragraph (2) or (3) of section 844(f) (relating to arson and bombing of government property risking or causing injury or death), section 1366(a) (relating to the destruction of an energy facility), section 2280 (relating to violence against maritime navigation), section 2332a (relating to weapons of mass destruction), or section 2332b (relating to acts of terrorism transcending national boundaries) of this title, section 236(a) (relating to sabotage of nuclear facilities or fuel) of the Atomic Energy Act of 1954 (42 U.S.C. 2284(a)), or section 46502 (relating to aircraft piracy) of title 49, shall be fined under this title or imprisoned not more than ten years, or both.

(b) A violation of this section may be prosecuted in any Federal judicial district in which the underlying offense was committed, or in any other Federal judicial district as provided by law.

(b) TECHNICAL AMENDMENT.—The chapter analysis for chapter 113B of title 18, United States Code, is amended by inserting after the item for section 2338 the following: "2339. Harboring or concealing terrorists."

Note: The USA PATRIOT Act was reauthorized by Congress in March 2006.

LIBRARY
Extra

within the United States. Former Commission Chairman Thomas Kean called it "shocking" that the nation remains so vulnerable. "We shouldn't need another wake-up call," said Kean. "We believe that the terrorists will strike again."[96] While it is impossible to discuss each of the reports mentioned here in detail in this textbook, they are available in their entirety at Library Extras 17–9 through 17–18 at cjtoday.com.

THE DEPARTMENT OF HOMELAND SECURITY

The Homeland Security Act of 2002, enacted to protect America against terrorism, created the federal Department of Homeland Security, which is charged with protecting the nation's critical infrastructure against terrorist attack. The new department began operations on March 1, 2003, with former Pennsylvania Governor Tom Ridge as its first director. The director, whose official title is secretary of homeland security, is a member of the cabinet. In 2005, Michael Chertoff became the new secretary of homeland security. A former federal prosecutor, Chertoff previously served as assistant attorney general for the Criminal Division at the U.S. Department of Justice and helped trace the 9/11 terrorist attacks to the al-Qaeda network.

Experts say that the creation of DHS is the most significant transformation of the U.S. government since 1947, when President Harry S. Truman merged the various branches of the armed forces into the Department of Defense in an effort to better coordinate the nation's defense against military threats.[97] DHS coordinates the activities of 22 disparate domestic agencies by placing administration of those agencies under five "directorates," or departmental divisions:

1. *Border and Transportation Security (BTS).* BTS is responsible for maintaining security of the nation's borders and transportation systems. The largest of the directorates, it is home to the Transportation Security Administration, the U.S. Customs Service, the border security functions of the former Immigration and Naturalization Service,[98] the Animal and Plant Health Inspection Service, and the Federal Law Enforcement Training Center.

2. *Emergency Preparedness and Response (EPR).* EPR works to ensure that the nation is prepared for, and able to recover from, terrorist attacks and natural disasters.

3. *Science and Technology (S&T).* This directorate coordinates the department's efforts in research and development, including preparing for and responding to the full range of terrorist threats involving weapons of mass destruction.

4. *Information Analysis and Infrastructure Protection (IAIP).* IAIP merges under one roof the functions of identifying and assessing a broad range of intelligence information concerning threats to the homeland, issuing timely warnings, and taking appropriate preventive and protective actions.

5. *Management.* The Management Directorate is responsible for budgetary, managerial, and personnel issues within DHS.

The members of the National Commission on Terrorist Attacks upon the United States (aka the 9/11 Commission), from left: Thomas H. Kean, Lee H. Hamilton, Fred F. Fielding, Bob Kerrey, John F. Lehman, and Richard Ben-Veniste. The commission's report, released on July 22, 2004, called for a major overhaul of U.S. intelligence agencies and for a realignment of federal expenditures on homeland security. What else did the report say?

CJ Today Exhibit 17–4

The Report of the National Commission on Terrorist Attacks upon the United States

On July 22, 2004, the National Commission on Terrorist Attacks upon the United States (better known as the 9/11 Commission) released its report. The commission was created by President George W. Bush and the Congress on November 27, 2002, and was charged with investigating the "facts and circumstances relating to the terrorist attacks of September 11, 2001, including those relating to intelligence agencies, law enforcement agencies, diplomacy, immigration issues and border control, the flow of assets to terrorist organizations, commercial aviation, the role of congressional oversight and resource allocation, and other areas determined relevant by the Commission."

In preparing their report, commission members reviewed more than 2.5 million pages of documents and interviewed more than 1,200 people in ten countries. The final 585-page report touched on a variety of topics. Central to the report, however, is a "global strategy" to defeat terrorism.

"The enemy is not just 'terrorism,' some generic evil," the commission wrote. A generic response to "terrorism" would blur the need for a focused U.S. antiterrorism response. "The catastrophic threat at this moment in history is more specific. It is the threat posed by *Islamist* terrorism—especially the al Qaeda network, its affiliates, and its ideology."

The commission noted that Islam is not the enemy and that Islam is not synonymous with terror. "Nor does Islam teach terror," said the Commission. "America and its friends oppose a perversion of Islam, not the great world faith itself."

The following paragraphs, taken directly from the commission's report, identify the radical ideology underpinning much of international terrorism today and lay out an important long-term strategy for dealing with the continuing terrorist threat.

> Osama Bin Ladin and other Islamist terrorist leaders, draw on a long tradition of extreme intolerance within one stream of Islam (a minority tradition). . . . That stream is motivated by religion and does not distinguish politics from religion, thus distorting both. It is further fed by grievances stressed by Bin Ladin and widely felt throughout the Muslim world—against the U.S. military presence

in the Middle East, policies perceived as anti-Arab and anti-Muslim, and support of Israel. Bin Ladin and Islamist terrorists mean exactly what they say: to them America is the fount of all evil, the "head of the snake," and it must be converted or destroyed.

It is not a position with which Americans can bargain or negotiate. With it there is no common ground—not even respect for life—on which to begin a dialogue. It can only be destroyed or utterly isolated.

Because the Muslim world has fallen behind the West politically, economically, and militarily for the past three centuries, and because few tolerant or secular Muslim democracies provide alternative models for the future, Bin Ladin's message finds receptive ears. It has attracted active support from thousands of disaffected young Muslims and resonates powerfully with a far larger number who do not actively support his methods. The resentment of America and the West is deep, even among leaders of relatively successful Muslim states. Tolerance, the rule of law, political and economic openness, the extension of greater opportunities to women—these cures must come from within Muslim societies themselves. The United States must support such developments.

But this process is likely to be measured in decades, not years. It is a process that will be violently opposed by Islamist terrorist organizations, both inside Muslim countries and in attacks on the United States and other Western nations. The United States finds itself caught up in a clash *within* a civilization. That clash arises from particular conditions in the Muslim world, conditions that spill over into expatriate Muslim communities in non-Muslim countries.

Our enemy is twofold: al Qaeda, a stateless network of terrorists that struck us on 9/11; and a radical ideological movement in the Islamic world, inspired in part by al Qaeda, which has spawned terrorist groups and violence across the globe. The first enemy is weakened, but continues to pose a grave threat. The second enemy is gathering, and will menace Americans and American interests long after Osama Bin Ladin and his cohorts are killed or captured. Thus our strategy must match our means to two ends: dismantling the al Qaeda network and prevailing in the longer term over the ideology that gives rise to Islamist terrorism.

Source: National Commission on Terrorist Attacks upon the United States, *The 9/11 Commission Report: Final Report of the National Commission on Terrorist Attacks on the United States* (Washington, DC: U.S. Government Printing Office, 2004), pp. 362–363.

Several other critical agencies have been folded into the new department or have been created under the five directorates:[99]

- *U.S. Coast Guard.* The commandant of the Coast Guard reports directly to the secretary of DHS. However, the Coast Guard also works closely with the undersecretary of BTS and maintains its existing identity as an independent military service. Upon declaration of war or when the president so directs, the Coast Guard will operate as an element of the Department of Defense, consistent with existing law.

- *U.S. Secret Service.* The primary mission of the Secret Service is the protection of the president and other government leaders, as well as security for designated national events. The Secret Service is also the primary agency responsible for protecting U.S. currency from counterfeiters and safeguarding Americans from credit card fraud.

- *Bureau of Citizenship and Immigration Services (CIS).* A new agency, CIS (also known as U.S. Citizenship and Immigration Services, or USCIS) dedicates its energies to providing efficient immigration services and easing the transition to American citizenship.

- *Bureau of Customs and Border Protection (CBP).* CBP, the unified border control agency of the United States, has as its mission the protection of our country's borders and the American people.

- *Bureau of Immigration and Customs Enforcement (ICE).* Also known as U.S. Immigration and Customs Enforcement, ICE (along with CIS) has roots in the now-defunct U.S. Immigration and Naturalization Service. ICE, the largest investigative arm of the Department of Homeland Security, is responsible for identifying and eliminating vulnerabilities in the nation's border, economic, transportation, and infrastructure security.

- *Office of State and Local Government Coordination.* This office ensures close coordination between local, state, and federal governments to ensure an effective terrorism-prevention effort and to provide quick responses to terrorist incidents.

- *Office of Private Sector Liaison.* The Office of Private Sector Liaison provides the business community with a direct line of communication to DHS. The office works directly with individual businesses and through trade associations and other nongovernmental organizations to foster dialogue between the private sector and DHS on the full range of issues and challenges that America's businesses face today.

- *Office of Inspector General.* The Office of Inspector General serves as an independent and objective inspection, audit, and investigative body to promote effectiveness, efficiency, and economy in DHS's programs and operations and to prevent and detect fraud, abuse, mismanagement, and waste.

All of the agencies described here can be found in the Cybrary at http://www.cybrary.info. You can visit DHS on the Web via Web Extra 17–15 at cjtoday.com. Learn what DHS is doing to keep America safe at Web Extra 17–16.

WEB
Extra
■ ■ ■ ■

THE NATIONAL STRATEGY FOR COMBATING TERRORISM

In 2003, the White House released its official *National Strategy for Combating Terrorism.*[100] The strategy includes a multipronged initiative aimed at reducing both the threat severity and international reach of international terrorist organizations. The avowed goals of the *National Strategy* are as follows:

- Defeat terrorists and their organizations by identifying, locating, and destroying them.

- Deny sponsorship, support, and sanctuary to terrorists by helping other nations fulfill their responsibilities and obligations to combat terrorism.

- Diminish the underlying conditions that terrorists seek to exploit by resolving regional disputes; by fostering economic, social, and political development; by encouraging market-based economies; by supporting good governance and the rule of law; and by "winning the war of ideas" to ensure that ideologies that promote terrorism do not find fertile ground in any nation.

- Defend U.S. citizens and interests at home and abroad by implementing strong and effective security measures and by enhancing measures intended to ensure the integrity, reliability, and availability of critical physical and information-based infrastructures (including transportation and information systems).

Figure 17–2, which is taken from the *National Strategy,* shows the assessed threat severity and geopolitical reach of two terrorist groups at the time of the report. The figure illustrates the federal government's two-pronged strategy of reducing the scope and the capability of such organizations.

The July 2004 report of the 9/11 Commission proposed sweeping changes within the U.S. intelligence community, including the creation of the position of national intelligence director (NID). Soon afterward, the Intelligence Reform and Terrorism Prevention Act of 2004 facilitated the creation of the National Counterterrorism Center (NCTC) under the newly created position of NID.[101] The NID acts as the principal adviser to the president, the National Security Council, and the Homeland Security Council for intelligence matters related to national security. The NCTC

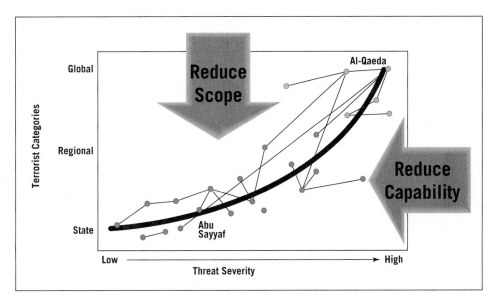

FIGURE 17–2

Reducing the scope and capability of terrorist organizations.

Source: National Strategy for Combating Terrorism (Washington, DC: The White House, 2003), p. 13.

serves as the primary organization in the U.S. government for integrating and analyzing all intelligence pertaining to terrorism and counterterrorism and for conducting strategic counterterrorism operational planning. Today's NCTC intelligence analysts have access to dozens of networks and information systems from across the intelligence, law enforcement, military, and homeland security communities. These systems provide foreign and domestic information pertaining to international terrorism and sensitive law enforcement activities.[102] Learn more about countering terrorist threats at Library Extra 17–19 at cjtoday.com. The *National Strategy* is available in its entirety at Library Extra 17–20. Visit the National Counterterrorism Center at Web Extra 17–17.

Foreign Terrorist Organizations

The Immigration and Nationality Act[103] and the Intelligence Reform and Terrorism Prevention Act of 2004[104] provide the U.S. Department of State with the authority to designate any group outside the United States as a **foreign terrorist organization (FTO)**. The process involves an exhaustive interagency review process in which all evidence of a group's activity, from both classified and open sources, is scrutinized. The State Department, working closely with the Justice and

LIBRARY Extra   **WEB** Extra

foreign terrorist organization (FTO)

A foreign organization that engages in terrorist activity that threatens the security of U.S. nationals or the national security of the United States and that is so designated by the U.S. secretary of state.

Air travelers being screened by Transportation Security Administration employees in Chicago's O'Hare International Airport. The hijackings of four airplanes by Islamic terrorists on September 11, 2001, led to tightened security controls over air travel nationwide and abroad. How did the hijackings reduce freedoms that Americans had previously taken for granted?

Treasury Departments and the intelligence community, prepares a detailed "administrative record" that documents the organization's terrorist activity.

Federal law requires that any organization considered for FTO designation must meet three criteria: (1) It must be foreign; (2) it must engage in terrorist activity as defined in Section 212 (a)(3)(B) of the Immigration and Nationality Act;[105] and (3) the organization's activities must threaten the security of U.S. nationals or the national security (national defense, foreign relations, or economic interests) of the United States. Table 17–2 lists 40 FTOs, as designated by the U.S. Department of State. For more detailed descriptions of these organizations, see the State Depart-

---

TABLE 17–2 Designated Foreign Terrorist Organizations

1. Abu Nidal Organization (ANO)
2. Abu Sayyaf Group
3. Al-Aqsa Martyrs' Brigade
4. Ansar al-Islam
5. Armed Islamic Group (GIA)
6. Asbat al-Ansar
7. Aum Shinrikyo
8. Basque Fatherland and Liberty (ETA)
9. Communist Party of the Philippines/New People's Army (CPP/NPA)
10. Continuity Irish Republican Army
11. Gama'a al-Islamiyya (Islamic Group)
12. Hamas (Islamic Resistance Movement)
13. Harakat ul-Mujahidin (HUM)
14. Hizballah (Party of God)
15. Islamic Movement of Uzbekistan (IMU)
16. Jaish-e-Mohammed (JEM) (Army of Mohammed)
17. Jemaah Islamiya (JI)
18. al-Jihad (Egyptian Islamic Jihad)
19. Kahane Chai (Kach)
20. Kongra-Gel (KGK) (formerly Kurdistan Workers' Party, PKK, KADEK)
21. Lashkar-e Tayyiba (LT) (Army of the Righteous)
22. Lashkar i Jhangvi
23. Liberation Tigers of Tamil Eelam (LTTE)
24. Libyan Islamic Fighting Group (LIFG)
25. Mujahedin-e Khalq Organization (MEK)
26. National Liberation Army (ELN)
27. Palestine Liberation Front (PLF)
28. Palestinian Islamic Jihad (PIJ)
29. Popular Front for the Liberation of Palestine (PFLP)
30. Popular Front for the Liberation of Palestine–General Command (PFLP–GC)
31. al-Qaeda
32. Real IRA
33. Revolutionary Armed Forces of Colombia (FARC)
34. Revolutionary Nuclei (formerly ELA)
35. Revolutionary Organization 17 November
36. Revolutionary People's Liberation Party/Front (DHKP/C)
37. Salafist Group for Call and Combat (GSPC)
38. Shining Path (Sendero Luminoso, SL)
39. Tanzim Qa'idat al-Jihad fi Bilad al-Rafidayn (QJBR) (al-Qaeda in Iraq; formerly Jama'at al-Tawhid wa'al-Jihad, JTJ, al-Zarqawi Network)
40. United Self-Defense Forces of Colombia (AUC)

Source: U.S. Department of State. Current as of October 1, 2007.

ment publication *Patterns of Global Terrorism,* which can be accessed at Library Extra 17–21 at cjtoday.com. The insignia of various terrorist organizations are shown in Figure 17–3.

Under federal law, FTO designations are subject to judicial review. In the event of a challenge to a group's FTO designation in federal court, the U.S. government relies on the administrative record to defend the designation decision. These administrative records contain intelligence information and are therefore classified. FTO designations expire in two years unless renewed.

Once an organization has been designated as an FTO, a number of legal consequences follow. First, it becomes unlawful for a person in the United States or subject to the jurisdiction of the United States to provide funds or other material support to a designated FTO. Second, representatives and certain members of a designated FTO, if they are aliens, can be denied visas or kept from entering the United States. Finally, U.S. financial institutions must block funds of designated FTOs and their agents and must report the blockage to the Office of Foreign Assets Control within the U.S. Department of the Treasury.

The State Department also has the authority to designate selected foreign governments as state sponsors of international terrorism. As of mid-2007, Cuba, Iran, North Korea, Sudan, and

17 November

Abu Nidal
Organization (ANO)

Al-Aqsa Martyrs' Brigade

Al-Jihad

Al-Qa'ida

Aum Shinrikyo
A.K.A. Aum Supreme Truth

Democratic Front for the
Liberation of Palestine
(DFLP)

Euzkadi Ta Askatasuna
(ETA)

FARC
Revolutionary
Armed Forces
of Colombia

First of October
Anti-Fascist Resistance
Group

HAMAS

Hizb Ut-Tahrir

Hizballah
(Party of God)

Lashkar-e-Tayyiba
(LT or LeT)
Army of the Righteous

Kahane Chai
(KACH)

Kurdistan Worker's Party
(PKK)

FIGURE 17–3

Terrorist organization insignias.

Source: Office of the Director of National Intelligence, National Counterterrorism Center, *Counterterrorism 2007*
(Washington, DC: NCTC, 2007), pp. 116–117.

Liberation Tigers of Tamil
Eelam (LTTE)

Loyalist Volunteer Force
(LVF)

Mujahedin-e Khalq
Organization (MEK)

National Liberation Army
(ELN)

New People's Army
(NPA)

Orange Volunteers
(OV)

Palestine Islamic
Jihad
(PIJ)

People against
Gangsterism and Drugs
(PAGAD)

Popular Front for the
Liberation of Palestine
(PFLP)

Popular Front for the
Liberation of Palestine-
General Command
(PFLP-GC)

Revolutionary People's
Liberation Party/Front

Shining Path
(Sendero Luminoso)

Tupac Amaru
Revolutionary Movement
(MRTA)

Ulster Defense Association
(UDA)

FIGURE 17–3

Terrorist organization insignias. (continued)

Syria were designated as state sponsors of international terrorism. According to the State Department, Iran remains the most active state sponsor of terrorism.[106] The State Department says that the Iranian government provides continuing support to numerous terrorist groups, including the Lebanese Hizballah, Hamas, and the Palestinian Islamic Jihad, all of which seek to undermine the Middle East peace process through the use of terrorism. Syria provides safe haven and support to several terrorist groups, some of which oppose Middle East peace negotiations. The State Department notes, however, that Libya is attempting to mend its international image following its surrender in 1999 of two Libyan suspects for trial in the bombing of Pan Am Flight 103. In early 2001, one of those suspects was convicted of murder, and judges in the case found that he had acted "in furtherance of the purposes of . . . Libyan Intelligence Services." Also in 2003, Libya agreed to foreswear its well-developed nuclear arms program in an effort to attract foreign investment. Cuba, however, continues to provide safe haven to several terrorists and U.S. fugitives and maintains ties to other state sponsors of terrorism and to Latin American insurgents. North Korea harbored several hijackers of a Japanese Airlines flight to North Korea in the 1970s and maintains links to terrorist groups. It also continues to sell ballistic missile technology to countries designated by the United States as state sponsors of terrorism, including Syria and Libya. Finally, Sudan continues to provide a safe haven for members of various terrorist groups, including the Lebanese Hizballah, Gama'a al-Islamiyya, Egyptian Islamic Jihad, the Palestinian Islamic Jihad, and Hamas, although it has been engaged in a counterterrorism dialogue with the United States since mid-2000. Learn more about terrorism from the Terrorism Research Center via **Web Extra 17–18** at cjtoday.com. Visit the State Department's Counterterrorism Office via **Web Extra 17–19**.

WEB
Extra
■ ■ ■ ■

The Future of International Terrorism

Terrorist groups are active throughout the world (Figure 17–4), and the United States is not their only target. Terrorist groups operate in South America, Africa, the Middle East, Latin America, the Philippines, Japan, India, England, Nepal, and some of the now independent states of the former Soviet Union. The Central Intelligence Agency reports that "between now and 2015 terrorist tactics will become increasingly sophisticated and designed to achieve mass casualties."[107] The CIA also notes that nations "with poor governance; ethnic, cultural, or religious tensions; weak economies; and porous borders will be prime breeding grounds for terrorism."[108] In the area of Islamic terrorism, the CIA expects that "by 2020 Al-Qaeda will have been superseded by similarly inspired but more diffuse Islamic extremist groups."[109] Read two CIA reports on the global trends that are likely to increase the risk of terrorism at Library Extras 17–22 and 17–23 at cjtoday.com.

LIBRARY
Extra
■ ■ ■ ■

The current situation leads many observers to conclude that the American justice system is not fully prepared to deal with the threat represented by domestic and international terrorism. Prior intelligence-gathering efforts that focused on such groups have largely failed or were not quickly acted on, leading to military intervention in places like Afghanistan and Iraq. Intelligence failures are at least partially understandable, given that many terrorist organizations are tight-knit and very difficult for intelligence operatives to penetrate.

SUMMARY

- Islamic law descends directly from the teachings of the Prophet Muhammad and looks to the Koran to determine which acts should be classified as crimes. Today's Islamic law is a system of duties and rituals founded on legal and moral obligations—all of which are ultimately sanctioned by the authority of religious leaders who may issue commands known as *fatwas.* Islamic law recognizes seven *Hudud* crimes—or crimes based on religious strictures. In Middle Eastern countries today, punishments for *Hudud* offenses are often physical and may include lashing, flogging, or even stoning. All other crimes fall into an offense category called *tazirat. Tazir* crimes are regarded as any actions not considered acceptable in a spiritual society. They include crimes against society and against individuals, but not those against God.

- The United Nations (UN) is the largest and most inclusive international body in the world. Since its inception in 1945, it has concerned itself with international crime prevention and world criminal justice systems, as illustrated by a number of important resolutions and documents, including the International Bill of Human Rights, which supports the rights and dignity of everyone who comes into contact with a criminal justice system; the Standard Minimum Rules for the Treatment of Prisoners; and the UN Code of Conduct for Law Enforcement Officials, which calls on law enforcement officers throughout the world to be cognizant of human rights in the performance of their duties. The World Crime Surveys, which report official crime statistics from nearly 100 countries, provide a periodic global portrait of criminal activity. Other significant international criminal justice organizations are the International Criminal Police Organization (Interpol), which acts as a clearinghouse for information on offenses and suspects who are believed to operate across national boundaries, and the European Police Office (Europol), which aims to improve the effectiveness and cooperation of law enforcement agencies within the member states of the European Union. Finally, the International Criminal Court (ICC) was created in 2000 under the auspices of the United Nations. The ICC, whose operations are only now beginning, is intended to be a permanent criminal court for trying individuals who commit the most serious crimes of concern to the international community, such as genocide, war crimes, and crimes against humanity—including the wholesale murder of civilians, torture, and mass rape.

- Globalization, or the internationalization of trade, services, investment, information, and other forms of human social activity, has been occurring for a long time but has recently increased in pace due largely to advances in technology, such as new modes of transportation and communication. Transnational crime, which may be one of the most significant challenges of the twenty-first century, is a negative consequence of globalization. Transnational

A PowerPoint presentation that supports this chapter is available from your Prentice Hall representative.

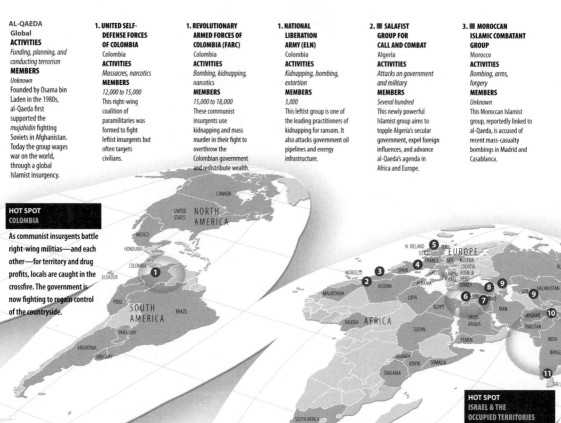

AL-QAEDA
Global
ACTIVITIES
Funding, planning, and conducting terrorism
MEMBERS
Unknown
Founded by Osama bin Laden in the 1980s, al-Qaeda first supported the *mujahidin* fighting Soviets in Afghanistan. Today the group wages war on the world, through a global Islamist insurgency.

1. UNITED SELF-DEFENSE FORCES OF COLOMBIA
Colombia
ACTIVITIES
Massacres, narcotics
MEMBERS
12,000 to 15,000
This right-wing coalition of paramilitaries was formed to fight leftist insurgents but often targets civilians.

1. REVOLUTIONARY ARMED FORCES OF COLOMBIA (FARC)
Colombia
ACTIVITIES
Bombing, kidnapping, narcotics
MEMBERS
15,000 to 18,000
These communist insurgents use kidnapping and mass murder in their fight to overthrow the Colombian government and redistribute wealth.

1. NATIONAL LIBERATION ARMY (ELN)
Colombia
ACTIVITIES
Kidnapping, bombing, extortion
MEMBERS
3,000
This leftist group is one of the leading practitioners of kidnapping for ransom. It also attacks government oil pipelines and energy infrastructure.

2. ■ SALAFIST GROUP FOR CALL AND COMBAT
Algeria
ACTIVITIES
Attacks on government and military
MEMBERS
Several hundred
This newly powerful Islamist group aims to topple Algeria's secular government, expel foreign influences, and advance al-Qaeda's agenda in Africa and Europe.

3. ■ MOROCCAN ISLAMIC COMBATANT GROUP
Morocco
ACTIVITIES
Bombing, arms, forgery
MEMBERS
Unknown
This Moroccan Islamist group, reportedly linked to al-Qaeda, is accused of recent mass-casualty bombings in Madrid and Casablanca.

HOT SPOT COLOMBIA

As communist insurgents battle right-wing militias—and each other—for territory and drug profits, locals are caught in the crossfire. The government is now fighting to regain control of the countryside.

The latest wave of international terrorism has focused the world's attention on a tactic that uses death and destruction as political tools. But terrorism itself, with roots deep in history and geography, is hardly new.

HOT SPOT ISRAEL & THE OCCUPIED TERRITORIES

Fueled by nationalism and mistrust, the cycle continues: Palestinian insurgents use terrorism against Israeli troops, settlers, and civilians in the occupied territories and Israel—while Israeli forces target militants, often inflicting civilian casualties.

6. ISLAMIC RESISTANCE MOVEMENT (HAMAS)
Israel, West Bank, Gaza Strip
ACTIVITIES
Suicide attacks
MEMBERS
Several thousand
Seeking to destroy Israel and extend Muslim rule across the Middle East, Hamas has mounted dozens of suicide attacks against Israeli civilians.

6. PALESTINE ISLAMIC JIHAD
Israel, West Bank, Gaza Strip
ACTIVITIES
Suicide attacks
MEMBERS
Several dozen
Led by operatives based in Lebanon and Syria, this radical group aims to replace Israel with a Palestinian Islamic state.

6. AL AQSA MARTYRS' BRIGADES
Israel, West Bank, Gaza Strip
ACTIVITIES
Shootings, suicide attacks
MEMBERS
Unknown
This group, linked to Palestinian leader Yasser Arafat's Fatah movement, arose during a Palestinian intifada in 2000.

6. KACH AND KAHANE CHAI
Israel, West Bank
ACTIVITIES
Shootings, assaults
MEMBERS
Several dozen
Outlawed since the massacre of 29 Muslims at Hebron in 1994, these groups seek to expand Israel by driving Palestinians from the West Bank and Gaza Strip.

6. HEZBOLLAH
Lebanon
ACTIVITIES
Bombing, hijacking, suicide attacks
MEMBERS
Several hundred
Formed in 1982 after the Israeli invasion of Lebanon, this Iran-backed group claimed victory when Israel pulled out in 2000. Its goal: destruction of the Jewish state.

6. ■ ASBAT AL ANSAR
Lebanon
ACTIVITIES
Assassination, bombing
MEMBERS
About 300
These al-Qaeda-linked extremists attack both domestic and international targets within Lebanon.

FIGURE 17–4

International terrorist groups and areas of operation.

4. BASQUE FATHERLAND AND LIBERTY (ETA)
Spain, France
ACTIVITIES
Assassination, bombing, extortion
MEMBERS
Dozens
Founded in 1959, this group has targeted Spanish officials and security forces in its fight for an independent Basque state in northern Spain and southwestern France.

5. REAL IRA
Northern Ireland
ACTIVITIES
Assassination, bombing, robbery
MEMBERS
100 to 200
An offshoot that formed after the Irish Republican Army declared a cease-fire in 1997, the RIRA has killed dozens in its fight for a united Ireland, free from British

WHERE THEY ARE

This map shows a sample of the many groups that use terror to achieve their goals, attracting an array of nationalists, political ideologues, and religious zealots. Some groups are multifaceted, incorporating politics and social programs along with violence; others are purely brutal. Today one type of group—related to a movement called Islamism—has earned an especially high profile for its drive to impose theocracy on Muslim lands and excise "impure" Western influences. According to the CIA, the deadliest of these groups—al-Qaeda—operates in 68 countries worldwide.

HOT SPOT
INDIA & PAKISTAN

Nuclear rivals India and Pakistan duel over the region of Kashmir, a flash point for conflict between Indian troops and Pakistan-based terrorist groups. Attacks against the pro-U.S. government of Pakistan are also on the rise.

ASIA

5. ULSTER DEFENCE ASSOCIATION
Northern Ireland
ACTIVITIES
Bombing, narcotics, shootings, intimidation
MEMBERS
Several hundred
Largest of the Protestant paramilitary groups that favor retaining British rule. Though bound by a cease-fire, the group often engages in violence against Catholics.

8. KURDISTAN WORKERS' PARTY (PKK)
Turkey
ACTIVITIES
Assassination, bombing
MEMBERS
More than 5,000
Also known as Kongra-Gel, this separatist group operates from northern Iraq and targets Turkish security forces and civilians in its fight for an independent Kurdish state.

9. ■ CHECHEN SEPARATISTS
Russia
ACTIVITIES
Bombing, kidnapping, murder
MEMBERS
Several thousand
Seeking independence from Russia, rebels have killed Moscow-backed Chechen officials, including Chechnya's president, and killed and kidnapped Russian civilians.

9. ■ ISLAMIC MOVEMENT OF UZBEKISTAN
Central Asia
ACTIVITIES
Bombing, kidnapping
MEMBERS
More than 1,000
This homegrown Islamist coalition seeks to replace Uzbekistan's secular regime and advance the regional goals of al-Qaeda.

10. ■ LASHKAR E-JHANGVI
Pakistan
ACTIVITIES
Massacres, bombing
MEMBERS
Fewer than a hundred
A small but brutally effective Sunni group, LEJ has attacked Shiite mosques and foreigners in a bid to destabilize Pakistan. Also linked to the 2002 murder of journalist Daniel Pearl.

HOT SPOT
INDONESIA & PHILIPPINES

Recent acts of terrorism have claimed hundreds of lives in Indonesia, prime target for indigenous groups like Jemaah Islamiyah that are now affiliated with al-Qaeda. In the Philippines, Muslim and Marxist rebels are an ongoing threat to stability.

MALAYSIA
⑫ PHILIPPINES
INDONESIA

AUSTRALIA

10. ■ JAISH-E-MOHAMMED
Pakistan
ACTIVITIES
Massacres, bombing
MEMBERS
Several hundred
This Islamist group is blamed for the bombing of an Indian state legislature in Kashmir that killed 38. Now split into two factions, this group, like others, fights to make predominantly Muslim Kashmir part of Pakistan.

10. LASHKAR E-TAIBA
Pakistan
ACTIVITIES
Massacres, bombing
MEMBERS
Several hundred
With training camps in Afghanistan, LET specializes in daredevil missions with devastating results, directed mainly against Indian troops and civilians in Kashmir.

11. LIBERATION TIGERS OF TAMIL EELAM
Sri Lanka
ACTIVITIES
Assassination, bombing
MEMBERS
10,000 to 15,000
Favoring suicide attacks, members seek an independent Tamil state in Sri Lanka. A precarious cease-fire is now in place.

12. ■ JEMAAH ISLAMIYAH
Southeast Asia
ACTIVITIES
Bombing
MEMBERS
Unknown
Responsible for a series of deadly bombings across Southeast Asia—including the Bali night-club attacks in 2002—al-Qaeda's local partner seeks an Islamic superstate spanning the region.

7. TAWHID W' AL JIHAD
Iraq
ACTIVITIES
Kidnapping, bombing
MEMBERS
Unknown
Jordanian Abu Musab al Zarqawi leads this loose network of jihadists, most of whom are Iraqi. Their common goal: to expel U.S. forces and create a Sunni Islamic state in Iraq. Many of its fighters are veterans of an older group, Ansar al Islam.

12. ABU SAYYAF
Philippines
ACTIVITIES
Kidnapping, bombing, piracy
MEMBERS
300 to 500
High-profile kidnappings of foreigners for ransom keep this group well financed—though the profit motive may be clouding Abu Sayyaf's founding vision of an Islamic state in the southern Philippines.

12. ■ MORO ISLAMIC LIBERATION FRONT
Philippines
ACTIVITIES
Bombing
MEMBERS
Around 12,000
Though it officially disavows terrorism, this insurgent group is linked to attacks on Philippine cities through its support for Jemaah Islamiyah. Now in peace talks with the government, the MILF aims for ethnic autonomy.

LEGEND

■ **Countries where al-Qaeda cells are known to be operating**
■ **Countries where al-Qaeda cells may be operating**
■ **Group affiliated with al-Qaeda**

crime is unlawful activity undertaken and supported by organized criminal groups operating across national boundaries. Criminal opportunities for transnational groups have come about in part by globalization of the world's economy and by advances in communications, transportation, and other technologies. Today's organized international criminal cartels recognize no boundaries and engage in activities like drug trafficking, money laundering, human trafficking, counterfeiting of branded goods, and weapons smuggling.

• This chapter defines *terrorism* as a violent act or an act dangerous to human life, in violation of the criminal laws of the United States or of any state, that is committed to intimidate or coerce a government, the civilian population, or any segment thereof, in furtherance of political or social objectives. Terrorism, which today is the focus of significant criminal justice activity, brings with it the threat of massive destruction and large numbers of casualties. Domestic and international terrorism are the two main forms of terrorism with which law enforcement organizations concern themselves today. Specific forms of terrorist activity, such as cyberterrorism and attacks on information-management segments of our nation's critical infrastructure, could theoretically shut down or disable important infrastructure services like electricity, food processing, military activity, and even state and federal governments. The vigilance required to prevent terrorism, both domestic and international, consumes a significant number of law enforcement resources and has resulted in new laws that restrict a number of freedoms that many Americans have previously taken for granted.

KEY TERMS

comparative criminologist, 162

cyberterrorism, 180

domestic terrorism, 176

ethnocentric, 163

European Police Office (Europol), 172

extradition, 175

foreign terrorist organization (FTO), 189

globalization, 173

Hudud crime, 165

infrastructure, 181

International Criminal Police Organization (Interpol), 171

international terrorism, 176

Islamic law, 165

narcoterrorism, 182

Tazir crime, 167

terrorism, 175

transnational crime, 174

QUESTIONS FOR REVIEW

1. What are the principles that inform Islamic law? How do these principles contribute to the structure and activities of the criminal justice systems of Muslim nations that follow Islamic law?

2. What important international criminal justice organizations does this chapter discuss? Describe the role of each in fighting international crime.

3. What is globalization, and how does it relate to transnational crime? What relationships might exist between transnational crime and terrorism?

4. What is terrorism? What are the two major types of terrorism discussed in this chapter?

QUESTIONS FOR REFLECTION

1. Why is terrorism a law enforcement concern? How is terrorism a crime? What can the American criminal justice system do to better prepare for future terrorist crimes?

2. What are the causes of terrorism? What efforts is the U.S. government making to prevent and control the spread of domestic terrorism? Of international terrorism?

3. What are the benefits of studying criminal justice systems in other countries? What problems are inherent in such study?

Discuss your answers to these questions and other issues on the CJ Today e-mail discussion list (join the list at cjtoday.com).

WEB QUEST

Use the Cybrary (http://www.cybrary.info) to identify countries other than the United States that make information on their criminal justice system available on the Web. (You might want to begin by clicking on the "International" category.) List the sites that you find, and describe the justice system of each nation.

Then use the Cybrary to identify countries other than the United States that make crime statistics available on the Web. List the statistics sites that you find for each country, and include a summary of the statistics available for each. Submit your findings to your instructor if asked to do so.

To complete this Web Quest online, go to the Web Quest module in Chapter 17 of the *Criminal Justice Today* Companion Website at cjtoday.com.

Chapter 17: Terrorism and Multinational Criminal Justice

CHECKING YOUR READING STRATEGIES
DISCUSSION AND CRITICAL THINKING QUESTIONS

1. **Preview the chapter** as you have been instructed. *Without reading the chapter itself*, write an outline of the chapter. Leave room to fill in the details later. Use your typographical cues to help you. (Do not include the "Summary" or any other review materials in your outline.)

2. **Preview the chapter again,** this time focusing on all the graphic illustrations. Read all the captions and information in tables; look carefully at all photographs and drawings. Next, let your eyes scan over the columns of text. See if you can find where in the paragraphs the illustrated material is explained. What cues are given in the text to tie the illustrations to the words?

3. *Circle the best answer for each of the following questions.*

   1. According to the outline listed at the beginning of the chapter, this chapter will cover how many points?
      a. Four
      b. Ten
      c. Twenty-one
      d. Not enough information to answer the question

   2. What is the *overall purpose* of the chapter's introduction?
      a. To set up the focus for the chapter
      b. To explain how other cultures view terrorism
      c. To explain how people protest
      d. To tie in the quotations that open the chapter

   3. How many types of graphic illustrations are used in this chapter? Look through the entire chapter. Select all that apply.
      a. Photographs
      b. Charts
      c. Graphs
      d. Organizational charts
      e. Shaded boxes (of formulas, theories, etc.)
      f. Maps
      g. Branching/tree diagrams
      h. In-chapter assessments/quizzes
      i. Diagrams
      j. Tables
      k. Flow charts
      l. Pie charts
      m. Process diagrams
      n. Margin notes

4. What typographical cues are used in the chapter to highlight important information for you? Select all that apply.

a. Boldface print
b. Font size
c. Bulleted lists
d. Color of print
e. Shading
f. Symbols (light bulb, question mark, star, etc.)
g. Italicized print
h. Font style
i. Underlining
j. Boxes
k. Arrows to show direction/order

4. **Preview the "Summary" and both sets of questions.** Read over the review of the concepts and the questions. These are the key points the authors feel you should draw from the chapter. How do the authors tie the concepts back to the text so you would know where to find the information? Go back and look for it. Make a checkmark in the margin so you will remember this is a key point when you read the chapter.

5. Now go back to the first page of the chapter and **read the chapter**. Move through the chapter section by section. Read first, then decide what information is important for you to know and what is explanatory to illustrate the point. Next, return to the outline you drafted for question 1. Fill in the outline with the information you have determined to be important for you to remember. Consider your method as well. **How** did you determine which information was important enough to record?

6. Did you read the "CJ Today Exhibit" sections? How about the "CJ News"? If not, go back and do them. Why do you think these are included in the text? Of what benefit are they to you and your reading of the chapter?

7. Consider epigrams (quotations) that open the chapter. How do they relate to the rest of the chapter? Why do you think the author included them? How do they help you learn?

8. Finally, **after reading** the chapter, answer the "Questions for Review" and the "Questions for Reflection." How well did you do?

GROUP PROJECTS

1. Compare your outline with that of your classmates. Are they all the same? If not, how do they differ? Why do you think that may be? Next, compare how well you and your classmates did when answering the questions at the end of the text's chapter. Did those of you with the more detailed outline do better? Why or why not?

2. Within your group, discuss the benefits of previewing the illustrations in the text before reading, as opposed to waiting to explore them as they come up in the reading.

3. As a group, consider what the authors do to make this chapter interesting and appealing to you. Consider both the visual components and the information itself. How do page layout and writing style make assigned reading more enjoyable?

4. Discuss with your group the usefulness of the "Where They Are" map in Figure 17-4.

5. Discuss with your group how helpful the chapter's information will be for you to understand what you hear in the news about terrorism. Have the authors left out any thing you have heard about?

6. As a group, consider the assessments supplied in the text. Why are they included? How do they aid your reading?

Unit VII
Reading Strategies for Technical Fields and Computer Science

from

GO! With Microsoft Office 2007 Introductory

Second Edition

by

Shelley Gaskin, Robert L. Ferrett, Alicia Vargas, and Suzanne Marks

Reading in the technical fields is a bit different than most of the disciplines we have looked at here because the text is part textbook, part operations manual. This might be closer to reading your math text than one of the others discussed here. The primary purpose of the technical courses is to teach you what you need to know to do a job, to give you some hands-on experience before sending you out on your own. There will be the information regarding the equipment or systems themselves, procedures to follow for installation, set-up, trouble-shooting, and the techniques you will need to use to perform these tasks. The primary thought patterns are problem solving and process.

These texts often open a chapter with a brief case or model to show you how the topic to be covered is used outside of the classroom, as our PowerPoint chapter does here. Then they pretty much plunge in to tell you what to do and how to do it. You do not get much of an introductory build-up here. As with math texts though, each point is explained and immediately followed with a graphic illustration of what is to be done. You will be walked through the steps, taught different techniques, and then there will be an assortment of practice exercise or projects of varying difficulty which will enable you to practice the skills just taught. Watch for boxed areas, such as those labeled "Note" or "Alert!" in the chapter here, since they will highlight important things for you to be aware of as you work through the stages of the task.

These texts are packed with factual information. They are pretty cut-and-dried, straight-to-the-point procedural explanations of what to do and how to do it. Take the time to preview the reading assignment. Prepare to read slowly, looking frequently back and forth between the text and the illustrations. Make note of the names of the parts of objects or steps in a procedure or system. Be prepared to have to re-read. If you are required to read an instruction manual, note that these are not read from cover to cover. Usually you will turn to the index to find where the information is located for whatever your purpose is, turn to those pages, and read just what you need to perform the task in question. If the directions are difficult, take them step-by-step, even redrawing or rewriting them if necessary.

chapterfifteen

Getting Started with Microsoft PowerPoint 2007

OBJECTIVES

At the end of this chapter you will be able to:

1. Open, View, and Save a Presentation
2. Edit a Presentation
3. Format a Presentation
4. Create Headers and Footers and Print a Presentation

OUTCOMES

Mastering these objectives will enable you to:

PROJECT 15A
Open, Edit, Save, and Print a Presentation

5. Create a New Presentation
6. Use Slide Sorter View
7. Add Pictures to a Presentation
8. Use the Microsoft Help System

PROJECT 15B
Create and Format a Presentation

Skyline Bakery and Cafe

Skyline Bakery and Cafe is a chain of casual dining restaurants and bakeries based in Boston. Each restaurant has its own in-house bakery, which produces a wide variety of high-quality specialty breads, breakfast sweets, and desserts. Breads and sweets are sold by counter service along with coffee drinks, gourmet teas, fresh juices, and sodas. The full-service restaurant area features a menu of sandwiches, salads, soups, and light entrees. Fresh, high-quality ingredients and a professional and courteous staff are the hallmarks of every Skyline Bakery and Cafe.

Getting Started with Microsoft Office PowerPoint 2007

Presentation skills are among the most important skills you will ever learn. Good presentation skills enhance all of your communications—written, electronic, and interpersonal. In our technology-enhanced world of e-mail and wireless phones, communicating ideas clearly and concisely is a critical personal skill. Microsoft Office PowerPoint 2007 is a presentation graphics software program used to create electronic slide presentations and black-and-white or color overhead transparencies that you can use to effectively present information to your audience.

Project 15A **Expansion**

In Activities 15.1 through 15.17, you will edit and format a presentation that Lucinda dePaolo, Chief Financial Officer, has created that details the Skyline Bakery and Cafe's expansion plan. Your completed presentation will look similar to Figure 15.1.

For Project 15A, you will need the following file:

p15A_Expansion

You will save your presentation as
15A_Expansion_Firstname_Lastname

Skyline Bakery and Cafe

Expansion Plans

Mission

To provide a nutritious, satisfying, and delicious meal experience for each of our customers in a relaxing and temptingly aromatic environment.

Company Information

‣ Founded in Boston by Samir Taheri in 1985
‣ Current locations in Massachusetts and Maine
‣ Expansion plans in 2009
  ▫ Rhode Island
  ▫ Virginia
‣ **Awards received this year**
  ▫ Golden Bakery
  ▫ Cuisine Excellence

Expansion Plans

‣ 2009
  ▫ Rhode Island and Virginia
‣ 2010
  ▫ New Hampshire and New Jersey

‣ 2011
  ▫ West Virginia and Ohio
‣ 2012
  ▫ New York and Connecticut

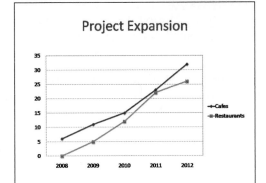

Figure 15.1
Project 15A—Expansion

Objective 1
Open, View, and Save a Presentation

Microsoft Office PowerPoint is a ***presentation graphics software*** program that you can use to effectively present information to your audience. The purpose of any presentation is to influence your audience. Whether you are presenting a new product to coworkers, making a speech at a conference, or expressing your opinion to your city council, you want to make a good impression and give your audience a reason to agree with your point of view. The way in which your audience reacts to your message depends on the information you present and how you present yourself. In the following activities, you will start Microsoft Office PowerPoint 2007, become familiar with the PowerPoint window, and then open, edit, and save an existing PowerPoint presentation.

Activity 15.1 Starting PowerPoint and Identifying Parts of the PowerPoint Window

In this activity, you will start PowerPoint and identify the parts of the PowerPoint window.

> ## Note — Comparing Your Screen with the Figures in This Textbook
>
> Your screen will match the figures shown in this textbook if you set your screen resolution to 1,024 × 768. At other resolutions, your screen will closely resemble, but not match, the figures shown. To view your screen's resolution, on the Windows desktop, right-click in a blank area, click Properties, and then click the Settings tab.

1 On the left side of the Windows taskbar, point to, and then click, the **Start** button.

2 From the displayed **Start** menu, locate the **PowerPoint** program, and then click **Microsoft Office PowerPoint 2007**.

Organizations and individuals store computer programs in a variety of ways. The PowerPoint program may be located under All Programs, or Microsoft Office, or from the main Start menu.

3 Take a moment to study the main parts of the screen as shown in Figure 15.2 and described in the table in Figure 15.3.

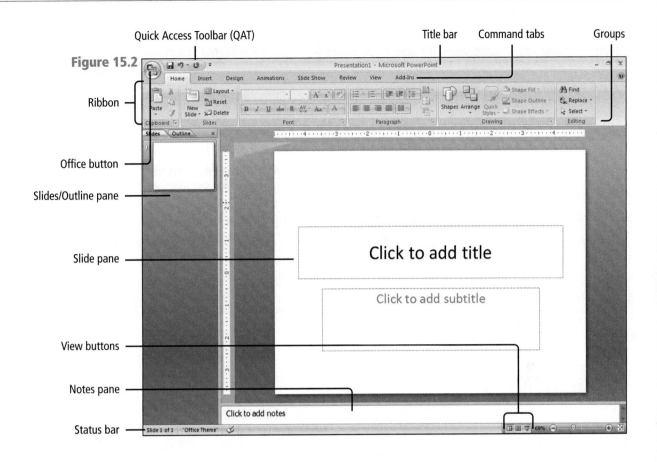

Figure 15.2

Quick Access Toolbar (QAT) · Title bar · Command tabs · Groups · Ribbon · Office button · Slides/Outline pane · Slide pane · View buttons · Notes pane · Status bar

Click to add title

Click to add subtitle

Click to add notes

Microsoft PowerPoint Screen Elements

Screen Element	Description
Command tab	Displays the commands most relevant for a particular task area, such as inserting, designing, and animating.
Group	Related command buttons associated with the selected command tab.
Notes pane	Displays below the Slide pane and allows you to type notes regarding the active slide.
Office button	Displays a list of commands related to things you can do with a presentation, such as opening, saving, printing, or sharing.
Quick Access Toolbar (QAT)	Displays buttons to perform frequently used commands with a single click. Frequently used commands in PowerPoint include Save, Undo, and Repeat. For commands that you use frequently, you can add additional buttons to the Quick Access Toolbar.
Ribbon	Organizes commands on tabs, and then groups the commands by topic for performing related presentation tasks.
Slide pane	Displays a large image of the active slide.

(Continued)

(Continued)

Microsoft PowerPoint Screen Elements

Screen Element	Description
Slides/Outline pane	Displays either the presentation outline (Outline tab) or all of the slides in the presentation in the form of miniature images called *thumbnails* (Slides tab).
Status bar	A horizontal bar at the bottom of the presentation window that displays the current slide number, number of slides in a presentation, Design Template, View buttons, and Zoom slider. The status bar can be customized to include other information.
Title bar	Displays the name of the presentation and the name of the program. The Minimize, Maximize/Restore Down, and Close buttons are grouped on the right side of the title bar.
View buttons	A set of commands that control the look of the presentation window.

Figure 15.3

Alert!

Does your screen differ?

The appearance of the screen can vary, depending on settings that were established when the program was installed. For example, the Add-Ins tab may or may not display on your Ribbon. Additionally, the Quick Access Toolbar can display any combination of buttons, and may occupy its own row on the Ribbon.

Activity 15.2 Opening a Presentation

To open a presentation that has already been created in PowerPoint, use the Office button. As you work on a presentation, save your changes frequently.

1 In the upper left corner of the PowerPoint window, click the **Office** button, and then click **Open** to display the Open dialog box.

2 In the **Open** dialog box, at the right edge of the **Look in** box, click the **Look in arrow** to view a list of the drives available on your system, as shown in Figure 15.4.

Your list of available drives may differ.

Your list of available drives will differ   Look in arrow

Figure 15.4

Look in box

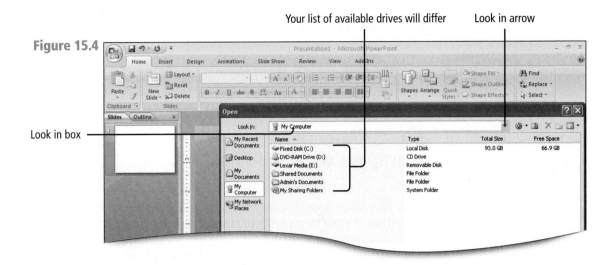

3 Navigate to the location where the student files for this textbook are stored. Click **p15A_Expansion**, and then click the **Open** button or press Enter to display Slide 1 of the presentation in the PowerPoint window.

PowerPoint displays the file name of the presentation in the title bar at the top of the screen.

4 Look at the **Slides/Outline pane** on the left side of the window and notice that the presentation contains four slides. Additionally, at the right side of the window, a scroll bar displays a scroll box and up and down pointing arrows for navigating through your presentation.

Below the scroll bar, the Previous Slide ⬆ and Next Slide ⬇ buttons display. See Figure 15.5.

Figure 15.5

Scroll box

Slides/Outline pane

Scroll bar

Previous Slide button

Next Slide button

⑤ In the scroll bar, click the **Next Slide** button ⬇ three times so that each slide in the presentation displays. Then click the **Previous Slide** button ⬆ three times until Slide 1 displays.

When you click the Next Slide or the Previous Slide button, you can scroll through your presentation one slide at a time.

Activity 15.3 Viewing a Slide Show

When a presentation is viewed as an electronic slide show, the entire slide fills the computer screen, and a large audience can view your presentation if your computer is connected to a projection system.

① On the Ribbon, click the **Slide Show tab**. In the **Start Slide Show group**, click the **From Beginning** button.

The first slide fills the entire screen and animation effects display the picture, and then the title and subtitle. *Animation effects* introduce individual slide elements one element at a time. These effects add interest to your slides and draw attention to important features.

Another Way — **To Start a Slide Show**

On the right side of the status bar, from the View buttons, click the Slide Show button. You can also display the first slide that you want to show, and then press F5 .

② Click the left mouse button or press Spacebar to advance to the second slide, noticing the transition as Slide 1 moves off the screen and Slide 2 displays. An animation effect stretches the graphic images across the screen from left to right.

Transitions refer to the way that a slide appears or disappears during an onscreen slide show. For example, when one slide leaves the screen, it may fade or dissolve into another slide.

③ Click the left mouse button or press Spacebar and notice that the third slide displays and the slide title drops onto the screen from the top of the slide and a picture appears from the lower right corner. Click again or press Spacebar and notice that the first bullet point displays. Continue to click or press Spacebar until each bullet point displays on the slide and the next slide—*Project Expansion*—displays.

④ Click or press Spacebar to display the chart, and then click or press Spacebar one more time to display a black slide.

After the last slide in a presentation, a *black slide* with the text *End of slide show, click to exit.* displays. A black slide is inserted at the end of every slide show to indicate that the presentation is over.

5 On the black slide, click the left mouse button to exit the slide show and return to Slide 1.

Activity 15.4 Creating Folders and Saving a Presentation

In the same way that you use file folders to organize your paper documents, Windows uses a hierarchy of electronic folders to keep your electronic files organized. When you save a presentation file, the Windows operating system stores your presentation permanently on a storage medium. Changes that you make to existing presentations, such as changing text or typing in new text, are not permanently saved until you perform a Save operation.

1 In the upper left corner of the PowerPoint window, click the **Office** button , and then click **Save As** to display the **Save As** dialog box.

2 In the **Save As** dialog box, at the right edge of the **Save in** box, click the **Save in arrow** to view a list of the drives available to you, as shown in Figure 15.6.

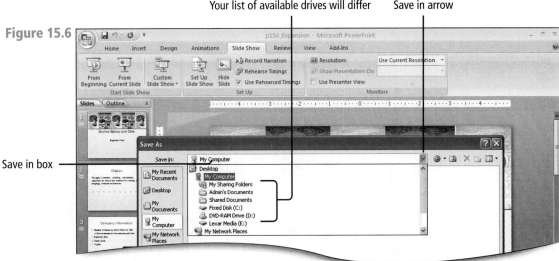

Figure 15.6

Your list of available drives will differ   *Save in arrow*

Save in box

3 Navigate to the drive on which you will be storing your folders and projects for this chapter—for example, a USB flash drive that you have connected, a shared drive on a network, or the drive designated by your instructor or lab coordinator.

4 In the **Save As** dialog box, on the toolbar, click the **Create New Folder** button . In the displayed **New Folder** dialog box, in the **Name** box, type **PowerPoint Chapter 15** as shown in Figure 15.7, and then click **OK**.

The new folder name displays in the Save in box, indicating that the folder is open and ready to store your presentation.

Figure 15.7

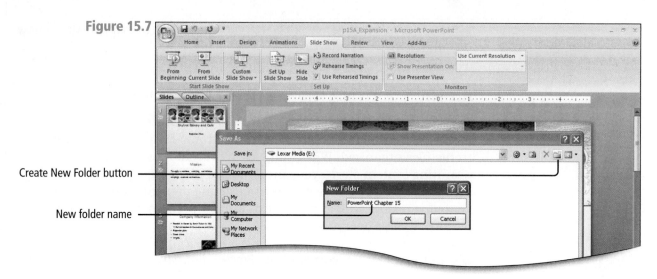

Create New Folder button

New folder name

5 In the lower portion of the **Save As** dialog box, locate the **File name** box. If necessary, select or delete the existing text, and then in the **File name** box, using your own first and last names, type **15A_Expansion_Firstname_Lastname** as shown in Figure 15.8.

Throughout this textbook, you will be instructed to save your files, using the file name followed by your first and last names. Check with your instructor to see if there is some other file-naming arrangement for your course.

The Microsoft Windows operating system recognizes file names with spaces. However, some Internet file transfer programs do not. To facilitate sending your files over the Internet if you are using a course management system, in this textbook you will be instructed to save files by using an underscore instead of a space.

Figure 15.8

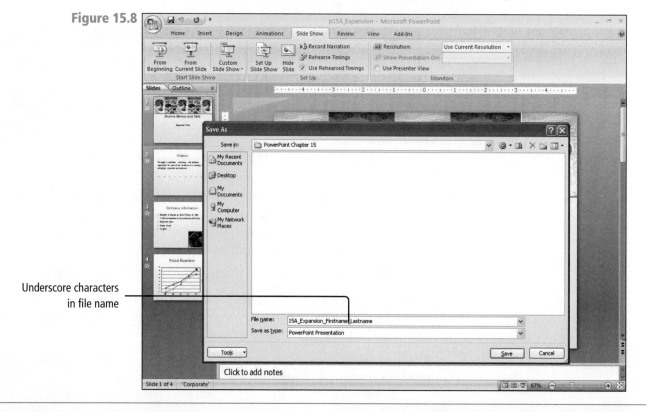

Underscore characters in file name

6 In the lower portion of the **Save As** dialog box, click the **Save** button, or press Enter.

Your presentation is saved on the storage device that you selected, and it is contained in the *PowerPoint Chapter 15* folder with the new file name. The new file name also displays in the title bar.

Objective 2
Edit a Presentation

In *Normal view*, the PowerPoint window is divided into three areas—the Slide pane, the Slides/Outline pane, and the Notes pane. When you make changes to the presentation in the Slides/Outline pane, the changes are reflected immediately in the Slide pane. Likewise, when you make changes in the Slide pane, the changes are reflected in the Slides/Outline pane.

Activity 15.5 Editing Slide Text

Editing is the process of adding, deleting, or changing the contents of a slide. When you click in the middle of a word or sentence and start typing, the existing text moves to the right to make space for your new keystrokes. In this activity, you will edit text in the Slide pane.

1 In the **Slides/Outline pane**, if necessary, click the **Slides tab** to display the slide thumbnails.

You can use the slide thumbnails to navigate in your presentation. When you click on a slide thumbnail, the slide displays in the Slide pane.

2 In the **Slides/Outline pane**, on the **Slides tab**, click **Slide 2** to display the company's mission statement. Move your pointer into the paragraph that contains the company's mission statement, and then click to the left of the word *experience* as shown in Figure 15.9.

On this slide a red wavy underline indicates that there is a misspelled word. Do not be concerned at this time with the misspelling—you will correct it in a later activity.

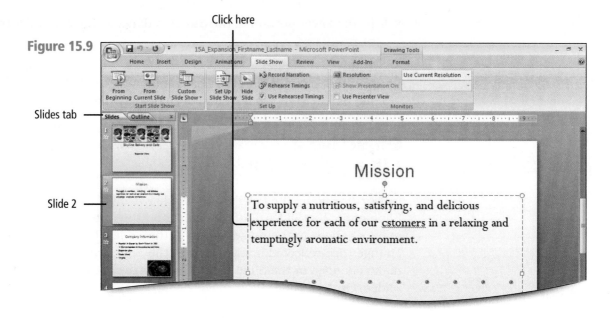

Figure 15.9

3 Type **meal** and notice that as you type, the existing text moves to the right to accommodate the text that you are inserting. Press Spacebar to insert a space between *meal* and *experience*.

After you type the space, the word *meal* moves to the first line of the paragraph because there is enough space in the first line to accommodate the text.

4 In the **Slides/Outline pane**, on the **Slides tab**, click **Slide 3**. In the bulleted list, in the third line, click to the right of the word *plans* and press Spacebar. Type **in 2009**

5 On the **Quick Access Toolbar**, click the **Save** button 💾 to save the changes you have made to the presentation since your last save operation.

Activity 15.6 Inserting a New Slide

To insert a new slide in a presentation, display the slide that will come before the slide that you want to insert.

1 If necessary, display **Slide 3**. On the Ribbon, click the **Home tab**.

On the Home tab, the Slides group includes the New Slide button. The New Slide button is divided into two parts: the upper part contains the New Slide icon, which inserts a slide without displaying options; the lower part contains the words New Slide and a down-pointing arrow that when clicked, displays a gallery. The *gallery*— a visual representation of a command's options—displays slide layouts. *Layout* refers to the placement and arrangement of the text and graphic elements on a slide.

2 In the **Slides group**, click the lower part of the **New Slide** button to display the gallery.

Alert!

Did you insert a slide without displaying the gallery?

The New Slide button is divided into two parts. If you click the upper part, a new slide is inserted, using the layout of the previous slide. To view the gallery, you must click the lower part of the New Slide button. Do not be concerned if the gallery did not display—the correct type of slide was inserted. Read Step 3, and then continue with Step 4.

3 Point to **Title and Text** as shown in Figure 15.10, and then click to insert a slide with the Title and Text layout. Notice that the new blank slide displays in the Slide pane and in the Slides/Outline pane.

The new slide contains two *placeholders*—one for the slide title and one for content. A placeholder reserves a portion of a slide and serves as a container for text or other content, including pictures, graphics, charts, tables, and diagrams.

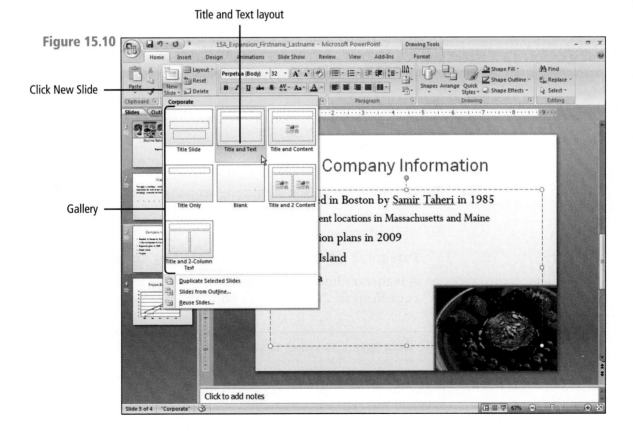

Figure 15.10

4 In the **Slide pane**, the title placeholder displays the text *Click to add title*. Click in the title placeholder. Type **Expansion Plans** and then click in the *Click to add text* content placeholder.

5 Type **2009** and then press Enter.

6 Type **Rhode Island and Virginia** and then press Enter.

7 Type **2010** and then on the **Quick Access Toolbar**, click the **Save** button to save your presentation.

Activity 15.7 Increasing and Decreasing List Levels

Text in a PowerPoint presentation is organized according to outline levels, similar to the outline levels you might make for a book report. The highest level on an individual slide is the title. ***Bulleted levels***—outline levels represented by a bullet symbol—are identified in the slides by the indentation and the size of the text. Indented text in a smaller size indicates a lower outline level. It is easy to change the outline level of text to a higher or lower level. For example, you may create a presentation with four bullets on the same level. Then you may decide that one bulleted item relates to one of the other bullets, rather than to the slide title. In this case, a lower outline level should be applied. You can increase the list or indent level of text to apply a *lower* outline level, or decrease the list or indent level of text to apply a *higher* outline level.

1 If necessary, display **Slide 4**, click at the end of the last bullet point—*2010*—and then press Enter to create a new bullet.

2 Press Tab and notice that a lower level bullet point is created. Type **New Hampshire and New Jersey**

3 Click anywhere in the second bullet point—*Rhode Island and Virginia*. On the Ribbon, in the **Paragraph group**, click the **Increase List Level** button.

A lower outline level is applied to the text.

4 Display **Slide 3**. Notice that the second bullet point is a lower outline level than the first bullet point.

5 Click anywhere in the second bullet point. On the Ribbon, in the **Paragraph group**, click the **Decrease List Level** button.

A higher outline level is applied so that the second bullet point is equivalent to all of the other bullet points on the slide.

Another Way

To Decrease List Level

You can decrease the list level of a bullet point by holding down Shift and pressing Tab.

6 You can change the outline level of more than one bullet point by first selecting all of the text whose outline level you want to change. In the fourth bullet point, position the pointer to the left of *Rhode*, hold down the left mouse button, and then drag to the right and down to select the *Rhode Island* and the *Virginia* bullet points as shown in Figure 15.11. Release the mouse button.

Dragging is the technique of holding down the left mouse button and moving over an area of text so that it is selected. Selected text is indicated when the background changes to a different color than the slide background. When you select text, a ***Mini toolbar*** displays near the selection. The Mini toolbar displays buttons that are commonly used with the selected object, as shown in Figure 15.11. The Mini toolbar is semitransparent unless you move the pointer to it. When you move the pointer away from the Mini toolbar, it disappears. You will learn more about the Mini toolbar in a later activity.

Figure 15.11

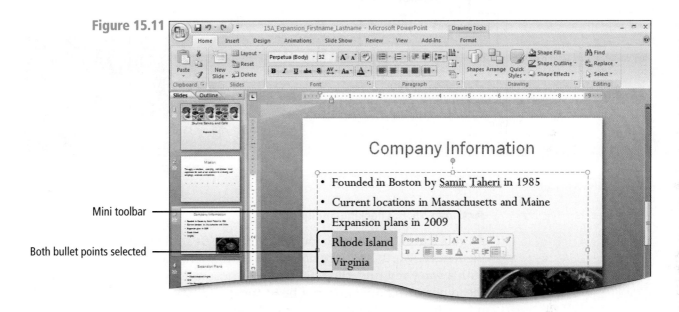

Mini toolbar

Both bullet points selected

Note — Demoting and Promoting Text

Increasing and decreasing the list level of a bullet point is sometimes referred to demoting and promoting text.

---

7 On the **Home** tab, in the **Paragraph group**, click the **Increase List Level** button .

Both bulleted items are demoted to lower levels.

8 Click at the end of the word *Virginia*. Press Enter to create a new bullet, and notice that the new bullet is indented at the same level as *Virginia*.

9 Click the **Decrease List Level** button to promote the new bullet. Type **Awards received this year** and then press Enter.

10 Click the **Increase List Level** button . Type **Golden Bakery** and press Enter. Type **Cuisine Excellence**

11 Compare your slide to Figure 15.12. **Save** your presentation.

Figure 15.12

Increase list level to indent ——

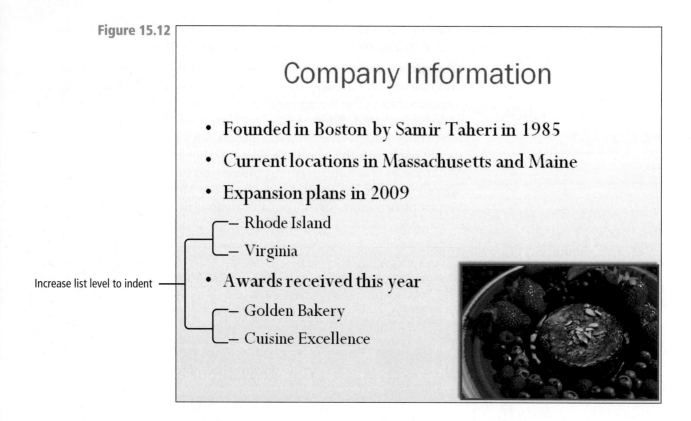

Activity 15.8 Checking Spelling

As you type, PowerPoint compares your words to those in the PowerPoint dictionary. Words that are not in the PowerPoint dictionary are marked with a wavy red underline. Sometimes these words are correct. For example, a person's name may not be in the dictionary and may be flagged as misspelled even though it is correctly spelled. The red wavy underline does not display when the presentation is viewed as a slide show.

One way to check spelling errors flagged by PowerPoint is to right-click the flagged word or phrase and, from the displayed shortcut menu, select a suitable correction or instruction.

1 Display **Slide 2**. Notice that the word *cstomers* is flagged with a red wavy underline, indicating that it is misspelled.

2 Point to *cstomers* and click the right mouse button to display the **shortcut menu** with a suggested solution for correcting the misspelled word, and the Mini toolbar, as shown in Figure 15.13.

A shortcut menu is a context-sensitive menu that displays commands and options relevant to the selected object.

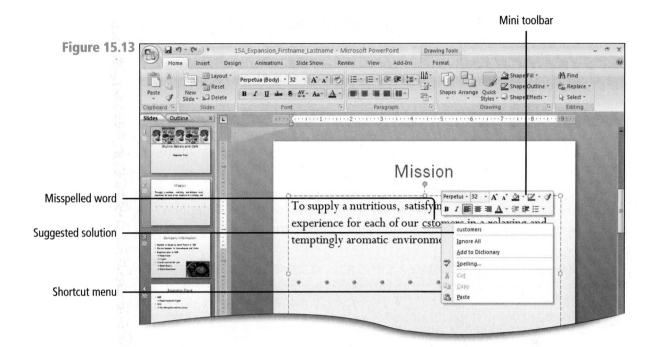

Figure 15.13

Misspelled word

Suggested solution

Shortcut menu

Mini toolbar

> 3 From the shortcut menu, click **customers** to correct the spelling of the word.

> 4 Display **Slide 3** and notice that the name *Samir Taheri* is flagged as misspelled, although it is spelled correctly.

> 5 Right-click *Samir*, and from the shortcut menu, click **Ignore All** so that every time the name *Samir* displays in the presentation, it will not be flagged as a misspelled word. Repeat this procedure to ignore the flagged word *Taheri*.

More Knowledge
Spelling Correction Options

The Ignore All option is particularly useful when proper nouns are flagged as spelling errors even when they are spelled correctly. If you are using PowerPoint 2007 on a system that you can customize—such as your home computer—you can add frequently used names and proper nouns to the PowerPoint custom dictionary by clicking the Add to Dictionary option from the shortcut menu.

> 6 Display each slide in the presentation and correct any spelling errors that you may have made when editing the slides.

> 7 **Save** your presentation.

Another Way
To Check Spelling

You can check the spelling of the entire presentation at one time. On the Ribbon, click Review, and then click the Spelling button to display a dialog box that will select each spelling error in your presentation and provide options for correcting it.

Activity 15.9 Editing Text by Using the Thesaurus

The **Thesaurus** is a research tool that provides a list of **synonyms**—words with the same meaning—for text that you select. You can access synonyms by using either the shortcut menu or the Review tab on the Ribbon.

1 Display **Slide 2**. In the first line of the paragraph, point to the word *supply*, and then click the right mouse button to display the shortcut menu.

2 Near the bottom of the shortcut menu, point to **Synonyms** to display a list of suggested words to replace *supply*. Point to **provide** as shown in Figure 15.14, and then click to change *supply* to *provide*.

Figure 15.14

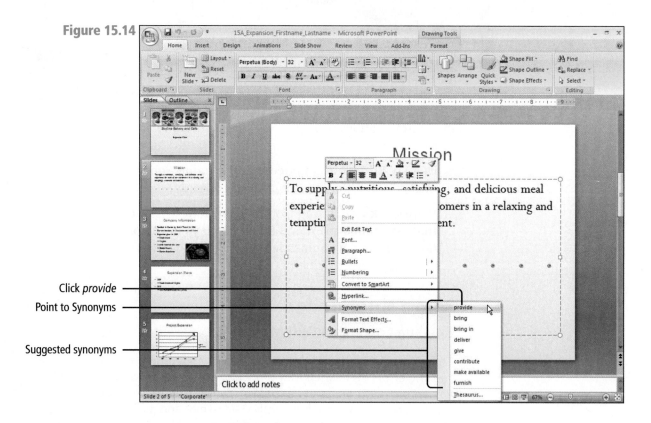

Click *provide*

Point to Synonyms

Suggested synonyms

3 **Save** the presentation.

Another Way — **To Access the Thesaurus**

After you select the word that you want to replace, on the Ribbon, click Review. Click Thesaurus to display the Research task pane, which contains a more comprehensive list of suggested synonyms.

Activity 15.10 Adding Speaker's Notes to a Presentation

Recall that when a presentation is displayed in Normal view, the Notes pane displays below the Slide pane. The Notes pane is used to type speaker's notes that can be printed below a picture of each slide. You can refer to these printouts while making a presentation, thus reminding you of the important points that you want to make while running an electronic slide show.

1 Display **Slide 4**. Look at the PowerPoint window and notice the amount of space that is currently dedicated to each of the three panes—the Slides/Outline pane, the Slide pane, and the Notes pane. Locate the horizontal and vertical borders that separate the three panes.

These narrow borders are used to adjust the size of the panes. If you decide to type speaker notes, you may want to make the Notes pane larger.

2 Point to the border that separates the **Slide pane** from the **Notes pane**. The resize pointer displays as an equal sign with an upward-pointing and a downward-pointing arrow, as shown in Figure 15.15.

Use the resize pointer to resize the Notes pane

Figure 15.15

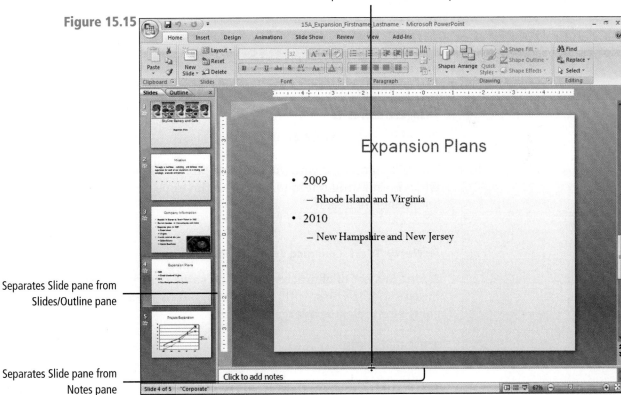

Separates Slide pane from Slides/Outline pane

Separates Slide pane from Notes pane

3 Press and hold down the left mouse button and drag the pointer up approximately 1 inch, and then release the left mouse button to resize the pane.

4 With **Slide 4** displayed, click in the **Notes** pane and type **These expansion plans have been approved by the board of directors.** Compare your screen to Figure 15.16.

Figure 15.16

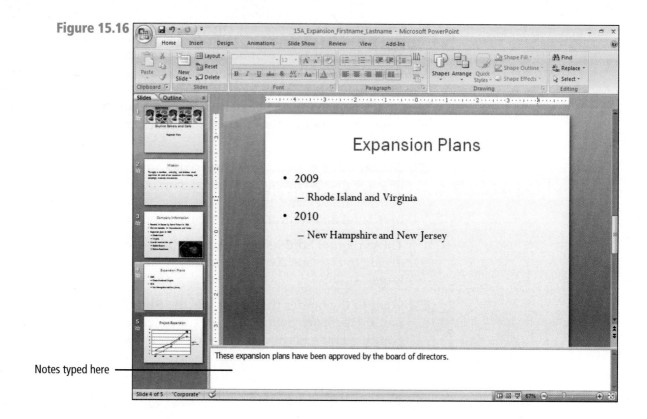

Notes typed here

---

5 **Save** 💾 the presentation.

Objective 3
Format a Presentation

You will do most of your *formatting* work in PowerPoint in the Slide pane. Formatting refers to changing the appearance of the text, layout, and design of a slide.

Activity 15.11 Changing Font and Font Size

A *font* is a set of characters with the same design and shape. Fonts are measured in *points*, with one point equal to 1/72 of an inch. A higher point size indicates a larger font size.

1 Display **Slide 1** and drag to select the title text—*Skyline Bakery and Cafe.*

2 Point to the Mini toolbar so that it is no longer semitransparent, and then click the **Font button arrow** Calibri (Headings) ▾ to display the available fonts, as shown in Figure 15.17.

The two fonts that display at the top of the list are the fonts currently used in the presentation.

Alert!

Did the Mini toolbar disappear?

When you select text, the Mini toolbar displays. If you move your pointer away from the selection and into the slide area without pointing to the Mini toolbar, it may no longer display. If this happened to you, select the text again, and then point to the Mini toolbar, making sure that you do not point to another area of the slide.

Figure 15.17

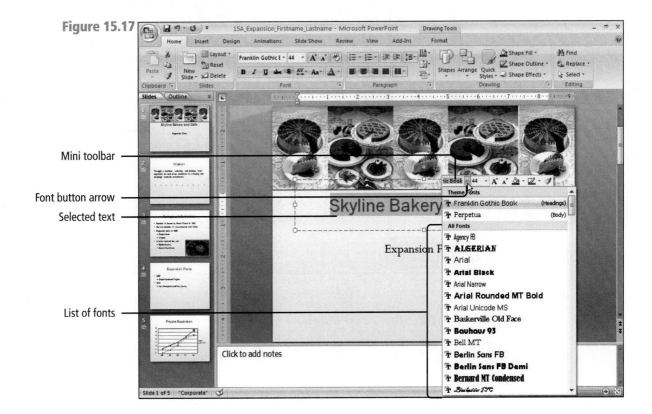

Mini toolbar

Font button arrow

Selected text

List of fonts

3 Scroll the displayed list as necessary, and then click **Book Antiqua**.

4 On the Ribbon, if necessary, click the **Home tab**. In the **Font group**, click the **Font Size button arrow** 44. On the displayed list, click **48**.

5 Select the subtitle text—*Expansion Plans*. On the Ribbon, in the **Font group**, click the **Font button arrow** Calibri (Headings). In the displayed list, scroll as necessary, and then point to—but do not click—**Arial Black**. Compare your screen with Figure 15.18.

Live Preview is a feature that displays formatting in your presentation so that you can decide whether or not you would like to apply the formatting. In this case, Live Preview displays the selected text in the Arial Black font, even though you did not click the font name. The font will actually change when you click the font name.

Live Preview displays the selection in the selected font

Figure 15.18

Font name

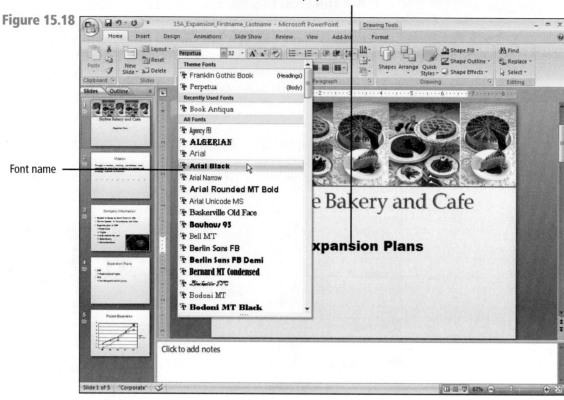

6 Click **Arial Black**.

7 **Save** 💾 the changes you have made to your presentation.

Activity 15.12 Applying Font Styles

Font styles emphasize text and are a visual cue to draw the reader's eye to important text. Font styles include bold, italic, and underline.

1 On **Slide 1**, drag to select the title—*Skyline Bakery and Cafe*. On the **Home tab**, in the **Font group**, point to the **Bold** button [B] as shown in Figure 15.19, and then click to apply bold to the title.

Figure 15.19

Click the Bold button

Selected text

▣ Select the subtitle—*Expansion Plans*. On the Mini toolbar, click the **Bold** button **B**, and then click the **Italic** button **I** to apply both bold and italic to the selection. Notice that on the **Home tab**, in the **Font group**, the **Bold** and **Italic** buttons are selected.

The Bold, Italic, and Underline buttons are ***toggle buttons***; that is, you can click the button once to turn it on and click it again to turn it off.

▣ With the subtitle still selected, on the **Home tab**, in the **Font group**, click the **Bold** button **B** to turn off the bold formatting.

▣ **Save** 🖫 your changes.

Another Way

To Apply Font Styles

There are four methods to apply font styles:

- On the Home tab, in the Font group, click the Bold, Italic, or Underline button.
- On the Mini toolbar, click the Bold or Italic button.
- From the keyboard, use the keyboard shortcuts of ⌨Ctrl + ⌨B for bold, ⌨Ctrl + ⌨I for italic, or ⌨Ctrl + ⌨U for underline.
- On the Home tab, in the Font group, click the Dialog Box Launcher to open the Font dialog box, and then click the font styles that you want to apply.

Activity 15.13 Aligning Text and Changing Line Spacing

Text alignment refers to the horizontal placement of text within a place-holder. Text can be aligned left, centered, aligned right, or justified. When text is justified, the left and right margins are even.

▣ Display **Slide 2** and click in the paragraph.

▣ On the **Home tab**, in the **Paragraph group**, click the **Center** button ≡ to center align the paragraph within the placeholder.

3 In the **Paragraph group**, click the **Line Spacing** button. In the displayed list, click **1.5** to change from single-spacing between lines to one and a half spaces between lines.

4 **Save** your changes.

Activity 15.14 Modifying Slide Layout

Recall that layout refers to the placement and arrangement of the text and graphic elements on a slide. PowerPoint includes a number of pre-defined layouts that you can apply to your slide for the purpose of arranging slide elements. For example, a Title Slide contains two place-holder elements—the title and the subtitle. Additional slide layouts include Title and Content, Title and 2 Content, Comparison, and Picture with Caption. When you design your slides, consider the content that you want to include, and then choose a layout that contains elements that best display the message that you want to convey.

1 Display **Slide 4.**

2 On the **Home tab**, in the **Slides group**, click the **Layout** button to display the **Slide Layout gallery**. The gallery displays an image of each layout and the name of each layout.

3 Point to each layout and notice that a **ScreenTip** also displays the name of the layout.

A ScreenTip is a small box, activated by holding the pointer over a button or other screen object, that displays information about a screen element.

4 Point to **Title and 2-Column Text**—as shown in Figure 15.20—and then click to change the slide layout.

The existing text displays in the placeholder on the left and a blank content placeholder is displayed on the right.

Figure 15.20

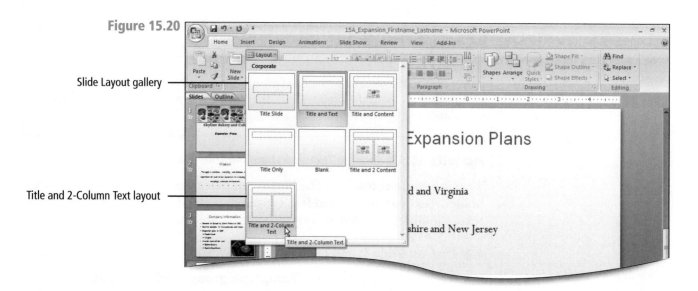

Slide Layout gallery

Title and 2-Column Text layout

5 Click in the placeholder on the right. Type **2011** and then press Enter. Press Tab to increase the list level. Type **West Virginia and Ohio** and then press Enter.

6 Press ⇧ Shift + Tab to decrease the list level. Type **2012** and then press Enter. Press Tab to increase the list level. Type **New York and Connecticut**

7 Click outside of the placeholder so that it is not selected, and then compare your slide to Figure 15.21.

8 **Save** 💾 your changes.

Figure 15.21

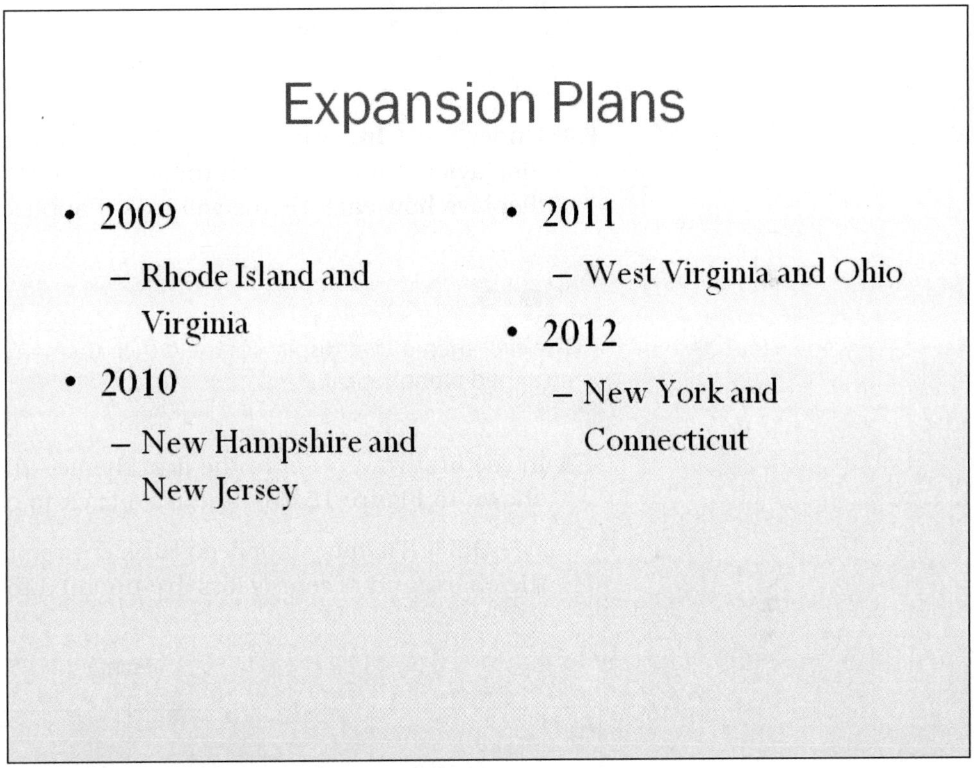

Expansion Plans

- 2009
  - Rhode Island and Virginia
- 2010
  - New Hampshire and New Jersey

- 2011
  - West Virginia and Ohio
- 2012
  - New York and Connecticut

Activity 15.15 Changing the Presentation Theme

A *theme* is a set of unified design elements that provides a look for your presentation by using color, fonts, and graphics. The overall *presentation* theme may include background designs, graphics, and objects that can be customized, using one of the three additional types of themes available in PowerPoint 2007. The color themes include sets of colors; the font themes include sets of heading and body text fonts; and the effect themes include sets of effects that can be applied to lines and other objects on your slides. Themes are found on the Design tab.

1 On the Ribbon, click the **Design tab**. In the **Themes group**, to the right of the last displayed theme, point to the **More** button ⮟ as shown in Figure 15.22, and then click to display the **Themes gallery**.

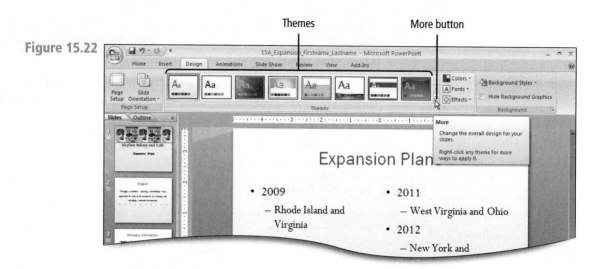

Figure 15.22

2 Under **Built-In**, *point* to several of the themes and notice a ScreenTip displays the name of each theme and that the Live Preview feature displays how each theme will look if applied to your presentation.

Note

The first theme that displays is the Office theme. Subsequent themes are arranged alphabetically.

3 In the first row, point to the first theme—the **Office Theme**, as shown in Figure 15.23—and then click to change the theme.

The Office Theme is applied to the entire presentation, and all text, the chart, and accent colors are updated to reflect the change.

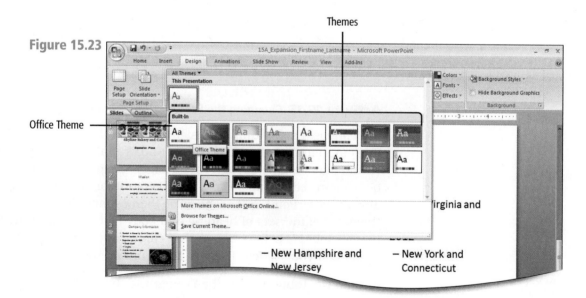

Figure 15.23

4 In the **Slides/Outline pane**, click to select **Slide 3**, and then press and hold down ⇧ Shift and click **Slide 4**. Compare your screen with Figure 15.24.

Both slides are selected as indicated by the contrasting colors that surround the slides in the Slides/Outline pane.

Figure 15.24

Selected slides

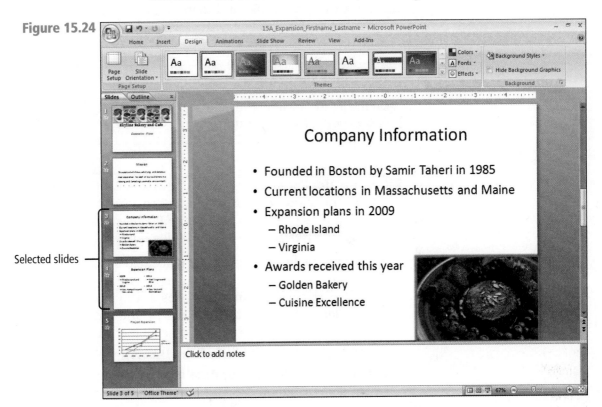

5 On the **Design tab**, in the **Themes group**, click the **More** button ▼ to display the **Themes gallery**. In the first row, *point* to the fifth theme—**Concourse**—and then click the right mouse button to display the shortcut menu. Click **Apply to Selected Slides**.

The Concourse Theme is applied to Slides 3 and 4.

6 **Save** 🖫 your presentation.

Objective 4
Create Headers and Footers and Print a Presentation

A ***header*** is text that prints at the top of each sheet of ***slide handouts*** or ***notes pages***. Slide handouts are printed images of multiple slides on a sheet of paper. Notes pages are printouts that contain the slide image in the top half of the page and notes that you have created in the Notes pane in the lower half of the page.

In addition to headers, you can create ***footers***—text that displays at the bottom of every slide or that prints at the bottom of a sheet of slide handouts or notes pages.

Activity 15.16 Creating Headers and Footers

In this activity, you will add a header to the handouts and notes pages that includes the current date and a footer that includes your name and the file name.

1 Click the **Insert tab**, and then in the **Text group**, click the **Header & Footer** button to display the **Header and Footer** dialog box.

Another Way ─── **To Display the Header and Footer Dialog Box**

On the Insert tab, in the Text group, you can click either the Date & Time button or the Number button.

2 In the **Header and Footer** dialog box, click the **Notes and Handouts tab**. Under **Include on page**, click to select the **Date and time** check box, and as you do so, watch the Preview box in the lower right corner of the Header and Footer dialog box.

The Preview box indicates the placeholders on a slide. Recall that a placeholder reserves a location on a slide for text or other content. The two narrow rectangular boxes at the top of the Preview box indicate placeholders for the header text and date. When you select the Date and time check box, the placeholder in the upper right corner is outlined, indicating the location in which the date will display.

3 If necessary, click the **Update automatically** button so that the current date prints on the notes and handouts each time the presentation is printed.

4 If necessary, click to *clear* the **Header** check box to omit this element. Notice that in the Preview box, the corresponding placeholder is no longer selected.

5 If necessary, click to select the **Page number** and **Footer** check boxes, noticing that when you do so, the insertion point displays in the Footer box. Using your own first and last names, type **15A_ Expansion_Firstname_Lastname** and then compare your dialog box with Figure 15.25.

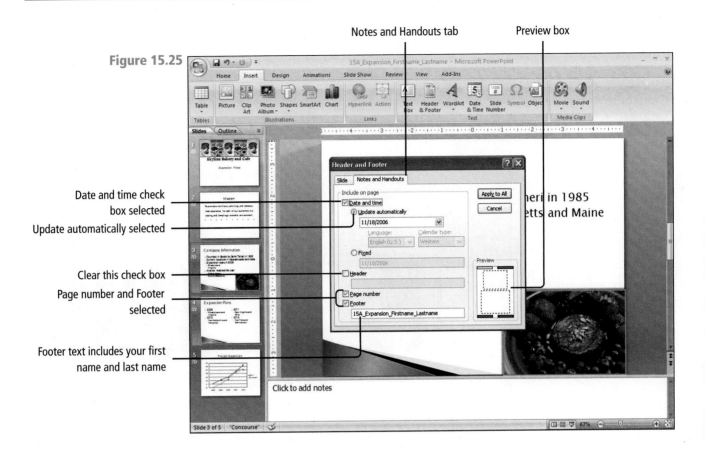

Figure 15.25

Notes and Handouts tab   Preview box

Date and time check box selected
Update automatically selected
Clear this check box
Page number and Footer selected
Footer text includes your first name and last name

6 Click **Apply to All**. **Save** your changes.

More Knowledge
Adding Footers to Slides

You can add footers to slides by using the Slide tab in the Header and Footer dialog box. Headers cannot be added to slides.

Activity 15.17 Previewing and Printing a Presentation and Closing PowerPoint

1 Click the **Office** button, point to the **Print arrow** as shown in Figure 15.26, and then click **Print Preview.**

Print Preview displays your presentation as it will print, based on the options that you choose. In the Print Preview window, you can change the direction on which the paper prints—landscape or portrait—you can choose whether you will print slides, handouts, note pages, or the presentation outline, and you can choose to print your presentation in color, grayscale, or black-and-white. By default, PowerPoint prints your presentation in grayscale.

Figure 15.26

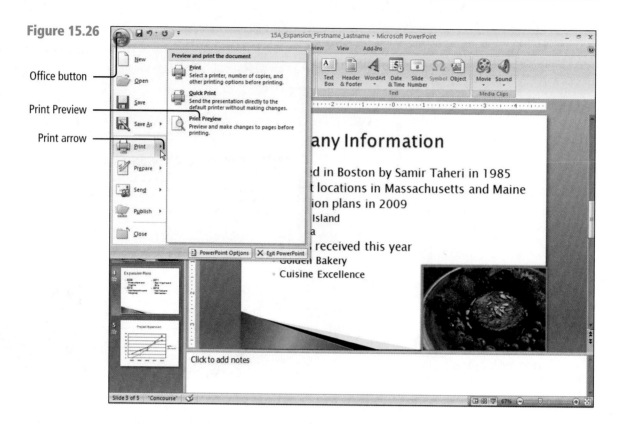

Office button

Print Preview

Print arrow

In the **Page Setup group**, click the **Print What arrow**, and then click **Handouts (6 Slides Per Page)** as shown in Figure 15.27. Notice that the preview of your printout changes to reflect your selection.

Note — Printing Slide Handouts

Printing a presentation as Slides uses a large amount of ink and toner. Thus, the majority of the projects in this textbook require that you print handouts, not slides.

Figure 15.27

Print What arrow

Click Handouts
(6 Slides Per Page)

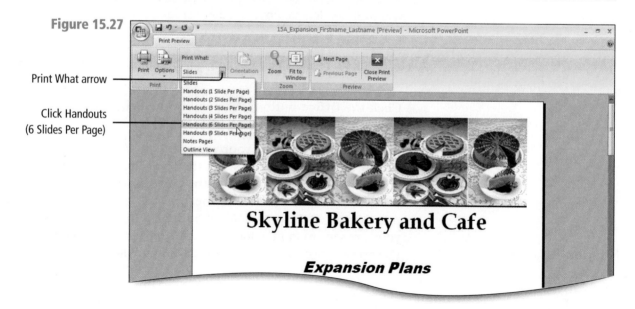

3 Check your *Chapter Assignment Sheet* or *Course Syllabus*, or consult your instructor, to determine if you are to submit your assignments on paper or electronically by using your college's course information management system. To submit electronically, go to Step 8, and then follow the instructions provided by your instructor.

4 In the **Print group**, click the **Print** button, and then in the **Print** dialog box, click **OK** to print your handouts.

5 In the **Page Setup group**, click the **Print What Arrow**, and then click **Notes Pages** to preview the presentation notes for Slide 1.

Recall that you created Notes for Slide 4.

6 At the right side of the **Print Preview** window, drag the scroll box down until **Slide 4** displays.

7 In the **Print group**, click the **Print** button. In the middle of the **Print** dialog box, under **Print range**, click **Current slide**, and then click **OK** to print the Notes pages for Slide 4.

8 Click **Close Print Preview** to close the Print Preview window and return to the presentation.

Another Way ── **To Print a Presentation**

Click the Office button, and then click Print to display the Print dialog box. The options that are available in Print Preview can be accessed and modified in the Print dialog box.

9 **Save** your presentation. On the right edge of the title bar, click the **Close** button ☒ to close the presentation and **Close** PowerPoint.

Note — Changing Print Options

When you preview your presentation, check to be sure that the text displays against the slide background. If it does not, on the Print Preview tab in the Print group, click Options. Point to Color/Grayscale, and then click Color or Color (On Black and White Printer).

End You have completed Project 15A

Project 15B **Overview**

In Activities 15.18 through 15.25 you will create a presentation that provides details of the Skyline Bakery and Cafe projected expansion. You will add a graphic image to the presentation, insert slides from another PowerPoint presentation, and rearrange and delete slides. Your completed presentation will look similar to Figure 15.28.

For Project 15B, you will need the following files:

p15B_Skyline
p15B_Cake
p15B_Template

You will save your presentation as
15B_Overview_Firstname_Lastname

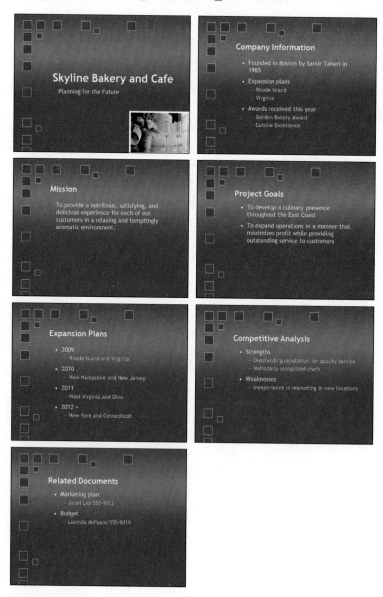

Figure 15.28
Project 15B—Overview

Objective 5
Create a New Presentation

Microsoft Office PowerPoint 2007 provides a variety of options for starting a new presentation. You can use a ***template*** that is saved on your system or that you access from Microsoft Online. A template is a file that contains the styles in a presentation, including the type and size of bullets and fonts, placeholder sizes and positions, background design and fill color schemes, and theme information. You can also start a blank presentation that has no text, background graphics, or colors that you can then customize yourself.

Activity 15.18 Starting a New Presentation

In this activity, you will create a new presentation based on a template from Microsoft Office Online.

1 **Start** PowerPoint. From the **Office** menu 🔲, click **New** to display the **New Presentation** window. See Figure 15.29.

At the left of the New Presentation window is a list of the Template categories installed on your system or available from Microsoft Office Online. The center section displays either subcategories or thumbnails of the slides in the category that you select. When you click on a template, the right section displays a larger view of the selected template and in some cases, additional information about the template.

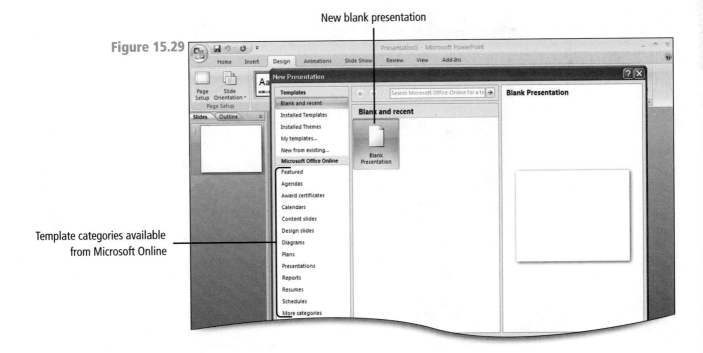

Figure 15.29

New blank presentation

Template categories available from Microsoft Online

2 Under **Templates**, click **Installed Templates**, and then click each displayed template to preview it.

3 In the left panel under **Microsoft Office Online**, click several of the categories. Notice that as you do so, the title of the center panel changes to the name of the category that you have chosen, and in some instances, subcategories display.

Alert!

Are you unable to access the templates from Microsoft Office Online?

If you are unable to access the templates from Microsoft Office Online, the template for this project is available from your student data files. In the New Presentation window, click Cancel to close the New Presentation window. Click the Office button, and then click Open. Navigate to your student files and open the p15B_Template file. Then, skip to Step 6.

4 Under **Microsoft Office Online**, click **Presentations**, and then in the center panel, point to **Other presentations** to display the Link Select pointer as shown in Figure 15.30.

Figure 15.30

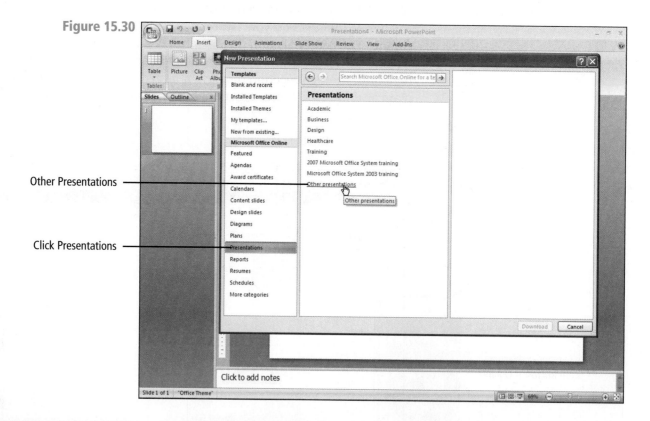

Other Presentations

Click Presentations

Another Way

To Locate Templates

In the New Presentation window, you can search for templates by using keywords. Click the Office button, and then click New. At the top, center of the New Presentation Window, type the keyword and then press Enter to view the presentation templates with the keyword that you typed.

5 Click **Other Presentations**. In the center section of the New Presentation window, click **Project overview presentation**, and then in the lower right corner of the window, click **Download** to access the template from Microsoft Office Online.

Alert! ── **Does a Microsoft window display?**

If a window displays regarding the validation of your software, click Continue. If you are unable to download the template, close all message windows and the New Presentation window. Click the Office button, and then click Open. Navigate to your student files, open the p15B_Template file, and then continue with Step 6.

6 If necessary, close any windows that display after the template is downloaded.

The new presentation includes 11 slides with ideas for content when making a project overview presentation. Scroll through the presentation to view the suggested content. Later, you will delete slides that are not relevant to the presentation and you will modify slide text so that the content is specific to this presentation topic.

7 On **Slide 1**, drag to select the text in the title placeholder—*Project Overview*—and then type **Skyline Bakery and Cafe** to replace it. Drag to select the three lines of text in the subtitle placeholder, and then type **Planning for the Future**

8 Display **Slide 2**. Select the text *Ultimate goal of project*, and then type **To develop a culinary presence throughout the East Coast**

9 Select the remaining two bullet points on the slide, and then type to replace them with the text **To expand operations in a manner that maximizes profit while providing outstanding service to customers**

10 Display **Slide 4**. In the bulleted list, select the *Competitors* bullet point and its second-level bullet point—*You may want to allocate one slide per competitor*—and then press Delete. Select *Your strengths relative to competitors*, and then type **Outstanding reputation for quality service** and then press Enter. Type **Nationally recognized chefs**

11 Replace the text *Your weaknesses relative to competitors* with **Inexperience in marketing in new locations**

12 In the scroll bar, click the **Next Slide** button ⬇ several times until **Slide 11** displays. Select and delete the *Post-mortem* and *Submit questions* bullet points and their subordinate bullet points. Under the *Marketing plan* bullet point, select *Location or contact name/phone*, and then type **Janet Liu/555-9012** Under the Budget bullet point, select *Location or contact name/phone*, and then type **Lucinda dePaolo/555-9019**

13 Click the **Office** button 🅑, and then click **Save As** to display the **Save As** dialog box. Click the **Save in arrow**, and then navigate to your *PowerPoint Chapter 15* folder.

14 In the **File name** box, delete any existing text, and then using your own first and last names type **15B_Overview_Firstname_Lastname** and then click **Save**.

Activity 15.19 Inserting Slides from an Existing Presentation

Teamwork is an important aspect of all organizations, and presentations are often shared among employees. Another employee may create several slides for a presentation that you are developing. Rather than re-creating the slides, you can insert slides from an existing presentation into the current presentation. In this activity, you will insert slides from an existing presentation into your 15B_Overview presentation.

1 Display **Slide 1**. Click the **Home tab**, and in the **Slides group**, click the **New Slide arrow** to display the **Slide Layout gallery** and additional options for inserting slides as shown in Figure 15.31.

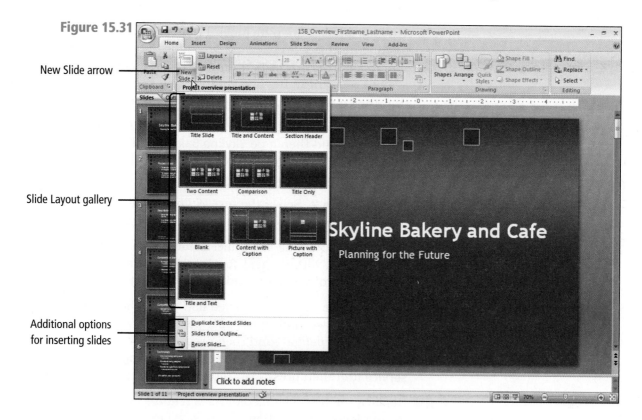

Figure 15.31

New Slide arrow

Slide Layout gallery

Additional options for inserting slides

2 Below the gallery, click **Reuse Slides** to open the **Reuse Slides** task pane on the right side of the PowerPoint window.

A *task pane* enables you to enter options for completing a command.

3 In the **Reuse Slides** task pane, click the **Browse** button, and then click **Browse File**. In the **Browse** dialog box, navigate to where your student files are stored, and then double-click **p15B_ Skyline**.

The slides contained in the p15B_Skyline presentation display in the Reuse Slides task pane. The title of each slide displays to the right of the slide image.

4 In the **Reuse Slides** task pane, point to **Slide 2** and notice that a zoomed image is displayed, as is a ScreenTip with the presentation title and the slide title. See Figure 15.32.

Figure 15.32

Reuse Slides task pane

Zoomed image of slide

5 Click **Slide 2—Mission**—and notice that it is inserted into the current presentation after Slide 1.

The theme of the current presentation is applied to the slide that you inserted. If you want to retain the theme and other formatting from the slide that you insert, you can click to select the *Keep source formatting* check box at the bottom of the Reuse Slides task pane.

More Knowledge
Inserting All Slides

You can insert all of the slides from an existing presentation into the current presentation at one time. In the Reuse Slides task pane, right-click one of the slides that you want to insert, and then click Insert All Slides.

6 In your **15B_Overview** presentation, in the **Slides/Outline pane**, scroll the slide thumbnails to display **Slide 11**. Click **Slide 11** to display it in the **Slide** pane. In the **Reuse Slides** task pane, click **Slide 3—Company Information**, and then click **Slide 4—Expansion Plans** to insert both slides after Slide 11.

Your presentation contains 14 slides.

7 In the **Reuse Slides** task pane, click the **Close** button ☒. **Save** 🖫 your presentation.

Note — Inserting Slides

You can insert slides in any order into your presentation. Just remember to display the slide that will precede the slide that you want to insert.

Objective 6
Use Slide Sorter View

Slide Sorter view displays all of the slides in your presentation in miniature. You can use Slide Sorter view to rearrange and delete slides, to apply formatting to multiple slides, and to get an overall impression of your presentation.

Activity 15.20 Selecting and Deleting Slides

To select more than one slide, click the first slide that you want to select, press and hold down ⇧ Shift or Ctrl, and then click another slide. Using ⇧ Shift enables you to select a group of slides that are adjacent. Using Ctrl enables you to select a group of slides that are nonadjacent (*not* next to each other). When multiple slides are selected, you can move or delete them as a group. These techniques can also be used when slide miniatures are displayed on the Slides tab.

1 Recall that the View buttons are located on the status bar in the lower right corner of the PowerPoint window. Locate the **View** buttons, and then click the **Slide Sorter** button ▦ to display all of the slide thumbnails. Alternatively, on the Ribbon, click the View tab, and then in the Presentation Views group, click Slide Sorter.

2 Click **Slide 4** and notice that a thick outline surrounds the slide, indicating that it is selected. On your keyboard, press Delete to delete the slide.

3 Click **Slide 5**, and then hold down ⇧ Shift and click **Slide 10** so that slides 5 through 10 are selected. Compare your screen to Figure 15.33.

Figure 15.33

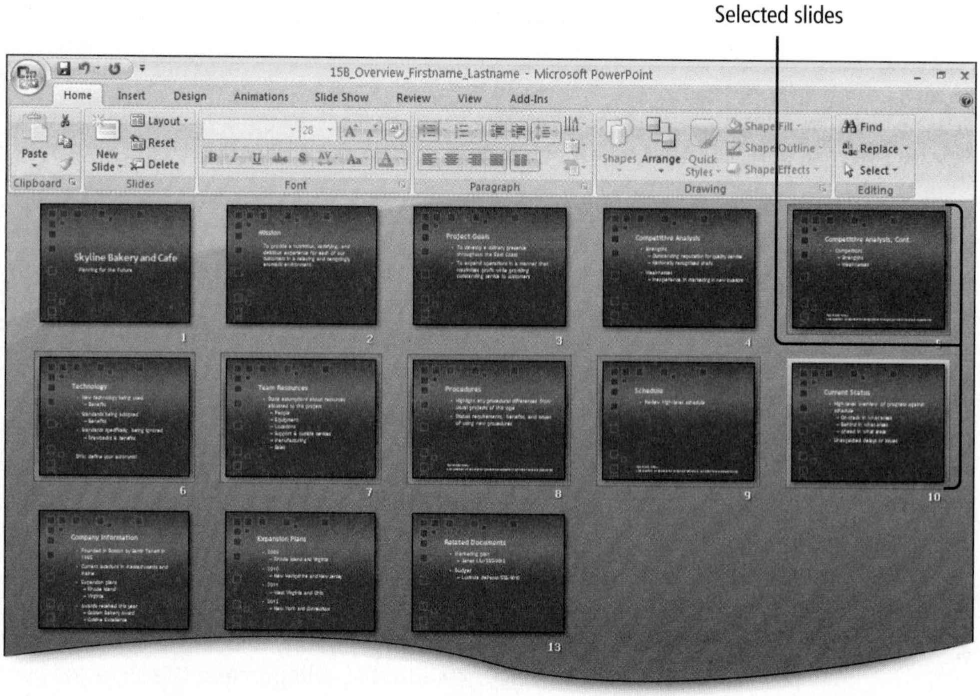

4 Press [Delete] to delete the selected slides.

Your presentation contains seven slides.

5 **Save** 🖫 your changes.

Activity 15.21 Moving Slides

1 Click **Slide 5** to select it.

2 While pointing to **Slide 5**, press and hold down the left mouse button, and then drag the slide to the left until the displayed vertical bar is positioned to the left of **Slide 2**, as shown in Figure 15.34. Release the left mouse button.

The slide that you moved becomes Slide 2.

Figure 15.34

Selected slide

Vertical bar positioned between Slides 1 and 2 to move slide to this position

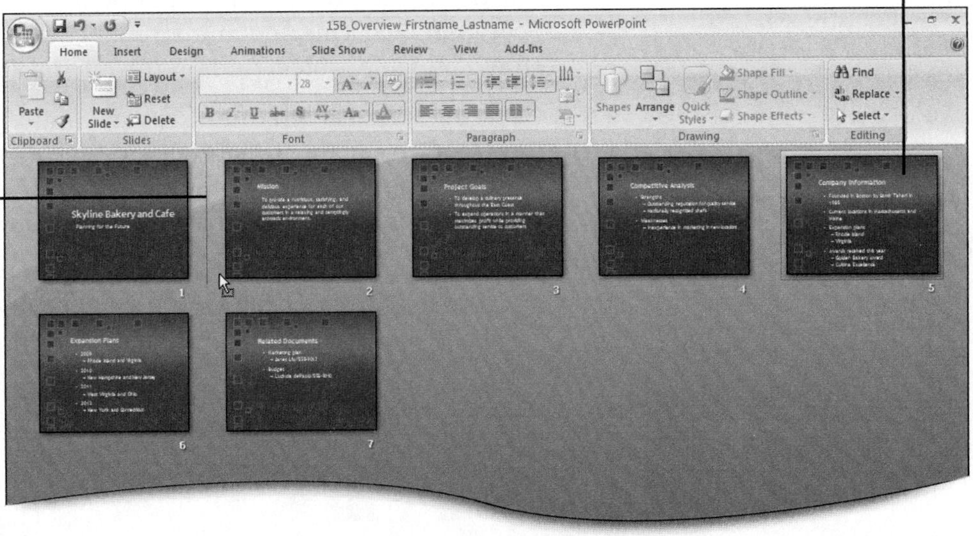

3 Select **Slide 6**. Using the same technique that you used in Step 2, drag to position the slide between **Slides 4** and **5**.

4 In the status bar, click the **Normal** button 🖳. **Save** 🖫 your presentation.

Objective 7
Add Pictures to a Presentation

Images can be inserted into a presentation from many sources. One type of image that you can insert is *clip art*. Clip art can include drawings, movies, sounds, or photographic images that are included with Microsoft Office or downloaded from the Web.

Activity 15.22 Inserting Clip Art

In this activity you will access Microsoft Office Online to insert a clip art image on the title slide.

1 Display **Slide 1**. On the Ribbon, click the **Insert tab**, and then in the **Illustrations group**, click **Clip Art** to display the **Clip Art** task pane.

2 In the **Clip Art** task pane, click in the **Search for** box and type **wedding cake** so that PowerPoint 2007 can search for images that contain the keywords *wedding cake*.

A message may display asking if you would like to include additional clip art images from Microsoft Office online. If this message displays, click Yes.

3 In the **Clip Art** task pane, click the **Search in arrow**, and if necessary, click to select the **Everywhere** check box. Click the **Search in** arrow again to collapse the search list.

When you click the Everywhere option, *All collections* displays in the Search in box. This action instructs PowerPoint to search for images stored on your system and on the Microsoft Office Online Web site.

4 Click the **Results should be arrow**, and then click as necessary to *deselect*—clear the selection by removing the check mark—the **Clip Art**, **Movies**, and **Sounds** check boxes so that only the **Photographs** check box is selected as shown in Figure 15.35.

With the Photographs check box selected, PowerPoint will search for images that were created with a digital camera or a scanner.

Type **wedding cake**
to search for images

Figure 15.35

All collections selected

Photographs selected

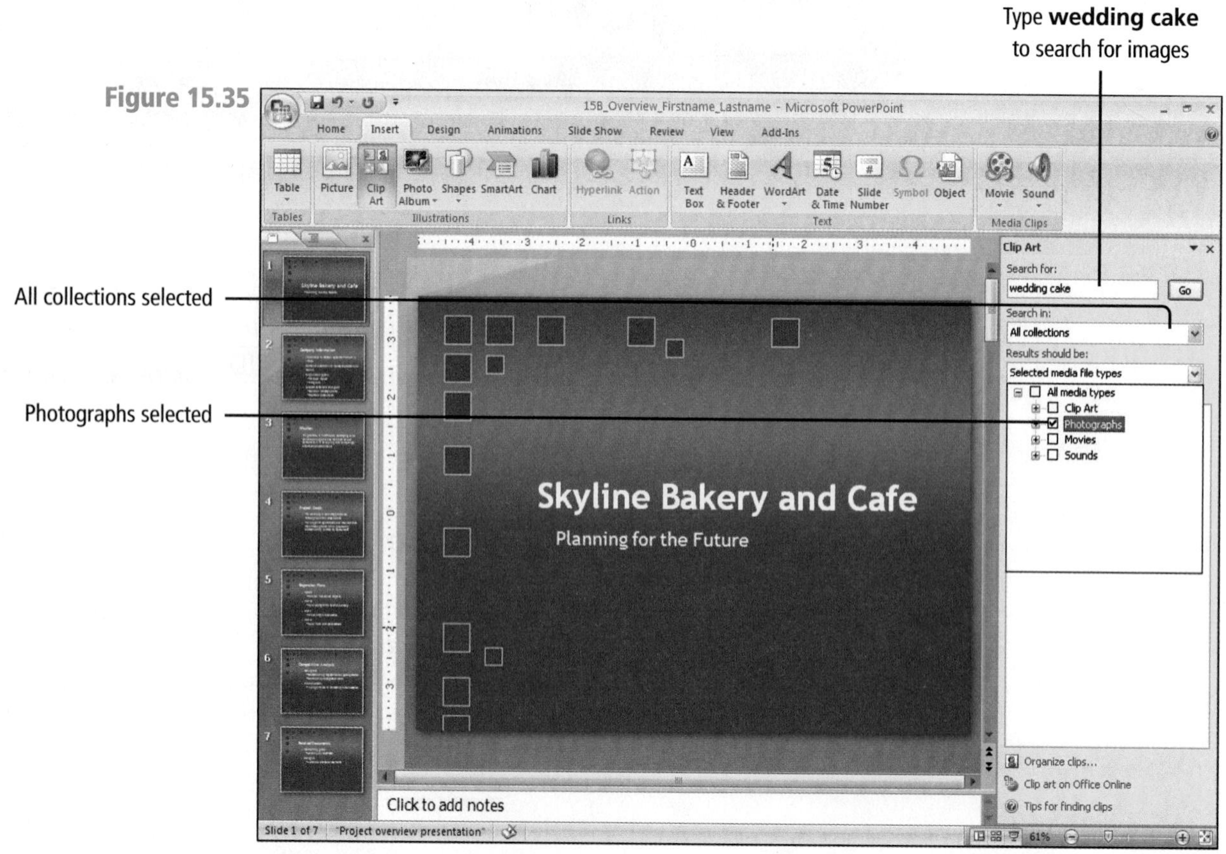

5 In the **Clip Art** task pane, click **Go**. After a brief delay, several images display in the Clip Art task pane. Locate the image of the wedding cake shown in Figure 15.36.

Selected image

Figure 15.36

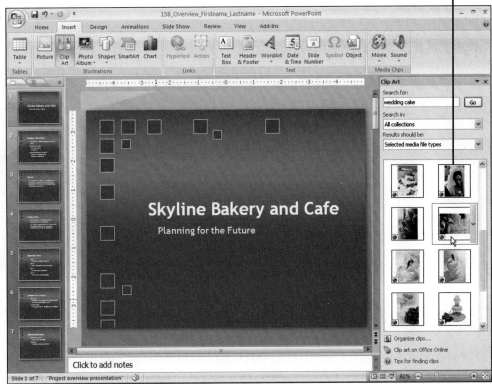

Was the wedding cake picture unavailable?

If you are unable to locate the picture for this project, it is available from your student data files. On the Insert tab, in the Illustrations group, click Picture. Navigate to your student files, and then double-click the p15B_Cake file.

6 Click the wedding cake picture to insert it in the center of Slide 1, and then notice that the Ribbon has changed and the picture is surrounded by white square and circular handles, indicating that it is selected.

Because the picture is selected, ***contextual tools*** named *Picture Tools* display and add a ***contextual tab***—*Format*—next to the standard tabs on the Ribbon as shown in Figure 15.37.

Contextual tools enable you to perform specific commands related to the selected object, and display one or more contextual tabs that contain related groups of commands that you will need when working with the type of object that is selected. Contextual tools display only when needed for a selected object; when you deselect the object,

Contextual tool

Figure 15.37

Contextual tab

the contextual tools no longer display. In this case, the Format contextual tab contains four groups—Adjust, Picture Styles, Arrange, and Size. In a later activity, you will use the Picture Styles group to format the wedding cake picture.

7 **Close** ☒ the Clip Art task pane. **Save** 🖫 your changes.

Activity 15.23 Moving and Sizing Images

When an image is selected, it is surrounded by white *sizing handles* that are used to size the image. In the corners of the image, the handles are circular. When you point to a circular sizing handle, a diagonal pointer displays, indicating that you can resize the image by dragging up or down. In the center of each side of the selected image, the handles are square. When you point to a square handle, a left- and right-pointing arrow or an up- and down-pointing arrow displays. These arrows indicate the direction in which you can size the image. When you point to an image without positioning the pointer over a handle, a four-headed arrow displays, indicating that you can move the image.

1 If necessary, click to select the picture of the wedding cake so that the handles display.

2 Position the pointer anywhere over the image to display the Move pointer 🛇. Drag down and to the right until the lower right corner of the picture is aligned with the lower right corner of the slide as shown in Figure 15.38. Release the mouse button.

3 If necessary, select the picture, and then point to the upper left circular handle to display the Diagonal Resize pointer 🡔.

Figure 15.38

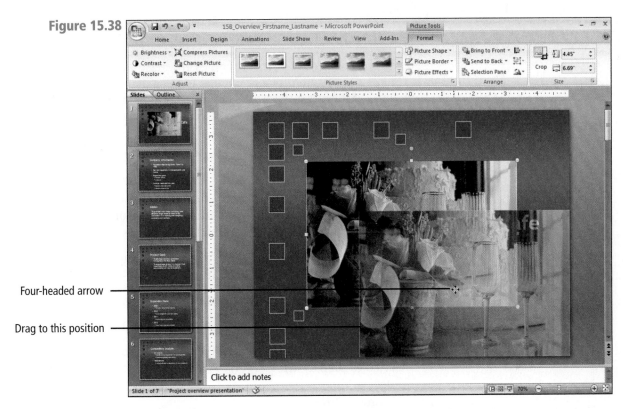

Four-headed arrow

Drag to this position

4 Drag down and to the right, noticing that as you do so, a semitransparent image displays the size of the picture. Continue to drag until the semitransparent image is approximately half the height and width of the original picture as shown in Figure 15.39. Release the mouse button to size the picture.

5 **Save** 💾 the presentation.

Figure 15.39

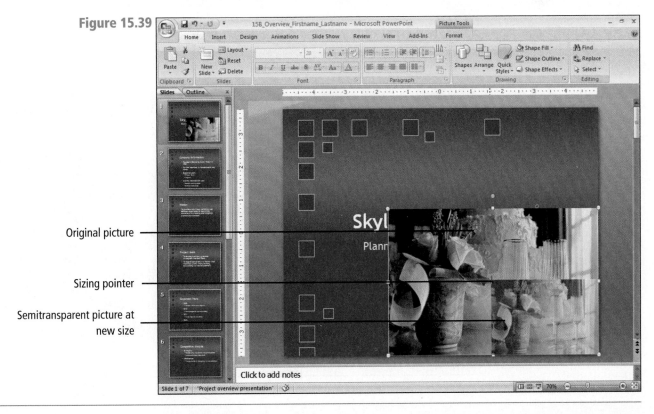

Original picture

Sizing pointer

Semitransparent picture at new size

Workshop — Sizing a Picture

Using one of the corner sizing handles ensures that the original proportions of the image are maintained. When a top or side sizing handle is used, the picture is stretched either taller or wider, thus distorting the image.

Activity 15.24 Applying a Style to a Picture

Recall that when a picture is selected, the Picture Tools contextual tool and the Format contextual tab display on the Ribbon. You can use the Format tab to change the color and brightness of your picture; apply a shape, border, or effect; arrange multiple images; or size your picture.

1 If necessary, click the picture of the wedding cake to select it and notice that the Picture Tools are available.

2 On the **Format tab**, in the **Picture Styles group**, click the **More** button to display the **Picture Styles gallery**.

3 In the displayed gallery, move your pointer over several of the picture styles to display the ScreenTip and to use Live Preview to see the effect of the style on your picture. Then, in the first row, click **Simple Frame, White**.

4 Click on a blank area of the slide so that the picture is not selected, and then compare your slide to Figure 15.40. Make any necessary adjustments to the size and position of the picture.

Figure 15.40

Adjust picture size

5 Click the **Insert tab**, and then, in the **Text group**, click the **Header & Footer** button to display the **Header and Footer** dialog box. Click the **Notes and Handouts tab**. Under **Include on page**, click to select the **Date and time** check box, and if necessary, click the **Update automatically** button so that the current date prints on the notes and handouts each time the presentation is printed. If necessary, *clear* the **Header** check box to omit this element from the header and footer. Click to select the **Page number** and **Footer** check boxes, noticing that when you do so, the insertion point displays in the Footer box. Using your own first and last names, type **15B_Overview_ Firstname_Lastname** and then click **Apply to All**.

6 Check your *Chapter Assignment Sheet* or *Course Syllabus* or consult your instructor to determine if you are to submit your assignments on paper or electronically. To submit electronically, go to Step 8, and then follow the instructions provided by your instructor.

7 From the **Office** menu, point to the **Print arrow**, and then click **Print Preview** to make a final check of your presentation. In the **Page Setup group**, click the **Print What arrow**, and then click **Handouts, (4 slides per page)**. Your presentation will print on two pages. Click the **Print** button, and then click **OK** to print the handouts. Click **Close** ☒ to close Print Preview.

8 **Save** 🖫 the changes to your presentation, and then from the **Office** menu, click **Exit PowerPoint**.

Objective 8
Use the Microsoft Help System

As you work with PowerPoint 2007, you can get assistance by using the Help feature. You can ask questions and Help will provide you with information and step-by-step instructions for performing tasks.

Activity 15.25 Accessing PowerPoint Help

In this activity, you will use the Microsoft Help feature to learn more about this feature.

1 **Start** PowerPoint. In the upper right corner of your screen, click the **Microsoft Office PowerPoint Help** button ⍰. Alternatively, press F1.

You can browse the PowerPoint Help topics by clicking any of the listed items; or, near the top of the Help window, you can click in the search box and type a keyword to search for a specific item. If you have access to the Internet, PowerPoint will search Office Online for your help topic.

2 Near the upper left corner of the Help window, in the **Search** box, type **Printing Slides** as shown in Figure 15.41.

Search box

Figure 15.41

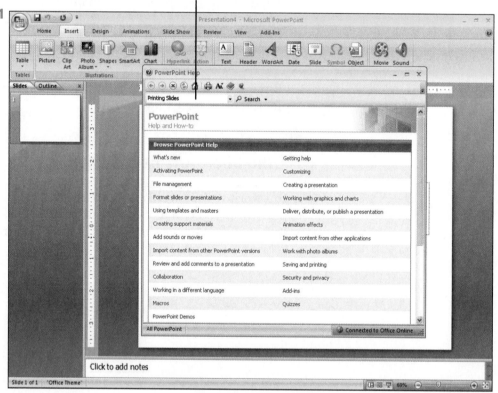

3 Press Enter or click **Search**. On the list of results, click **Print your slides** and then read the information that displays.

4 On the PowerPoint Help title bar, click the **Close** button ☒. On the right side of the title bar, click the **Close** button ☒ to close PowerPoint.

 You have completed Project 15B

There's More You Can Do!

From the student files that accompany this textbook, open the folder **02_theres_more_you_can_do**. Locate the Try IT! exercises for this chapter and follow the instructions to learn additional skills.

Try IT!—Set Slide Orientation and Size

In this Try IT! exercise, you will change the size and orientation of a slide.

Content-Based Assessments

Summary

In this chapter, you started PowerPoint and opened a PowerPoint presentation. You entered, edited, and formatted text in Normal view and worked with slides in Slide Sorter view; you added speaker notes; and you viewed the presentation as a slide show. The spelling checker tool was demonstrated, and you practiced how to change font style and size and add emphasis to text.

You created a new presentation, added content and clip art, and moved and deleted slides. You also added a footer to the notes and handouts pages and created a chapter folder to help organize your files. Each presentation was saved, previewed, printed, and closed. Finally, the Help program was introduced as a tool that can assist you in using PowerPoint.

Key Terms

Content-Based Assessments

Matching

Match each term in the second column with its correct definition in the first column. Write the letter of the term on the blank line in front of the correct definition.

_____ **1.** A feature that introduces individual slide elements one element at a time.

_____ **2.** The PowerPoint view in which the window is divided into three panes—the Slide pane, the Slides/Outline pane, and the Notes pane.

_____ **3.** Outline levels represented by a symbol that are identified in the slides by the indentation and the size of the text.

_____ **4.** A feature that displays buttons that are commonly used with the selected object.

_____ **5.** A context-sensitive menu that displays commands and options relevant to the selected object.

_____ **6.** The action of holding down the left mouse button and moving the mouse pointer over text to select it.

_____ **7.** A set of characters (letters and numbers) with the same design and shape.

_____ **8.** A unit of measure to describe the size of a font.

_____ **9.** A container that reserves a portion of a slide for text, graphics, and other slide elements.

_____ **10.** A slide that is inserted at the end of every slide show to indicate that the presentation is over.

_____ **11.** The changing of the appearance of the text, layout, and design of a slide.

_____ **12.** A feature that displays formatting in your presentation so that you can decide whether or not you would like to apply the formatting.

_____ **13.** A feature that changes the horizontal placement of text within a placeholder.

_____ **14.** Printouts that contain the slide image in the top half of the page and notes that you have created in the Notes pane in the lower half of the page.

_____ **15.** A feature that displays your presentation as it will print, based on the options that you select.

A Animation

B Black slide

C Bulleted levels

D Dragging

E Font

F Formatting

G Live Preview

H Mini toolbar

I Normal view

J Notes pages

K Placeholder

L Point

M Print Preview

N Shortcut menu

O Text alignment

Content-Based Assessments

Fill in the Blank

Write the correct word in the space provided.

1. Microsoft Office PowerPoint 2007 is a presentation _____ program that you can use to effectively present information to your audience.

2. Miniature images of slides are known as _____.

3. A slide _____ controls the way in which a slide appears or disappears during an onscreen slide show.

4. The process of adding, deleting, or changing the contents of a slide is known as _____.

5. A _____ is a visual representation of a command's options.

6. The placement and arrangement of the text and graphic elements on a slide refer to its _____.

7. Tools that enable you to perform specific commands related to the selected object are _____ tools.

8. A file that contains the styles in a presentation, including the type and size of bullets and fonts, placeholder sizes and positions, background design and fill color schemes, and theme information, is known as a _____.

9. The _____ is a research tool that provides a list of synonyms for a selection.

10. Words with the same meaning are known as _____.

11. Font _____ add emphasis to text, and may include bold, italic, and underline.

12. A _____ button is one in which you can click the button once to turn it on and click it again to turn it off.

13. Text that prints at the top of a sheet of slide handouts or notes pages is known as a _____.

14. Text that displays at the bottom of every slide or that prints at the bottom of a sheet of slide handouts or notes is known as a _____.

15. The view in which all of the slides in your presentation display in miniature is _____ _____ view.

Content-Based Assessments

Skills Review

Project 15C — Hospitality

In this project, you will apply the skills you practiced from the Objectives in Project 15A.

Objectives: 1. *Open, View, and Save a Presentation;* **2.** *Edit a Presentation;* **3.** *Format a Presentation;* **4.** *Create Headers and Footers and Print a Presentation.*

In the following Skills Review, you will edit a presentation created by Shawna Andreasyan, the Human Resources Director, for new Skyline Bakery and Cafe employees. Your completed presentation will look similar to the one shown in Figure 15.42.

For Project 15C, you will need the following file:

p15C_Hospitality

You will save your presentation as 15C_Hospitality_Firstname_Lastname

Figure 15.42

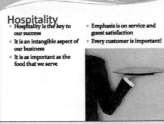

Content-Based Assessments

chapterfifteen   **Skills Review**

(Project 15C–Hospitality continued)

1. **Start** PowerPoint. Click the **Office** button, and then click **Open.** Navigate to the location where your student files are stored and open the file **p15C_Hospitality**. Click the **Office** button, and then click **Save As.** Navigate to your **PowerPoint Chapter 15** folder and using your own first and last, save the file as **15C_Hospitality_Firstname_Lastname.**

2. Click the **Design tab.** In the **Themes group**, to the right of the last displayed theme, click the **More** button to display the **Themes gallery**. Recall that after the first theme—Office—the remaining themes display alphabetically. Under **Built-in**, locate and click the **Flow** theme to apply the theme to the entire presentation.

3. Display **Slide 2**, and then click in the paragraph. Click the **Home tab**, and then, in the **Paragraph group**, click the **Center** button to center align the paragraph within the placeholder. In the **Paragraph group**, click the **Line Spacing** button, and then click **2.0** to apply double-spacing to the paragraph. Then, click in the slide title, and click the **Center** button to center align the title.

4. On **Slide 2**, drag to select all of the text in the paragraph. Point to the Mini toolbar, and then click **Bold** and **Italic** to apply both font styles to the paragraph.

5. Display **Slide 4** and notice the red wavy underline under the last word of the last bullet. Point to *atmoshere*, and then click the right mouse button to display the shortcut menu. Click **atmosphere** to correct the spelling of the word.

6. On **Slide 4**, in the third bullet point, right-click the word *good* to display the shortcut menu. Near the bottom of the menu, point to **Synonyms**, and then in the synonyms

list, click **excellent** to use the Thesaurus to change *good* to *excellent*.

7. With **Slide 4** still displayed, on the **Home tab**, in the **Slides group**, click **Layout** to display the **Slide Layout gallery**. Click the **Two Content** layout.

8. Click in the placeholder on the right. Type **Do you** and then press Enter. Press Tab to increase the list level. Type **Greet every guest** and then press Enter. Type **Make every guest feel welcome**

9. In the placeholder at the left of **Slide 4**, drag to select the last three bulleted items. On the **Home tab**, in the **Paragraph group**, click the **Increase List Level** button to demote the three bulleted items one level below the first bulleted item.

10. With **Slide 4** still displayed, on the **Home tab**, in the **Slides group**, click the **New Slide arrow**, and then in the gallery, click **Title and Content** to create a new Slide 5.

11. On **Slide 5**, click in the title placeholder, type **Why Our Customers Return** and then click in the content placeholder. Type the following five bulleted items, pressing Enter at the end of each line to create a new bullet. Do not press Enter after the last item.

    We exceed their expectations

    They enjoy our relaxing atmosphere

    They feel comfortable in their surroundings

    We ensure fresh, high-quality food

    Our customer service is outstanding

12. With **Slide 5** displayed, click in the **Notes** pane and type **Remember that every single one of our customers is a VIP!** Make spelling corrections as necessary on the slide and in the notes.

Content-Based Assessments

Skills Review

(Project 15C–Hospitality continued)

13. Display **Slide 1** and drag to select the sub-title text—*New Employee Training*. On the Mini toolbar, click the **Font size button arrow**, and then change the font size to **44**.

14. Click the **Insert tab**, and then, in the **Text group**, click **Header & Footer** to display the **Header and Footer** dialog box.

15. Click the **Notes and Handouts tab**. Under **Include on page**, click to select the **Date and time** check box and, if necessary, click the **Update automatically** button so that the current date prints on the notes and handouts each time the presentation is printed. If necessary, clear the **Header** check box to omit this element from the header and footer. If necessary, click to select the **Page number** and **Footer** check boxes, noticing that when you do so, the insertion point displays in the Footer box. Using your own first and last names, in the Footer box type **15C_Hospitality_Firstname_Lastname** and then click **Apply to All**.

16. On the Ribbon, click the **Slide Show tab**, and then in the **Start Slide Show group**, click **From Beginning**. Press Spacebar or click the left mouse button to advance

through the presentation and view the slide show.

17. Check your *Chapter Assignment Sheet* or *Course Syllabus* or consult your instructor to determine if you are to submit your assignments on paper or electronically. To submit electronically, go to Step 20, and then follow the instructions provided by your instructor.

18. From the **Office** menu, point to the **Print arrow**, and then click **Print Preview** to make a final check of your presentation. In the **Page Setup group**, click the **Print What arrow**, and then click **Handouts, (6 slides per page)**. Click the **Print** button, and then click **OK** to print the handouts.

19. In the **Page Setup group**, click the **Print What arrow**, and then click **Notes Pages**. Click the **Print** button, and in the **Print** dialog box, under **Print range**, click the **Slides** option button. In the **Slides** box, type 5 to instruct PowerPoint to print the notes pages for Slide 5. Click **OK**, and then close Print Preview.

20. **Save** changes to your presentation, and then from the **Office** menu, click **Exit PowerPoint**.

End You have completed Project 15C

Content-Based Assessments

Skills Review

Project 15D — Funding

In this project, you will apply the skills you practiced from Objectives found in Project 15B.

Objectives: 5. *Create a New Presentation;* **6.** *Use Slide Sorter View;* **7.** *Add Pictures to a Presentation.*

In the following Skills Review, you will create the preliminary slides for a presentation that Lucinda dePaolo, Chief Financial Officer for Skyline Bakery and Cafe, will use to provide an overview of financial plans to a group of investors. Your completed presentation will look similar to the one shown in Figure 15.43.

For Project 15D, you will need the following files:

p15D_Background
p15D_Proposal_Template
p15D_Calculator

**You will save your presentation as
15D_Funding_Firstname_Lastname**

Figure 15.43

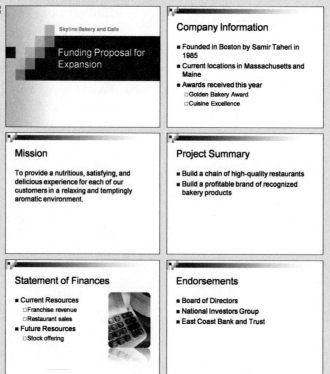

Content-Based Assessments

Skills Review

(Project 15D–Funding continued)

1. **Start** PowerPoint. From the **Office** menu, click **New** to display the **New Presentation** window. Under **Microsoft Office Online**, click **More Categories**, and then under **More categories**, click **Proposals**. Click the **Grant proposal** template, and then in the lower right corner of the **New Presentation** window, click **Download** to access the template from Microsoft Office Online. If a Microsoft Office window displays, click Continue. Alternatively, if you are unable to access the templates from Microsoft Office Online, the template for this project is available from your student data files. Click the Office button, and then click Open. Navigate to your student files and open the p15D_Proposal_Template presentation.

2. On **Slide 1**, drag to select the text *Organization Name*, and type **Skyline Bakery and Cafe** to replace it. Select the text that you just typed, and on the Mini toolbar, click the **Font Size button arrow**, and then click **24**. Drag to select the text in the title placeholder, and then type **Funding Proposal for Expansion**

3. Click the **Office** button, and then click **Save As**. In the **Save As** dialog box, click the **Save in** arrow, and then navigate to the location where you are storing your files for this chapter. In the **File name** box, delete any existing text, and then using your own first and last names type **15D_Funding_Firstname_Lastname** and then click **Save**.

4. Scroll through the presentation to view the content suggested for a funding proposal. Notice that in Slide 2, an introduction and mission statement are suggested. This content exists in another presentation and can be inserted without retyping the slides.

5. Display **Slide 1**. On the **Home tab**, in the **Slides group**, click the **New Slide arrow** to display the **Slide Layout gallery** and additional options for inserting slides. At the bottom of the gallery, click **Reuse Slides** to open the **Reuse Slides** task pane.

6. In the **Reuse Slides** task pane, click the **Browse** button, and then click **Browse File**. In the **Browse** dialog box, navigate to where your student files are stored and double-click **p15D_Background**. In the **Reuse Slides** task pane, point to either of the two slides that display and click the right-mouse button. From the shortcut menu, click **Insert All Slides** to insert both slides into the presentation. **Close** the **Reuse Slides** task pane.

7. On the status bar, locate the **View** buttons, and then click the **Slide Sorter** button to display the 15 slides in the presentation. Click to select **Slide 4**, and then press Delete to delete the slide. Click **Slide 5**, hold down Shift and click **Slide 7** so that slides 5 through 7 are selected. Press Delete to delete the selected slides.

8. Click **Slide 6**, hold down Shift and click **Slide 9** so that slides 6 through 9 are selected. With the four slides still selected, hold down Ctrl, and then click **Slide 11**. Press Delete to delete the selected slides. Six slides remain in the presentation.

9. Click **Slide 3** to select it. While pointing to **Slide 3**, press and hold down the left mouse button, and then drag the slide to the left until the displayed vertical bar is positioned to the left of **Slide 2**. Release the left mouse button to move the slide.

10. In the status bar, click the **Normal** button, and then **Save** your presentation. Display **Slide 4**, and then select the text in the

Content-Based Assessments

Skills Review

(Project 15D–Funding continued)

content placeholder. Replace the selected text with the following two bullets:

Build a dominant chain of high-quality restaurants

Build a profitable brand of recognized bakery products

11. Display **Slide 5,** change the title to **Statement of Finances** and then select the text in the content placeholder. Replace the selected text with the following bullet points, increasing and decreasing the list level as indicated:

Current Resources

> **Franchise revenue**

> **Restaurant sales**

Future Resources

> **Stock offering**

12. Click the **Insert tab**, and then in the **Illustrations group**, click **Clip Art** to display the **Clip Art** task pane. In the **Clip Art** task pane, click in the **Search for** box, and then type **calculator**

13. In the **Clip Art** task pane, click the **Search in arrow**, and if necessary, click the **Everywhere** check box so that it is selected. Click the **Results should be arrow**, and then click as necessary to *clear* the **Clip Art**, **Movies**, and **Sounds** check boxes so that only **Photographs** is selected. Click **Go** to display the photographs of calculators. Click the picture of the white calculator with an adding machine tape on a blue background. Check Figure 15.43 at the beginning of this project if you are unsure of the picture that you should insert. **Close** the **Clip Art** task pane. (Note: If you cannot locate the picture, on the Insert tab, in the Illustrations group, click Picture. Navigate to your student files and then double-click p15D_Calculator.)

14. Position the pointer anywhere over the picture to display the ⊕ pointer. Drag to the right so that the picture is positioned approximately one-half inch from the right edge of the slide.

15. If necessary, click the picture of the calculator to select it and to activate the Picture Tools. On the Ribbon, click the **Format tab**, and then in the **Picture Styles group**, in the first row, click **Reflected Rounded Rectangle**.

16. Display **Slide 6**. Select the bulleted list text, and then replace it with the following bulleted items:

Board of Directors

National Investors Group

East Coast Bank and Trust

17. Click the **Insert tab**, and then in the **Text group**, click **Header & Footer** to display the **Header and Footer** dialog box.

18. Click the **Notes and Handouts tab**. Under **Include on page**, click to select the **Date and time** check box and, if necessary, click the **Update automatically** button so that the current date prints on the notes and handouts each time the presentation is printed. If necessary, clear the **Header** check box to omit this element from the header and footer. Click to select the **Page number** and **Footer** check boxes. Using your own first and last names, in the Footer box, type **15D_Funding_Firstname_Lastname** and then click **Apply to All**.

19. Check your *Chapter Assignment Sheet* or *Course Syllabus* or consult your instructor to determine if you are to submit your assignments on paper or electronically. To submit electronically, go to Step 21, and then follow the instructions provided by your instructor.

Content-Based Assessments

Skills Review

(Project 15D–Funding continued)

20. From the **Office** menu, point to **Print**, and then click **Print Preview** to make a final check of your presentation. In the **Page Setup group**, click the **Print What arrow**, and then click **Handouts, (6 slides per page)**. Click the **Print** button, and then click **OK** to print the handouts. **Close** Print Preview.

21. **Save** changes to your presentation, and then from the **Office** menu, click **Exit PowerPoint**.

End **You have completed Project 15D**

Content-Based Assessments

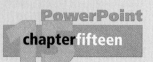

Mastering PowerPoint

Project 15E—Recruitment

In this project, you will apply the skills you practiced from the Objectives found in Project 15A.

Objectives: 1. *Open, View, and Save a Presentation;* **2.** *Edit a Presentation;* **3.** *Format a Presentation;* **4.** *Create Headers and Footers and Print a Presentation.*

In the following Mastering PowerPoint project, you will edit a presentation created by Shawna Andreasyan regarding the new online recruiting program at Skyline Bakery and Cafe. Your completed presentation will look similar to Figure 15.44.

> **For Project 15E, you will need the following file:**
>
> p15E_Recruitment

You will save your presentation as
15E_Recruitment_Firstname_Lastname

Figure 15.44

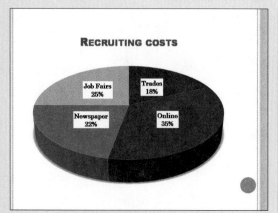

Content-Based Assessments

Mastering PowerPoint

(Project 15E–Recruitment continued)

1. **Start** PowerPoint and **Open** the file **p15E_Recruitment**. Save the presentation as 15E_Recruitment_Firstname_Lastname

2. On **Slide 1**, change the **Font Size** for the title to **48** so that the entire title fits on one line. Add the subtitle **Online Recruiting Plan** and then apply **Italic** to the subtitle.

3. Add a **New Slide** to the presentation with the **Title and Content** layout. The slide title is **Need for Online Recruiting** In the content placeholder, type the following bullet points and correct any spelling errors that you make while typing:

   Expansion into new geographic locations

   Cost savings over traditional methods

   New graduates search online for jobs

   Reach a more diverse applicant pool

4. On **Slide 3**, **Center** the slide title, and then change the **Font** to **Arial Black**. Add the following speaker's notes, correcting spelling errors as necessary. **We currently use three major recruiting methods. This chart indicates the amount that will be spent on each method once online recruiting is established.**

5. Add a **New Slide** to the presentation with the **Title and Content** layout. The slide title is **Online Recruiting Advantages** In the content placeholder, type the following bullet points, and then correct any spelling errors that you make while typing. After you type the text increase the list level of the fourth bullet point—*Automated database.*

   Access to more qualified applicants

   Streamlined application process

   Improved manageability

   Automated database

   Easily maintained and updated

6. Display **Slide 3**, and then on the Ribbon, click the **Design tab**. Using the **More** button, display the **Themes gallery**. Under **Built-In**, apply the **Oriel** theme to **Slide 3** only. (Hint: Right-click the theme, and then click **Apply to Selected Slides.**)

7. Display **Slide 1** and view the slide show, pressing Spacebar to advance through the presentation. When the black slide displays, press Spacebar one more time return to the presentation.

8. Create a **Header and Footer** for the **Notes and Handouts**. Include only the **Date and time updated automatically**, the **Page number**, and a **Footer** with the filename **15E_Recruitment_Firstname_Lastname** using your own first and last names.

9. Check your *Chapter Assignment Sheet* or *Course Syllabus* or consult your instructor to determine if you are to submit your assignments on paper or electronically. To submit electronically, go to Step 11, and then follow the instructions provided by your instructor.

10. **Print Preview** your presentation, and then print **Handouts, (4 slides per page)** and the **Notes Pages** for **Slide 3**.

11. **Save** changes to your presentation, and then **Close** the presentation.

End You have completed Project 15E

Content-Based Assessments

chapter fifteen | Mastering PowerPoint

Project 15F — Kitchen

In this project, you will apply the skills you practiced from Objectives in Project 15B.

Objectives: 5. *Create a New Presentation;* **6.** *Use Slide Sorter View;* **7.** *Add Pictures to a Presentation.*

In the following Mastering PowerPoint project, you will create a presentation that Peter Wing, Executive Chef for Skyline Bakery and Cafe, will use to describe the different types of chefs employed by the restaurant. Your completed presentation will look similar to Figure 15.45.

For Project 15F, you will need the following files:

p15F_Chefs
p15F_Tools
p15F_Nutrition_Template

**You will save your presentation as
15F_Kitchen_Firstname_Lastname**

Figure 15.45

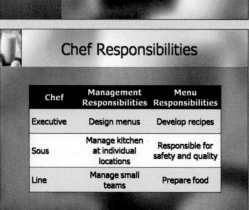

Content-Based Assessments

chapterfifteen   ## Mastering PowerPoint

(Project 15F–Kitchen continued)

1. **Start** PowerPoint and begin a new presentation based on the **Nutrition** design template. You may search by using the keyword *Nutrition* or you may find the template in the **Design slides, Academic** category. If you do not have access to the online templates, open **p15F_Nutrition_Template** from your student files. **Save** the presentation as **15F_Kitchen_Firstname_Lastname**

2. The title for the first slide is **The Kitchen is Open!** and the subtitle is **Skyline Bakery and Cafe**

3. From your student files, add all of the slides in the **p15F_Chefs** presentation into the current presentation. Then, display the presentation in **Slide Sorter view** and rearrange the slides so that the *Kitchen Organization* slide is the second slide, and the *Director of Kitchen Operations* slide is the fourth slide.

4. Display **Slide 2** in **Normal** view and insert a clip art image by searching for **Photographs** in **All collections**, using the keyword **skillet** Insert the picture that contains a chef's hat, skillet, wooden spoon,

knife, and guest check. If you cannot find the picture, insert the picture found in your student files, p15F_Tools.

5. Drag the picture to the lower right corner of the slide, and then apply a **Picture Style—Bevel Rectangle**. (Hint: Picture Styles are found in the Format tab of the Picture Tools contextual tool.)

6. Create a **Header and Footer** for the **Notes and Handouts**. Include only the **Date and time updated automatically**, the **Page number**, and a **Footer** with the filename **15F_Kitchen_Firstname_Lastname** using your own first and last names.

7. Check your *Chapter Assignment Sheet* or *Course Syllabus* or consult your instructor to determine if you are to submit your assignments on paper or electronically. To submit electronically, go to Step 9, and then follow the instructions provided by your instructor.

8. **Print Preview** your presentation, and then print **Handouts, (4 slides per page)**.

9. **Save** changes to your presentation, and then **Close** the file.

End **You have completed Project 15F**

Content-Based Assessments

chapterfifteen   ## Mastering PowerPoint

Project 15G — Flyer

In this project, you will apply the skills you practiced from the Objectives found in Projects 15A and 15B.

Objectives: 2. *Edit a Presentation;* **3.** *Format a Presentation;* **4.** *Create Headers and Footers and Print a Presentation* **5.** *Create a New Presentation;* **7.** *Add Pictures to a Presentation.*

In the following Mastering PowerPoint project, you will create a single slide to be used as a flyer for the annual employee baking contest. Your completed presentation will look similar to Figure 15.46.

For Project 15G, you will need the following files:

New blank PowerPoint presentation
p15G_Cookies

**You will save your presentation as
15G_Flyer_Firstname_Lastname**

Figure 15.46

Content-Based Assessments

 **Mastering PowerPoint**

(Project 15G–Flyer continued)

1. **Start** PowerPoint and begin a new blank presentation. Change the **Layout** of the title slide to the **Comparison** layout. Change the **Design** of the presentation by applying the **Oriel** theme. **Save** your presentation as **15G_Flyer_Firstname_Lastname**.

2. The title of the slide is **Annual Employee Baking Contest** Change the **Font** to **Bradley Hand ITC** and the **Font Size** to **36**. Apply **Bold**, and then **Center** the title.

3. In the orange box on the left side of the slide, type **How do you participate and join the fun?** In the orange box on the right side of the slide, type **Bring your favorite yummy dessert! Center** the text in both boxes.

4. In the content placeholder on the left side of the slide, type the following bullet points:

   Bake your favorite secret recipe!

   Bring it to work on December 15!

   Our chefs will be judging all day!

   Great prizes in lots of different categories!

5. Click in the content placeholder on the right side of the slide and insert a clip art by using the keyword **christmas cookies** Search for **Photographs** in **All collections**. Click the picture with the star-shaped cookies on the brown background. If you cannot find the picture, insert the picture found in your student files, **p15G_Cookies**.

6. Move the picture so that it is centered below the *Bring your favorite yummy dessert!* text. Then, apply **Picture Style— Drop Shadow Rectangle**.

7. Insert a **Footer** on the Slide (*not* the Notes and Handouts), that includes the file name **15G_Flyer_Firstname_Lastname** Because of the layout of this slide, the footer will display vertically on the right side of the slide.

8. Check your *Chapter Assignment Sheet* or *Course Syllabus* or consult your instructor to determine if you are to submit your assignments on paper or electronically. To submit electronically, go to Step 10, and then follow the instructions provided by your instructor.

9. **Print Preview** your presentation. There is only one slide in the presentation, so print **Slides**.

10. **Save** and **Close** your presentation.

End You have completed Project 15G

Content-Based Assessments

chapter fifteen   Mastering PowerPoint

Project 15H — Fresh

In this project, you will apply the skills you practiced from the Objectives found in Projects 15A and 15B.

Objectives: 2. *Edit a Presentation;* **3.** *Format a Presentation;* **4.** *Create Headers and Footers and Print a Presentation* **5.** *Create a New Presentation;* **6.** *Use Slide Sorter View;* **7.** *Add Pictures to a Presentation.*

In the following Mastering PowerPoint project, you will create a presentation that describes some of the steps taken by Skyline Bakery and Cafe to ensure that their food is fresh. Your completed presentation will look similar to Figure 15.47.

For Project 15H, you will need the following files:

New blank PowerPoint presentation
p15H_Text
p15H_Apple_Template
p15H_Vegetables
p15H_Tomato

You will save your presentation as
15H_Fresh_Firstname_Lastname

Figure 15.47

Content-Based Assessments

Mastering PowerPoint

(Project 15H–Fresh continued)

1. **Start** PowerPoint and begin a new presentation by searching for a template with the keyword **Apple** Click the template with the three green apples. If the template is not available, from your student files, open **p15H_Apple_Template**.

2. The title of this presentation is **Keeping It Fresh!** and the subtitle is **Skyline Bakery and Cafe Save** the presentation as **15H_Fresh_Firstname_Lastname**

3. Add the two slides from the **p15H_Text** presentation. Display **Slide 3**, and then in the left bulleted list placeholder, increase the list level of the *Patisserie chef*, *Executive chef*, and *Line chef* bullet points. In the right bulleted list placeholder, increase the list level of the *Federally regulated* bullet point.

4. Add a **New Slide** with the **Title and Content** layout, and in the title placeholder, type **Our Commitment** In the bulleted list placeholder, type the following bullet points:

   Fresh food, unforgettable taste, served in a clean and cozy setting

   Quality ingredients picked by our discerning staff of chefs

   Cooked to perfection at all times

5. In **Slide Sorter** view, switch **Slides 2 and 4** so that **Slide 2** becomes the last slide and the **Our Commitment** slide becomes the second slide. Return the presentation to **Normal** view.

6. On **Slide 2**, in the second bullet point, use the shortcut menu to view **Synonyms** for the word *picked*. Change the word *picked* to **selected**.

7. Display **Slide 4**. Insert a clip art image by using the keyword **cabbage** Search for

Photographs in **All collections**. Click the picture with many different types and colors of vegetables. Move the picture down and to the left so that it covers the apples and is positioned in the lower left corner of the slide. If you cannot locate the picture, it is available in your student files. The filename is **p15H_Vegetables**.

8. Insert the vegetable picture again so that there are two of the same pictures on the slide. Move the picture down and to the right so that it is positioned in the lower right corner of the slide.

9. Insert another clip art image, this time by using the keywords **cherry tomato** Search for **Photographs** in **All collections**. Click the picture with tomatoes that look like they are spilling out of a bowl as shown in the figure at the beginning of this project. If you cannot locate the picture, it is available in your student files. The filename is **p15H_Tomato**. Drag the tomato picture straight down so that it overlaps the two vegetable pictures and its bottom edge aligns with the bottom edge of the slide. Apply **Picture Style—Simple Frame, Black**.

10. Create a **Header and Footer** for the **Notes and Handouts**. Include only the **Date and time updated automatically**, the **Page number**, and a **Footer** with the file name **15H_Fresh_Firstname_Lastname** and then view the slide show.

11. Check your *Chapter Assignment Sheet* or *Course Syllabus* or consult your instructor to determine if you are to submit your assignments on paper or electronically. To submit electronically, go to Step 13, and then follow the instructions provided by your instructor.

Content-Based Assessments

Mastering PowerPoint

(Project 15H–Fresh continued)

12. Display **Slide 1**, and then view the slide show. **Print Preview** your presentation, and then print **Handouts, (4 slides per page)**. If the text or pictures do not display, on the Print Preview tab, in the Print group click Options, point to Color/Grayscale, and then click Color or Color (On Black and White Printer).

13. **Save** changes to your presentation. **Close** the presentation.

End **You have completed Project 15H**

Content-Based Assessments

Mastering PowerPoint

Project 15I — Holiday

In this project, you will apply the skills you practiced from Objectives found in Projects 15A and 15B.

In the following Mastering PowerPoint project, you will create a presentation that details the holiday activities at Skyline Bakery and Cafe. Your completed presentation will look similar to Figure 15.48.

For Project 15I, you will need the following files:

New blank PowerPoint presentation
p15I_December
p15I_Green_Template
p15I_Coffee
p15I_Ornaments

You will save your presentation as
15I_Holiday_ Firstname_Lastname

Figure 15.48

Content-Based Assessments

Mastering PowerPoint

(Project 15I–Holiday continued)

1. **Start** PowerPoint and begin a new presentation by searching for the green and gold holiday template. If the template is not available, from your student files, open **p15I_Green_Template**. The title of the presentation is **Holiday Happenings** and the subtitle is **With Skyline Bakery and Cafe** Insert all of the slides from the presentation **p15I_December**. **Save** the presentation as **15I_Holiday_Firstname_Lastname**

2. On **Slide 2**, increase the list level for bullet points 2, 3, and 4 and for the last two bullet points. Change the **Layout** to **Two Content**, and then in the right placeholder insert a clip art photograph of a white coffee mug on a green background. If you cannot find the image, it is located with your student files—**p15I_Coffee**. Size the picture so that it is approximately as wide as the word *December* and as tall as the text in the left placeholder. Apply **Picture Style—Compound Frame, Black** and position the picture, using Figure 15.48 at the beginning of this project as your guide.

3. Display **Slide 3** and change the **Layout** to **Comparison**. In the *Click to add text* box on the left side of the slide, type **Traditional Elegance** and then in the box on the right side of the slide type **Bountiful Buffet Center** and **Underline** the text in both boxes, and then change the **Font Size** to **28**.

4. Insert a **New Slide** with the **Content with Caption** layout. In the *Click to add title* box, type **Luncheon** and then change the **Font Size** to **36**. In the text placeholder on the left side of the slide, type the following paragraph:

Luncheons during December are reminiscent of years gone by. Join us for a pleasing array of old-fashioned festive delights, served by candlelight while holiday music plays.

5. Select the paragraph, and then change the **Font** to **Constantia** and the **Font Size** to **20**. Apply **Bold** and **Italic**, and then change the **Line Spacing** to **1.5**.

6. In the content placeholder on the right side of the slide, insert a clip art of five, brightly colored glass ornaments. Apply **Picture Style—Reflected Bevel, Black** and use Figure 15.48 at the beginning of this project as your guide for sizing and positioning the picture. If you cannot locate the picture, the file name in your student files is **p15I_Ornaments**.

7. Insert a **New Slide** with the **Title Slide** layout. In the title placeholder, type **Savor the Holidays** and in the subtitle placeholder type **Skyline Bakery and Cafe**

8. Move **Slide 4** so that it is between **Slides 2** and **3**. Add the **Date and time updated automatically**, the **Page number**, and the file name **15I_Holiday_Firstname_Lastname** to the **Notes and Handouts Footer**. Check the presentation for spelling errors, and then view the slide show from the beginning.

9. Check your *Chapter Assignment Sheet* or *Course Syllabus* or consult your instructor to determine if you are to submit your assignments on paper or electronically. To submit electronically, go to Step 11, and then follow the instructions provided by your instructor.

10. **Print Preview** your presentation, and then print **Handouts, (6 slides per page)**.

11. **Save** changes to your presentation, and then **close** the file.

End You have completed Project 15I

Content-Based Assessments

 **Business Running Case**

Project 15J—Business Running Case

In this project, you will apply the skills you practiced in Projects 15A and 15B.

From the student files that accompany this textbook, open the folder **03_business_running_case.** Locate the Business Running Case project for this chapter. Follow the instructions and use the skills you have gained thus far to assist Jennifer Nelson in meeting the challenges of owning and running her business.

Rubric

The following outcomes-based assessments are *open-ended assessments*. That is, there is no specific correct result; your result will depend on your approach to the information provided. Make *Professional Quality* your goal. Use the following scoring rubric to guide you in *how* to approach the problem, and then to evaluate *how well* your approach solves the problem.

The *criteria*—Software Mastery, Content, Format and Layout, and Process—represent the knowledge and skills you have gained that you can apply to solving the problem. The *levels of performance*—Professional Quality, Approaching Professional Quality, or Needs Quality Improvements—help you and your instructor evaluate your result.

	Your completed project is of Professional Quality if you:	Your completed project is Approaching Professional Quality if you:	Your completed project Needs Quality Improvements if you:
1-Software Mastery	Choose and apply the most appropriate skills, tools, and features and identify efficient methods to solve the problem.	Choose and apply some appropriate skills, tools, and features, but not in the most efficient manner.	Choose inappropriate skills, tools, or features, or are inefficient in solving the problem.
2-Content	Construct a solution that is clear and well organized, contains content that is accurate, appropriate to the audience and purpose, and is complete. Provide a solution that contains no errors of spelling, grammar, or style.	Construct a solution in which some components are unclear, poorly organized, inconsistent, or incomplete. Misjudge the needs of the audience. Have some errors in spelling, grammar, or style, but the errors do not detract from comprehension.	Construct a solution that is unclear, incomplete, or poorly organized, containing some inaccurate or inappropriate content; and contains many errors of spelling, grammar, or style. Do not solve the problem.
3-Format and Layout	Format and arrange all elements to communicate information and ideas, clarify function, illustrate relationships, and indicate relative importance.	Apply appropriate format and layout features to some elements, but not others. Overuse features, causing minor distraction.	Apply format and layout that does not communicate information or ideas clearly. Do not use format and layout features to clarify function, illustrate relationships, or indicate relative importance. Use available features excessively, causing distraction.
4-Process	Use an organized approach that integrates planning, development, self-assessment, revision, and reflection.	Demonstrate an organized approach in some areas, but not others; or, use an insufficient process of organization throughout.	Do not use an organized approach to solve the problem.

Outcomes-Based Assessments

PowerPoint
chapter**fifteen**

Problem Solving

Project 15K — Catering

In this project, you will construct a solution by applying any combination of the Objectives found in Projects 15A and 15B.

For Project 15K, you will need the following file:

New blank PowerPoint presentation

**You will save your presentation as
15K_Catering_Firstname_Lastname**

Using the information provided, create a presentation that contains four to six slides that Nancy Goldman, Chief Baker, can use to describe the catering services offered by Skyline Bakery and Cafe. The presentation will be used at a business expo attended by representatives of many companies that frequently host business luncheons and dinners for their clients. The presentation should include a title slide, a slide that describes why customers would be interested in Skyline Bakery and Cafe's catering services, at least two slides with sample menus, and an ending slide that summarizes the presentation. The tone of the presentation should be positive and sales oriented so that the audience is encouraged to try Skyline's catering service.

The presentation should include a theme or template that is creative and is appropriate to the upbeat tone of the presentation. Use at least two different slide layouts to vary the way in which the presentation text is displayed. Search for clip art that visually represents the types of menu items described. Add the file name to the Notes and Handouts footer and check the presentation for spelling errors. Save the presentation as **15K_Catering_Firstname_Lastname** and submit it as directed.

End **You have completed Project 15K** ————————

Problem Solving

Project 15L—Picnic

In this project, you will construct a solution by applying any combination of the Objectives found in Projects 15A and 15B.

For Project 15L, you will need the following file:

New blank PowerPoint presentation

You will save your presentation as
15L_Picnic_Firstname_Lastname

In this project, you will create a one-slide flyer to be distributed to employees of Skyline Bakery and Cafe advertising the upcoming employee picnic. The picnic is held every summer at a large, regional park. The tone of the flyer is fun! Use two fonts that are informal and inviting and large enough to easily read if the flyer were posted on a bulletin board. Include in the flyer a slide title that will make the employees feel welcome and excited about attending. Choose a content layout that includes multiple placeholders for the information that you need to provide. The flyer should include information on location, date, time, and types of activities. Include a picture that is reminiscent of a picnic or large outdoor gathering. Refer to Project 15G for ideas on how to lay out the flyer.

Add the file name to the footer and check the presentation for spelling errors. Save the presentation as **15L_Picnic_Firstname_Lastname** and submit it as directed.

End **You have completed Project 15L** _____

Problem Solving

Project 15M—Customer Service

In this project, you will construct a solution by applying any combination of the Objectives found in Projects 15A and 15B.

For Project 15M, you will need the following files:

New blank PowerPoint presentation
p15M_Mission_Statement

You will save your presentation as
15M_Customer_Service_Firstname_Lastname

In this project, you will create a six-slide customer service presentation to be used by Shawna Andreasyan, Director of Human Resources for Skyline Bakery and Cafe. All employees will be attending customer service training seminars and this presentation is a brief introduction to the overall topic of customer service.

Good customer service is grounded in the Skyline Bakery and Cafe's mission statement. The mission statement has been provided for you in presentation p15M_Mission_Statement and should be inserted early in the presentation. Think about the mission statement, and then in the next slide, use a title slide layout to make a brief statement that summarizes how the mission statement is tied to customer service. Then consider some of the following principles of good customer service. A company should make a commitment to customer service so that every employee believes in it and is rewarded by it. Employees should also understand that everyone is involved in good customer service. The company is not just about the product; people are critically important to the success of any business and good customer service ensures that success. Furthermore, employees who are rewarded for good customer service will likely continue to work with good practices, perhaps leading to increased sales.

Using the information in the previous paragraph and other information that you may gather by researching the topic of "restaurant customer service," create at least two additional slides that Shawna Andreasyan can use to describe the importance of good customer service and how it is rewarded at Skyline Bakery and Cafe. When creating the design template, search Microsoft Online for customer service or training templates; there are several available. The tone of this presentation is informative and serious. Keep this in mind when choosing a template, theme, fonts, and clip art. Add the date and file name to the Notes and Handouts footer and check the presentation for spelling errors. Save the presentation as **15M_Customer_Service_Firstname_Lastname** and submit it as directed.

End You have completed Project 15M

chapter fifteen

Problem Solving

Project 15N — Menus

In this project, you will construct a solution by applying any combination of the Objectives found in Projects 15A and 15B.

For Project 15N, you will need the following file:

New blank PowerPoint presentation

**You will save your presentation as
15N_Menus_Firstname_Lastname**

In this exercise, you will create a presentation that contains special menus that are used for different holidays. Recognizing that holiday menus are frequently used in a number of presentations throughout the year, Peter Wang, Executive Chef, has decided to create sample menus in one presentation so that the menus are available when the marketing staff need to insert them into PowerPoint presentations.

Choose five holidays and create slides that include one holiday menu per slide. You may research holiday menus on the Internet, visit local restaurants to find out if they have special holiday menus, or you may use your own experience with family traditions in creating these menus. The slide title should identify the holiday and every slide should include a picture that portrays the holiday meal or represents the holiday in some way. Alternatively, consider using a Two Content layout in which the menu is in one column and a quote describing why the menu is special is in the other column. Keep your theme simple so that it does not interfere with the pictures that you have selected. Because these slides will likely be used in different presentations throughout the year, you may choose different fonts and font styles that characterize each holiday.

Add the date and file name to the Notes and Handouts footer and check the presentation for spelling errors. Save the presentation as **15N_Menus_Firstname_Lastname** and submit it as directed.

End **You have completed Project 15N** _____

Problem Solving

Project 15O — Opening

In this project, you will construct a solution by applying any combination of the Objectives found in Projects 15A and 15B.

For Project 15O, you will need the following file:

New blank PowerPoint presentation

You will save your presentation as
15O_Opening_Firstname_Lastname

In this project, you will create a presentation to be shown by Skyline Bakery and Cafe's Chief Executive Officer, Samir Taheri, at a Chamber of Commerce meeting. The presentation will explain the details of the company's grand opening of two new locations in Rhode Island taking place in June. The presentation should contain six to eight slides and the first two to three slides should include background information that may be taken from the following paragraph that describes the company and the new restaurant's location.

Skyline Bakery and Cafe is a chain of casual dining restaurants and bakeries based in Boston. Each restaurant has its own in-house bakery, which produces a wide variety of high-quality specialty breads, breakfast sweets, and desserts. Breads and sweets are sold by counter service along with coffee drinks, gourmet teas, fresh juices, and sodas. The full-service restaurant area features a menu of sandwiches, salads, soups, and light entrees. Fresh, high-quality ingredients and a professional and courteous staff are the hallmarks of every Skyline Bakery and Cafe.

The new restaurant is located in an outdoor lifestyle center where many residents gather in the evening to socialize. The restaurants are opening in June, so consider a summer theme as you develop ideas about the kinds of events that the owners may host during the grand opening. Include in the presentation four slides representing four different days of events—two at each of the new locations. The Comparison and Two Content slide layouts may be very effective for these four slides. Use fonts and clip art to enhance your presentation but do not clutter the presentation with excess images or many different types of fonts. Add the date and file name to the Notes and Handouts footer and check the presentation for spelling errors. Save the presentation as **15O_Opening_Firstname_ Lastname** and submit it as directed.

End **You have completed Project 15O** ————————

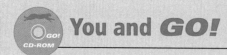

PowerPoint
chapterfifteen

You and *GO!*

Project 15P — You and *GO!*

In this project, you will construct a solution by applying any combination of the Objectives found in Projects 15A and 15B.

From the student files that accompany this textbook, open the folder **04_you_and_go**. Locate the You and *GO!* project for this chapter and follow the instructions to create a presentation about a place to which you have traveled or would like to travel.

End You have completed Project 15P ———————————

GO! with Help

Project 15Q — *GO!* with Help

The PowerPoint Help system is extensive and can help you as you work. In this project, you will view information about getting help as you work in PowerPoint.

1 **Start** PowerPoint. At the right end of the Ribbon, click the **Microsoft Office PowerPoint Help** button to display the **PowerPoint Help** dialog box. In the **Search** box, type **keyboard shortcuts** and then press Enter.

2 In the displayed search results, click **Keyboard shortcuts for PowerPoint 2007**. Maximize the displayed window and read how you can use keyboard shortcuts in PowerPoint.

3 If you want, print a copy of the information by clicking the **Print** button at the top of the **Microsoft Office PowerPoint Help** window.

4 **Close** the Help window, and then **Close** PowerPoint.

End You have completed Project 15Q ———————————

Outcomes-Based Assessments

Group Business Running Case

Project 15R—Group Business Running Case

In this project, you will apply the skills you practiced from the Objectives in Projects 15A and 15B.

Your instructor may assign this group case project to your class. If your instructor assigns this project, he or she will provide you with information and instructions to work as part of a group. The group will apply the skills gained thus far to help the Bell Orchid Hotel Group achieve its business goals.

End **You have completed Project 15R**

Outcomes-Based Assessments

Chapter 15: Getting Started with Microsoft PowerPoint 2007

CHECKING YOUR READING STRATEGIES
DISCUSSION AND CRITICAL THINKING QUESTIONS

1. **Preview** the chapter as you have been instructed. *Without reading the chapter itself*, write an outline of the chapter. Leave room to fill in the details later. Use your typographical cues to help you. (Do not include the "Summary" in your outline.) How detailed is it? What do you discover about trying to outline a technical chapter that is different from the previous chapters we have considered? Will an outline also work for this discipline, or do you need another organization plan? What other methods might be helpful? Mind maps? Flash cards? Chart? Table? Get creative and explore options that would work best for you.

2. **Preview** the chapter again, this time focusing on all the graphic illustrations. Read all the captions and information in tables, then look carefully at all graphs, tables, and drawings. Next, let your eyes scan over the text. See if you can find where in the paragraphs the illustrated material is explained. What cues are given in the text to tie the illustrations to the words?

3. *Circle the best answer for each of the following questions:*

   1. According to the objectives listed at the beginning of the chapter, this chapter will cover how many points?
      a. Four
      b. Three
      c. Eight
      d. Not enough information to answer the question

   2. According to the listing at the beginning of the chapter, this chapter will have how many outcomes?
      a. Ten
      b. Two
      c. Six
      d. Not enough information to answer the question

   3. What is the *overall purpose* of the chapter's introduction about Skyline Bakery and Café?
      a. To demonstrate how communication affects business
      b. To set up the project for the chapter
      c. To introduce PowerPoint

   4. How many types of graphic illustrations are used in this chapter? Look through the entire chapter. Select all that apply.
      a. Photographs
      b. Diagrams
      c. Charts
      d. Tables
      e. Graphs
      f. Flow charts
      g. Process diagrams
      h. Pie charts
      i. Shaded boxes (of formulas, theories, sample problems, etc.)

5. What typographical cues are used in the chapter to highlight important information for you? Select all that apply.

a. Boldface print

b. Italicized print

c. Font size

d. Font style

e. Bulleted lists

f. Underlining

g. Color of print

h. Boxes

i. Shading

j. Arrows to show direction/order

k. Symbols (light bulb, question mark, star, etc.)

4. **Preview** the "Summary," and the rest of the "Content Based Assessments." Read over the review of the concepts and the questions. These are the key points the authors feel you should draw from the chapter. How do the authors tie the concepts back to the text so you would know where to find the information? Go back and look for it. Make a checkmark in the margin so you will remember this is a key point when you read the chapter.

5. Now go back to the first page of the chapter and **read** the chapter. Move through the chapter section by section. Read first, then decide what information is important for you to know and what is explanatory to illustrate the point. Then, return to the outline you drafted for question 1. Fill in the outline with the information you have determined to be important for you to remember. If you have ruled out the outline, still take notes. Rework sample problems or formulas in your notebook. Make flash cards of formulas. This is a discipline that requires practice, practice, practice! Consider your method as well. **How** did you determine which information was important enough to record?

6. What is the difference between an objective and an outcome for this textbook?

7. What is more helpful to you in this text—the descriptions in-text or the examples? Why?

8. What is the point of the "Alerts!"? How about the "Another Way," "More Knowledge," "Note," and "Workshop" boxes? Why do you think the authors include those?

9. Next, consider the figures such as in Figure 15.2 and the others like it. What purpose do they serve? How do these help you understand the explanation of the steps in the process? How effective are these graphics, and why? Make note of other such graphics used in the text and compare them as well, considering which are more helpful for remembering information.

10. Did you read the boxes of information? If not, go back and do so now. What type of information is in these boxes? Why are they included in the chapter? How do they assist your learning?

11. You will see items marked "activity" within the chapter. What purpose do they serve? How do they help you learn the material?

12. What purpose does the "There's More You Can Do!" box serve?

13. Finally, **after reading** the chapter, answer the review questions at the end of the chapter under "Matching" and "Fill in the Blank." How well did you do? Which of the strategies used by the authors, or you, helped you the most? Remember these for the future. (Your professor may

also want you to try the "Skills Review" or "Mastering PowerPoint" activities to reinforce what you should have learned in this chapter since the probability of you needing to use Power-Point in the future is pretty high. Reviewing the "Rubric" at the end of the chapter would be a good way for you to anticipate how your own PowerPoint presentations may be assessed in the future.)

GROUP PROJECTS

1. Compare your outline, notes, or flash cards with those of your classmates. Are they all the same? If not, how do they differ? Why do you think that may be? Did someone develop a strategy that you think could work well for you? Ask that person to show you how to use it. Don't be afraid to share strategies; it is not cheating. Next, compare how well you and your classmates did when answering the questions at the end of the text's chapter. Did those of you with the more detailed outline or notes do better? Or were other strategies more helpful? Why or why not?

2. As a group, discuss the benefits of previewing the illustrations in the text before reading, as opposed to waiting to explore them as they come up in the reading.

3. Discuss how helpful it was to practice the activities before tackling the exercises.

4. With the group, consider what the authors do to make this chapter interesting and appealing to you. Consider both the visual components and the information itself. How do page layout and writing style make assigned reading more enjoyable?

5. Discuss with your group what you have learned about the importance of knowing how to construct a PowerPoint presentation. Why might it be important for you to understand how and why to master this skill?

Textbook Credits

Unit I: Allied Health & Nursing
Chapter 6: "Health Care Delivery Systems," pp.100–16 in *Kozier & Erb's Fundamentals of Nursing: Concepts, Process, and Practice*, 8th ed., by Berman, et al., ISBN: 0-13-171468-6.

Unit II: Business & Foodservice
Chapter 14, "Marketing Foodservice," pp. 601–23 in *Foodservice Organizations: A Managerial and Systems Approach*, 6th ed., by Gregoire and Spears, ISBN: 0-13-193632-8.

Unit III: Humanities
History & Visual Arts: Chapter 14, "European Cultural and Religious Transformations," pp. 396–431 in *Civilization: Past & Present (Volume I: To 1650)*, 11th ed., by Brummett, et al., ISBN: 0-321-23627-0.

Literature: Two Works: "Salvation," by Langston Hughes, pp. 187–89 and 193–94; "The Masque of the Red Death," by Edgar Allan Poe, pp. 398–401 and 407–08 in *American 24-Karat Gold: 24 Classic American Short Stories*, 2nd ed, by Sisko, ISBN: 0-321-36524-0.

Two Works: "Richard Cory," by Edwin Arlington Robinson, p. 692; "Sympathy," by Paul Laurence Dunbar, p. 719 in *An Introduction to Literature*, 14th ed, by Barnet, Burto, and Cain, ISBN: 0-321-35601-2.

Unit IV: Mathematics & Automotive
Chapter 14: "Math, Charts and Calculations," pp. 104–08 in *Automotive Technology*, 3rd ed., by Halderman, ISBN: 0-13-175477-7.

Unit V: Natural Sciences
Chapter 21, Nutrition, Digestion, and Excretion," pp. 393–416 in *Life on Earth*, 5th ed., by Audesirk, Audesirk, and Byers, ISBN: 0-13-175535-8.

Unit VI: Social Sciences & Criminal Justice
Chapter 17, "Terrorism and Multinational Criminal Justice," pp. 614–51 in *Criminal Justice Today: An Introductory Text for the 21st Century*, 10th ed., by Schmalleger, ISBN: 0-13-513030-1.

Unit VII: Technical Fields & Computer Science
Chapter 15, "Getting Started with Microsoft PowerPoint 2007," pp. 915–991 in *GO! With Microsoft Office 2007 Introductory*, 2nd ed., by Gaskin, et al, ISBN: 0-13-241887-8.

Photo Credits